Law on Display

1 0 1 0 1 0 1 0 1 0 1 0 1
1 0 1 0 1 0 1 0 1 0 1
1 0 1 0 1 0 1 0 1
1 0 1 0 1 0 1
1 0 1 0 1
1 0 1
1

Ex Machina: Law, Technology, and Society
General Editors: Jack M. Balkin and Beth Simone Noveck

The Digital Person:
Technology and Privacy in the Information Age
Daniel J. Solove

The State of Play : Law and Virtual Worlds
Edited by Jack M. Balkin and Beth Simone Noveck

Cybercrime: Digital Cops in a Networked Environment
Edited by Jack Balkin, James Grimmelmann, Eddan Katz,
Nimrod Kozlovski, Shlomit Wagman, and Tal Zar

Law on Display:
The Digital Transformation of Legal Persuasion and Judgment
Neal Feigenson and Christina Spiesel

Law on Display

The Digital Transformation of Legal Persuasion and Judgment

Neal Feigenson and Christina Spiesel

NEW YORK UNIVERSITY PRESS

New York and London

NEW YORK UNIVERSITY PRESS
New York and London
www.nyupress.org

Library of Congress Cataloging-in-Publication Data

Feigenson, Neal.
Law on display : the digital transformation of legal persuasion
and judgment / Neal Feigenson and Christina Spiesel.
p. cm.
Includes bibliographical references and index.
ISBN-13: 978–0–8147–2758–4 (cl : alk. paper)
ISBN-10: 0–8147–2758–1 (cl : alk. paper)
1. Electronic discovery (Law)—United States. 2. Electronic records—
Law and legislation—United States. 3. Electronic evidence—Law and
legislation—United States. 4. Evidence, Documentary—United States.
5. Video tapes in courtroom proceedings—United States.
I. Spiesel, Christina. II. Title.
KF8902.E42F44   2009
347.73'64—dc22   2009015573

New York University Press books are printed on acid-free paper,
and their binding materials are chosen for strength and durability.
We strive to use environmentally responsible suppliers and materials
to the greatest extent possible in publishing our books.

Manufactured in the United States of America
10 9 8 7 6 5 4 3 2 1

For Ellen, Gabby, and Tom
—N.F.

For Sydney, Elie, and Sirri
—C.S.

Contents

Figures

For color versions of most of the figures and additional material
go to the book's web site at www.lawondisplay.com/

Preface

Law has traditionally been about words: trial testimony and oral argument, statutes and judicial opinions, negotiations and jury deliberations. Now, as never before, it's also about pictures displayed on screens: dashboard camera videotapes, digitally enhanced crime scene photos, computer animations, PowerPoint slide shows, and much more. And not just pictures, but multimedia displays combining photographs and videos, drawings and diagrams, the sounds of witnesses' voices, and, indeed, anything that will help lawyers to present their cases and convince their audiences. Law's incorporation of digital visuals and multimedia is advancing rapidly and continuously taking new forms; 3-D virtual reality evidence is on the horizon, and, thanks to videoconferencing technology and the Internet, entire legal proceedings may soon go online.

This is a major change in legal culture. Thinking with pictures—looking at them, trying to interpret them, and using them to reach decisions—is very different from thinking with words alone. Understanding them requires new skills. That's unsettling to many lawyers and judges; law school doesn't train them to deal with pictures, and their experiences in practice may not have prepared them well, either. The change is also unsettling to jurors. True, digital technologies promise jurors unprecedented access to the facts they must decide; think of a videotape enhanced to identify a culprit or a brain scan image that reveals otherwise hidden injuries. And when trial information is presented on a courtroom screen, it's likely to appeal to people who are accustomed to learning about the world through audiovisual media on television and computer screens. But jurors also know that digital pictures can be crafted to show practically anything the presenter wants, and this suspicion battles with their intuitive belief in the truth of what they see. It troubles the public, too, to imagine that judgments of guilt or innocence may turn on the kinds of audiovisual displays that they're used to seeing in movies and advertisements. How can justice be done in this new environment?

This book grapples with that question. We describe the changing legal culture, using detailed case studies to explore how lawyers are deploying new media and how judges and jurors are responding. We also take a broader perspective, analyzing how digital technologies and new habits of using them in everyday life are reshaping the nature of legal knowledge and altering the ever-shifting relationships between law and the wider culture. We discuss what lawyers, judges, and the legal system can do to obtain the greatest benefit from the new technologies while reducing the threats they pose to good judgment. And we look ahead to law's future, in which multimedia on screens may well play an even greater role. We identify the issues that the legal system and the public must confront to maintain law's legitimacy as justice goes online.

As we contemplate the arc of the book, we cannot help but ask whether digital pictures and multimedia are in general good or bad for law. There is no simple answer. Since it's clear, though, that digital pictures are here to stay, the question becomes how the law can best accommodate them, along with words spoken and written. Unless the legal system makes the effort to embrace and understand the new media, it's going to encounter even more trouble as lawyers routinely deploy their digital tools. If, on the contrary, the law takes up the challenge to be alert, wise, and full of inquiry about the uses of new media, judgment and justice may be enhanced. This book is a first effort to suggest what should be done—not because we have all the answers but because, we hope, we have some of the right questions.

Our interdisciplinary approach to our subject reflects our different backgrounds and areas of expertise, which have come together over a decade of talking, teaching, and writing. One of us (Spiesel) is an artist in both analog and digital media and a semiotician; in an earlier stage of the digital revolution, she was an officer in a small software development company. Spiesel first started thinking about the intersection of law and visuality after hearing a lecture by Bernard Hibbets, a law professor, at a meeting of the College Art Association in 1996. She then created a course, Envisioning Law, which she taught at the Yale Law School in spring 1998. The other of us (Feigenson), a law professor with an interest in cognitive and social psychology, audited the course. We then collaborated with Richard Sherwin, also a law professor, to develop it into a new course, Visual Persuasion in the Law, which has been taught since 2000 at Quinnipiac University School of Law and at New York Law School.

In this book, as in our course, we draw on the wisdom of many disciplines to understand the confluence of law, digital media, and culture:

rhetoric and narrative theory, the psychobiology of vision and the psychology of persuasion and decision making, information design and media studies. We hope that readers will be not only stimulated by our efforts to bring knowledge together from so many domains but also inspired to improve upon them. We are also aware that what we say about particular tools may well be outpaced by technological change. While some of our predictions may prove mistaken, we're confident that our general observations about the roles of new media in law will be more enduring.

Most of the book has not previously appeared in published form, but portions of some chapters have been adapted from the following sources: Brian Carney and Neal Feigenson, "Visual Persuasion in the Michael Skakel Trial," *Criminal Justice* 19, no. 1 (Spring 2004): 22–35 (discussion of *Skakel*, chapter 3); Lisa Podolski and Neal Feigenson, "Digitally Processed Images in Connecticut Courts After *Swinton*," *Connecticut Trial Lawyers Association Forum* 25, no. 1 (Winter 2007): 33–41 (discussion of *Swinton*, chapter 4); Neal Feigenson, "Brain Imaging and Courtroom Evidence: On the Admissibility and Persuasiveness of fMRI," *International Journal of Law in Context* 2, no. 3 (2006): 233–55 (discussion of fMRI, chapter 4); Richard K. Sherwin, Neal Feigenson, and Christina Spiesel, "Law in the Digital Age," *Boston University Journal of Science and Technology Law* 12, no. 2 (Summer 2006): 227–70 (discussion of Maxus and *Skakel* cases, chapter 5).

The book, as we said, is built around detailed studies of the audiovisual displays used in actual cases, and we are grateful to the lawyers, trial consultants, and others who have provided us with their materials as well as information and insights into their cases: law professors Donald Braman, Dan Kahan, and David Hoffman and attorney Craig T. Jones (*Scott v. Harris*, chapter 2); attorney Michael Conroy and video archivist Eileen Clancy (*People v. Dunlop*, chapter 2); trial consultant Christopher Ritter of The Focal Point and attorneys Bob Pommer and Jack Worland (*SEC v. Koenig*, chapter 3); trial consultants Larry Collins and Brent Larlee of Animation Technologies and attorney Tom Ullmann (*State v. Bontatibus*, chapter 3); trial consultant Brian Carney of WIN Interactive, Inc. (*State v. Skakel*, chapters 3 and 5); attorneys Hugh Keefe and Michael Georgetti and Connecticut Superior Court Judge Christine Keller (*State v. Murtha*, chapter 3); Barbara Williams, managing partner, Image Content Technology LLC, and attorney Norm Pattis (*State v. Swinton*, chapter 4); communications consultant Cliff Atkinson of BBP Media and attorney Mark Lanier (*Ernst v. Merck, Inc.*, and *Cona and McDarby v. Merck, Inc.*, chapter 5). Four of our nine cases were tried in Connecticut courts, but, while the selection is partly a matter of convenience (it's our home state and we tend to have more contact with local lawyers than distant ones), we believe that comparable visuals and multimedia are being employed throughout the United States (not to mention the United Kingdom and Australia), so that the full range of cases we analyze offers readers a reasonably representative glimpse of law in the digital visual age.

We would also like to thank the many people who have taught us about our topic, read and commented on portions of the manuscript, or helped us in other ways: David Bolinsky of XVIVO; Bill Buckley; Todd Constable; Brenda Danet; Brett Dignam; David Dill; Ellen Eisenberg; Michael Fischer; Joann Gaughran; Federal District Court Judge Nancy Gertner; Andy Goodman; Daniel Kiecza; Fred Lederer; Jim Lehrer of the Media Arts Center; Andrea Levine; Nancy Marder; Jeff Meyer; Linda Meyer; Keith Murphy; Elaine Pagliaro and Paul Penders of the Connecticut Department of Public Safety; Damian Schofield; Elie Spiesel; Sirri Spiesel; Sydney Spiesel; David Tait; and Wendell Wallach. We have greatly benefited from all of their wisdom; any errors in the book are of course our responsibility, not theirs. We would like to give special thanks to Debbie Gershenowitz and Gabrielle Begue, our editors at NYU Press, whose careful revisions and constant good judgment considerably improved the book. Our Visual Persuasion in the Law students have provided us with continuing inspiration through their visual work and their contributions to class discussions over the years. We are also grateful to Dean Brad Saxton of the Quinnipiac University School of Law for his generous support throughout the writing of the book and to successive deans of the Yale Law School, Anthony Kronman and Harold Koh, who gave Spiesel access to all that a research scholar needs to carry on her work.

Finally, we dedicate this book to our wonderful families, without whose support, encouragement, patience, and generosity this book would never have been completed.

1

The Digital Visual Revolution

Millions of people saw Rodney King beaten by members of the California State Police. Over and over, they watched portions of George Holliday's amateur videotape on television.[1] The jury in the 1992 criminal trial of four of the police officers repeatedly viewed the tape, too—unedited, as shown by the prosecution; in slow motion and as freeze-frames accompanied by expert testimony, as shown by the defense. No matter what you saw when you watched—a helpless black man being beaten by racist cops or a drug-crazed violent offender being lawfully subdued and arrested—the scenes on the tape remain emblematic of all that ensued. Millions more watched the 1995 trial of O. J. Simpson for the murder of his former wife, Nicole Brown Simpson, and her friend Ronald Goldman. In her closing argument, prosecutor Marcia Clark urged the jury to "put the pieces together" while, on a large courtroom screen, puzzle pieces made from a photograph of the defendant fell, one by one, into place. Yet, jurors and the public watching on television also remembered a moment earlier in the trial when Simpson, at the prosecution's invitation, had tried and failed to put on the black glove allegedly used by the killer. The trial became a battle between the picture of the puzzle and the images that Johnnie Cochran, the defense lawyer, knew the jury and the public had in mind when he proclaimed, "If it doesn't fit, you must acquit." These contested pictures and performances are what we think of when we think about these cases. They shaped the verdicts and remain a part of our collective imagination and memory.[2]

In the years since these famous trials, the variety and the importance of visual displays in American courtrooms have exploded. Lawyers continue to use drawings, photographs, videos, in-court demonstrations, and other traditional methods of visually persuading their audiences. But now, in tens of thousands of cases, civil and criminal, high-profile and routine, lawyers are also using digital technologies to create and present their evidence and arguments. Consider just a few examples:

- The prosecution in a murder trial digitally enhances autopsy photographs of human bite marks on a woman's breast and, using Photoshop, overlays them with translucent images of the defendant's teeth to prove that the defendant was the killer.
- A blaze in a store leads to a fireman's death. In the ensuing arson-murder trial, the defense attorney displays on a large screen a photo sequence of the spreading fire with a running transcript of the firemen's communications with each other, synchronized to an audio track of their words. Jurors can see and hear how (according to the defendant) the slow response to an accidental fire probably caused the tragedy.
- The plaintiff's lawyer in a products liability suit against a major pharmaceutical company accompanies his opening statement and closing argument with running PowerPoint slide shows, using iconic stock photos and cartoons to visualize crucial aspects of his case.
- In another murder trial, the prosecution uses interactive software to combine digitized audio evidence, photos, and text to create the impression that the defendant had, in effect, confessed to the crime.

It is no accident that digital visual and multimedia displays are proliferating in law. Pictures—moving and still, on television, in movies and on DVDs, on the Internet, and in print media—increasingly dominate our culture, from news and entertainment to education and politics. Law is a part of this culture. What is different today is that digital tools have made it easier and cheaper for just about everyone to create, modify, and deploy pictures of all kinds. The widespread use of these tools has made them familiar parts of our mental and cultural landscapes. People now have different expectations about what information looks like, where they should look for it, and how quickly they should be able to get it. The new technologies change what people see and hear, how they think and feel about it, and how it matters to them. Legal practitioners are adopting these technologies to assemble their cases, to negotiate with adversaries, and to persuade arbitrators, judges, and juries. And why wouldn't they? Digital visuals·have become a kind of vernacular which everyone can understand.

This visual and digital transformation of law practice heralds nothing less than a revolution in the ways that lawyers argue, jurors and judges decide, and the public thinks about the law. In this book we seek to understand the implications of the wholesale entry of pictures into legal practice and of the technologies that make it possible. We look at specific cases to explore the evidentiary and rhetorical functions of visual displays of all sorts, from digitally enhanced photos and computer animations to PowerPoint, multimedia, and virtual reality. We study digital visual tools as shapers and carriers of meaning. We examine how digital technologies change how legal knowledge is created and how legal decision makers render justice.

In this introductory chapter, we offer essential background for understanding law's visual and digital transformation, presenting ideas and themes that we will pursue through case studies later in the book. We begin with pictures. We discuss how pictures make meaning differently than words do and how pictures and words can be combined to complement or challenge each other's meanings and to generate new meanings not yielded by either the pictures or the words alone. We explain a bit about visual perception and visual thinking, about the differences between perceiving pictures and perceiving reality directly—and about how people tend to ignore those differences, and why that matters.

We then proceed to the contribution made by the ubiquity of digital technologies. Digitization allows people, as never before, to *write with pictures* (a phrase anticipated by the legal scholar Lawrence Lessig):[3] to create pictures anew or to manipulate existing ones originating in any medium whatsoever, to combine them freely with words or other pictures, and to use the resulting pictures to refer to other images in an ongoing, culturewide conversation. We discuss three interrelated features of this greatly enhanced ability to write with pictures. First, because digital technologies make it much easier to produce, modify, and disseminate pictures (and sounds), people without special training or skills can express their thinking visually and share it with others. As a result, there are many more pictures in circulation, and the effects that these pictures have on people's thoughts, feelings, and decisions become that much more important to people's everyday lives (whether people are aware of these effects or not) and to the culture as a whole. Second, because digitization allows pictures to be so readily adapted to any communicative or argumentative context, the *rhetorical potential* of pictures has been tremendously expanded and put in the hands of many more people. Third, by enabling so many people to be producers and not merely consumers of visual and multimedia messages, digitization and the Internet have contributed to a *democratization of meaning making*, changing expectations and debates about whose versions of reality, and whose fantasies, have what kind of authority in the culture.

We conclude by outlining the challenges that these features of digital culture pose for the law. Digital pictures and multimedia offer judges and jurors unprecedented access to reality and thus the promise of grounding their decisions more firmly in the facts. At the same time, the ease with which digital pictures can be manipulated casts that very access into doubt. Lawyers who use new technologies can be more persuasive because they can present their cases in the media with which their audiences are most familiar. Yet, courtroom arguments that resemble popular entertainments or advertising may seem to threaten basic notions of how a justice system should operate. And the more pictures on screens play a part in legal judgment—or even subsume it, as dispute resolution goes online— the more traditional gatekeepers, judges and lawyers, will be faced with the task of accommodating the wide range of meaning-making habits that all participants in the justice system bring to the screen from their every-day lives.

To identify these developments and challenges and to understand their significance, we draw on insights from many disciplines, including psychology, cognitive science, and media studies. Our method is, broadly speaking, ethnographic, observing legal practices while seeking to ground in relevant literatures the inferences we draw from what we see. We are aware that any such borrowings across disciplinary boundaries involve a risk of mistranslation, of using concepts out of context.[4] Nevertheless, we believe that those interested in what is happening in law today have no choice but to cross those boundaries; there is no other way to appreciate what the uses of new media mean for the practice of law. The nature of our subject invites complexity: Every use of pictures in law has, at the very least, evidentiary, cognitive, rhetorical, technological, and ethical dimensions. But we will try to keep things as straightforward as possible, starting with the basic ingredients: pictures and words.

Pictures and Words

Law, like most other disciplines or practices that aspire to rationality, has tended to identify that rationality (and hence its virtue) with texts rather than pictures, with reading words rather than "reading" pictures, to the point that it is often thought that thinking in words is the only kind of thinking there is.[5] This poses a major obstacle to understanding what is happening as digitization transforms our world into one dominated by pictures. To explain how digital culture is changing law, then, we need first to say a few things about pictures and visual thinking: what pictures are, how people process pictures differently than they do written or spoken words, and what can happen when words and pictures interact.

A word about pictures. Let's begin with terminology—specifically, "pictures" and "images"—a matter that may on the surface seem quite simple but that is actually very complicated. In common usage, a "visual image" can refer to an artifact, such as the snapshot you hold in your hand and look at; to your mental image of that photo; or to your visual memories drawn from your experience of looking at the photo or the thing that the photo depicts. All of these types of images can also be understood as having relationships to other visual artifacts in a larger cultural context. Our visual images are infused with the cultural meanings of our picture-making activities (think of the changing connotations of "snapshot," for instance) as well as the visual conventions of television and film.

Even with regard to visuals "out there" (as opposed to visualizations and visually inspired ideas "inside our heads"), things can get complicated. If someone makes a painting, it's pretty clear that it exists in the materials out of which it is made; we can see the stuff, even individual paint strokes if we get close enough, and if we could touch it, we would get all kinds of tactile information as well. Film or videos, or images on a computer monitor for that matter, can look a lot like paintings, but for their audiences they are just incorporeal colored light. As viewers, we can't touch their physical form, but they can stimulate our beliefs and emotional responses just as powerfully as more material artifacts can. Because of these complexities of visual stimuli both inside and outside our heads, as well as our responses to those stimuli and the contexts in which we encounter and think about them (including cultural memory and individual experience), it is hard to deploy a simple vocabulary that always distinguishes which level of picturing or imaging we are talking about. As a general matter, then, in this book we will use "pictures" to mean visually perceived artifacts, external visual representations, reserving "image" for mental imagery (that is, internal, immaterial visual representations), and we will strive to make the object of discussion clear from the context.[6]

Then there is the problem of the many kinds of objects that we call pictures. When he spoke about picturing for the DeVane lecture series celebrating Yale University's Tercentennial, Richard Benson, then dean of the School of Art, categorized all representations, including written or printed words, as pictures. Most often we will use the term "picture" to refer to a two-dimensional visual artifact that its viewers understand to be a representation.[7] These representations are often nonverbal but need not be; words printed on a page (or displayed on a screen) exist within the frame of the page or the screen and thus are picture-like in our usage.

We can think of the realm of pictures as encompassing three large domains. First are visual representations that are *descriptive* of what we might see with our eyes looking out on the world, with or without technological prostheses. These descriptive pictures appear to make meaning in a "bottom-up" fashion that starts with perception. Then there are pictures that are *diagrammatic*, graphic representations of more or less abstract thoughts—measurements, relationships, and so on. These make meaning in a "top-down" fashion that starts with cognition. Finally, there are pictures that consist of *notations*, such as words, mathematical expressions, and musical scores.[8] And these domains overlap: A single frame may include more than one kind of representation, and, in any one domain, meanings may be generated in multiple ways. And, increasingly, digital tools allow people to make hybrid representations that employ elements of two or all three domains. The world of picturing thus embraces everything from doodles to fine art and includes all of the charts and graphs, photographs and videos, film clips and computer-generated animations, and scientific data displays and virtual reality views that we discuss in this book. Sometimes we will use the word "picture" to refer to an entire framed visual representation, whatever sort of hybrid of descriptive, diagrammatic, and/or notational forms it may be. Sometimes "picture" or "pictorial" will be used to contrast descriptive and diagrammatic representations on the one hand from verbal or other notational ones on the other, within the same frame.

Pictures versus words. On the face of it, we might say that words and pictures are both ways in which people give form to their ideas and feelings and convey those ideas and feelings to others. Both are means of capturing or fixing experience, of creating or documenting data, and of bringing phenomena into relationships and then of communicating any or all of that to other people so that behavior can be harmonized toward common goals. People can also freely play with both words and pictures; either can be used to express passing thoughts and to appeal to the imagination. And pictures, like words, can make meanings symbolically; both can be used to create analogies and metaphors.

Yet, we intuitively understand that pictures and words are not the same. Words always refer to something else. They are arbitrary signs.[9] They are essentially abstract. They have a grammar (different rules depending upon the specific language, but always a grammar),[10] and the grammar specifies not only how words may be constructed out of smaller semantic units but also the order in which the words may unfold and hence the meaning of the words in sequence. Ideas expressed in words are thus what we call time-based, because time—the linear order of expression—governs the unfolding of meaning. When we read, we can focus on each word or group of words to the exclusion of all else if we need to. We can also scan quickly, picking up some words and not others, and our previous reading experience will fill in the gaps or signal us to go back for more information. But whenever we are reading, we cannot grasp the whole idea until we have gone through all of its parts and correctly filled in any gaps with our prior knowledge.

Pictures are different. Generally speaking, the first thing we see is their *all-overness*, the large compositional whole that must then be parsed for its parts. And, when we parse, we cannot help but do that with the whole picture in mind. As with reading words, we are primed when we look at pictures by what we have already seen, and we can and do fill in information that may, for any number of reasons, be missing from our visual perceptions. (Consider, for instance, how we see a continuous visual field even though our retinas receive no input at the "blind spot" where the optic nerve connects to the eye.) But we can enter a picture anywhere we want to, drawn to any feature of it that catches our eye, whether the attraction is based on our own interests and predilections, formal qualities of the picture itself, or some combination thereof. With words, we can't get the idea without getting to the end of the spoken or written thought. With pictures, by contrast, we can stop "reading" when we think we recognize the subject matter, although we may then fail to decode other meanings that the picture may be intended to convey or be capable of conveying. And this happens very quickly: While our eyes and brains can process either verbal or visual information faster than the conscious mind is capable of noticing (as evidenced by the efficacy of both verbal and visual stimuli in subconscious priming studies), we can get the gist of a visual display in a single fixation lasting less than a third of a second.[11] It takes much longer to process the semantic equivalent presented in verbal form.

An important implication of all of this is that pictures are especially well suited for conveying meaning through associational logic, often infused with emotions that are triggered beneath our conscious awareness. Words, of course, can also prompt emotional associations, but pictures do this more rapidly. The same areas of the brain that process visual perceptions are also responsible for mental imagery, and these are connected to the amygdala and other areas of the brain critical for emotion.[12] And, because visual information acquires emotional valence before that information ever gets to the cortex,[13] the whole picture passes along its emotional colors even as we begin to decode its parts. The initial emotional loading can occur nearly immediately and may influence further readings of the picture quite apart from any later contribution that cortical reflection makes. Moreover, because we can stop reading the picture when we think we've got the subject matter, whereas we have to get more or less to the end of the verbal string to get the meaning of the sentence, other meanings and associations that are conveyed (subliminally or not) by the rest of the picture are that much less likely ever to be identified or scrutinized.

Belief in pictures and the problem of naïve realism. For several reasons, pictures in general are capable of inducing belief more intuitively and more effectively than words alone. Pictures that are descriptive (in the sense that we have used that term) resemble unmediated reality more than words can[14] and are therefore more likely to provoke cognitive and especially emotional responses similar to those aroused by the real thing depicted.[15] And, within the category of descriptive pictures, documentary photos, videos, and film can appear to be caused by the external world without the taint of human mediation or authorial interpretation.[16] Consequently, they tend to be accepted as highly credible evidence of the reality they depict, even though they lack the other sensory modalities that the viewer would encounter in real life.[17] Moreover, although people's cognitive default is to believe initially whatever they hear, read, or see, only later engaging in the effort needed to suspend or reject belief,[18] pictures tend to be more resistant than words to the forces of disbelief. Pictures tend to be more vivid than words and, especially in the case of the rapid picture sequences in video and film, they can be more involving and entertaining, decreasing the mental resources available for doubt. And, if we quickly stop thinking about a picture once we think we've gotten the point, we are less likely to reflect on it critically—including how the picture's emotional associations may be contributing to our belief in the picture's truthfulness.

The intuitive tendency to believe in whatever things, events, or ideas a picture (perhaps especially a descriptive, documentary picture) depicts or suggests—that is, to be more inclined, at least initially, to accept pictures than words as reliable evidence of reality—derives from two closely related habits of mind that, singly or in combination, may be called *naïve realism*. The first is the common-sense notion that there's an objective world out there and that anyone with open eyes can know it and see it.[19] Seeing is believing. This is naïve realism: "realism" because it plausibly posits the existence of a world at least partly independent of our knowledge of it; "naïve" because it attributes that knowledge exclusively to features of the world and not also to the ways we come to know it, which include the physical and social contexts of our perceptions and our prior knowledge and expectations ("believing is seeing"). Believing in the truthfulness of our perceptions is intuitive. Our brains process direct sensory inputs more quickly than they do the kinds of language-mediated thoughts that lead to reflection, critique, and suspicion; the frontal lobe where such delayed responses occur is located farthest from the brain regions where sensory inputs are registered.[20] And it would surely be odd if human brains and bodies had evolved so that quickly trusting our perceptions were a generally dysfunctional trait. At the same time, intuition, as the cognitive psychologist Daniel Kahneman has observed, is like perception: fast, effortless, and automatic.[21] Intuitive judgment just "feels right." Our minds, largely beneath the threshold of our consciousness, somehow simplify complex tasks to facilitate judgments that we confidently believe are correct.[22]

It follows that the more like everyday perception our encounter with a representation is, the more likely we are to believe (again, initially and unreflectively) in the truth or reality of what it depicts or describes. And people's uptake of pictures is more like everyday perception than is their uptake of words alone. (Again, we are taking descriptive pictures such as news or documentary photos and film as paradigmatic here, although our remarks also apply to a lesser extent to other sorts of pictures.) Because pictures are tied to vision, the primary sense through which we experience the world outside ourselves, pictures can seem transparently obvious and completely "natural." This brings us to the second mental habit that may be called naïve realism: People tend (again, initially and unreflectively) to conflate representations with direct perceptions of reality, to "look through" the mediation at what is depicted. To see the picture is to see the real thing, unmediated. What a picture depicts just seems to have presence, a kind of being in the world.[23] As a consequence, the meaning of the picture is understood to be identical to its content. The realism in this way of understanding pictures is the entirely plausible belief that (most) descriptive, documentary pictures that purport to describe external reality actually do so, if incompletely; the naïveté comes from ignoring how (to paraphrase Marshall McLuhan) the medium affects the message—how the meanings a picture conveys are shaped by the tools, techniques, and social contexts of representation.

At a very basic level, to approach pictures from the standpoint of naïve realism is to ignore the most fundamental aspect of all pictures, which is that they are *framed*: bounded, separated from reality by something that cues the reader that they are artifacts to be interpreted. Being aware of the frame and its implications includes recognizing, first, that every picture that people make is an abstraction from nature: A part of the possible perceptual field has been selected; the totality of sensory data has been reduced to one or two dimensions (either sight or sight and sound); and extraneous elements have (usually) been eliminated so that the signal is (relatively) clear. Understanding the picture requires identifying and appreciating the significance of each of these abstractions and the choices that the picture maker has made regarding each. Second, the presence of the frame defines relationships between the parts of the picture and the whole, changing the relative importance of the elements in the spatial field and defining the point of view—the position of the viewer—from which things are observed. Third, an awareness of the frame means recognizing that every picture comes cognitively and emotionally loaded with different levels of meanings. Some derive from the particular genre of representation (e.g., think of the similarities and differences between a photograph made with an analog camera and an oil painting based on a meticulous rendering of information from a photograph). Some are grounded in people's past experiences with that sort of representation or genre of picture. Some arise from the creator's specific compositional choices using the medium in which the work is realized. And some of the meanings are provided or shaped by the context of and purposes for the viewing.

The capacity of pictures to induce intuitive belief sets up a complex dynamic that we will follow throughout the book. It helps to explain why pictures have come to predominate over written texts in so many aspects of our culture—why our culture, and increasingly now the law as well—has gone visual. Pictures can often communicate many kinds of ideas and persuade more effectively than words alone because pictures tend to be intuitively credible, often compelling, and seemingly automatically understood. To the extent that difficult problems of judgment can be pictured—that is, translated into visual descriptions, diagrams, or both—those judgments seem to become more tractable, even effortless. Decisions that would otherwise be difficult become intuitive. A lawyer who visually represents arguments as boxes or building blocks and stacks them on top of one another so that the stack for the client's side of the case is taller than the opponent's stack seeks to convert a difficult, intangible judgment—whose arguments are stronger?—into a simple, visual one: Whose pile is taller? The visual representation is self-validating: The side with the taller pile wins.

But pictures also generate meanings beyond the ones most immediately grasped and beyond those that the picture makers intended. By exposing and challenging the naïvely realistic view of pictures, we can bring these other meanings or interpretations to awareness. And, often, this is accomplished precisely by showing *more pictures*—which then generate their own plethoras of meanings, obvious and subtle, which are themselves subject to further contestation, potentially ad infinitum. The lawyers who represented the police officers in the first Rodney King case, for instance, did exactly this when they showed still frames and slow-motion sequences from the amateur video that the prosecution had played unedited, in real time. The still frames and the video excerpts constituted new pictures, albeit derived from the same source material, and (together with the accompanying expert testimony) they offered jurors an entirely different understanding of the events depicted.

Pictures and words together. Pictures, when deployed by lawyers, always come in the context of lots of words: the words of statutes and prior judicial decisions, contracts and documentary evidence, depositions and trial testimony; the words that constitute the competing narratives of the case; and the words that lawyers and witnesses use to introduce the pictures. Some of those words (or others) may be in the frame together with a descriptive or diagrammatic picture, yielding one of those hybrids we mentioned earlier. A picture may be intended simply to illustrate words, whether or not those words are in the same frame, or it may do something else. In fact, pictures may pose complex arguments all on their own. Let us begin with a picture from the realm of the fine arts that puts the problem squarely in front of us: René Magritte's 1929 painting *The Treachery of Images* (Figure 1.1).

In the oil painting's frame, there are two "statements": a representation of a pipe used for smoking tobacco and the French words (translated) "This is not a pipe." It doesn't matter which you "read" first, the pipe or the phrase. The phrase you have to read word by word. As noted earlier, the sequence is important; the syntax makes the meaning. The pipe you "read" in one glance. But to what is the *entire* painting, consisting of all

Figure 1.1. René Magritte, "The Treachery of Images" (1929) (courtesy of the Los Angeles County Museum of Art. © René Magritte Estate/Artists Rights Society (ARS), New York/ADAGP, Paris).

of the elements within the frame, pointing? What do we think Magritte means? Let's explore this a bit.

Neither the painted object nor the painting as a whole is a real pipe, of course. That makes the words true. But the painting contains a picture of a pipe, which the words seem to deny. Does the pipe look more solid and real to you than the words? Or do the words compel your belief more completely because they are propositional, giving you a task you can test for yourself? Does putting both the picture of the pipe and the words into a frame as seemingly equal partners create a contest between the two modalities, and, if so, does either prevail? And what might Magritte mean by his title, *The Treachery of Images*? Perhaps the treachery is that the pipe is there but we cannot grab it, since it is actually just pigment on canvas (or, in the reproduction you are more likely to encounter, ink on a page or pixels on a screen). Or perhaps it's that the painting creates a desire (to touch or otherwise experience the presence of the real pipe) that it then leaves unfulfilled. Or perhaps the words can neither entirely contain the picture of the pipe nor constrain the meaning of the painting as a whole. Maybe pictures are treacherous because they upset stable meanings—because the painting keeps on speaking in its own voice no matter what we call it, eluding our grasp. The painting's ambiguities are intentional. If you have enjoyed looking at this reproduction of this painting, then the pleasure probably lies in these tensions between words and pictures and in Magritte's elegant presentation of these dilemmas of meaning.

It is precisely in this gap between pictures and words that much of our communication through media takes place. Things can be "said" in pictures that cannot, for a variety of reasons, be named with words, and people often exploit those interstices between saying and showing to talk about the world. Both modes of representation are crucial to developing the play of the multiple meanings in *The Treachery of Images*. The painting would be dull, and surely would never have wound up so widely reproduced in books, if either were missing. Magritte's painting presages a signal feature of the digital age: the ability to write with pictures in combination with words to an unprecedented degree. But, before we go further into the hybrid forms—pictures with words, media with other media—that are now so common and crucial to our digital cultural landscape, we need to consider briefly some broader contexts.

The Visual Turn

The ascendancy of visual culture. Magritte made his painting long before the digital revolution. He used analog materials and addressed the problem of meaning in analog terms. That the painting is self-consciously wise in the ways of meaning making, however, is no surprise. Even as Magritte worked, scholars in many disciplines had begun to question the longstanding suspicion of picturing and the privileging of words over pictures in Western culture.[24] The oft-mentioned "visual turn" in our culture refers as much to this validation of the visual as a means of communication and a way of knowing the world as it does to the sheer increase in the number of visual representations at large in society.

There are any number of reasons why the visual should have become increasingly validated in more recent times. Partly, it has to do with the authority of science in Western culture since the Enlightenment and the crucial role of both visual technologies, such as newly invented telescopes and microscopes, and picturing—including maps of geographic discovery and practices of "virtual witnessing" of experiments—in scientific and technological advances from the sixteenth century to the twentieth.[25] It also has to do with the increasing contacts between different societies across the earth: Visual artifacts circulate far beyond their territories of origin, suggesting visual access to knowledge of the Other; visual symbols facilitate communication across language barriers (think, e.g., of the standard icons for men's and women's restrooms or the worldwide use of the red hexagonal sign with white letters: "STOP"). Scholars in many fields have turned their attention to what had previously been regarded as popular (or "low") culture, treating everything from kitsch and comic books to movies and television as proper subjects for serious academic study. Philosophers, psychologists, and, more recently, cognitive scientists and neuroscientists have all suggested that there is more than meets the eye in both looking at pictures and thinking our thoughts.[26]

In any event, the sheer number of pictures has increased exponentially, and their influence across all cultural domains has spread accordingly. Visual representations have challenged and, more recently, overtaken purely verbal ones as the dominant means of communication in Western culture. It is by now a commonplace that, as a result of image-making and image-distribution media from photography and offset printing to photocopying, broadcast television, and film, a person in contemporary culture sees more constructed images in a day than someone living a few centuries ago did in a lifetime.[27] For decades, people have been relying more on television than on print media for their knowledge of the world and spending more time watching audiovisual entertainments—first movies, then television, and, more recently, video and computer games—than reading.[28] The effects of this profusion of pictures are profound and ongoing. We focus on two.

Visual media shape thinking and judgment. Most visual media share certain effects on viewers' perceptions and judgments. Thanks to Marshall McLuhan, it is also widely understood that the particular medium shapes the message:[29] that different media exert different kinds of influences on the messages they convey. For example, print culture usually operates in a field of concepts and categories.[30] Television, by contrast, excels in depicting personal dramas, offering viewers story lines and character types that are familiar and immediately accessible. Television achieves unique emotional power and intimacy by way of the closeup, which brings viewers directly into the emotional field of the characters on the screen. This is not just a matter of aesthetics. Dramatizing the personal tends to obscure the general. By presenting social problems in terms of personal history and individual character development, television resists sociopolitical complexity, which is notoriously difficult to dramatize in visual form.

People's media-spawned expectations are guided by the visual codes of all the media they regularly encounter: print advertising, television, and film, especially major Hollywood movies, and now computer gaming and the Internet, as well. The visual codes that come from popular culture become a part of people's visual common sense, which is to say they are unconsciously assimilated. People understand cross-cutting and parallel editing; they do not need anyone to explain these storytelling devices. The camera is inside the audience's heads, and viewers are prepared to reconstruct reality in accordance with the perceptual and cognitive codes they have internalized. In short, what people find to be credible and persuasive in visual displays is guided by the habits of thinking and feeling that have been inculcated by their experiences with the media they have encountered.

Truth and fiction in visual culture. Although visual representation is (as noted earlier) often associated with advances in scientific and other knowledge, the visual turn in Western culture, especially in recent decades, has also been characterized by an increasingly pervasive conflation of fact and fiction. Consider that advertising is arguably (in the words of the rhetorician Stephen McKenna) "the most successful rhetorical enterprise on the face of the planet"[31] and that the mass media (and, increasingly, much of the Internet) are driven by advertising. In the world of advertising, critical thinking—the audience's ability to scrutinize the factual content of the claims being made, to distinguish reality from fantasy—is not the goal of most messages or, arguably, of the message system as a whole. This is plain from the form as well as the content of (especially television and Internet) advertising: There are too many ads, cutting too rapidly from one picture to another, for people to reflect carefully on what they're seeing and hearing; at the same time, the ads are designed to be vivid, humorous, and entertaining in order to stand out from the cacophony. Audiences who are both entertained (or at least distracted) and cognitively overloaded are less willing and less able to examine critically the meanings generated by these visual messages. In a culture permeated by modern advertising, the prominent audiovisual style of communication is not conducive to clear thinking about what's true, what's partly true, what's misleading, and what's altogether false.

Confusions of fact and fiction are rampant in the realm of visually mediated news and politics. To be sure, deliberate efforts to present lies as truth, ideology as history, are as old as recorded human civilization. Not only misdirection but outright forgeries have been a staple of political (and academic) life for many centuries. Visual and multimedia spectacles have been a part of politics at least since Alexander the Great and the Egypt of the pharaohs.[32] But the ostensible credibility of pictures that seem to present reality directly and unmediated, such as news photography and documentary video, combined with people's growing dependence on those pictures for their knowledge of the real, has multiplied the possibilities for managing people's impressions of the world. Never before has common-sense naïve realism, with its presumption to be able to tell fact from fiction, been so relied upon to prevent us from actually seeing the difference. Consider, for example, the repeated broadcast of simulations in place of real battle coverage during the first Gulf War, which gave the American viewing public a convincing impression of the effectiveness, efficiency, and bloodlessness of our military's might.[33] Or, in the domain of entertainment, consider the skill with which television networks have enticed viewers to watch "reality TV" programs that ostensibly provide windows onto reality—urban policing in *COPS*, military actions in Afghanistan in the short-lived *Profiles From the Front Lines*, competitions between "real" people (i.e., not professional actors) to endure challenging environments in *Survivor*—scripted according to the conventions of dramatic fictions.[34]

Advertisers have blurred boundaries between media genres that used to help audiences decide whether to take up incoming messages as news, entertainment, or sales pitch. Both industry and government prepare and package video news releases which then appear as straight reportage on local news outlets, cloaking ads for policy positions in the guise of fact.[35] Consider also the long advertising sections in magazines that present themselves as informational brochures about a foreign country (tourism industry) or medical problems that can be "solved" with a new drug (pharmaceutical industry). Product placements insinuate advertising into entertainments to reach viewers who try to TiVo themselves free of such solicitations. Indeed, a hallmark of the infotainment culture is not only the surreptitious exploitation of the fact/fiction confusion but its explicit celebration. We see this in docudramas and dramatic fictions "based on a true story" and in *The Daily Show With Jon Stewart*, which proclaimed itself "The Leader in Fake News" and yet (or therefore?) became the most trusted news source for millions during the 2004 American presidential campaign, largely because of the skill with which the show humorously deconstructed the purportedly "reality-based" rhetoric of politicians and of mainstream news outlets.[36] This culture, with its sleight-of-hand about what's real and, in many cases, its tendency to distance audiences from reality, might be especially problematic when those same people become decision makers in real legal cases, where their judgments have actual consequences for others. On the other hand, *The Daily Show's* visual deconstructions also indicate how visual technologies can be deployed to hone people's critical awareness of mediated information.

In a visual culture, the features of specific visual media and the ways they shape the messages people receive—and hence the beliefs people form and the decisions they make—are crucial to understanding how the culture works. Yet, the effects of visual media in our culture often remain obscured because of the persistence of habits of naïve realism, the nature and aims of so many pictures designed to advertise, and the absence of training in visual literacy from most curricula. Visual literacy has not always been on education's menu;[37] lawyers, judges, and jurors who possess this literacy do so only by accident or because of personal interest, not through required training.[38] The upshot is that many participants in the legal system and much of the general public may be less than fully prepared to think critically about the possible meanings of the pictures they see or, consequently, to assess the truthfulness of pictures and multimedia when it matters. The digitization of media and society has only amplified this challenge.

The Digital Revolution

The proliferation of digital media has accelerated society's reliance on the visual, magnifying both the benefits and the problems of that reliance. But, more than that, the spread of digital visual and multimedia technologies is transforming the very nature of mediated expression and communication.

Picturing tools for everyone. Digital technologies have made the means of making and widely distributing all kinds of pictures, previously in the hands only of a relative few, available to practically everyone. To give you some size of the market for digital imaging software, the market research group NPD estimated that 29.5 million digital cameras would be sold in the United States in 2006.[39] By early 2009, according to Lyra Research, an industry research firm, the cumulative number of mobile phones equipped with still or video cameras was expected to "surpass the cumulative number of both conventional and digital cameras shipped in the entire history of photography—and camera phones have been on the market for less than a decade."[40] The futurist Ray Kurzweil has marshaled evidence from many sources to show that communication and computing technologies have been advancing in power, decreasing in cost, and spreading in use at exponential rates.[41]

In a digital culture, the tools of picturing are not only nearly ubiquitous but, for the most part, easy to use. (Indeed, they have become ubiquitous *because* they are easy to use.) Digital cameras eliminate the need for lab work. People can take photos and then send them immediately to friends or family; news photographers in remote locations can get their pictures to professional photo agencies more easily and quickly than ever before. If you don't own a printer for pictures, drug store photo centers will print them for you, often more cheaply than you could do it yourself. Cell phone cameras are used not only for spur-of-the-moment and sentimental snapshots but also for citizen surveillance of events occurring in public spaces. Millions of people edit their photos using either professional editing software like Adobe Photoshop or freeware like Google's Picasa.[42] They edit their videos in the camera using built-in functions, or they use simple, standard-issue software programs that come with their computer's operating systems; they can also use professional video editing tools like Adobe's Premier and Apple's Final Cut Pro, available for their home computers. Children are being taught PowerPoint in the primary grades, and school projects increasingly take advantage of the multimedia capabilities of laptop computers, which have become essential equipment for students. Before cameras were consumer products, drawing was mandatory for professional and skilled crafts work, so drawing was part of the standard curriculum. This mastery required considerable training of the hands, and it took quite a bit of time and practice to learn to draw with fluidity and understanding. Today, students can make pictures that display high-level conceptual understanding without first acquiring that mastery.[43]

When these digital picturing tools meet the World Wide Web, pictures go from being circulated only among friends and family to reaching a potentially unlimited global audience. The Web site YouTube ("broadcast yourself"), which hosts video of just about any kind, made by anyone, from home movies to clips of favorite ads and episodes from television shows, was created in February 2005, and by July 2006 had overtaken MySpace as the most popular community Web site in the world.[44] Young professionals use the site to show off their production and editing skills. This, in turn, has upended marketing wisdom. When a pilot of a comedy show, *Nobody's Watching*, was posted on YouTube in June 2005, viewers' reviews in the first week pushed it from just another post to a "featured" video, and, after the number of responses reached 300,000, television executives decided that industry focus groups had been trumped by the public and rescheduled the pilot for broadcast.[45] And digital files don't have to remain passively deposited for audience viewing. Because everything on the Web is made of essentially the same stuff—the 1s and 0s of digital code—files can be downloaded, joined, and recombined in virtually unlimited ways by people who never meet each other.

Scientists, too, have been the beneficiaries of visualizing tools far more complex than the telescopes and microscopes introduced at the beginning of the scientific revolution. X-rays have been around since the end of the nineteenth century, but digital diagnostic imaging technologies, from ultrasound to CT scans (computerized tomography), PET scans (positron emission tomography), MRIs (magnetic resonance imaging), and fMRIs (functional MRIs), have yielded millions of new visual medical records. Computer animation programs allow the fruits of scientific research to be readily and compellingly visualized for educational or advertising purposes.[46]

Indeed, digital picturing tools have been eagerly adopted in just about every field that uses pictures. Mechanical engineers, architects, and screenwriters and producers all have specialized software that has made the traditional, hands-on methods of these professions nearly obsolete.[47] In many ways, modern warfare is information warfare, in which military decisions are made on the basis of continual computer monitoring, analysis, and graphic modeling far from the actual theater of war and in which orders are executed by troops far from the command. The U.S. Army has even collaborated with video game designers to produce *America's Army*, a popular video game which the Army uses as a recruiting and training tool.[48]

Digital picturing tools are everywhere in our work and leisure lives. And the complete penetration of digital thinking into our entertainments and disciplines of knowledge means that the ways we conceive of the world as a whole are being transformed.

Writing with pictures. By giving people this unprecedented capacity to translate events and things, ideas and observations, into visual forms, to combine pictures and words in any way desired, and to exchange those pictures and words worldwide, digital technologies have made picturing a very different kind of practice. Pictures can now make meanings in newly complicated ways. Understanding pictures, therefore, becomes a more complex and nuanced business than ever.

One feature of our picture-laden digital visual environment is that we increasingly see composite pictures—not just words and pictures juxtaposed, as in Magritte's painting, but hybrids in which the conventional codes of various kinds of pictures may be combined or in which a picture from one kind of discourse winds up in another. Educated people are used to *intertextuality*, the explicit or implicit reference in one text to another, such as Herman Melville's use in *Moby Dick* of the cadences of the Bible. Intertextuality is also a feature of visual texts: Think of the many paintings of artists' ateliers or grand galleries that depict walls filled with pastiches of other paintings. But it is hardly limited to elite entertainments. Television programs and movies abound with cross-references to other shows and movies. Movies also borrow the representational conventions of particular film genres to convey specific meanings and emotional effects (for instance, *The Blair Witch Project* used the jerky pictures produced by a handheld camera to evoke the realism of cinema verité).

Sometimes a work in a given medium borrows or alludes not merely to other works or even to other genres within that medium but to the visual forms and interpretive codes of other media. The media theorists Jay David Bolter and Richard Grusin have called this *remediation*.[49] By this they mean the couching of newer media in terms of older ones, such as the presentation of the personal computer screen as a desktop, Web sites as pages, or (to pick a less obvious example) the unfolding of many video games in terms of Hollywood screenwriting conventions.[50] We will use the term to refer also to the incorporation by older media of the forms and codes of newer ones—for instance, the adoption by television news and other programs of interfaces with split screens, stable or scrolling text on the bottom, and other features that visually evoke the multiple windows of personal computing. In digital culture, the ease with which materials from any source whatsoever can be mixed and the profusion of media and interfaces (including television monitors, computer screens, cell phone displays, and Wi-Fi-enabled PDAs) mean that opportunities for compositing forms and meanings from multiple media abound.

Here's an example of what happens to meaning when this hybrid character of visual representation itself becomes a mode of discourse. Figure 1.2 is a picture of President George W. Bush as he appeared on the front

Figure 1.2. President Bush appears on the front page of the July 10, 2002 *New York Times* (video still courtesy of CNBC).

page of the *New York Times* on July 10, 2002. This still image appears as a screen capture of a televised speech by the president on the topic of corporate responsibility. The Worldcom and Enron debacles were then in full swing, so we can understand why the president would be addressing this issue and why the *Times* would consider that newsworthy.

But where is the president, actually? The wallpaper behind him looks somewhat like a graphic from a corporate annual report; it may or may not be real wallpaper in a real room. With blue screen technology,[51] the president could be anywhere at all. (The caption tells us that he was speaking to a "Wall Street audience," which strongly suggests, although it does not entail, that the speech was made in lower Manhattan; in any event, this information comes from the text below the frame and not from the picture itself.)

Now notice (as the caption writer at the *Times* did, at some level) the tickers at the bottom of the depicted television screen, which provided television viewers with scrolling stock data, and, just above these on the right, the three composite stock data figures, each accompanied by a little triangular arrow pointing down. Notice, too, below these, the CNBC logo, which seems to be "on" the tickers but "underneath" the data reported on those tickers. As all of these elements appear on the television screen, do they simply record the president's appearance, or do they also reflect an editorial comment by CNBC ("thumbs down" today)? And what is it about a televised picture, or this televised picture in particular, that made the editors at the *Times* choose it (as opposed to, say, a print photographer's shot of the actual speech) as the picture to include with the written story? Plainly, the televised coverage of the speech, and not only the speech itself, was part of the story. What we seem to have is (1) the president making a speech (2) that is nested in a news broadcast that is commenting on that speech, (3) which comment is itself alluded to by the *New York Times* (the caption reads "President Bush's televised image shared the screen with stock market data") in a picture and caption (4) that accompany articles reporting and analyzing the event. If we add the publication of the picture in this book, the picture is appearing on five different levels of communication, all at once.

There is no way to verify what the newspaper intended by printing this picture. A little to the right of it, above the fold, an article gives the expected prominence to the president's remarks. Different readers would bring different expectations to the paper's coverage of the event. Did the editors choose this picture because it would encourage each group of readers to believe that the picture was addressed to them in particular? Those who admire the president would see his serious expression and the strong phrase "Corporate Responsibility" both behind him (in the wallpaper) and in front of him (in the caption provided by CNBC), so he is squarely "inside the message." Those who approve of his message (or what they might infer it to be simply from seeing the picture and the phrase) might read the downward-pointing arrows as referring to the morally downward path of corporate irresponsibility and the attendant loss of profitability, a downturn which the president is now, responsibly, seeking to correct.

Those critical of the president might see him fenced in by the words behind him and the words and numbers in front, trapped within the corporate world; the arrows would reflect a "thumbs down" attitude toward that world, the president's capture by it, and the president in general. In short, the *Times* could make all of its readers happy with this picture.

This is writing with pictures, and it's happening all the time in our media-rich and media-savvy culture. By not explicitly naming meaning with words, the *Times* could exploit the multiple messages of a single picture because that picture contained multiple meanings, each of which is constructed from all of the same visual elements. That is, it is possible to generate two internally consistent but opposite readings of the whole picture (as we have suggested) that leave out no major elements of the picture. To create those multiple meanings, the newspaper relied on the television broadcast's use of immediately intelligible visual forms, some of which represented those of the president's actual appearance (assuming the physical reality of the "corporate responsibility" wallpaper) and some of which were created anew, such as the now-familiar remediation of ticker tape in the scrolling stock market data. The newspaper added some of its own, including, most importantly, the choice, cropping, and location of the picture on the front page. To convey those meanings effectively, the *Times* was counting on its readers' ability to unpack these multilayered, multimedia codes.

The complexities and ambiguities of these intersecting and overlapping visual forms, however, pose the risk that meanings will be missed or misconstrued. Indeed, the creators of these kinds of implicit communications may be counting on some audiences getting the message and others missing it; those who are "in the know" can be targeted, while others remain unaware that a coded message has been sent. To talk about the ambiguous meanings in pictures like these, we have to stop and pay attention to all that they might suggest to us, to go beyond our first impressions of the subject matter—to think of these pictures as something to be read and not merely seen. This is hard to do when the pictures are flashing by at the rate of 29.95 frames per second; it is hard to do if we merely turn the page too quickly on a picture in a print medium.

As a ubiquitous digital practice, writing with pictures changes how meanings are made and exchanged throughout the culture. It elevates the importance of picturing, and specifically digital picturing, as a way of representing, communicating, and thinking. It makes the task of decoding visual messages more complex and in turn makes the enterprise of persuading more complex as well. And it disperses the authority to make and interpret meanings.

Digital visual thinking. By greatly increasing the number and variety of pictures, digitization makes responding to pictures an ever more important part of the ways people think, feel, decide, and act in their everyday lives. We have already described how many more pictures there are, from snapshots to medical diagnostics to PowerPoint slide shows. We have also briefly mentioned how what people think they know and how they know it are shaped by the media to which they are exposed. At a minimum, the basic features of visual as opposed to purely verbal communication—its relative vividness, its ease and speed of comprehension (on at least some levels), and so on—should play a larger role in people's thinking and decision making as the number of pictures there are to see increases. Indeed, as the human-made environment changes, so do the brains of the people who grow up in that environment.[52] Thus, adolescents today, who are exposed to much more fast-paced visual information than were adolescents twenty years ago, are faster and more accurate at basic object recognition tasks.[53]

Yet, it is how we use technologies and not merely how we are exposed to them that is most profoundly related to how we think. Anthropologists have long observed that what people do with the tools they use contributes significantly to how they think and who they are.[54] Hence, "advances in human intelligence and the evolution of technology are intimately related."[55] The spread of digital technologies for making, manipulating, and disseminating pictures, therefore, is likely to have important consequences for human cognition (and metacognition). In *Orality and Literacy*, Walter Ong famously argued that "writing restructures consciousness";[56] the adoption of writing transformed the habits of thought of previously oral cultures. If that's true of writing with words, what about writing with pictures? How does thinking change when people can so readily express ideas and observations in visual form, make and modify their own or others' pictures, combine pictures and words however they wish, and rapidly exchange those word-picture combinations around the world?

It may be too soon to generalize,[57] but one speculation seems reasonable: The more consciously people write with pictures and seek to understand what others have written, the less tenacious should be the cognitive default of naïve realism. As the philosopher and historian of science Ian Hacking has argued, when representations are undifferentiated, the problem of realism does not arise; in other words, we are all naïve realists, because the one representation of which we're aware naturally appears to us as true. "But as soon as representations begin to compete, we ha[ve] to wonder what is real."[58] As digital technologies bring more pictures of any given thing or event into more rapid circulation, those pictures are more likely to compete, making it possible (for lawyers, we would say necessary) to ask how each mode mediates reality and with what consequences.

More than this, the widespread awareness that pictures are modified and manipulated in the course of being used to communicate should change the perceived connection between pictures and reality. The average person may not (yet) be adept at using advanced professional editing software like Adobe Photoshop, but, in all likelihood, he or she will have heard of "photoshopping" as a verb referring to altering a picture. In an era when digital pictures are infinitely malleable, when, in the words of the architectural scholar and new media theorist William Mitchell, "the referent has come unstuck,"[59] the naïvely realistic sense of the documentary picture as metonymic truth (that is, the photographic representation standing unproblematically in the place of the reality it represents) is challenged by the understanding of the picture as a construct, a text to be actively construed rather than a window onto the world that merely needs to be looked through.

Pictures have become "unstuck" in another sense as well. As senders and not just receivers of articulated visual messages, people who use digital technologies understand that pictorial elements, not to mention pictures and words,[60] have fluid and contingent relationships to each other (as well as to reality). A photo of what appears to be a tourist with a backpack standing on the observation deck of the World Trade Center on the morning of September 11, 2001, oblivious to the plane approaching from behind, circulates on the Internet. Many viewed it as poignant and tragic realism—until the appearance of pictures showing "Tourist Guy" at the bombing of the U.S.S. *Cole*, the sinking of the *Titanic*, Godzilla's conquest of Tokyo, and other improbable venues, not to mention pictures showing Osama bin Laden in Tourist Guy's place at the World Trade Center.[61] Such mashups of depictive elements and of conceptual and emotional registers (running joke, political criticism) and the rapid succession and proliferation of variant pictures suggest a shift in popular expectations about what any one picture may mean, with what sort of authority, and for how long. And the division of our computer, television, and even movie screens into multiple windows (as we saw in the Bush photo in the *Times*, discussed earlier) brings a heterogeneity of pictures and words into the visual present, where each can refer to, comment on, support, or destabilize the meanings of the others.[62]

Rhetorical potential. "Where once only words were malleable enough to be widely wielded as a rhetorical tool, . . . the digital image [has become] prevalent, easy to manipulate, and consequently, easy to recontextualize."[63] We saw in the example of the *Times's* photo of President Bush some of the complex ways in which rhetoric changes when people can write with pictures. Not only pictures and words but different sorts of pictures, drawn from or alluding to different media, can be put into new sorts of relationships, generating new ranges of meanings, furthering arguments in new ways. This can also be seen in practically any segment of any network or cable news show: live programming, clips of previous programs, and digitally processed photos, videos, and graphics, each staged and framed in distinctive ways, are edited and blended with each other as well as with words, both spoken and text, to create multilayered messages. The potential for conveying meanings implicitly increases; so, too, does the potential ambiguity of the picture's meanings, which picture makers may creatively exploit or ignore at their peril.

Democratization of meaning making. Digital technologies have put the ability and hence the power to make visual meanings into more hands than ever before. This democratization did not begin with digitization, of course. During the many centuries in which the ability to fix images or texts in lasting form was largely confined to political and cultural elites, ordinary people might carve on gravestones or write graffiti on nearly anything. The invention of the printing press and the later availability of cheap paper made possible the many newspapers of the eighteenth century and their dissemination of an increasing diversity of political opinions.[64] The rapid spread of photography in the mid- to late nineteenth century, which allowed many more people to afford portraiture, gave dignity and significance to lives that would otherwise have passed unrecorded. And the mass production of cheap cameras and the standardization of photo processing technology in the first half of the twentieth century allowed millions to compose and record images of their own choosing.[65]

But digital picture-making tools, together with the Internet, have vastly expanded not only people's ability to communicate and argue visually but also their ability to reach a potentially worldwide audience. Personal Web pages, blogs, and chat rooms by the millions allow individuals without power, wealth, or credentials (the traditional prerequisites for airing one's views broadly) to use words to expound on, criticize, and reconceptualize the messages of the powerful, wealthy, and credentialed, as well as their own. And pictures are increasingly becoming a part of this mix, as people create still photos, videos, and animations and repurpose the creations of others to parody, entertain, inform, and express opinions.

Consider, for instance, in the realm of politics, the most iconic of the infamous Abu Ghraib prison photos, that of the hooded prisoner standing on a box with what he was told were live electrodes attached to the ends of his hands. It is not entirely clear why this photo and others were taken or posted in the first place;[66] in some ways, the most obvious precursors are the postcards of lynchings.[67] What is clear is that, among the disturbing pictures that emerged from Abu Ghraib, this was the most striking visually, and it was easily turned into an icon that could be circulated just like Tourist Guy. This time, the image circulated into the world of high art, as well as that of major media entertainment, achieving a form of perfection when the actual subject of the photograph posed with a copy of the photograph to make his own political statement.[68]

Popular participation in making meaning extends beyond such discrete episodes to encompass mediated culture in general.[69] People now expect to contribute as they never have before to the entertainments they enjoy. Television shows and advertisements routinely invite viewers to go to Web sites where they can find more information, participate in polls, or join a chat group discussing the topic. Perhaps the epitome of this genre is *American Idol*, as of this writing the most popular television show of its kind, in which contestants' fates are decided on a week-to-week basis by the votes of the viewing audience.[70] We have already mentioned YouTube and its growing role not only as a forum for the recirculation of all sorts of videos but as an influence on the mass media industry and even on the progress of the 2008 presidential campaign in the United States. DVDs, with all their extra materials and their menus, allow people to select what they want to see, which can be both less and more than the original movie; people can even make their own versions of the movie.[71] Moreover, the millions of people who spend innumerable hours in online gaming environments are developing an intuitive sense that knowledge is acquired by interacting with one's environment (a view propounded often in the past twenty years in academia but never experienced to this extent by the population at large) and that only their active intervention makes the worlds they perceive and inhabit "real."[72]

These new distributions of meaning making have necessarily been accompanied by a decline in the authority of the traditional gatekeepers of information. Take the news, for instance. Formerly, there was a whole ecology of print news: The papers at the top were the "papers of record," covering not just local news but also national and international news; then there were regional papers, strictly local papers, and special-interest papers. People knew this hierarchy. Major columnists, like television commentators, could sway public opinion or could deliver authoritatively the information that people needed. Newspapers were supported by advertising revenues. Today, information services on the Internet such as Craigslist and eBay have challenged the very existence of newspapers by drawing advertising revenue away from both the papers' classified ads sections and their display ad space in the rest of the paper. The nature of the news itself has changed. The domination of the big media by a few owners has resulted in a profusion of alternative press in the self-publishing world of the Internet, where everyone from crackpots and disinformation experts to people willing and able to do serious investigative reporting are free to express their views. And they do, across a full spectrum of opinion. Because they are networked, they can, in the aggregate, constitute a sort of social "weather report" in dialogue with major media.[73] These new sources are easily illustrated and so offer more and different data for their bona fides, although the same problems of authentication remain and are, in fact, increased. The now "venerable" Google News shows readers links to thirty-six countries' news in their local languages. Its front page shows what other readers think is important or have found useful. Other aggregators like Digg and Reddit reflect recommendations made by readers of the Web, catching interesting stuff in a less focused newsgathering than Google's. These forms of gatekeeping are in sharp contrast to the top-down editorial decisions at traditional newspapers. And what appears on the Google News front page is changing all the time; log off and then on again and what you see may be completely different.[74]

The law, too, has been affected by this newfound access to information. Several years ago, a fifteen-year-old boy became the most sought-after purveyor of online legal advice, trumping actual lawyers with a mix of common sense and insights gleaned from television law programs.[75] When anyone can make meaning and share it with everyone, differentiating the authoritative from the bogus, the factual from the fictional, becomes increasingly problematic.

There is a paradox here: Access to more information does not imply more knowledge. People can be easily taken in by messages that merely seem authoritative, whether because of the putative source of the message or the style of its presentation. The Internet facilitates productive communication between geographically separated people; it multiplies the power of digitization and picturing technologies to distribute cognition as never before.[76] But, by the same token, the Internet empowers groups of people who exchange ideas with one another within narrowly defined perspectives, with the consequence that skewed understandings can be easily validated and propagated. People's increasing ability to shape their digital worlds self-referentially—for instance, to personalize the news they read by signing up for alerts, setting homepages, or using Real Simple Syndication software, which "subscribes" users to sites they choose, allowing them to receive updates or new content automatically—need not entail democratization in any constructive political sense. Rather, it can lead to an exclusion of alternative points of view and the belief that different views need not be considered, ultimately an antidemocratic kind of solipsism, what the legal scholar Cass Sunstein has referred to as "information cocoons."[77] And, while surfing the Internet has given many people the experience of acquiring knowledge as a highly interactive pursuit, the fact that the information is coming in on a computer screen that looks a whole lot like a television screen may induce in others a kind of passivity.

In sum, people are immersed in digital pictures; they are also creating and disseminating digital pictures and multimedia themselves. In digital culture, the rules and practices for getting information and deciding whether to believe it and for crafting pictures and words and adjusting them to one's persuasive goals are rapidly changing. The relationships between speaker and audience, message sender and recipient, are being transformed in the worlds of news, entertainment, education, advertising, and politics. And all of this is happening in the law as well.

Law in a Digital Age

Lawyers are part of the broader culture. They are human beings subject to the same kinds of experiences and pressures as their audiences. Because the exercise of their profession involves them in the exercise of power, however, they need to understand the verbal and visual tools they deploy to accomplish their aims and what the effects of those tools might be. Lawyers also need to understand what their adversaries are doing. They cannot, for instance, comfortably retain a naïvely realistic approach to pictures when doing so will adversely affect their clients and the quality of justice that the legal system provides.[78]

That's one reason why this book is not about how to use particular digital devices—how to make a good PowerPoint, for instance. Instead, we hope to offer a way of thinking about larger developments taking place in digital culture so that lawyers, as well as judges, jurors, and the public, can understand those developments and think critically about them.

Legal knowledge in a digital age. The law has always purported to be very much (although certainly not exclusively) concerned with the truth: with grounding judgments in what actually happened. And, in the pursuit of truth, the law has long privileged words over picturing: the words of eye-witnesses and experts on the stand, of lawyers in their briefs and oral arguments, of judges in their written opinions. Yet, since at least the nineteenth century, as the legal scholar Jennifer Mnookin has written, the law has also turned to pictures (perhaps especially pictures as scientific and forensic evidence) in a quest for the kind of indisputable access to reality that witnesses, with their imperfect memories and susceptibilities to bias, may fail to provide. Courts received these pictures with anxiety, at once hoping and believing that they could convincingly reveal the truth even while fearing that they might be too persuasive, especially considering how easily they could be manipulated. This ambivalence toward courtroom visuals has been expressed ever since in the doctrinal category of *demonstrative* evidence: Pictures, when admissible at all, are shown to juries but typically only as illustrations of oral testimony, not as independent, substantive proof.[79]

In a digital multimedia age, the law must struggle with this same tension between words and pictures, between the need for access to the real and the ever-present risk of deception, but in a still more urgent fashion. By increasing the number of pictures available for lawyers' use, digital technologies multiply the occasions for both hope and doubt. Digital hardware and software allow lawyers to provide judges and jurors with visual access to aspects of reality that would otherwise remain obscure. They allow lawyers to translate highly technical and detailed information into visual form and thereby enhance judges' and jurors' ability to grasp that information and use it correctly in reaching decisions. At the same time, by making it so much easier to rework pictures and to display them in multiple formats, digital image processing programs can engender skepticism about any item of demonstrative evidence. Has the picture been altered to further the advocate's argument at the expense of accuracy or fairness to the opponent? Or, might judges' and jurors' preoccupation with the picture overwhelm their ability to attend to other relevant aspects of proof? If decision makers' exposure to persuasive digital displays, by appealing to their intuitive grasp of what's real, makes them feel more comfortable with and confident in their decisions, does this imply that the judgments will be more accurate or otherwise better according to any other criteria relevant to justice?

Some commentators, worried about the malleability of digital photographs and videos, have called for their per se exclusion from evidence. One judge was so suspicious that a lawyer might have incorporated subliminal messages into a computer animation that he insisted on previewing every cell of the animation—more than 30,000 of them.[80] Apart from such threats of outright manipulation, there is the ever-present concern that any given visual display may be prejudicial or misleading. Yet, judges lack clear guidelines for deciding when this is so, resulting in treatment of particular visual technologies and displays that varies not only from jurisdiction to jurisdiction but from one judge to another.

These are real concerns. One theme that runs through the following chapters is that a basic awareness of how pictures make meaning, combined with a close study of particular visual displays, can provide an antidote to naïve realism and thus permit a more intelligent and nuanced inquiry into the cognitive, emotional, and rhetorical effects of the pictures and multimedia displays shown in court. It may even be that the law, with its adversarial litigation and deeply rooted procedures and norms that encourage jurors to pay careful attention to what is said and shown, can offer a model for reasoned deliberation and judgment in an inescapably digital visual culture.

Legal argument in a digital age. Legal decisions are always about more than the facts and the law. Judges and jurors need to be convinced that their decisions are justified not only factually and legally but also morally. Lawyers, therefore, aim to marshal and present all of their evidence in the service of a theory of the case that encapsulates the rightness of their clients' cause, and they deliver arguments to persuade judges and jurors that justice favors their clients' positions. Thanks to digital technologies, more and more lawyers are creating visual and multimedia displays for explicitly argumentative as well as evidentiary uses. They are incorporating photos, video, and animation into integrated presentations on courtroom screens, and, when they do so, they draw on the same expository and rhetorical techniques with which their audiences are familiar from watching television and movies and using the Internet.

How should legal doctrine and courtroom practice adapt to a world in which lawyers are increasingly using the same picture-based media in which people are immersed in their everyday work and leisure lives, including those of advertising and entertainment? Should the law strive to purify legal judgments from these taints of popular media? Or, if it is believed that proliferating digital technology has opened a Pandora's box of persuasive tools that is unlikely to be closed, can the law develop concepts and practices that accommodate those tools within defensible notions of justice and fairness? Part of the answer may lie in enhancing the digital visual literacy of lawyers, judges, jurors, and the public, but by itself this is unlikely to be a stable or wholly satisfactory solution. How, for instance, should an adversarial system respond to parties' unequal access to the most expensive and sophisticated hardware and software?

From the advocates' perspective, persuasion in a digital culture is both a more adventuresome enterprise and a highly fraught one. The breakdown of received methods of gatekeeping information in the culture at large means that it is much harder for lawyers to make accurate assumptions about what the audiences for their legal arguments already believe. Lawyers may suppose, for instance, that primetime television still provides a cultural lingua franca, but it is no longer necessarily the leading indicator of what and how most people are thinking. Audiences exposed to the stupendous variety of digital visual and multimedia messages in their everyday lives may be more willing to encounter new kinds of arguments and proofs in legal contexts. Or, aware of how easy it is to mold pictures and words to suit any purposes and bereft of traditional cues for gauging the authority of messages sent by others, they may be much less inclined to take a lawyer's word (or picture) for anything. How can lawyers overcome this skepticism and use their digital toolbox to their best advantage?

Legal judgment in a digital age. The law has always tightly regulated who has the power to make representations and meanings. Through rules of evidence, ingrained procedures and conventions, and judicial oversight, the law seeks to control who may speak, when, and how, and with what effects. Will jurors who are accustomed to making their own evaluations of visual and multimedia information and to making and remaking pictures themselves be as ready to accede to the guidance of judges, lawyers, and experts as to how courtroom pictures should be read? Will they attend to evidence and argument with greater skepticism? How might the legal system be expected to adapt to a culture in which anyone with access to a computer and the Internet can communicate as authoritatively as anyone else and people expect to surf the Internet to find out what they need to know? When lawyers, for ease of trial presentation, routinely put their demonstrative evidence on interactive CD-ROMs, as some are already doing, will jurors expect to be able to play the disk themselves in the jury room (as has happened in one high-profile case in Great Britain)?[81] And, as bandwidth increases, will an overburdened judiciary continue to expand the role of virtual proceedings, converting not only witness examinations but entire trials, including jury deliberations and judgment, to the interface of the screen?[82] What might be the effects of doing so on decision making and justice?

Outline of the Book

In the following chapters, we explore different aspects of law's digital visual and multimedia revolution. The book moves generally from the most familiar technologies (video in chapter 2) to the most advanced (interactive online and virtual environments in chapter 6), and from their uses as evidence (chapters 2 through 4) to their deployment in arguments (chapter 5). But different technologies and their uses cannot be neatly divided among the different chapters, because they're not neatly separated in law practice. Throughout the book, we emphasize how every item of visual evidence is rhetorical—that is, offered to further an argument—and on more than one occasion we will encounter advocates who mix various software tools and presentation media. Successive chapters build on previous ones so that, as readers go through the book, they will acquire an increasingly deep and articulated understanding of our main themes. The last chapter, on the ethics of legal visuals and multimedia, is both retrospective, referring back to the uses of new media illustrated earlier in the book, and prospective, offering suggestions for enhancing the practice of law in the digital visual age.

Much of the book is built around detailed case studies. Only by seeing what lawyers are actually doing with new media can we comprehend how the larger themes of the book play out. We will see how and why lawyers with particular claims to prove and arguments to make, operating under particular evidentiary, material, or other constraints, choose the visual and multimedia tools they do and with what potential effects on their audiences' thoughts, feelings, and decisions. As the examples already mentioned in this introduction suggest, we need to look very closely at the pictures lawyers use to appreciate the knowledge those pictures can produce, the arguments they can convey, and the multiple readings they invite. By moving back and forth between the details of particular pictures and the cases in which they appear, on the one hand, and more theoretical analyses of those pictures' meanings and effects, on the other, we hope to enrich readers' appreciation of the complexities of legal advocacy and judgment today.

Let's start, then, with the pictures that seem the simplest: videotapes made to document reality. These photographic pictures can seem to give us reality directly and unproblematically. They can even seem to speak for themselves. We will see why the self-evident meaning of photographic pictures is such an enticing notion, and we'll begin the interpretive work needed to appreciate its rhetorical aims.

2

The Rhetoric of the Real
Videotape as Evidence

When a lawyer shows the jury a crime scene photograph, when an expert produces surveillance tape to prove that an intruder was, indeed, present as the prosecutor claims, when an oil spill despoils a shore and photographs of oil-soaked birds are produced to show ecological damage—all of these pictures are documentary. They offer visual evidence to support an argument about a legal story. Lawyers need these pictures to be clear, but they need more than just clear visual images; their pictures serve rhetorical purposes as well as convey reliable factual evidence.

In this chapter, we examine pictures that are photographic. Because they seem to record what our eyes see, many people believe that they can provide judges and jurors with the most direct access to what really happened and thus constitute the most convincing sort of evidence. The idea of eye-witness is so deeply embedded in our culture, and especially our legal culture,[1] that it confers special powers on such pictures. Photographs are the kinds of pictures that most tightly bind the evidence to the story of the case that the proponent tells and hence to the proponent's argument about why the client is in the right.

We argue that there is more than meets the eye in these pictures. We need to decode them, taking into account what is visible in the frame, our knowledge of the medium, and the context in which the pictures are presented. We call this chapter "The Rhetoric of the Real" to underscore that our focus is on how the realism of documentary pictures is deployed in legal arguments. These arguments, moreover, can spill out into the world if the case is of more than purely legal interest. The pictures may be dropped into the media stream as part of a story's coverage or to influence public opinion. When this happens, these same pictures can help shape social reality outside the case itself. Our case studies involve videotape, but our general observations apply equally to still photographs.

We look first at two legal cases involving digital videotape made by police officers. In *Scott v. Harris*,[2] the crucial evidence was videotape made by cameras mounted on the dashboards of police cruisers; in *People v. Dunlop*, the evidence was videotape that the police, using handheld cameras, made during the protests at the 2004 Republican National Convention, in New York City. *Scott* turns on how video evidence is evaluated when both sides agree that the court is seeing a fair and accurate copy of the video in question. *Dunlop* involves the opposite circumstance: video evidence that has been deceptively altered to support a desired outcome. Finally, we briefly discuss surveillance carried out by citizens to document events on the fly: tapes made by camcorder, cell phone, or mounted dashboard cameras in private vehicles, which have become evidence in the court of public opinion if not also the courtroom.

Scott v. Harris

The story. On Thursday, March 29, 2001, Victor Harris was driving his Cadillac east on Georgia Highway 34, southwest of Atlanta, at 73 m.p.h. in a 55 m.p.h. zone on a four-lane road going toward Peachtree City, a town in greater Atlanta. Around 10:40 p.m., Harris was spotted by Coweta County Deputy Sheriff Clinton Reynolds, who flashed his lights to slow him down.[3] At first, Reynolds just tailed Harris—in his words, he was just signaling Harris to slow down.[4] Instead, Harris continued driving, beginning what became a high-speed chase. Harris later said that he was "scared" (he was afraid of having his car impounded) and that is why he didn't stop.[5] Reynolds decided to pursue Harris and caught up with him just after crossing Sullivan Road, a major local road.[6] Reynolds turned on his emergency lights and siren, automatically activating his dashboard camera. Reynolds radioed his dispatcher with the report that he was pursuing a vehicle and gave its license number. Officer Timothy Scott picked up the radio call and joined the chase even though Reynolds had not called for assistance; Scott didn't know why the car was being pursued.

Highway 34 becomes Highway 54 as it approaches Peachtree City. Harris turned off 54 into a drugstore parking lot in a small shopping complex, either to elude his pursuers or to cut through to Highway 74, a two-lane, north-south road perpendicular to Highway 54. Reynolds was on his tail, but Scott, still hurrying to catch up, overshot the entrance and entered the parking lot from the other side, which put him in a position to block Harris's egress. Instead of stopping, Harris pulled to the left; he brushed past Scott's car—there is some dispute about exactly what happened—and made it onto 74, speeding up again. Scott turned around and followed Reynolds out of the parking lot and onto 74.

Once on Highway 74, all three cars moved at speeds upwards of ninety miles per hour: Harris in front, then Reynolds, and, last, Scott following closely behind. No other cars crossed the highway from intersecting roads; traffic had been stopped by Peachtree City police officers. Scott asked permission from Reynolds to take the lead. Now the three cars were engaged in a full-fledged, high-speed race, the officers' sirens blaring, their dashboard cameras running. Scott requested permission by radio from the sergeant tracking the chase to perform a "PIT" (Precision Intervention Technique) maneuver, designed to put a moving car into a skid. Although permission was granted, Scott decided that it would have been too dangerous; Harris's car could have skidded uncontrollably on the two-lane highway, perhaps endangering others, including the officers themselves. Instead, Scott gave a push with his bumper to the left side of Harris's rear bumper, forcing Harris's car off the road.[7] The car went airborne, then down an incline, crashing into an embankment. The chase was over, the Cadillac wrecked, and its driver, nineteen-year-old Victor Harris, had been made a quadriplegic.[8]

Victor Harris sued Officer Scott and others in federal court, claiming that the police had violated his constitutional rights by using excessive force to end the chase.[9] The trial judge ruled that crucial facts—in particular, whether Harris's driving posed a serious enough risk to public safety to justify the police's method of ending the chase—were legitimately in dispute and thus for a jury to decide. The judge therefore allowed the case to go forward. Scott appealed to the Eleventh Circuit Court of Appeals, which agreed with the district court judge that the case should go to trial. Scott petitioned the Supreme Court to review the appellate decision, and the Court took the case. On April 30, 2007, after reviewing the videotapes (as well as transcripts of the hearing in the trial court), the Court reversed the lower courts and ruled in favor of Scott, ensuring that no jury would hear and decide the case.[10]

How much of a threat did Harris's driving pose to public safety? Did the officers act reasonably under the circumstances? Let's turn to the evidence that the Supreme Court thought dispositive: the dashboard camera video, that (seemingly) neutral observer of the events.

The videos. The Court looked at two digital videos, one from Reynolds's police cruiser and one from Scott's.[11] They are in color, although the color is hard to see because the cameras were recording at night in an intermittently illuminated landscape. Both have audio tracks. Combined,[12] their running time is just under sixteen minutes; the longer (Reynolds's) runs just under nine minutes. Each tape covers the action from the point of view of the car in which the camera was mounted (not, strictly speaking, the driver's point of view). The equipment operates only when emergency lights and sirens are turned on, so the tapes didn't record everything the officers did while on duty. The tape from Reynolds's car begins earlier and arrives at the accident scene after the crash has occurred; it includes footage of what happened in the parking lot as seen from behind Harris's car. The tape from Scott's car shows him racing to catch up with Reynolds, the parking lot confrontation with Harris's car, the subsequent chase, and the bumping of Harris's car off the road; it concludes with some of the aftermath, when Harris's car is already resting at the bottom of the embankment.

The tapes are very dark, and it is hard to see details apart from glowing bubbles of hot and cold light (giving clues about their sources—cars, trucks, street signs, street lights) that enter and leave the visual field. We see clusters of lights from what must be small commercial areas and then expanses of darkness where there are few lights, mostly those from oncoming vehicles in the opposite lanes. There is little or no evidence of sidewalks along the roadway, and we can't see the lights from any houses, so either they are set well back from the road or their inhabitants were already in bed. A map[13] indicates that the area where Harris is first observed speeding is a typical suburban/rural labyrinth of curving streets, with few through or cross streets. The road on which he was driving was the main through street.

Over the course of both tapes, we generally see light, mixed traffic: mostly cars, a few passing trucks. There is no evidence of pedestrians. The parking lot where the encounter took place serves businesses that were all closed. Two Peachtree police cars were parked in the lot but their occupants were initially unaware of any pursuit in their midst.[14] When the chase resumes, other police cars have already stopped crossing traffic at the few intersections, allowing Harris and the police officers to continue unimpeded. It doesn't seem that driving conditions were bad, although the roads may have been wet; both police cars have droplets on their windshields, but neither is operating wipers. Oncoming vehicles do not seem to stir up puddles or spray our three drivers.[15]

We see on the tapes three different styles of driving. Reynolds, prior to the action in the parking lot, stays behind Harris but keeps up with him. Reynolds's driving seems measured and appropriate to the task he set for himself. Even in the more excited concluding portions of the tape, when everyone was going at higher speeds, his car seems very much under control. Scott's driving, in contrast, seems more on the edge: He frequently drives in the turning lane and twice almost loses control of his car. (He goes so fast that he misses Harris's and Reynolds's turns into the shopping center, and, on emerging from the shopping center later, he turns wide, less in control.) Harris, who did run at least one red light (although we cannot see this very well on the tape),[16] uses his turn signals to indicate his intentions to other drivers, a sign that he is paying attention to the world outside his car, and does not lose control until he is forced off the road.

What can be seen on the tapes of the encounter in the shopping center parking lot? We can watch the officers' efforts to box Harris in both from the rear view (Reynolds's tape) and from the front (Scott's). As Scott, risking a head-on collision, attempts to cut off Harris's egress by blocking his path, Harris turns to the left and goes by. We can hear a very small sound of metal brushing, but the video doesn't indicate any bounce or other evidence of contact. Seen from the back, it's possible that Harris's right rear fender or bumper touched Scott's right front bumper.

What can be seen of the end of the chase? Everything speeds up; we experience the cars' acceleration as we watch. Scott asks Reynolds if he can take the lead because his car "is already tore up." We see Scott carefully position himself to apply force to the left side of Harris's car, which would cause it to turn, as it did. We see Harris's car move off to the right, and then nothing—until we see smoke rising and other officers outside their cars at the scene. The scene includes what looks like a utility pole with a light on, which suggests that Scott could have seen the embankment, if only at the last minute. We have gone from darkness down a black roadway to dramatic illumination of a smoking accident site lit by an overhead light and headlights, with figures moving in and out of view as police try to open Harris's car to render aid. It's impossible to tell whether we are looking at the front or the rear of the wrecked car. We can hear a combination of police radio conversation and sounds from an FM radio being picked up by the dashboard camera mikes. (We will return to the soundtrack later.)

We have tried to describe for you what can be seen on the videotapes. Now let's think about them on other levels. To begin with, they seem to be reliable evidence. Viewers can see consistent time/date stamps in white in front of the picture, changing as time elapses. Although each tape starts and stops at particular times, the time code between beginning and end is unbroken, indicating that the tapes have not been internally edited and, indeed, were produced by cameras that started automatically (as they were designed to do). We are, therefore, inclined to believe that what we see on the tapes was really in front of the camera. Indeed, neither party disputed the tapes' authenticity.

There is a gap, however, between our perception of the tapes' authenticity and our own experience driving cars. The footage must have been made with a camera with Steadicam[17] features: The camera remains stable and does not respond to the movements of the car. Inside this media frame, we mostly see some bright lights bobbling along in a totally black visual field of nighttime darkness. We hardly seem to be riding in a car. Our vantage point is similar to that of the player in a first-person shooter video game.

The reference to gaming is important because of *point of view*. Point of view not only describes the viewer's position; it also evokes a range of cultural associations. Video gaming is a relatively new medium in our culture but an increasingly important one.[18] In video gaming, in contrast to watching films or television, our own actions, combined with effects built into the game's design, create the narrative. We interact with situations, objects, or other characters; we are agents, even heroes, immersed in a complex environment.[19] That the dashboard video camera's output is so steady increases the fantasy-like quality of what we see. At the same time, the first-person point of view, combined with the lack of sensations that would reflect the car's response to the roadway, increases the perception of a godlike overview. Viewers of the tapes can thus be both more fully immersed in and more convinced of the authority of the view they experience. Viewers might even subconsciously feel that they are in control of the whole game and that, because it is a game, nothing really bad can happen to the first-person character in the drivers' seat. This might also increase the psychological distance between the pursuer and the pursued, making Harris just one more object to be dealt with.[20]

We turn now from our description of and reflections on what can be seen on the tapes to what the Justices of the Supreme Court, in their written opinions and remarks during oral argument, said that they saw.

The case in the Supreme Court. The central legal issue, as we have noted, was whether the police were justified in using potentially deadly force to stop the chase; this, in turn, depended largely on whether Harris's driving posed enough of a threat to public safety to warrant that sort of force. The defendant, Officer Scott, argued that no reasonable jury could find that his actions were unjustified and, therefore, that there was no need to hold a trial. The trial judge disagreed, ruling that a jury should watch the video and consider all of the other evidence to decide whether the police had acted reasonably (and therefore constitutionally). Three federal appeals court judges agreed with the trial judge.

Eight of nine Justices of the Supreme Court disagreed, ruling in favor of Scott and thereby ensuring that there would be no trial. The majority opinion was written by Justice Antonin Scalia. Justices Ruth Bader Ginsberg and Stephen Breyer wrote concurring opinions. Only Justice John Paul Stevens dissented.

The Supreme Court's response to the tapes perfectly exemplifies how the rhetoric of the real can shape the law. The eight Justices in the majority believed that the tapes by themselves made the reality of the case perfectly clear: Harris's driving so threatened public safety that the police acted reasonably in running him off the road, and no reasonable person could see things otherwise. The Supreme Court's usual job is to resolve questions of law, not to try facts. Here, however, the Court thought it so obvious that the videotapes showed the facts of the matter that it arrogated to itself a decision ordinarily left for the jury. The Court also took the unprecedented step of posting the video evidence (along with its opinion) on the Court's Web site, inviting members of the public to see what the cameras had recorded and, implicitly, to verify with their own eyes that Scott had used appropriate force. The eight Justices in the majority clearly believed that the public would see the videotape just as they did, and so they deployed the rhetoric of the real to enhance public support for their decision.

The majority considered the videotapes to be truth-telling witnesses to the action in the story, reliable as evidence and then as warrants for their final decision. Just what did these Justices see that caused them to think as they did?

Justice Scalia, writing the majority opinion, characterizes what he sees on the video as "closely resembling a Hollywood-style car chase of the most frightening sort, placing police officers and innocent bystanders alike at great risk of serious injury."[21] Anyone who goes to the movies or watches television has come to expect that Hollywood-style chases will thrill us with odd combinations of danger in which various vehicles threaten people, objects, and other vehicles in the scene. Near-misses (and destructive collisions) are elaborated not only out of plot necessities but for the pleasure of the audience; we enjoy being startled.[22] The clarity of the photographic picture on film lets us delectate over each element in the chase, and we are able to enjoy the tensions from the safety of our seats. We are drawn in because we assume the point of view of the camera and we identify with the characters we've come to know from earlier scenes in the film. And our uncertainty about the outcome is heightened through skillful cross-cutting, as exemplified by the classic sequence in *The French Connection*. Justice Scalia, in fact, specifically referred to that movie during oral arguments.[23] Whatever led him to associate the video with a particular Hollywood movie or movies in general, his remark directs our attention away from the tapes as we may perceive them to what we already know or think. He evokes our memories of all kinds of other stories in which good and bad guys chase each other and thus cues our intuitive ideas about who's in the right, who's a wrongdoer, and what the backstory might be. Viewers may bring these narrative frames to bear not only on the specific issue of how much danger Victor Harris was posing to the public but also on the "moral reasonableness" of letting Officer Scott off the hook.[24] In short, narrative is substituted for a direct parsing of the content of the actual videos—for seeing what is there.

When Justice Scalia suggests that he was "frighten[ed]," he enters the scene personally; he is no longer just a spectator. Watching the tapes as if they were a Hollywood movie encourages this kind of participation (as does the tapes' evocation of video gaming, as we mentioned earlier).[25] Justice Scalia asks us to share his viewpoint and his emotional response, and so to believe him, rather than locating our (or his) response in a thorough analysis of what can be seen and heard on the tape.

Even as Justice Scalia asserts that the tapes resemble Hollywood films, he also assumes that they offer us reality unaltered and unprocessed. Yet, he does not seem to realize the contradiction between these two stances. The Hollywood movies he has in mind are narrative fictions, not even documentaries (which are themselves highly constructed versions of reality).[26] Of course they don't give us reality unmediated. But neither do the tapes from Reynolds's and Scott's dashboard cameras, a point that neither Justice Scalia nor the other Justices in the majority seem to recognize.[27] Most of the Justices thought that the videotape simply showed them what really happened, regardless of any verbal gloss that Harris's lawyer or the lower courts might have put on things. Consider this exchange:

MR. JONES (representing respondent Harris): This is an interlocutory appeal, this an interlocutory appeal under *Mitchell v. Forsythe*, and the Court is bound by its own ruling to accept the facts as found by the court below, and decide the narrow issue of law here which is, one, is there a constitutional violation on these facts. And two, was the law clearly established.

JUSTICE SCALIA: Even if having watched the tape, there is no way that, that factual finding can be accurate?[28]

The immediacy and intensity of seeing the video gave Justice Scalia the confidence to override the lower court's findings of fact, communicated in mere written form. Shortly after this exchange, Justice Breyer joins in:

MR. JONES: But those are not the facts that were found by the court below in this—

JUSTICE BREYER: Well that's, that's what I wonder. If the court says that isn't what happened, and I see with my eyes that is what happened, what am I supposed to do?[29] . . . But suppose I look at the tape and I end up with Chico Marx's old question with respect to the Court of Appeals: Who do you believe, me or your own eyes?[30]

It is hard to question what is before your own eyes. As we discussed in chapter 1, we are wired to believe what we see. To doubt requires that we step back from the vividness of experience and from our emotional attachment to that experience. Doubting takes analytical energy. Eight of nine Justices reviewed the tapes and concluded that the tapes showed them the truth. Justice Scalia seems to assume that, once it was established that the tapes had not been doctored, it was clear that anyone viewing the tapes would see the same truth. In explaining the Court's posting of the videos on its Web site, Scalia writes: "We are happy to allow the videotape to speak for itself."[31]

Only Justice Stevens, writing in dissent, notices that seeing the tapes and inferring judgments about risk and responsibility from what one sees require all kinds of interpretive acts. In contrast to the majority's analysis, Justice Stevens carefully substantiates his interpretation of the tapes by referring to specific aspects of what can be seen and heard on them, and he relates these to the written accounts of the events in the briefs. For instance, Justice Stevens notes that passing another car on a two-lane road is different from doing so on a four-lane road and that the tapes show Harris passing appropriately for the road on which he was driving. Justice Stevens observes that cars on the shoulder would have pulled over because of the blaring sirens, which the other Justices appear to have ignored, and not necessarily because Harris (and the pursuing officers) forced them off the road. (In fact, the tapes do not show any cars forcing others off the road until Scott's car rams Harris's.)[32] Implying a generational difference in experience, he suggests that his colleagues may never have driven and passed on two-lane roads themselves, appealing to their life experience (as Justice Scalia does, too, when alluding to Hollywood movies). He suggests further that his "colleagues were unduly frightened by two or three images on the tape that looked like bursts of lightning or explosions, but were in fact merely the headlights of vehicles zooming by in the opposite lane."[33] Just as Justice Stevens paid close attention to the behavior of other cars seen on the road, he also seems to have heeded the soundtrack. For the other Justices, did the sounds of the sirens become entangled with the bursts of light, increasing their sense that they were watching something "explosive" and thus dangerous to the public at large?

The role of sound. While our main focus in this book is on pictures, we have also alluded to sound (encompassed, for instance, in the term "multimedia"). As legal professionals begin to exploit the possibilities of multimedia presentation, they will deploy sound as well as picture files.[34] So we need to say a few words about sound in general and then about the audio in *Scott*.

Hearing differs from seeing. We use our eyes to see the world, and, when we do, we see things situated in a spatial continuum that seems to extend in space in any direction we turn our heads. What we see is "out there" and can be located in relation to other things we see, contextualized by the spatial cues that define our perception. (For instance, more distant things appear smaller.) In contrast, when we hear something, the sound stands out from the ambient acoustic array (all the background sound), which we ordinarily don't even notice. We can turn our heads to hear the sound better, and we can try to locate the sound by pinpointing its source or inferring its distance from its volume, but what attracts our interest is a discrete aural phenomenon, something that causes us to pay attention.[35] And, because sounds are evanescent, *recorded* sounds can seem especially present because they reflect phenomena that we are used to thinking of as events.[36] Sounds make us focus on fleeting data because we know that they won't last; when hearing recorded sounds, we may think that we might have ignored the sound entirely had it not been recontextualized by being recorded and re-presented to us. Recorded sounds, like pictures, are "framed"—they are recorded under certain conditions and played back under different conditions—but this framing is even less obvious when we hear recorded sounds than when we look at pictures, which tends to make recorded sound seem that much more immediate and therefore "real."[37]

Audio plays an unexpectedly interesting part in the tapes in *Scott*. While the cars are speeding down the highway, we hear, with varying degrees of clarity, radio messaging between the two police cars and their dispatcher. We hear the sirens to which Justice Stevens refers, but not very well; it's impossible to tell from which cars they are emanating. At the accident site after the end of the chase, the sound tracks become more complex. It is hard to identify who is speaking; officers are outside their cars using handheld radios, but the sound is being picked up inside the cars, and we hear the cars' radios more clearly than we did during the chase.[38] As the ambient sound changes, we hear a rhythm inside Reynolds's car that sounds a bit like a human heartbeat but is actually rock music. Reynolds's voice, if it is his voice, sounds both scared and excited, and, with the rhythm beating under it, we readily identify with the peril he has experienced. On the tape from Scott's car we hear his car radio: a few ads and the beginning of a Smash Mouth song, "Then the Morning Comes," including the line "You're going to do it again."[39] All of these incidental sounds make the events depicted on the tape seem especially present and real.[40]

The tapes online. As we've noted, the Court took the unprecedented step of posting the videos on the Court's Web site as a way of responding to Justice Stevens's reading of the tapes. Perhaps the Court thought that the scope of police authority to use deadly force was of such public interest and concern that it was worth posting the videos to secure popular support for the decision. Did the posting also reflect the influence of YouTube-generation law clerks who thought that it would be "cool" to answer Justice Stevens in this way? Did the Court, although asserting that "the videotape speaks for itself," also hope to frame the public's viewing by coupling the tapes to the opinion, thereby upholding their words over the pictures even as the Court sought to join in the new visual vernacular?

Justice Scalia was surely confident that the public would view the tapes the way that the majority did, but, if so, we must ask whether the majority may have failed to appreciate how, in the age of the Internet, pictorial meanings multiply even further in the court of public opinion.[41] The legal scholars Dan Kahan, David Hoffman, and Donald Braman carried out an empirical study of the public's responses to the *Scott* tapes.[42] They found that three-quarters of their sample agreed with the Court's conclusion that the police's use of deadly force was justified.[43] There were, however, sharp differences in opinion, especially between viewers of different races and political orientations,[44] suggesting that reasonable people could disagree about how to read the tape—and that the Court's naïve realism may have led them to misjudge this.

Interestingly, the video file posted on the Supreme Court's Web site is not the same as the videos submitted as evidence in the case.[45] The posted tape appears to have been "styled."[46] First, the posted tapes are black and white; the dashcam video evidence is in color. Second, they contain smudgy white visual "noise" running along the bottom, metadata that are generated when a digital file is transferred to VHS (analog) media. (The video posted on the Web has been redigitized from that analog material.) Third, the posted tapes contain double sets of time code data: the original time codes and, partly overlapping those, a second set added when the tapes were (as we suspect) transferred to VHS. Finally, the posted tape ends with material from Scott's dashboard camera but omits approximately the last two minutes. What's left out are some of the postcrash scenes showing the faces of some of the officers; a view of two officers inspecting the front of Scott's cruiser, one of whom then gestures with a "thumbs-up"; and, last, the soundtrack provided by Scott's car radio.

We don't know who substituted the online version for the evidentiary "original" or why, so our remarks about the significance of the changes must remain speculative. But it does seem that the alterations make the facts that can be gleaned from the tapes more ambiguous, while removing some images and sounds that the public might have found problematic. For instance, the change from color to black and white makes it much harder to see that the police could probably tell that there were culverts and embankments along the road. This arguably undermines Scott's assertion that his chase-ending maneuver did not constitute deadly force because, "as the videotape shows, the road where the contact took place appeared [at night] to be level."[47] For some viewers, the change from color to "artsy" black and white may also have evoked the older photographic convention associating "serious" material (such as older movies, noir fiction, and fine art photography) with black and white. The double sets of time counters make it harder to read either one, canceling their informational value and discouraging most casual viewers from attending to any evidentiary significance they may have.

Deleting the end of the tape from Scott's cruiser could well be justified: It protected the privacy of those officers who might be visually identifiable from the complete tape, and the aftermath of the chase arguably isn't germane to the tapes' evidentiary value, anyway. Cutting off the end of the tape, however, also eliminated the aforementioned thumbs-up, which, given viewers' awareness that Victor Harris lay grievously injured in the background, could have provoked negative associations.[48] In addition, it eliminated the coincidental juxtaposition of the lyric on the radio and the scene in front of the camera, which also could have prompted associations prejudicial to the police. One further issue may be relevant: Nowhere in the court documents is Victor Harris's race mentioned, and it can't be determined from the tapes.[49] For those who know, and for others who may learn or guess, however, the awareness that he is African American could change the context of the events, providing another cultural narrative frame for the chase and its tragic conclusion. The concluding minutes of the dashcam videotape—white policemen going about their business while a young black man lies helpless—could well have been especially provocative.

Whatever the intended or unintended meanings of the "translation" from the original to the posted version of the videotapes, did the Court have any obligation to identify the version posted as different from the original? Or should the audience be left to its own devices in parsing the tapes in their new context? We discuss this and related questions in chapter 7. The differences between different available versions of the videotape evidence, however, will become a crucial feature of the search for truth in the next case.

The meanings of pictures and words. Our analysis of *Scott v. Harris* is meant to exemplify the always fraught interrelationships between words and pictures. Did the cars "brush" or "collide" in the parking lot? What do these differing verbs evoke, and does the videotape support one over the other? It's hard to tell. When we try to make sense of any pictures, we are always engaged in back-and-forth conversations between those pictures and spoken or written words and between images in memory and thoughts we articulate to ourselves, using one to understand the other. In this case, the majority of the Supreme Court moved quickly away from the pictures to their own verbal framing of those pictures, leaving the actual videotape behind so that the "Hollywood-style car chase" scenario took over. Justice Scalia seemed overeager to slot his visual perceptions into a narrative pigeonhole. He truncated the back-and-forth movements between pictures and words by saying: "The videotape speaks for itself." What he meant was: "It means what I say it means." The pictures, having "spoken" through his own translation into words, don't have to "say" anything else. Having pinned down the video with his words, Justice Scalia implicitly believes that the video evidence is then contained, its meanings limited to those consonant with the Court's verdict and opinion.[50] Because we can watch the same material ourselves, however, the Court's opinion fails to constrain our view. Its decision becomes less convincing, more subject to question, because of discrepancies between what we can see and what we are told to see. The pictures continue to speak.

The majority opinion in *Scott v. Harris* reflects an important theme of this book: The naïve realist position in regard to all pictures, but especially photographic pictures, diminishes our understanding of what those pictures can communicate. Therefore, we must examine *all* pictures (and, indeed, all representations that matter to our decisions) to ascertain the range of meanings they may provoke, well beyond those that might immediately occur to a naïve realist. In this case, the assumption that the video unproblematically and unequivocally showed "the real" led a majority of the Court to dismiss the other possible realities consistent with the visual evidence. The Court's decision prevented a jury that knows the roads and traffic in Georgia from discussing and evaluating how risky Harris's driving was to the public and how reasonable Scott's decision was to end the chase by bumping him off the road. As Justice Stevens noted, his colleagues "usurped the jury's fact finding function and, in doing so, implicitly labeled the four other judges to review the case unreasonable."[51] We don't know what led the Court to convert the videotape to words too rapidly; it may have been a perceptual bias in favor of paying more attention to the picture than the sounds, or a desire to impose upon the video a narrative frame that supported the Court's decision. In any case, the effect was to peremptorily reduce the complexity of the video as evidence.[52]

Conflicts over the meaning of images will increase as pictures become ever more important to the law. If pictures propagate meaning freely, how are we to know which interpretations most deserve our belief?[53] Participants in the legal system need to become more visually and media literate. The first step is to understand that the meanings of all pictures are the result of a maker, a medium, a subject, a context, and our reception of them. Videotape from dashboard-mounted video cameras can seem objective because the cameras seem not to be operated by human beings, who by definition have a subjective position. As we've pointed out, though, those cameras have a point of view that engages us in familiar ways: We become the driver, the game player, observing from inside the scene. Every aspect of these moving pictures can affect our response. It matters how clearly we can see their contents. And it matters what is inside the frame and what is left out: how Harris's taillights twinkling in the distance differ from what we see up close, just before the push that sent him off the road. Some of what we see may remind us of other Hollywood movies or YouTube clips. It's natural for people to draw on familiar associations to make sense of what they see and hear, but what exactly in or about the video is causing that association? What is actually visible or audible, as opposed to what the pictures and sounds on the tape remind us of? Conversations about just these sorts of questions need to take place for video evidence to be evaluated properly. The dashboard camera videotapes at issue in *Scott* were made as a matter of routine to create a record of events as they unfolded, especially high-energy events with lights and sirens.[54] They are counted on to provide evidence when questions about police conduct arise. In our next example, we move from tape made by a fixed camera activated through electronic choices independent of human action to video cameras in the hands of police officers on the streets of New York City. We also move from the interpretation of pictures of unquestioned authenticity to deliberate efforts to alter perceived reality by doctoring pictures.

The 2004 Republican National Convention and the Case of Alexander Dunlop

Setting the stage. When the Republican Party chose to locate its 2004 convention in New York City with its many resonances—especially those of 9/11, which had been used as a rhetorical touchstone for many presidential speeches—everyone knew that it was going to be a very complicated social picture indeed.[55] Not only are New York City voters overwhelmingly Democratic, but the city has hosted many demonstrations over the years. There was every reason to expect that many opponents of the Bush Administration would show up along with the delegates, press, and the regular late-summer tourist crowd, as well as the just plain curious who would show up because something was going on.

Charged with maintaining order and providing security for important people under uncertain conditions, the New York Police Department swung into action well before the Republican National Convention arrived in New York.[56] It began a massive surveillance program, monitoring groups and individuals by tracking them on the Internet, attending their events, gathering published materials, and traveling to other states and to Europe.[57] "[T]he NYPD was preparing for the 2004 Republican National Convention as if the world were about to end. One document called for a 'doomsday' plan to deal with more than 5,000 arrests."[58] Masses of anti-Bush protestors arrived: Somewhere between 400,000 and 800,000 demonstrators showed up at the largest gathering, depending upon whether you believe the estimates of the *New York Times* or the NYPD, respectively.[59] But doomsday didn't happen; police arrested 1,806 people over the days of the convention, 152 of whom were ultimately convicted of minor offenses.[60]

For the NYPD, as for other participants in the drama of the convention and the events surrounding it, videotaping was an important tool for constructing reality for the national and even international audiences sure to be watching. Just like demonstrators and tourists, police officers, both uniformed and undercover, took advantage of the availability of small, handheld video cameras which allowed them to move freely.[61] They were able to focus on whatever in their visual field captured their interest. They "edited" by simply moving the camera and filming short takes rather than single long shots. They made "motivated tapes," exercising judgment about where to stand, what to frame in the viewfinder, when to start and stop recording. Their videos were therefore very unlike the continuous stream captured by an activated dashcam, which we saw in *Scott*. The police may have initially thought of using their cameras as a kind of crowd-control device ("We're recording you") rather than as a way of creating usable evidence, but, once they started taping, potential evidence is what they made.

Everyone—the Republican Party, the police, the delegates, the press, the protestors, the tourists—arrived at the convention with cameras. Some, such as the mayor and the police, wanted to use pictures to make reality conform to a pre-envisioned image that would serve their purposes.[62] Some, including organized groups of protestors, planned to shoot their own video to be used, if necessary, as counterevidence. Some didn't plan at all. All became part of an intentionally staged theater of pictures that unfolded in the public space of the streets.[63]

Dunlop's story. On Friday, August 27, 2004, Alexander Dunlop took his bicycle, left his apartment at Second Avenue and 10th Street at 8:45 p.m., and headed to his favorite place for sushi. Dunlop didn't realize, however, that his bike was constructing an identity for him. On that night he could easily have been confused with a member of Critical Mass, a loose collective of bike riders who make monthly Friday night rides in Manhattan (and other cities around the world)—without a permit to demonstrate— on behalf of alternative modes of transportation in an era of global warming.[64] Because it was only two days before the biggest demonstration planned for the convention weekend was to occur, police may have wanted to handle the Critical Mass gathering in a way that would send messages through major media coverage, before the majority of demonstrators arrived in the city, about the trouble that demonstrators could get into.[65]

When Dunlop emerged from his apartment with his bike, the streets were jammed with people, the air, in his own account, "full of electricity."[66] In pursuit of his sushi, Dunlop asked a policeman what was happening; "'they said they didn't know.'" Tenth Street was blocked off, and there was a barricade on 9th Street, so Dunlop "asked a police officer how to get out." The officer told him where to go. He found himself in a cul-de-sac of sorts and asked the same officer why he had been sent that way, when he'd asked the officer how to leave the area. The officer told him, "'I told you to go there so I could arrest you.'" And Dunlop was arrested. He was taken "slowly" along with hundreds of other people to Pier 57, where the city planned to gather detainees for processing. Dunlop described spending many hours standing because the floor was too filthy and greasy to lie down on.[67] Dunlop came out at 6:00 p.m. on Saturday (just under twenty-four hours after he was detained) and was told by a public defender that the charges against him were disorderly conduct, parading without a permit, resisting arrest, and obstructing government administration.

This was a catchall set of charges, a big enough bundle to scare demonstrators into settling their cases, to make them satisfied with an ACD (adjournment in contemplation of dismissal for time served) rather than go to the expense (for all concerned) of time and money involved in a trial. Such a settlement would spare the justice system an overload of cases; it would also leave the accused with a misdemeanor charge that would be eventually expunged from the record if the person got into no further trouble. Dunlop, a divinity student at the time, did not want any arrest on his record. He was not involved in politics and knew that he had done nothing wrong that night. So, when the prosecutor offered him a plea of disorderly conduct with time served (a lesser charge), Dunlop chose to go to trial rather than confess to charges of which he felt himself to be entirely innocent. In fact, not only did Dunlop know that he was innocent of any wrongdoing; he was aware of the consequences to his life of a criminal conviction, however minor:

> I wouldn't have been able to get the job that I wanted, perhaps. Any background check, the record would have come up, the criminal record would have come up. And I graduated from Harvard, and then I would have had a criminal record, and I wouldn't have been able to go to work at any bank or law firm that I might have wanted to. I've heard stories where this kind of criminal record comes up when you try to cross a border. A friend of mine was telling me about a friend of his who had a visa denied to go to another country because of a disorderly conduct charge coming up at a political protest. So, it really restricts what you're able to do, and what job you can get, the travel you can do. It might have ruined my life. It really might have.[68]

Dunlop looked for a new lawyer to represent him. He found Michael Conroy, who took the case pro bono on the recommendation of a friend in September 2004.[69]

The videotape. On the face of it, this looked like a case of Dunlop's word against that of the police. Attorney Conroy asked the prosecutor's office if his client appeared on any of the videos taken by the NYPD. An assistant district attorney forwarded to Conroy a tape of very poor quality with occasional jumps that didn't mean anything to Conroy or Dunlop at the time.

The tape that the assistant DA had provided was a VHS tape. It's very dark and difficult to see what's going on, even though the events being filmed took place in lit urban areas (in contrast, for instance, to the Georgia highways at night in *Scott*).[70] Running along the bottom are smeary white artifacts, just like those in the posted *Scott* tape, that reflect the tracking data from the original digital tape. Here, the artifacts would have arisen from the same kind of transfer from one kind of media to another that we suggested might have caused the markings on the *Scott* tape when it was prepared for posting on the World Wide Web. In this case, however, the person who prepared the tape may have been deliberately trying to obscure some information. If the digital data was recorded onto a VHS tape using the lowest setting (SLP), the result would have been even lower resolution and a general degrading of the digital data.[71] The tape lacks any visible date/time stamps and has fuzzy audio to go with the fuzzy video. In the jumble of police, demonstrators, and onlookers, the tape shows Dunlop from the back under arrest with his hands cuffed behind him, sitting on the ground with several other arrestees.

Many groups and individuals had organized before the convention, planning to create an alternative video record of events in the streets by making their own documentary footage. Citizens with cameras, by showing the scene broadly, may help to substantiate the basic facts of the events; their footage can be used to put together a more coherent narrative based on many sources. If there are good tapes of the same episodes as those shown on the police department tapes, then there is more than one "voice" telling the pictorial story. It's not easy to videotape under these circumstances, though. Police may try to prevent the taping; equipment in the hands of amateurs may not function properly; or, in the excitement of the moment, the operator may forget all of the things that can interfere with capturing footage that's usable later. I-Witness Video, a group dedicated to citizen documentation of demonstrations and police behavior, had trained some two hundred volunteers in how to create usable evidentiary tape.[72] It is difficult for inexperienced people to record good tape because street events unfold in unpredictable ways, so the camera may or may not "see" what is important in the scene. Because the importance of some details may not emerge until later, trainees are encouraged to keep the camera on, recording broadly what unfolds. Among other things, the training emphasizes the need to set and use the time/date stamp for footage and to capture shots of street signs and other identifiers for place and time.

Before the convention, the New York City chapter of the National Lawyers Guild began to plan for lawyers to be available in the streets as witnesses and advisers during the anticipated mass arrests. They also organized a repository for citizens' tapes of the events for use in eventual court cases. Eileen Clancy from I-Witness Video, a trained video archivist, helped to put together what became a vast video archive, a blend of police tapes, professional documentary tapes, and amateur materials.

Alexander Dunlop, having decided to go to trial, heard about the archive and came looking for other tapes of the scene of his arrest. In Clancy's words:

I received some police videotapes . . . that were given over by the District Attorney to a lawyer as evidence in another case[;] I reviewed those, and I spotted [Dunlop] in a couple of places. So, I took a look to see when he was coming up for trial, and it was about a day-and-a-half. So I called his attorney right away, Michael Conroy, and said, "I have your guy on tape in a couple of places, including the arrest." And he said, "Really?" And I said, "Yes." So he said, "Well, I better come look at that." And I said, "Well, do you have any tapes? Because we'd like to also see, you know, what other tapes are out there." He says, "Well, I have a tape. It's not helpful, particularly."[73]

Conroy and Dunlop brought their tape to the archive, and they watched it with Clancy. It looked a lot like her tape—yet there seemed to be a problem, so they put two VCRs side by side and ran the tapes simultaneously. The comparison showed that the tape that the prosecutor had given to Conroy had been edited. Scenes that might be considered exculpatory had been omitted: Dunlop just standing with his bike looking at what was going on around him and shots of his arrest when he was clearly not resisting.[74] The omissions were covered by degrading the videotape by copying and recopying it so that the data were ever further removed from the original. The resulting product could very well be explained away as "lousy police equipment and poor technicians," possibly very plausible excuses in another context. And, as we have already noted, the tape that had been supplied to Conroy had no time/date stamps on it.[75]

Here is attorney Conroy's account of what happened next:

In court, unknown to the District Attorney, there was a reporter from the *New York Times,* so the problem of the two tapes got on record, both of the court and in the public eye.[76] I said, "Your Honor, I'd like to find out whether this is a complete video tape that the DA gave me." The DA, on record, said, "We're tired of these accusations and we're tired of the way the defendant is looking at me." [Conroy, quoting himself] "Your Honor, I have two video tapes, the one they [the District Attorney's office] gave me and one from the National Lawyers Guild. The first has two sequences missing which show that my client didn't do it." The Judge said, "Approach the bench." I said, "I gave them every opportunity to explain/correct [the matter]. Now I know that the original jump was a cut." District Attorney: "Can't be. Not the police tape." Michael Conroy: "The National Lawyers Guild tape *is* the police tape." They watched the tapes.

The District Attorney said, "I have to go back to my supervisor." The next day the judge dismissed the case.[77]

Whoever made the edited tape clearly intended it to support a conviction or, perhaps, to pressure Dunlop to accept a plea. After a shot of the crowd (an "establishing shot," if you will) Dunlop was shown, from the back, sitting on the ground along with others arrested. Maybe someone thought that guilt by association would do the trick. While it is possible that Dunlop's demeanor on the stand would have been powerful enough to undermine the credibility of the edited tape if shown in court, it would have been hard to quarrel with the government's tape, for a variety of reasons. First, the hold of naïve realism makes it difficult to question photographic pictures, as we have already observed; our belief in their truthfulness is deeply naturalized. Second, the tape would have been submitted by powerful authorities representing both police and prosecution, and finders of fact and the public tend to believe what these authorities present. Third, the tape itself doesn't seem overtly argumentative. There's no voice-over narration, no fancy editing. In fact, every effort was made to cover the edits by making the tape seem even more amateurish. The tape, moreover, is noisy both visually and aurally, the product of a handheld camera on crowded streets where many people were yelling, with traffic sounds heard in the background. And, because it looks amateur in the sense of being both untaught and naïve, not manipulative or manipulating, the tape looks more rather than less authentic. Amateur filming has been a public marker of credibility in legal matters at least since the nation watched George Holliday's amateur tape of the beating of Rodney King. How can something so awkward be falsified? All of these factors would make the tape more credible to an uncritical audience.

How does the rhetoric of the real figure in *People v. Dunlop*? The police videos at issue in the case seem to have been made as part of an image-management and image-creation process in which evidentiary value played a very small role. Few facts can be established from the tapes themselves. The tapes do not clearly locate the scene in time and space. They don't follow individual actors in the unfolding drama; they don't do a good job of presenting the scene in general or narrating specific stories within that scene.

Yet, when the prosecutor turned the tape over to Michael Conroy, Dunlop's lawyer, the presumption had to be that the tape had evidentiary value and was to be accepted as a truthful representation of reality. At this point, the rhetoric is: We've got your guy and, look, he's guilty. Except that even this statement has to be taken on faith because we do not see Dunlop misbehaving; we see only him sitting with other arrestees. To figure out how he got there, we are left to draw on our own images of what was going on in the streets that night. All the tape reliably tells us is that Dunlop was there, waiting with the others to be transported to the piers. It is a fragmentary story. The tip-off that there might have been more to the story comes from the jumps in the videotape that Conroy and Dunlop observed. Only when another, unedited copy of the same police videotape was found and compared to the version the prosecutor gave Conroy, however, could the reality of the unedited version definitively trump the apparent reality of the first tape. What is now exposed as purposeful editing renders the first tape's implicit argument—"We've got your guy, and he's guilty"—as false as a deliberately miscaptioned photo. In the end, faux realism becomes a style; its aim may be to convince us to look no further, but the recognition that it is a style may produce the opposite effect, calling the credibility of the evidence into question.

The reality claimed for the first tape is nothing more than rhetorical pretension, but the unedited tape itself shows us only fragments of the "real." Only by appealing to the larger social and historical contexts in which these tapes were made, which the pictures on the tape themselves can only barely evoke, can we make sense out of what happened. Government actors—the NYPD, prosecutors, the mayor's office, possibly representatives of the federal government as well—were hoping that the seduction of the moving picture would lull viewers into believing what (we would argue) they ought not to believe, not so much about the wrongfulness of Alexander Dunlop's behavior in particular as about the rightfulness of the police actions against convention demonstrators generally. The government was employing something that looked like reality (but wasn't) to persuade not just the judges in Dunlop's case and others' but, at least as important, the general public. The "real" to which the videotapes appealed was an image of policing and security in the face of disorder, framed as an especially dangerous threat in a post-9/11 world. The police enlisted video to prove to the public that they had done their jobs well.

Just as visual technologies are being used by those with power and authority, ordinary people have quickly learned to use them as tools for self-protection, social shaming, and speaking back to those with power. YouTube, the most successful site on the World Wide Web for easily sharing video (with minimal gatekeeping), has provided the means for amateur and even casual videographers to sway public opinion. It has enabled sur-veillance to propagate from the state to its citizens.[78] We now turn to these citizens' surveillance videos.

Citizens' Surveillance

When we view "documentary" footage shot by amateurs in response to events they are witnessing, that amateur status may endow the videos with a special credibility, different from that attributed to "official stories." (We saw in *Dunlop* how precisely this quality may have been exploited to give credibility to a tape that had been altered.) We watch those videos with the same fascination that we would more official accounts, and for the same reasons: to possess knowledge about the world and to satisfy our curiosity and voyeuristic desires.

As we saw in the events surrounding *People v. Dunlop*, videocameras are being wielded by people with actual power, such as the NYPD, and by those who lack power or who feel that they are at some social or po-litical disadvantage. Our frayed social contract is being renegotiated with cameras.[79] Citizens believe that they can use their videos to correct of-ficial stories or provide evidence for their side of the story. YouTube has provided a venue for citizens' video recordings. A search in the spring of 2007 under "police brutality" produced 3,000 clips to view but only 600 for "police injured" and about 55 for "police endangered." Near the top of the list on the day we checked[80] was a clip showing officers of the Los Angeles Police Department beating a suspect, already down and sub-dued, with repeated blows to the face.[81] At the end of the clip, a rolling text gives the names of the two police officers and the suspect; finally, a text statement claims that the suspect said, "I can't breathe." The page in which the video clip is embedded identifies it as an "amateur video"; the accompanying note says that "LA Police chiefs have admitted the video is disturbing."

In fact, we have no way of knowing much of anything about how this video was made or by whom. It was posted on YouTube by a user who claims to live in Canada; he doesn't claim to have made it himself. What truth value should we assign to this fifty-six-second fragment if it of-fers no authentication other than the name of the person who posted it and, in a sidebar, the police spokesperson's acknowledgment that it exists and that, in the spokesperson's opinion, it doesn't make the LAPD look good?[82] What will happen to the reception of videos in courts of law if anonymous citizen videos like this become the benchmark of the "real"? And, if jurors associate video evidence with clips they've seen on YouTube (as opposed to, say, Hollywood movies), will that make the evidence more credible or less?

To give you some sense of how complex it is to determine facts from odd bits of video that surface in cyberspace, we offer some examples of recent video documents that have received fairly wide Internet distribution. Some have even received print media coverage, and all have influenced public opinion. In November 2006, a student was tased by UCLA campus police. He was working in the campus library. School rules required him to have his student identity card on his person after hours, and he had forgotten to bring it. In a post-9/11 world, security personnel may have been primed to be aggressive, especially when dealing with a young man who seemed Middle Eastern (in fact, the student was American born and of Iranian descent) and who was without his "papers." We don't know what the campus police were thinking, but, as the student was leaving the library, they set upon him with a taser. Several other students taped the episode on cell phones equipped with video cameras. Disappointed by the university's response to the incident, they posted these videos on YouTube,[83] which provoked the university to convene an official and public investigation.

The video portions of the clips are very difficult to make sense of. Videophones at present can make only rather small, low-resolution files, and, because they are handheld devices, the video pictures tilt and dip as the holder moves around in the excitement of the moment. So it is the audio, more than anything that we can see, that makes us feel present. We can't actually see the student being tased because library carrels and security personnel block our view. We hear the student tell the officers that he is leaving the building. Then we hear the student's cries of pain as he is tased, not once but five times, because he couldn't get up in response to a command to rise. (The tasing itself incapacitated him, preventing him from complying.) What should we believe about these videos? The videophones were being used to record the tasing at some distance, perhaps ten to twenty feet. We infer that they were covert recordings—that is, that the security guards did not know that they were being recorded—which also increases our willingness to believe that the depicted events are real, not staged. Finally, the posted videos were accompanied by an explanation that identified the scene, although not the names of the principals.

Our next example explores the ambiguities of fixed-camera surveillance material. In early September 2007, a young man, Brett Darrow, recorded a late-night incident between himself and a police officer in Missouri. Darrow, in response to previous episodes when he had felt harassed by officers, had installed in his own car, for his protection, video technology similar to that used by the police in *Scott*, although mounted behind him, not on the dashboard. On the night in question, he planned to meet a friend after work at a commuter parking lot. After he pulled in at about 2:00 a.m., a police officer approached him and demanded that he get out of the car and show identification. When Darrow responded by asking the officer if he'd done anything wrong, the officer lost control and threatened to jail Darrow on whatever charges he could think up. Darrow remained calm in the face of the officer's anger; eventually the officer backed off, and the evening (or at least the portion Darrow's camera captured) ended without any arrest or violence. The tape from the fixed camera shows us only the empty car interior, with a small glimpse of the parking lot outside and lights from the police car blinking in the rear view mirror. As in the UCLA cell phone videos, it's the audio track that tells the story: We can hear the whole conversation between Mr. Darrow and the officer.

After Mr. Darrow posted the video on YouTube, the chief of police received more than three hundred calls from irate citizens, and the officer was suspended.[84] Interestingly, the officer was eventually fired for having failed to turn on his own dashcam videocamera.[85] Mr. Darrow, who did turn his on, was able to use his tape as evidence in the court of public opinion. In this court, the tapes were convincingly real and did not involve any of the complexities of the videotapes in *Scott*—except that there's nothing much to see, only words to be heard. The very steadiness of the boring video picture, substantiating that the footage was made by a fixed camera, gave the tape a highly persuasive authenticity. The three hundred callers who contacted the chief of police clearly believed what they saw and heard on YouTube.

These examples of documentary video raise a host of questions for the law. How do we know whether fragments like these truthfully show what they purport to show or whether they have been staged or materially edited? They may come to us with or without labels but rarely have the kinds of context that would help us to frame them properly. Lacking that, we may fall back on our intuitive frames and scripts—police brutality, say—without ever realizing how poorly those frames may fit the (presumptively) real incident depicted. Cases may arise, moreover, in which video evidence from surveillance cameras operated by private businesses, surveillance cameras overlooking public streets and parking lots, police dashboard cameras, and cameras owned by private citizens all contain parts of a single legal story.[86] What will the legal system do when confronted with conflicting pieces of video evidence in which the question is not the alteration of the material but differences in point of view?

Our analyses of all of the examples of video in this chapter have questioned their presumptive realism by approaching them on three levels: a close description of what is presented inside the frame (and on the soundtrack); inferences based on what we know about their mediation (e.g., understanding the changes to the Dunlop tape); and, finally, an examination of their contexts. We conclude the chapter with a few more remarks about context—specifically, the public relations dimensions of legal videography, and hence the interplay between law and culture in the age of digital pictures. Citizens who post videos online in the hope that they may solve their problems by sharing their naïve realism with others, not to mention lawyers who, like the prosecutor in the Rodney King case, offer video evidence with a similar hope, would do well to ponder the broader contexts in which pictures operate and make meaning.

In *Scott*, as we have seen, the Supreme Court posted a version of the video evidence online as a way of inviting the public to understand and, ideally, to agree with their decision. The public relations aspects of *People v. Dunlop* are more complex. Here is an example. Before the convention, the city denied a permit to the organizers of the largest demonstration. They wanted to stage a peaceful gathering on the Great Lawn and Meadow in Central Park, the site of many large protests in the past and so a site of great symbolic significance. The city's public excuse for denying the permit was that the demonstration would damage the lawn, a position the Parks Department supported. We think it was equally possible that one of the motivations for the city's position was pictorial. The city's mayor, Michael Bloomberg, was up for reelection the next year. Formerly a Democrat, and with generally more liberal social values than the national Republican Party, he had to prove himself worthy of party support while not losing his Democratic base (even though, being a billionaire, he was not dependent on anyone's financial help). Half a million or more people gathered on the Great Lawn, if photographed from any of the tall buildings ringing Central Park, would have looked impressive indeed.[87]

Squeezing those people onto the streets, on the other hand, would make it hard for anyone without an airplane to get a good view of the river of humanity below (and the airspace was closed to all but security aviation and major media). Moreover, people gathered in a large crowd on a lawn can look pretty organized, just a large crowd in a defined space. Individuals would not stand out in the same way that they would as they moved down a narrower street. A large, peaceful protest on a green lawn wouldn't signal scary chaos or frightening, uncontrolled streets, made so by individuals who might look especially suspicious if their couture featured long hair, sandals, and anything else identifiably countercultural. As we have suggested, those who had an interest in showing that the city was under control needed pictures of trouble to underscore their message. Trouble inside the large crowd on the lawn would also have been harder for the police to contain: The police would have been surrounded—and that would not have made for a good picture, either.[88]

"Real" pictures, imagined pictures, multiple pictures—all of these pictures sporulate and propagate in the real environment. In the digital age, the "real" in the rhetoric of the real is itself acquiring new meanings. In his classic essay "Perspective as Symbolic Form," the art historian Erwin Panofsky argued that perception is conditioned by our habits of representation.[89] If so, then the multiple modes and arrangements of representation seen in this chapter indicate that what we think the real is supposed to look like is itself in dramatic flux. "Our new mode of perception," writes the media theorist Anne Friedberg, "is multiple and fractured. It is 'post-perspectival'—no longer framed in a single image with fixed centrality; 'postcinematic'—no longer projected onto a screen surface . . . ; [and] 'post-televisual'—no longer unidirectional in the model of sender and receiver."[90] We increasingly expect reality to be not simply revealed by a photographic picture opening a window onto the world but something we construct for ourselves using many sorts of pictures, accessed through the many windows on our computer screens.

Are judges, lawyers, jurors, and the public up to the challenges posed by this much more complex—perceptually, technologically, and rhetorically—notion of visual truth? In the next two chapters, we explore different aspects of this. In chapter 3, we study advocates' use of a range of digital tools to make pictures that explain the facts of their cases better. In chapter 4, we encounter the peculiar issues that pictures of scientific evidence raise for legal judgment.

3

Teaching the Case

Lawyers have an ethical obligation to pursue their clients' interests diligently within the bounds of the law,[1] trying to persuade judges and jurors (if not also opposing counsel) that their clients' positions are justified. To do this, they have to help decision makers understand what happened and why it matters.[2] Mediators, arbitrators, judges, and jurors depend on the lawyers to take fragments of reality indicated by witnesses, documents, and other sources and to translate those fragments into intelligible, coherent form. They depend on the lawyers to teach them the case.[3]

When lawyers do this, they can't rely exclusively on the kinds of photographic and videographic recordings of reality discussed in chapter 2. For one thing, these pictures, increasingly plentiful as they may be, are still exiguous. Most of legally relevant reality is not captured by a camera, either because no camera is around or because that reality is too large or too small, too distant, too ephemeral, or simply hidden from view. For another, photos and videos may not be able to convey a clear understanding of how processes and events unfold. A photo's visual density may enhance the impression of realism but obscure the essential aspects of how something (e.g., a machine, a body) works. Perhaps most important, lawyers often need to teach concepts, not just re-present things and events.

Explaining the case effectively often involves the use of what we described in chapter 1 as diagrammatic pictures, including charts, graphs, and maps. Like photos and videos, these sorts of pictures can tell us something about the world, but not necessarily by simulating an observable slice of it. Diagrams depict concepts: They convert ideas into visually perceptible form, making apparent the relationships between ideas, things, and events.[4] When lawyers want their audiences to understand quantitative data, they can plot those data and display them in the form of a bar graph, pie chart, visual table, or other graphic that clearly conveys the numbers and the relationships between them.[5] They can visually arrange relevant facts in the form of lists, flowcharts, or timelines. They can turn photos or videos into illustrations of specific facts: A figure in a group picture or an object in a complex scene can be singled out from reality's visual clutter; a crucial sentence from a document can be called out and highlighted. And they can map the connections between relevant legal concepts and the facts of the case.

In this chapter, we present several case studies that illustrate how digital technologies such as Adobe Illustrator and Microsoft PowerPoint, trial presentation programs such as TrialDirector, and animation software enhance lawyers' ability to explain their cases to their audiences. Using new media, lawyers teach differently and better in many ways: by putting information on screens, mobilizing and juxtaposing evidence, combining verbal and pictorial information, creating sequences of pictures, interacting with their displays, and animating elements of pictures or entire presentations. We conclude the chapter by arguing that these features of digitization are transforming not only how legal decision makers learn about case-relevant reality but also the very nature of what counts as reliable legal knowledge.

Accounting Made Simple:
Adobe Illustrator and PowerPoint in a Securities Fraud Case

Before Enron, one of the largest financial fraud cases in American history was brought by the Securities and Exchange Commission against James Koenig, former chief financial officer, and other officers of Waste Management, Inc., the nationwide trash hauling and disposal company.[6] The SEC contended that, from 1992 through 1996, Koenig had engaged in a series of complex accounting schemes intended to understate corporate expenses and thus increase reported profits. Corporate accounting is supposed to be performed in accordance with generally accepted accounting principles (GAAP) and other standard accounting rules. Koenig, the SEC charged, had departed from these principles in his treatment of depreciation, capitalization of interest, and several other aspects of the business— ten separate areas of accounting in all. After Koenig left Waste Management, a new management team launched an investigation into Koenig's accounting practices, and, in February 1998, the Board of Directors declared a $1.4 billion restatement (a public readjustment of past financial statements) covering the period 1992–1996.[7]

In March 2002, the SEC brought a civil complaint charging James Koenig with sixty counts of securities fraud in connection with his alleged manipulations of Waste Management's financial statements.[8] Koenig's law-yers countered that he was being made the fall guy for the real culprits, the new management team and the new members of the Board. Koenig, they argued, had fully complied throughout with all accepted account-ing principles, using his best judgment, which he had honed over twenty years of helping to build Waste Management into an immensely success-ful company. What didn't comply with GAAP was the corporate restate-ment, which the new officers and directors dictated upon their arrival at Waste Management. They knew that they were going to sell the company; their strategy was to write off assets and thereby avoid future depreciation expenses, thus making the company appear more profitable (and more at-tractive to prospective buyers) without affecting its actual cash flow. And that's just what happened: The price of Waste Management stock went *up*, not down, the day after the restatement was announced, Waste Manage-ment was sold profitably, and the company thrived.

From April through June 2006, the jury listened to testimony and ar-guments. On June 29, 2006, more than four years after the lawsuit began, the jury found Koenig liable on all counts.[9]

The plaintiff SEC faced the daunting challenge of teaching jurors how to understand accounting, a subject they might find boring and difficult. To this end, the SEC lawyers, Jack Worland, Richard Skaff, and Bob Pom-mer, teamed up with a trial communication consultant, G. Christopher Ritter, and his company, The Focal Point.[10] Ritter, a former trial lawyer and adjunct professor of trial practice, had considerable experience in helping lawyers to strategize their cases and in crafting graphics, both high-tech and traditional, for courtroom use. Ritter used Adobe Illustrator to create approximately 180 slides for the opening statement and more than 100 for the closing argument. Both slide shows presented a clear, coherent visual strategy: consistent color scheme and slide layout, concise titles in identi-cal font at the top of every slide, and graphics that unfolded from left to right and top to bottom, using iconic illustrations, bold arrows, and other standard visual elements. In court, Worland used PowerPoint to display these slides, giving jurors simple, memorable pictures to associate with every important aspect of his oral presentation.[11]

Building visual explanations. Repeatedly throughout the opening state-ment, jurors saw sequences of anywhere from two or three to a dozen slides illustrating each of the ten accounting issues in the case.[12] Each se-quence followed the same logic of *comparison and contrast*: First the nor-mal, standard, accepted, and lawful accounting procedure was explained, step by step; then, starting from the same diagrammatic structure and iconic language, the defendant Koenig's divergence from the norm was shown. Sometimes the contrast unfolded over several slides. Elsewhere, the contrast took place in a single slide, creating an immediately intelligible visual juxtaposition.[13] And, occasionally, even when the contrast was relatively simple, a brief, two-slide series (which could be created in PowerPoint within a single slide, using simple animation) was used for dramatic effect. One of the accounting issues, for instance, concerned how much money the company was supposed to set aside as reserves for self-insurance and tax purposes. In successive pairs of slides, jurors first saw a simple diagram indicating "What Mr. Koenig should have done." This was illustrated from left to right in a straight line: Consult with Waste Management's internal experts about likely risk and tax liabilities, then confirm his estimates with the outside accountants before putting an accurate report of the reserve in the books. Then jurors saw "What Mr. Koenig actually did": A large red X appeared over the icon for "Accurate Reports," and a bold black arrow, with a locked black box superimposed on it, slanted down to the lower right of the slide, where the text read, "Mr. Koenig books lower estimate and raises profits."[14]

Jack Worland could have drawn diagrams of proper accounting procedures on a flip chart or other analog medium, shown how Koenig's conduct differed, and thus given jurors visual hooks for the essential aspects of each issue. Using digital software, however, he had much more control over the amount and type of information visible at any one time, a crucial aspect of effective visual instruction.[15] And just imagine how much physical effort would have been required to draw and write all of the elements of all of the diagrams (180 slides in the opening statement) needed to illustrate the plaintiff's case or even to be constantly taking down and putting up poster boards. Even if this activity did not exhaust the lawyer, it would likely have distracted the jurors as they watched him dance with large paper pages or boards and would have needlessly slowed down the proceedings.

In addition, by projecting the slides onto a large courtroom screen, lawyers using digital technology were able to maintain jurors' visual focus on a single location throughout the extensive presentation. In *SEC v. Koenig*, the courtroom screen was indeed large, on the order of fourteen feet across—"almost like a megaplex," according to Bob Pommer of the SEC—and situated across the courtroom from the jury box and adjacent to the defense table. Projecting slides onto this courtroom screen also led to unforeseen rhetorical effects that could not possibly have occurred if the lawyers had used only flip charts or poster board. For instance, at one point during opening statements, when the large screen displayed a diagram of one of the ways in which Koenig's conduct departed from accepted procedures, a giant black arrow slanting down toward Koenig's picture in the slide also appeared to point directly to his head as he sat at counsel's table.[16]

Finally, the copy-and-paste function of (word- and) picture-processing software made it easy to employ identical visual elements over and over again: iconic figures representing personnel or documents, photos of Koenig and others, and graphic devices such as blue arrows and red Xs. This created a visual *vocabulary* for the presentation with which jurors could become familiar, helping them to assimilate each new piece of information as it fit into the ecology of the case. Even more important, it facilitated implicit communication. Consider the locked black box that accompanied Koenig's photo throughout the slide show.[17] As a familiar verbal trope, "black box" means something hidden from outsiders, not to be looked into.[18] Picturing the black box, though, served at least two other rhetorical purposes. First, the box looked a bit like a treasure chest or perhaps a safe, implicitly associating Koenig with the hoarding of not only secrets but money. Second, the black box appeared next to Koenig's photo almost twenty times. It would have been obnoxious if not objectionable for Jack Worland to *say* "black box" so often in connection with Koenig. Manually putting the picture of the box in front of jurors that many times (say, by attaching it with Velcro to a board) would similarly have called too much attention to it. In contrast, digital technology allowed the SEC to associate the black box with Koenig repeatedly yet less obtrusively, more matter-of-factly, so that for jurors, the locked black box, with its negative connotations, became Koenig's attribute.[19]

Integrating explanation, symbolism, and story. The same techniques of illustration used to explain an accounting practice can also tell a story. One of the major issues in the case—in fact, running to more than half a billion dollars, the single largest item in the $1.4 billion restatement[20]— involved how Waste Management depreciated its assets. The key concept here is *salvage value*: what Waste Management's trucks and other equipment were worth at the end of their useful lives. Salvage value must be subtracted from the starting value of the asset when first used in order to determine the amount the company must deduct as depreciation expenses over the life of the asset. The higher the salvage value, the less there is to depreciate, and the lower the depreciation expenses the company reports. The SEC claimed that Koenig deliberately and persistently inflated the salvage values of Waste Management's trucks and other equipment so that the company could report lower depreciation expenses and, hence, higher profits.

Salvage values and depreciation may not sound like the stuff of drama. Yet, as depicted in the SEC's visuals, accounting manipulations become an engrossing morality tale, in which Koenig behaves badly, even forcing others to do his evil bidding, but gets his comeuppance in the end.

Jurors have just heard Jack Worland explain, and have seen several slides illustrating, the basics of asset depreciation and the importance of salvage values. They have also seen and heard that, had Koenig relied on the usual sources of information regarding the salvage value for Waste Management's trucks, he would have arrived at a figure of about $5,000 per truck. Instead, Koenig declared that the figure should be $25,000 or higher and then set about to substantiate his number—to fit the facts around the policy, as it were. The new slide sequence begins, as usual, with a simple illustration in the upper left: an icon labeled "Mr. Chappel," the Waste Management employee who was looking into the basis for that $25,000 figure, and, just below, a picture of a garbage truck with a price tag attached and the caption, "$25,000 salvage value??" The next slide adds an arrow, emblazoned with the words "Get Support," running rightward from the Chappel icon to a photo of Mr. Repke, a financial analyst at the company whom Chappel consulted on the question. The slide after that adds another arrow with the same words, running rightward from Repke to a photo of Mr. McGivney, whom Repke consulted. McGivney analyzed the question and wrote a memo about it. The fourth slide in the sequence captures his opinion by adding a small text box under his picture, reading "Conclusion: salvage values aggressive"—accountant-speak for *too high*.[21]

Enter Koenig. His picture appears in the next slide, far below McGivney's at the bottom of the slide (again, way off the straight and narrow symbolized by the Chappel-to-Repke-to-McGivney line); next to it, a large "!?," vernacular for an unprintable expression of surprise and anger in reaction to McGivney's memo.[22] As Worland tells jurors that Koenig ordered Repke to collect and destroy all copies of the McGivney memo, the next slide adds to Koenig's picture his familiar visual attribute, the locked black box, and a bold black arrow appears, slanting upward toward the picture of Repke, with a large black text box superimposed on it, with white lettering declaring, "Make sure McGivney deletes!" Koenig also ordered Repke to go to McGivney's office and stand over him while he deleted the memo from his hard drive, which is what Repke and McGivney did.[23] On the right side of the seventh slide, demarcated by a blue rectangular frame, we see cartoon figures with faces meant to represent Repke and McGivney, both identifiable because their photos are still on the screen, just to the left. A determined Repke looms over a somewhat resigned McGivney as the latter feeds a yellow sheet into a shredder, and a document callout emerges, showing the words " . . . salvage values aggressive . . ." within a jagged, ripped-from-the-document border. And, below this, but still within the blue frame to indicate that this is part of the same episode, we see a picture of a computer screen dialogue box, asking, "Are you sure you want to delete 'Salvage Value Support?,'" with the familiar hand-shaped cursor poised over "Yes"—and next to this, for emphasis, a large "Delete" button (Figure 3.1).

Chris Ritter, the trial consultant, has said that his goal in designing this and other slide sequences was, where possible, to give natural storytellers like Jack Worland a platform for doing what they do so well, leading jurors to conclude, regardless of whether they had absorbed all of the niceties of accounting practice, "That can't be legal!" Postverdict interviews with the jurors in the *Koenig* case revealed that they still remembered this particular graphic from the opening statement and recalled that it was very powerful.[24]

As it turned out, Koenig didn't destroy every trace of the McGivney memo. One copy was left in Chappel's secretary's drawer, and it was later found during the SEC's investigation.[25] In the eighth and last slide in the sequence, the diagram/story we've been watching is faded almost completely out, remaining as a kind of shadow in the background, and the Repke/McGivney episode disappears entirely from the upper right. Instead, in the lower left, we see an illustration of a secretary seated at her desk; behind her is a file cabinet with the Waste Management logo on top; the bottom left drawer is open, and emerging from it is the same document callout we saw in the previous slide: "salvage values aggressive." The transition from the preceding slide to this one immediately shifts the audience's attention from the upper right of the slide (the document destruction scene), and indeed the entire diagram to which they've visually habituated, to the lower left, the document recovered. Composition and sequence thus provide a visual accompaniment that perfectly fits the logic of the lawyer's words. The visual metaphor of the callout, that very familiar symbol in presentational software, could not be more apt: From where

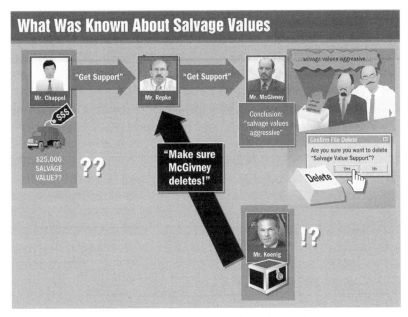

Figure 3.1. Explaining and storytelling: a slide from the SEC's opening statement in *Koenig* (courtesy of G. Christopher Ritter, The Focal Point, and attorneys Robert Pommer and Jack Worland).

it was long hidden, *the truth calls out*—to the SEC, and now to the jurors themselves.

In these and many other slide sequences, the SEC's digital visuals helped jurors to understand an immensely complicated case and did it in a way that made seeing things the SEC's way seem intuitive. Skillfully designed and deployed, the visuals integrated explicit and implicit meanings, explanation and persuasion. And they accomplished this through techniques, including sequentially constructed diagrams, repeated iconic pictures, and compelling large-screen display, that are distinctively digital.

Reconstructing Reality in the Bontatibus Case

Late in the afternoon on November 26, 1996, a fire broke out at the Floors and More store in Branford, Connecticut. As firefighters responding to the blaze worked their way inside the building, the roof collapsed on them, trapping several of them. One volunteer firefighter, Edward Ramos, died. Anthony "Gene" Bontatibus, Sr., the owner of the store, was a well-known person in Branford. A former selectman and former chair of the town's Planning and Zoning Commission, Bontatibus had started Floors and More and built it up into an apparently successful family business.[26]

On March 7, 1997, Bontatibus was arrested and charged with arson and murder after police investigators concluded that the fire had been deliberately set, caused by an ignitable liquid poured in the kitchen behind the store's showroom.[27] His trial ended in a hung jury. The state retried him. Out of funds, Bontatibus was now represented by a public defender, Thomas Ullmann. This time, a mistrial was declared after one of the jurors decided to conduct his own investigation into the flammability of vinyl flooring.[28] The state decided to prosecute Bontatibus a third time.

The Floors and More fire had already been investigated by several agencies before Bontatibus was initially charged,[29] but Ullmann decided before Bontatibus's second trial to take another look. He engaged Richard Custer, a fire safety consultant. After intensive research, Custer opined that the evidence was inconclusive as to whether the fire had started in the kitchen by the ignition of a flammable fluid (as the prosecution contended), by the ignition of residual gas from a leak that had been observed earlier that day, or by an electrical failure of a fluorescent light transformer.[30] Ullmann eventually settled on the theory that, whether caused by a gas leak or electrical failure, the fire had begun in the attic space below the roof of the store. His ability to persuade the jurors at Bontatibus's third trial of this, at least to the extent of creating reasonable doubt about the prosecution's account, would largely determine whether his client would spend decades in prison.[31]

Testimonial evidence included eyewitness accounts from the firefighters who were on the scene and expert testimony from fire safety experts and other investigators. Bontatibus himself, although not at the scene at the time of the fire, also testified about the prior gas leak in the building and his efforts to address it, claiming that he had left the store for home about half an hour to forty minutes before smoke was first observed coming from the building. The tangible evidence available to Ullmann as he began to plan his defense strategy included (1) several dozen photos taken during the fire itself by a local newspaper reporter who had rushed to the scene; (2) hundreds of photographs of the destroyed building taken by fire and police investigators; (3) videos taken by the state police after the fire and the following day; and (4) tape recordings of the initial 911 call to the fire department and of the communications between the firefighters from the Branford Fire Department who responded to the call and the commanders at the scene.[32]

Public defender Ullmann had two goals in developing the testimony of his expert witness, Richard Custer. He wanted jurors to understand and believe Custer's opinion that the fire started in the roof of the store and therefore had not been set deliberately. He also wanted them to accept the possibility that the fire department's own incompetence—most important, in waiting too long after seeing that the roof was on fire and therefore at risk of collapsing before ordering those inside to vacate—was largely responsible for the tragic death of the volunteer firefighter Ramos. (Given that jurors often find firefighters, as they do policemen, presumptively credible, any such suggestion would probably have to remain implicit and be handled very carefully.) Ullmann's audience, in short, needed a convincing *story* to understand how the fire started and what led up to Edward Ramos's death. To convey a compelling but legally relevant narrative, Ullmann chose digital picturing tools.

The law of demonstrative evidence. Visuals used during the presentation of evidence, as opposed to those used during opening statements or closing arguments, are called *demonstrative evidence.* This includes everything from photos and videos to X-rays and brain scans, from maps, charts, and graphs to 3-D models and computer animations. The law governing the admissibility of demonstrative evidence is somewhat inconsistent and confusing, varying from one state and even one courtroom to the next. The most common view is that demonstratives merely illustrate oral testimony and therefore are not required to meet the same standards of *authentication* before being shown to the jury that substantive evidence (such as a weapon or other object allegedly involved in the actual events) is.[33] Demonstrative evidence can be used at trial if it fairly and accurately represents what the witness says it represents.[34] Some courts, however, treat at least some demonstratives—especially those generated by sophisticated and/or unfamiliar technologies, such as computer animations or simulations presented by an accident or crime reconstruction expert—as substantive evidence and demand that they be authenticated more carefully.[35] And, unlike substantive evidence, demonstratives admitted during trial are generally not sent to the jury room for jurors to consider during deliberations.[36]

All judges seem to agree that fundamental concepts of relevance and fairness always apply to demonstrative evidence. The proponent of an item of demonstrative evidence establishes its relevance by showing that the item helps the jury to understand the testimony it illustrates.[37] Whether it is fair to let jurors see the item is often a more difficult question, as we will see later in this chapter (and throughout the book). The basic test is set forth in Federal Rule of Evidence 403, which provides that the judge may exclude the demonstrative if its probative value is substantially outweighed by the risk of creating unfair prejudice, confusing issues, or misleading the jury.[38] Finally, whether a visual display should be admitted or excluded is left to the discretion of the trial judge, whose decision is rarely reversed on appeal.[39]

Explaining the fire with digital illustrations. None of the hundreds of photos or video footage taken at the scene of the fire depicted the fire from inside the Floors and More store as it was starting. The documentary evidence appeared to be as consistent with the prosecution's theory of how the fire began as with the defendant's. To help jurors visualize Custer's explanation, Ullmann needed new pictures. He asked Animation Technologies, Inc. (ATI), a litigation consulting company with headquarters in Boston, to create a series of illustrations showing, step by step, how the fire could have started in the space below the roof of the building and led to the roof's collapse, resulting in the pattern of damage documented in the photographic and video evidence.

During direct examination, Custer set the stage by narrating half a dozen photographs of the destruction in the store's floor tile display room (behind the showroom and adjacent to the kitchen), as the photos were displayed on a large screen. This was the most straightforwardly depictive kind of picture—the most "real," in the sense discussed in chapter 2. Next came the most abstract and overtly explanatory: a diagram of the floor plan of the entire store, orienting the jurors to the relative locations of the tile room, showroom, and kitchen. Then Custer walked the judge and jurors through the eight illustrations prepared by ATI, which occupied a kind of middle ground between the depictive and the diagrammatic. The first seven show the tile room from a point of view high up on the side wall opposite the tile display stands. We first see the large room bathed in a calm light: floor, display stands and shelves with tile samples, front and side walls, and a large heating unit against the ceiling at the front of the room. Then signs of fire appear above as a jagged piece of the ceiling, edged in red, begins to break off. As the fire spreads, smoke pours down and a large piece of insulation (documented in one of the photographs already shown) falls. The roof weakens further, and the portion of the ceiling to which the heating unit is attached comes apart, causing the heater to plummet onto and to crush one of the tile display stands (again matching the photographic documentation that the jurors have already seen)

Figure 3.2. How the fire began and spread: illustration of the defendant's fire safety expert's testimony in *Bontatibus* (courtesy of Larry Collins, Animation Technologies, Inc., and attorney Tom Ullmann).

(Figure 3.2). The last drawing zooms in to a closeup of the heater on top of the tile stand, a visual exclamation point to conclude the sequence.

There are a number of reasons why these finely crafted digital illustrations could have helped jurors to understand and therefore accept Custer's expert opinion. Like any well-designed diagrams, the illustrations portray the critical information—the breaking apart of the ceiling because of the intense heat from above and the consequent falling of the heating unit onto the tile stands—with maximum clarity, avoiding peripheral or otherwise inessential details. They show a plausibly real world, but only the most essential information is portrayed. (The photographs taken after the fire, in contrast, show a chaos of undifferentiated debris amid the ruins of the store: everything in front of the lens that was sufficiently illuminated.) Like any historian, Custer worked backwards from the documented physical traces of the event to reconstruct the sequence of crucial moments leading up to it. ATI's pictures showed that sequence unfolding forward in time, more or less as it would have been visible to the unaided eye. And, while all of this could have been done using analog media and displayed in court on poster board, digital technology allowed the reconstructed history of the fire to be shown on the screen, within the kind of frame in which jurors are accustomed to watching news footage, documentaries, educational materials, and other presumptively accurate visual depictions of reality.[40]

Using digital multimedia to reconstruct reality.[41] Between the second and third trials, Ullmann attended a criminal defense lawyers' seminar in Atlanta at which another lawyer, using simulated case materials, demonstrated a multimedia recreation of a building fire and the fire department's laconic response to a victim's calls for help. Ullmann realized that, in the photographs of the Floors and More fire and the audiotapes of the 911 and fire department communications, he had all of the evidentiary support he needed to construct a similar multimedia display.

ATI's first version for the *Bontatibus* case contained over an hour of taped communications and more than 150 photographs. Ullmann thought that this would be too much for the jurors to absorb and that they (and perhaps also the judge) would find it tedious. He wanted to recreate events in a way that would hold his audience's attention and focus it on his theory of the case, but to ensure admissibility, he also wanted the re-creation to unfold entirely in real time, without internal edits. ATI condensed the demonstrative material into an audiovisual sequence lasting just over ten minutes. While Custer, the fire safety expert, was on the stand, jurors listened to the audiotape of the communications among the fire department personnel; in the bottom third of the screen, they read the transcript of the firefighters' words and saw the time code for each remark (crucial information, given Ullmann's implicit argument that the fire department's delays were partly responsible for firefighter Ramos's death); and, in the top two-thirds of the screen, they watched the events as depicted by a series of more than two dozen photographs taken by the newspaper photographer.[42]

The sequence picks up the story just after the firefighters have arrived on the scene. We see first the front of the Floors and More building from a distance of about fifty feet and then closer up, bluish-grey smoke billowing from the front door and roof, as the firefighters on the scene array themselves and their equipment. A hose snaking along the parking lot in the foreground lies flat, plainly without water inside.[43] More fire engines arrive and more firefighters enter the burning building, carrying an apparently full hose. Those in the building exchange information with Deputy Fire Chief Ronald Mullen, who is at the command post; in between these exchanges, we hear only the white noise of static and the automated voice announcing the time code every ten seconds. A red glow on top of

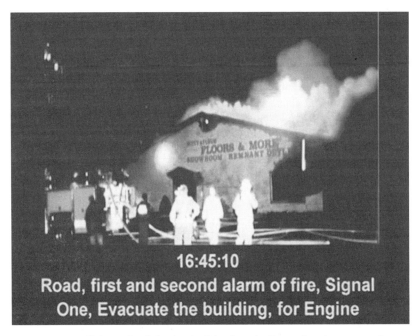

16:45:10
Road, first and second alarm of fire, Signal
One, Evacuate the building, for Engine

Figure 3.3. A still from the defendant's slide show in *Bontatibus* (courtesy of
Larry Collins, Animation Technologies, Inc., and attorney Tom Ullmann).

the building becomes brighter and larger, mixing with the smoke. Four
minutes in, Mullen says, "[W]e have a heavy volume of fire in the upper area." Jurors will learn from other witnesses that such an observation
should lead to an immediate order to vacate, because a burning roof may
collapse at any time.

Almost five minutes in, Deputy Chief Mullen announces that "we have
the, ah, front windows taken out; the, ah, condition should improve." It
does not. As the firemen make their way into the interior of the building,
the roof of the building glows yellow, then white, as smoke envelops the
outside. The fire on the roof continues to grow. The photographs follow one
another more quickly now, increasing the tension.[44] Six minutes in, Command says to those inside, "We have a heavy haul on the fire above you,"
and again at nearly nine minutes in, "There is a heavy volume of fire above
your head." Ten seconds after this, command finally orders the firefighters
inside the building to "back out"; another ten seconds pass before we hear
the signal tone that the firefighters knew meant that they should evacuate
the building,[45] followed by an explicit order to evacuate (Figure 3.3).

It is too late. The roof, engulfed in flames, collapses. Looking at what used to be the side of the store, we see only clouds of smoke, some bluish-grey, some darkly shadowed in the dusk, surrounding a white- and red-hot core. After about thirty seconds, a desperate cry is heard: "Deputy Chief Pepe to Command!" Now we see again the front of the building, with yellow-orange flames erupting from the roof into the sky, as Deputy Chief Mullen calls: "Pep where are ya? . . . Where are ya?" There is no answer. The screen goes black. Only after playing the entire sequence without interruption did defense attorney Ullmann go back and ask his expert witness to explain to the jurors how the documentary evidence of photographs and audiotapes supported his opinion about how the fire had started.

Using traditional analog media and traditional case presentation methods, it would have taken Ullmann hours to put this photographic and audiotape evidence before the jury. It would have been extremely difficult for jurors to integrate all of that material, if presented bit by bit, into a coherent notion of what happened. The multimedia display concentrated and thereby heightened the impact of the represented information much more than a seriatim presentation of photographs and then audiotapes would have. In addition, together with the series of digital illustrations discussed earlier, the multimedia sequence offered jurors a range of visual explanations of the disputed events—interior and exterior, diagrammatic and pictorial—each bolstering the credibility of the other.

Perhaps the most significant rhetorical aspect of the display is that presenting the photographic and audio evidence as a single, coherent story appealed to jurors' familiarity with audiovisual stories from their everyday experiences watching television, movies, and video clips on the Internet.[46] The events themselves left real traces: individual photographs from different photographers, some video, and audiotape recordings. But these traces were physically fragmented. Reconstructing reality in immediately, intuitively understandable form required that Ullmann and ATI select and assemble the fragments, generate the transcript of the audio communications, and integrate all of the material into a continuous sequence on the screen. By doing so, they enabled jurors to grasp the story arc, the narrative necessity,[47] of the tragic events, from the opening scene in which some of the firefighters' hoses have no water to the concluding cry of Deputy Fire Chief Ronald Mullen to Deputy Fire Chief William Pepe and the other firemen trapped inside the building, "Pep, where are ya?," answered only by an ominous silence.[48]

Explicitly, the multimedia sequence vividly and effectively illustrated the expert witness Custer's theory of how the fire began. Implicitly, the sequence also conveyed the other part of the defendant's theory of the case, an idea that would have been tactless (or worse) to express—that the fire department's mishandling of the situation was the real cause of Edward Ramos's death. Jurors saw and heard a dramatic story in which Command knew about the fire on the roof but delayed giving the order to vacate, followed by tragedy. Jurors' intuitive grasp of narrative logic, not to mention common sense, told them that the first was connected to the second.[49] In addition, by eliciting jurors' sympathy for the trapped victim, the display may have prompted jurors to attribute blame to the fire department and not the defendant.[50] This display thus offers yet another example of a principle we find whenever pictures are in play: the simultaneous creation of both explicit and implicit meanings. That these digital demonstratives taught the facts of the case so well is perfectly consistent with, and indeed strengthened, their capacity to persuade the audience of the rightness of the client's cause.[51]

The Difference That Digitization Makes

The *Koenig* and *Bontatibus* cases exemplify the broad claim made in our introductory chapter that digital technologies are changing how lawyers explain and how judges and jurors learn. It's worth stepping back from the case studies to discuss these ideas in more detail, drawing connections between the uses of digital technologies in court and related phenomena in the culture at large.

Digital and analog media share the basic virtue of facilitating visual learning. As the cognitive psychologist Allan Paivio and the educational psychologist Richard Mayer have explained, people possess dual information-processing channels, the auditory/verbal and the visual/pictorial.[52] These separate (but interacting) channels are used both to take in sensory inputs and to process them in working memory.[53] People learn better when information is presented pictorially (the mode corresponding to the visual channel) as well as verbally, because when both pictures and words are presented, people can construct mental models of the information in both their visual and their verbal channels and build connections between them.[54] Lawyers, accordingly, have long benefited from using analog visual displays to teach their cases: drawings, maps, charts, and diagrams on poster boards and blackboards, as well as 3-D models and other kinds of demonstratives.

What's different about digitization? As *Koenig* and *Bontatibus* illustrate, legal information is now on the screen; evidence is mobilized and juxtaposed as never before; lawyers can combine words and pictures with unprecedented flexibility; and they can make meanings by constructing sequences of pictures. The last three of these features are also found to a lesser extent in analog media, but digital tools make it much easier for lawyers to take advantage of all of them. And, because lawyers are doing that, digitization is changing how legal decision makers understand trial information.[55]

Putting information on the screen. Traditional analog demonstratives are displayed in a variety of settings: Photographs are handed from one juror to the next; 3-D models are carted into the central space bounded by the bench, the jury box, and counsels' tables; easels and blackboards are set up wherever they can be used for drawing and be visible to all. Digital demonstratives, by contrast, are displayed on screens.[56] Audiences take in visual information differently when they watch it on a screen compared to when they see it or hold it in real space, and these differences can affect how they interpret everything they see.[57] We trace these various (and conflicting) effects to two senses in which the screen *frames* what viewers see: as a physical border that limits and creates new relationships among the elements displayed inside it and as a carrier of personal and cultural associations.

Screens shape the display of digital information. Every screen, like the physical frame of an analog picture, imposes a boundary on the viewing space. The boundary partly defines our interpretation of the visual elements within. Consider, again, as we did in chapter 1, the Abu Ghraib prison photo of the hooded prisoner standing on a box with what he was told were live electrodes attached to the ends of his hands. Alone in the center of the picture, evoking Christ on the cross, the figure seems to be the focus of a kind of ritual—an effect enhanced by our apparent visual distance from the figure, far enough away to see the entire body on its pedestal.[58] A different version of the same scene, accompanying Susan Sontag's essay "Regarding the Torture of Others" in the *New York Times*, shows the prisoner slightly further away, less brightly lit—and, partly cut off by the right edge of the frame, an American soldier standing against a wall, clipping his nails and not looking at the prisoner.[59] The casual presence and demeanor of the soldier on the side of the scene and the displacement of the prisoner to the partly shadowed back of a hallway radically changes the picture's meanings. Now it implies, among other things, that such torture was an everyday occurrence at the prison, so routine that it doesn't warrant the soldier's attention, much less his concern.

The composition of visual elements within the frame can also affect the implied relationships among those elements. The placement of the prisoner and the soldier in the second Abu Ghraib photo, for example, draws our attention to the space between the two, thus linking the figures visually and suggesting something about the nature of the relationship between them: close enough to imply a causal connection (the soldier and those he represents are responsible for the prisoner's predicament) but distant enough to imply a moral disconnect (the lack of empathy on the part of the soldier for the prisoner).

In these respects, digital pictures resemble analog ones, but putting pictures on digital screens can also create distinctive effects. Screens differ from one another in size, aspect ratio, and color balance, all of which can affect what viewers see and how they interpret it. In addition, the "flattening" of all digitized data, whatever its origin, into a uniform, two-dimensional, nontactile screen format creates an experience very different from that of holding something (such as a photograph or an object) or of seeing a three-dimensional model that one can readily imagine touching.[60] On the other hand, pictures seen on screens are set off from the rest of the perceptual environment in a way that, say, photographs handed from one juror to another are not. And when we watch pictures on screens, although we know that someone has created those pictures, the "author" is not present; thus, lawyers who show pictures on screens are less likely to be intuitively understood as the creators or sponsors of those pictures than they are when they handle photographs or poster boards. For these reasons, what is seen on a courtroom screen may seem both more perceptually distant and further removed from the lawyer's own body and personality, which could increase its apparent objectivity. And, when pictures and words are projected onto a single screen for all to see, the audience shares a common visual focus, participating together in the visual activity much as they might at the movies.[61]

This leads us to the second sense in which screens frame what judges and jurors see in the digital age. Everyone has spent countless hours watching television and movie screens. From these experiences, people have developed beliefs and expectations that they unconsciously carry over to what they see on courtroom screens. For instance, some research indicates that people tend to believe what they see in the mass media,[62] to the point of incorporating mediated fictions into their beliefs about the world.[63] Simply by putting information on a screen, lawyers can tap into these tendencies. Furthermore, by presenting information in a format that audiences find very familiar, lawyers can put judges and jurors at ease,[64] making them readier to receive new information—and possibly less inclined to do so critically.[65] More specifically, audiences have become habituated to mass media conventions of how visual narratives unfold, making courtroom presentations that fit those notions easier to comprehend and possibly more credible as well. (We have seen this in *Bontatibus* and will encounter an even more dramatic example in the multimedia closing argument in the *Skakel* case, discussed in chapter 5.) In addition, when people watch screens, they are accustomed to seeing polished, even slick, presentations, which can set a high bar, especially for lawyers who create their own visuals. Just as lawyers who come to court with sophisticated digital graphics can impress jurors with their preparation and professionalism, so the lawyer whose slides or videos malfunction risks looking incompetent and foolish.[66]

Now people are also spending ever-increasing amounts of time in front of another sort of screen—the ones on their personal computers, primarily, but also their cell phones, BlackBerries, and other handheld devices. Their relationships to these screens are in many respects quite different from those they have with movies and television,[67] and the implications for the interpretation of words and pictures shown on courtroom screens are complicated. On the one hand, people who are inclined to believe that information on a computer screen is reliable simply because they see it as computer generated may be that much more disposed to believe what a lawyer displays on screen.[68] On the other, as we observed in chapter 1, the more people use Photoshop, Final Cut Pro, and other digital photo and video editing programs, the more aware they may be that all digital visual representations are constructed and the more likely they may be to view screen images with skepticism. This may be especially true of younger audiences, who have grown up with *The Daily Show* and video mashups on YouTube.

Mobilizing and juxtaposing the evidence. By translating all information from whatever original source to the common electronic denominator of 0s and 1s (as we noted in chapter 1), digitization makes it possible for advocates to mobilize information to an unprecedented degree and to integrate almost any kind of evidence into a single screen presentation. Digital tools enable lawyers to marshal more information from disparate sources and to make it all accessible to judges and jurors on the screen in whatever way, simultaneously or in sequence, will help them understand the case better. For instance, the *Bontatibus* sequence, as we have seen, drew on dozens of still photos, audio recordings, and specially made digital illustrations. (Later in this chapter, we will see how the prosecution in the *Skakel* case used digital technology to deploy a similarly wide range of demonstrative evidence.) In addition, digitization allows lawyers to "smooth out the edges" of older demonstrative evidence, such as old photos or documents, and to present that evidence accurately and with the same degree of clarity and "finish" as they can more recent evidence.[69]

Digitization also allows everyone, including lawyers, to juxtapose and compare information visually and thus make both similarities and differences between ideas more vivid and intuitive. Much of the SEC's visual presentation in *Koenig*, as we have seen, followed this strategy: The slides repeatedly contrast simple diagrams representing accepted accounting procedures and ones that start off the same way but then diverge, representing the defendant's unacceptable methods. An even better example of juxtaposition from that case is another pair of slides that the SEC created to show what was wrong with the defendant's continuing to capitalize interest on landfill construction loans after the landfills were open for business. Under accepted accounting practices, interest payments on construction loans are part of the value of the asset being built (which may then be depreciated) until the building is complete and operational, at which point the interest is counted as an ordinary business expense. Koenig, however, continued to capitalize interest on the landfills toward their asset value even as they filled up (and thus avoided counting those payments as expenses, consistent with his other machinations to inflate reported profits).[70] In the left half of the first slide of the pair, under the title "How Mr. Koenig Capitalized Interest," is a simple cartoon of an empty landfill; in the right half, the same landfill is shown half-full, and, underneath, a legend proclaims that, as the available space declined, the landfill's value, according to Koenig's methods, went *up*. To underscore the point, the next slide, with the same title, shows on the left a whole cookie with the legend "50¢" and, on the right, half a cookie with the legend "$1.00" (Figure 3.4).[71]

The simple visual analogy and comparison allows jurors to grasp intuitively the SEC's point that Koenig's accounting results were not just wrong but absurd. This logic of juxtaposition is so basic and familiar, and so easy to implement with digital tools, that one can forget how much harder it is to learn when one cannot see, at the same time and on the same screen, the items being compared.

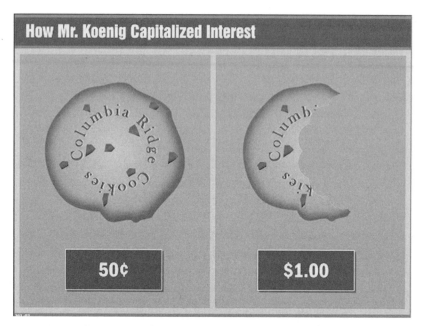

Figure 3.4. Juxtaposition and metaphor: a slide from the SEC's opening statement in *Koenig* (courtesy of G. Christopher Ritter, The Focal Point, and attorneys Robert Pommer and Jack Worland).

Combining pictures and words. In an analog world, there are demonstratives made of words, such as lists written on a flip chart. And there are pictures, like photos and drawings. Often the two don't meet. Graphs, charts, and diagrams use words and numbers to label bars and lines but rarely venture much more.

Digital tools change all of this. Digital technologies, especially widely available software programs such as PowerPoint, enable people without specialized graphic design skills or training (including most lawyers) to manipulate and arrange pictures, texts, and sounds in almost any way desired. Pictures, for instance, can be costlessly and almost effortlessly duplicated, resized, and relocated within the frame in whatever way best serves the lawyer's communicative purposes. Text can be displayed in a great variety of fonts (more than two hundred styles in the current version of PowerPoint, each available in regular, bold, italics, or bold italics), sizes, and colors, conveying whatever emphasis and other effects the lawyer chooses. And, if that's not enough, the words can be underscored or surrounded by borders in any style for additional emphasis. Video and audio clips can be retrieved and incorporated into the presentation, although not quite as easily as still pictures and text can.[72] Lawyers thus have great flexibility to annotate pictures, to illustrate texts, and, in general, to put words and pictures together to teach better, following principles of good information graphics.[73]

Digital tools invite lawyers to play with pictures and use them for new purposes.[74] For instance, as we saw in the SEC's graphics of the locked black box or the shredding of the salvage value report in *Koenig*, lawyers use pictures as eye-catching, memorable icons to label ideas that are especially significant or are repeated during the presentation.[75] Multiple copies of pictures can also be used instead of bars or lines to represent quantities in visual tables, helping jurors to notice and remember information that they might otherwise find hard to absorb.[76] And, by adding simple animation functions to any of these word-picture combinations, lawyers can direct audiences' attention to specific visual elements without changing their size or appearance, thereby maintaining the desired composition of the finished display.

Equally important and even more interesting rhetorically is how lawyers can use PowerPoint and other digital tools to *write with pictures* (as we discussed in chapter 1) and thus to create new and multiple meanings, both explicit and implicit. The deployment of iconic visual elements in the *Koenig* graphics—in particular, the defendant's photo with the picture of the locked black box, often positioned apart from a diagram representing how things should have been done—provides a relatively simple example of this.[77]

Putting pictures into sequences. When people learn, they first have to process information through their working memories. But working memory capacity is limited. By ordering and pacing information effectively over time, lawyers allow their audiences to conserve scarce mental resources and thus to absorb and retain new information better.[78] Digital technologies make it easier for lawyers to arrange and rearrange word-picture combinations into coherent, effective sequences that best fit whatever kind of material they need to teach.

If the task is to present an analytical framework for understanding the facts and the relevant concepts, as it was in *Koenig*, being able to arrange words and pictures into sequences that unfold over time, at a pace controlled largely by the presenter, offers a number of advantages. By controlling the flow of information, the lawyer can avoid giving audiences too much at any one time.[79] Lawyers can also use temporal sequence to reflect the underlying logic of the presentation, as we saw in *Koenig*. The one-frame-after-another exposition can give an audience the visual experience of a step-by-step process or the item-by-item accumulation of supporting evidence. Sequence (and animation) can also yield surprise, entertaining the audience while underscoring points of emphasis.[80] The SEC did this repeatedly by setting up the accepted, normal way of doing things and then interjecting a picture of Koenig and a representation of how his methods diverged from the norm.

When the task is to explain what happened and how, time-based pictorial presentations using digital technologies turn sets of pictures into stories. Traditional analog methods of displaying series of pictures have their own explanatory benefits, to be sure. A still diagram or photo array simultaneously depicting several stages of an event or process has the advantage of leaving all of the steps visible, permitting a direct visual comparison of multiple steps. It also allows the audience to proceed through the explanation at its own pace, even to go back and examine an earlier step more closely.[81] And a lawyer who displays enlarged photos of a series of events one after the other on a courtroom easel can at least hint at the actual flow of reality that the photos excerpt, while also calling the audience's attention to particular pictures.

A sequence of pictures on the screen, however, invites the audience to interpret the discrete visual items as constructing the kind of unified, coherent narrative that they are accustomed to seeing on television and in videos and films. When shown on the screen, transitions from one picture to the next become *cuts*. The use of this essential convention of cinematic exposition cues viewers' expectations about the meaning of what they are seeing, namely that the visual sequence constitutes a story about its ostensible subject, rather than a mere collection of items of visual evidence. The fact that the cuts between pictures may leave gaps in the chronology of the story doesn't matter because viewers are adept at bridging discontinuities in what they see as long as narrative continuity on the whole is maintained.[82] That is, viewers supply the continuity in a top-down fashion on the basis of their knowledge of the story elements and the kind of story being told.[83] So effective is this "illusion of continuity" that movie viewers tend not to notice the cuts at all—they think that they're seeing continuous depictions of action.[84] Viewers also understand, from their lifetimes of experience watching movies and television, the meaning of particular cutting techniques; they know, for instance, that the more rapid "cutting" in the latter portion of the second *Bontatibus* sequence signals an increase in dramatic tension.[85]

Construing a sequence of pictures—especially one, as in the photo sequence in *Bontatibus*, that is accompanied by a continuous, synchronous soundtrack (i.e., the sounds that could have been heard at the same time and place as the events depicted in the pictures)—in terms of their everyday viewing habits, the audience experiences a heightened sense of participation in the depicted events.[86] Participation, in turn, can enhance the audience's interest and emotional involvement in what is depicted.[87] Furthermore, viewers may form more specific associations with the narrative models and styles of popular movies and television programs, triggering expectations about the sort of story they are about to see (and hear)—and they are likely to find more credible narrative sequences that meet those expectations.[88]

All four of these features of digital visuals—the screen display, the increased mobilization and juxtaposition of information, the proliferation of multiple levels of meanings, and the range of effects created by seamless picture sequences—differentiate new courtroom media from old, giving lawyers more tools to present evidence in ways that jurors will find clear and compelling. Our next topic is an even more striking departure from traditional ways of making trial information visible: interactivity.

The Benefits of Interactivity: Trial Presentation Software

Thus far, we have examined how digital technologies help lawyers to assemble pictures and words into audiovisual explanations that they can then display at trial. But trials can be full of surprises. The order of witnesses and the testimony may change from one moment to the next; new arguments and new strategies may emerge as a result of what witnesses, opposing lawyers, or the judge says. Lawyers need to be able to adapt, and their deployment of visual displays needs to be flexible as well.

The answer is interactive trial presentation software. InData's Trial-Director came on the market in 1996, and Verdict Systems' Sanction followed in 1999,[89] integrating developments in presentation software, digital file storage, and graphics editing software already taking place in the culture at large.[90] These and other trial presentation programs allow lawyers to do just about everything they can do in PowerPoint. For instance, the programs let lawyers display different files side by side, zoom in and out, emphasize selected portions with callouts, and annotate anything displayed using a variety of markup tools,[91] thereby enabling the lawyers to take advantage of juxtaposition and word-picture recombination. Like

PowerPoint, these programs also allow lawyers to build narrative explanations out of sequences of pictures.

TrialDirector, Sanction, and similar programs also have two crucial (and related) features not found in PowerPoint. First, they function as case management software, giving lawyers access to the full database of materials that have previously been logged into the program (after first being digitized, if originally in analog format): text, audio, and video files of all kinds.[92] Second, the programs allow lawyers immediate and random access to these materials. Lawyers can retrieve any file on demand and display that file at any desired point in the proceedings. That is, the programs are nonlinear, whereas PowerPoint, except perhaps in the hands of its most capable users, remains relentlessly linear, making it difficult for the presenter to vary from the prepared sequence of slides.

These features certainly enhance the lawyer's ability to mobilize information.[93] They also enable the lawyer to interact with that information as the moment demands. In a typical use of TrialDirector or Sanction, for instance, a lawyer conducting direct examination of a witness can call up a digital file of any kind of demonstrative evidence—words, pictures, sounds—show it to the jury exactly when the witness needs it to help explain his or her testimony, and remove it instantly from view as soon as it is no longer needed. At the witness's instruction, the lawyer can also mark up the demonstrative, obtaining the rhetorical benefit of performing visual changes before the jurors' eyes (just as a lawyer could do by writing on a flip chart or blackboard, but which would be awkward and difficult using PowerPoint).

To examine in more detail how the interactivity of digital evidence presentation technologies enables lawyers to explain the facts of their cases more efficiently and effectively, we turn to the highly publicized murder prosecution of Kennedy cousin Michael Skakel.

Interacting With the Evidence in the Skakel Case

On October 30, 1975, Martha Moxley, a fifteen-year-old girl from the gated community of Belle Haven in Greenwich, Connecticut, was beaten to death with a golf club.[94] After nearly a quarter-century of official and unofficial investigations that were by turns fitful and resolute, Michael Skakel, a neighbor of Martha's and also fifteen years old at the time of Martha's death, was charged with her murder. The trial began on May 4, 2002. The case against Skakel was twenty-seven years old and lacked strong forensic evidence. Prosecutors did not have eyewitnesses who could unambiguously place the defendant at the scene of the crime. Skakel claimed that he was elsewhere at the time. In addition, even after defeating legal objections to trying the defendant as an adult for a crime allegedly committed so long ago as a juvenile,[95] the State would have to overcome jurors' possible reluctance to accept that a rotund, middle-aged family man not known as a violent criminal could once have bludgeoned a lovely young lady to death. All in all, the prosecution faced a challenging task in convincing a jury beyond a reasonable doubt that Skakel was the murderer.

To marshal its demonstrative evidence and display it to the jury in the most effective possible manner, the prosecution engaged Brian Carney, a legal visual technology consultant with WIN Interactive, Inc., to create a customized, interactive multimedia evidence presentation system.[96] Carney had been a prosecutor in Massachusetts for more than a decade; he had established a unit within the Suffolk County District Attorney's Office to develop high-tech visuals for trial use and then left to form his own consulting business. In *Skakel*, Carney worked with the prosecutors to design a comprehensive digital visual toolbox on CD-ROM that included more than one hundred crime scene and autopsy photographs, documents, diagrams, and digitized audio and video recordings. The toolbox was fully interactive: Every piece of evidence that was to be displayed or offered, except for live testimony, was available at the click of a mouse and could be made to appear on a large screen in the courtroom behind the witness.

All of this evidence was organized and simultaneously accessible to the prosecutors in two different, highly customized ways: a hierarchical menu system and a system of hyperlinked buttons which provided access across categories of materials.[97] Both of these navigational approaches made it easy for the trial lawyers, who ran the presentation in court, to locate within a few seconds any piece of evidence they wished to display. The prosecutors had been involved in the design of the interactive navigational systems; the program accommodated their desire to access specific types of evidence in whatever ways they might need to in the course of the trial. For example, to find the 1975 police photographs of the Moxley residence, prosecutors could click on the Moxley home in an aerial photograph of the Belle Haven neighborhood and immediately retrieve all available police photographs of that location (Figure 3.5).

During direct and cross-examination throughout the trial, the prosecution used the disk to clarify witness testimony and to help the jurors make sense of the State's version of the distant and disputed events. For instance,

Figure 3.5. Interactive demonstrative evidence in *Skakel*: By clicking on the aerial photograph, prosecutors immediately displayed elevation photographs of the victim's home (courtesy of Brian Carney, WIN Interactive, Inc.).

jurors needed to see the layout of the Moxley residence to understand where Martha Moxley's and her brother John's bedrooms were in relation to the trees in which Michael had told various people he was masturbating that night. Other testimony that these trees could not be climbed would, if believed, undermine Skakel's statements about those two sets of trees. As the witnesses testified about these matters, the prosecutor rolled a mouse over the zoomed-in aerial photograph of the Moxley home and clicked again, and the courtroom display zoomed in on a full-screen diagram of the home. Icons in the lower right corner of the screen represented each of the three floors of the house; by clicking on any one of these, the lawyer could immediately bring up that portion of the diagram.

The prosecution also needed jurors to understand and believe in its version of the series of events that could account for the fragmentary physical evidence found at the crime scene: the golf club head used to kill Martha, found in the center of the driveway in front of the Moxley home; some blood and a piece of golf club shaft nearby; outside the driveway, a large pool of blood and another piece of golf club shaft; and a "drag path" leading from that area to the tree where Martha's body was eventually found. Each of these items was mapped and labeled on an aerial photograph of the scene. During direct examination of Greenwich Police Detective Thomas Keegan, the prosecutor used the interactive program to build a graphic, one item of evidence at a time, showing where each item was located at the scene. The program, through linked commands, allowed the prosecutor to focus on each piece of evidence for as long as desired. For instance, when the label on the screen reading "golf club head" was clicked on, all of the other labels would disappear, focusing attention on where that one item was located, while a photograph of the golf club head appeared in the lower right corner of the screen. By the end of the witness's testimony, jurors understood where each piece of evidence had been found in relation to the others and were thus better able to fit these evidentiary traces with the prosecution's story of the crime.

The digital evidence presentation system improved the prosecution's ability to communicate and to explain relevant information to the judge and jurors. In addition to the benefits that PowerPoint would provide (e.g., large-screen display), the presentation system eliminated any possible confusion as to what particular part of the photograph or document was being discussed: The witness could simply point to the desired part of the picture on the screen by using a laser pointer; the lawyer could do the same by using a remote controlled mouse. This also helped everyone to draw connections between the testimonies of different witnesses as to the same matters, because all of the witnesses spoke to the same pictures. Interactive digital tools enabled the prosecution to conduct a more seamless performance, eliciting information from the witness stand and either supporting or contradicting it immediately through whatever pictures were best suited to do that job. This enhanced jurors' learning by bringing all relevant information into the closest possible association and by reducing distractors. Finally, participating in the preparation of the interactive disk forced prosecutors to gather and organize their demonstrative evidence well before trial, which helped them to prepare their witnesses better and thus to present those witnesses' evidence more effectively at trial.[98]

We will revisit the *Skakel* case in chapter 5 and see how the prosecution used the same interactive program in a highly dramatic fashion during its closing argument. And, in chapter 6, we will explore a possible legal future in which not only lawyers and witnesses but also judges and jurors interact with digital media. Next, though, we address another, increasingly common way in which lawyers use digital technologies to teach the facts of their cases: computer animation.

Moving Diagrams: Computer Animations

Digital visual and multimedia technologies can be used, as they were in *Koenig*, to present information and argument systematically, starting from concepts and moving to the evidence. Digital tools can also be used to represent reality in ways that resemble what people on the scene might perceive: the sorts of audiovisual accounts offered by the longer sequence in *Bontatibus* or, for that matter, by the videos in *Scott* and *Dunlop*, discussed in chapter 2.

Computer animations fall somewhere in between. They straddle the perceptual and the conceptual, the narrative and the paradigmatic.[99] They are diagrams that tell stories. They take features of visible reality, especially continuous movement, and use them to vivify schematic representations of data. Animations re-create reality in an abstracted and thus simplified form, clarifying case-relevant information and omitting whatever might obscure it.

Animations can be extremely effective teaching tools. Moving images are often better suited than other visual media for explaining critical information about processes or events, which happen through time.[100] In contrast to pictures made with cameras, animations, on the one hand, are not bound by the limits of what is visible under the available light and, on the other, can avoid extraneous information and focus on only what the proponent wants to make salient, while doing so with enough liveliness to keep viewers attentive. Animations are thus ideal for visualizing information that might otherwise be too technical or difficult for viewers to follow. They can clarify processes that are not naturally and readily visible because those processes occur too quickly or too slowly, from atomic reactions to the gradual leaching of a pollutant; occur on too large or too small a scale, from the unfolding of a storm to the replication of DNA; or are occluded by other objects, such as the internal workings of a machine. For all of these reasons, lawyers turn to animations to re-create events like accidents and crimes so that their essential features, the changing relative positions of vehicles or the path of a bullet, say, can be made clear. Yet, animations can also have no effect or even mislead viewers, as indicated by the psychological research we outline next.

The psychology of legal animations. From the handful of published experimental studies on the effects of computer animations on legal decision making, several findings, necessarily tentative, have emerged. First, animations can, but sometimes do not, influence judgments of fact and legal responsibility. For example, the psychologist Meghan Dunn and colleagues found that animations affected how mock jurors determined liability for a small-plane crash but did not affect their judgments concerning an auto accident.[101] A possible explanation for this is that when the type of situation seems familiar to jurors (as would more likely be true of a car crash than a small-plane crash), jurors act as if they are capable of reconstructing a satisfactory story about what led to the accident from the oral testimony and other evidence alone, so they do not have to rely on the animation.[102]

Second, animations can help or hinder accurate fact-finding, depending on the nature of the animation and the other, reliable evidence. The psychologists Saul Kassin and Meghan Dunn found that mock jurors in an insurance claim case who saw a "neutral" animation of a man falling to his death at a construction site (i.e., depicting only the trajectory of the body as it fell) were more likely to render a verdict consistent with the physical evidence (accidental death, as the plaintiff claimed, or suicide, as the insurance company asserted, respectively). When, however, the animation became more biased (i.e., depicting the man either slipping after losing his balance or taking a running leap off the building), mock jurors increasingly made judgments contrary to the physical evidence and in line with the what the animation depicted: Those who saw the animated display depicting the man losing his balance and falling were more likely to vote in favor of the plaintiff's theory of an accidental death, even when the physical evidence supported the defendant's theory that the man jumped.[103]

Third, jurors who watch animations may not be the best judges of whether the animations have influenced their thinking. In the first experiment mentioned, Dunn and her colleagues found that mock jurors in the plane crash case did not rate the animation as having been very influential when in fact it affected their liability judgments, whereas those in the car crash case thought that the animation was the most important item of evidence even though it actually had no effect on their decisions. In other words, the mock jurors got it exactly backwards.[104]

It is also not clear why computer animations affect legal judgments, to the extent that they do. Research on the effects of visual displays generally suggests that, because animations can present important information more vividly than nonmoving diagrams or words alone can, they lead to improved retention and recall.[105] According to other research on what cognitive psychologists call *processing fluency*, if animations make the depicted events easier for viewers to understand, viewers may infer from that easier processing that what is depicted is more likely to be true.[106] In addition, an animation whose continuous motion approximates that of a videotaped depiction of the event may also induce stronger emotional responses (where the event depicted is emotion-provoking) than would a nonmoving diagram, and those emotions may influence decision makers' judgments—just as videotaped evidence has been shown to do.[107]

This brings us to our last case study of the chapter, in which both animation and videotape were in play. Faced with a surveillance video that seemed to show conclusively that his client had behaved culpably, a defense lawyer used computer animation to re-create another version of events that he hoped jurors would find, if not equally "real," then at least convincing enough to support his theory of the case. The trial court's admission of the animation and the jury's subsequent acquittal of the defendant raise provocative questions about the persuasive power of digital visual evidence.

Animation Meets Video: Objective and Subjective Reality in the Murtha Case

In October 2006, Robert Murtha, a police officer in Hartford, Connecticut, was acquitted on charges including first-degree assault arising from his January 2003 shooting of a suspect attempting to flee in a stolen car.[108] Murtha had chased the other driver in his police cruiser until the driver stopped his car in a snow bank on the side of the road. As Murtha got out of his cruiser and approached the other car, the suspect pulled back onto the road and sped away. Murtha fired several shots at the driver's side window, striking and injuring the driver. In his original incident report, Murtha asserted that the suspect's car had hit him before pulling away, prompting him to shoot in self-defense. But Murtha changed his story when he became aware that a video from another police cruiser following the chase showed not only that the other car had not hit Murtha but that Murtha had run after the car and fired at the driver as the car sped away (Figure 3.6). At trial, Murtha claimed that, in the stress of the moment, he *thought* that the car was headed straight toward him when the driver

Figure 3.6. Video still from police dashboard camera in *Murtha* (courtesy of attorney Hugh Keefe).

first pulled back onto the road and that this reasonable (albeit mistaken) perception justified his use of deadly force in self-defense.[109]

The prosecution showed the jury surveillance video from the other police cruiser, depicting the chase and the shooting. Defense attorney Hugh Keefe recognized that he needed something visual to counter this compelling State's evidence—something to show the incident from Murtha's perspective. Animation could be used to show not what actually happened but rather what Officer Murtha (reasonably) *believed* had happened.

Jeffrey Taylor, a legal visual consultant, working closely with Murtha, produced a visual display of the shooting from Murtha's point of view. It begins with a clip from the surveillance video as the camera approaches to within perhaps twenty feet of Murtha's cruiser, which is stopped with its lights flashing, and the suspect's car, stopped in the snow on the side of the road. As the suspect begins to pull back onto the road, the action "freezes" and the video turns into an animation. The point of view changes from that of the dashboard camera mounted on the following police cruiser to that of a virtual camera generated by computer software. This virtual camera's (and our) point of view rises up and rotates to the left

Figure 3.7. Animation still from defendant's visual display in *Murtha* (courtesy of attorney Hugh Keefe).

around Murtha's cruiser, coming to rest behind a digital Officer Murtha as he stands, outstretched arm holding his gun, confronting the car (Figure 3.7). The viewer is now just behind Murtha, sharing his point of view in the crucial moment: The bright headlights of the suspect's car flash in our eyes, the left front headlight seemingly only a few feet away. Because the scene is frozen, the car could, for all that appears, be headed right at us. The animation holds this shot for a moment, then pulls away, up, back, and around again to the point of view from the surveillance camera, and we see the suspect's car continue down the road, away from us.

The prosecutor, James Thomas, objected to the animation, contending (out of the jury's hearing) that the animation was argumentative and inaccurate—not a fair representation of reality as indicated by the video.[110] The trial judge, Christine Keller, reviewed the animation-plus-video several times. On the basis of Murtha's testimony that the animation fairly and accurately depicted what Murtha thought he saw, Judge Keller found that the animation satisfied the test used in previous cases involving day-in-the-life movies and video reenactments of accidents: Was the animation a reasonably fair and accurate depiction of what it purported to show? She also found that it did not reflect any exaggeration or "artistic embellishment."[111] Accordingly, the judge allowed the jury to see the entire display, subject to a limiting instruction that the animation was being presented not as a precise reenactment of the incident but only to illustrate what Murtha claimed he honestly had believed was happening.[112]

There are several reasons why jurors might have found the animation to be a plausible representation of what Officer Murtha thought was happening at the time.[113] Murtha explained on the stand what had precipitated the car chase: He had just responded to a call involving seven men with guns at a housing project. When a backup officer drew his weapon, two of the men—the suspect and another—had jumped into a car and driven away. The shooting was therefore the culmination of a highly stressful sequence of events. Defense expert witnesses testified how, in stressful situations like Murtha's, officers can develop "tunnel vision," becoming so focused on one aspect of a situation that they misperceive or remain oblivious to others. This testimony helped jurors to understand how Murtha might have sincerely thought (as he initially reported) not only that the suspect's car had been heading straight toward him but that it had struck him, even though it had not.[114]

To illustrate his testimony about tunnel vision (what psychologists call *inattentional blindness*), one of the experts showed jurors another video, well known in academic psychology circles, in which a person in a gorilla suit walks through a circle of college students who are passing a basketball around.[115] If viewers are instructed beforehand to count the number of passes, many will fail to see the gorilla—even though, once seen, the gorilla is comically obvious. Judge Keller herself remarked, out of the jury's hearing: "I have to confess I didn't see the gorilla. . . . And I wasn't even counting basketballs."[116] This video is another example of how visual displays can help teach jurors what they need to know—in this case, what they needed in order to understand the expert's testimony about the effects of attentional focus on perception and memory. But showing this instructional video did more. By giving jurors a "direct experience" of what the expert was talking about,[117] the video prepared them for the direct visual experience that the animation provided of what the defendant Murtha was talking about.[118]

The reality that mattered in this case was, as it often is in trials, a hybrid of the objective and the subjective: The defendant was justified in shooting the fleeing driver if he reasonably believed that he needed to in order to defend himself. His testimony was sufficient proof of his belief, but whether that belief was reasonable depended (as it always does) on a consideration of the circumstances in which he acted. From the prosecution's point of view, the surveillance video seemed to be the most trustworthy evidence of those circumstances—the best proof of what really happened. Given this video evidence, what purpose did the animation serve?

Ostensibly, the defense did not offer the animation as a competing version of what really happened. Rather, the animation was offered to illustrate Officer Murtha's subjective perception of that reality.[119] But, more than that, the defendant's animation-plus-video offered jurors a visualization that integrated that subjective truth with the "objective truth" as represented by the dashboard camera's seemingly neutral report. As we saw in the discussion of the *Scott* case in chapter 2, dashcams are presumed to be objective because they simply record whatever is in front of them when they are (automatically) turned on; what they show is not shaped by an individual videographer's decision to point and shoot. This is the probative value of the defendant's display: It doesn't merely replicate the defendant's testimony in pictures rather than words but also helps the audience to understand that the defendant's perceptions were plausibly anchored in reality.

The medium is perfectly suited to the message: To show a hybrid kind of truth, the defense used a visual hybrid. The montage of animation and video clip bolsters the animation's credibility by grounding it in the presumptive truthfulness of the video. The transition from video to animation folds the two into the same level of represented reality: By starting with the surveillance camera's point of view and swinging around to the defendant's, the animation implicitly claims that both the defendant and the camera were "looking at the same reality." Connecting the animation to the video in this way also normalizes the more novel medium of animation by associating it with the very familiar (and presumptively reliable) medium of surveillance video—a kind of implicit remediation.[120]

Are these kinds of visual rhetorical effects reasons to welcome the animation in *Murtha*, or are they grounds for concern? Like any other evidence, the animation should have been admitted only if any risks it posed of causing unfair prejudice, confusing the issues, or misleading the jury did not outweigh its probative value.[121] Consider, in addition to the points already raised, the following. Jurors may perceive the animation to be more credible simply because they associate the medium of computer-generated graphics with (presumptively credible) scientific knowledge and expert scientific testimony. Any such effect would seem to be a kind of bias and hence misleading—but perhaps no more so than, say, jurors' reliance on expert witnesses' credentials, which are always admissible even though they may influence jurors' judgments of experts' credibility.[122] In addition, precisely what makes the animation probative for its ostensible purpose—showing the crucial events from the defendant's point of view— also inclines viewers to attribute less responsibility to the actor whose point of view the animation leads them to adopt and more responsibility to other actors or to the circumstances.[123] Jurors watching the animation stand with Murtha as he faces the threat of the (seemingly) oncoming car, and the sympathy they may feel with Murtha could lead them to improperly base their verdict on that emotion, rather than on reason.[124]

Furthermore, there are several striking discrepancies between the animated portion of the display and the video. For instance, the video makes it clear that Murtha was never standing in front of the suspect's car. In the animation, however, the suspect's car re-enters the road from the snow bank at a much sharper angle than seen in the unedited video, so that when the animation "freezes" the scene and the camera rotates to show Murtha standing still in the middle of the road, he appears partly in front of the suspect's car, his arm holding the gun already extended at the car's windshield. And, when the animation concludes as the suspect drives off, Murtha is depicted walking slowly alongside as he squeezes off three shots. In the unedited video, by contrast, Murtha is seen emerging from his cruiser only as the suspect's car regains the road and then running alongside and even approaching the suspect's car as he shoots repeatedly into the driver's side window. Judges exclude from evidence computer simulations that are offered as substantive depictions of reality but are not adequately supported by other reliable evidence.[125] Is it an adequate response in *Murtha* to say that we need not be troubled by the lack of evidentiary support for key aspects of the animation because the defense did not offer it as a true representation of external reality? Should the witness's testimony that the animation fairly and accurately represents what he *thought* he saw suffice, when the implicit visual rhetorical strategy depends, as we have argued, on encouraging viewers to merge his subjective account with objective reality?

Digital technology offered the trial judge in *Murtha* some options for dealing with this visual display. One of the great benefits of digitization, after all, is that digital pictures and multimedia can so easily be changed. The trial judge might have obtained the probative benefits of the defendant's video-plus-animation with fewer of the judgmental risks by asking defense lawyers to insert a slug (a bit of black video) between the video and the animation or to label the respective components "dashcam" and "animation." Either change would have made jurors less prone to elide the difference between the two modes of visual representation. For jurors to learn as much as they can from digital displays without being confused or misled, however, opposing counsel and judges must be ready, even in the heat of trial, to identify and evaluate those displays' multiple meanings and effects and be familiar enough with the technologies at hand to know what remedial measures, if any, are feasible. Some are already capable of rising to the occasion; soon, more will be, especially as more media- and technology-savvy young lawyers enter the profession.

As the cases we have examined in chapters 2 and 3 illustrate, digital media are transforming what judges' and jurors' knowledge of legally relevant reality looks and feels like. This is significant on at least three levels.

First, digital visuals and multimedia can improve decision makers' knowledge and understanding of reality. The videos in *Scott* and *Dunlop* let us know more about what happened than we could possibly know without that evidence. In *Bontatibus* and *Skakel*, digital tools were used to configure visual and audio evidence so that jurors could more readily integrate that evidence into coherent accounts of the crucial events, enhancing their understanding of those events. The digital presentation of evidence can also help jurors to evaluate *other* evidence, leading (all things being equal) to better decision making. The *Skakel* jurors, for instance, could better determine the credibility of the defendant's story about what he was doing in the tree behind the Moxley home (including looking through Martha's bedroom window) because they understood where the tree was in relation to the back of the home; the diagram and pictures juxtaposed on the screen made this clear. Digital visuals can impose order on a complex mass of material, as the SEC's slide show did in *Koenig*, giving decision makers a more complete and precise framework for applying the operative rules and norms to the facts.

Of course, it doesn't follow that legal decision makers will now have complete and unequivocal knowledge of case-relevant reality. Even surveillance videos (like any other visual evidence) require interpretation, and reasonable interpretations can differ—the basic point that the Supreme Court missed in *Scott*. The original photographic and audio evidence in *Bontatibus* was unquestionably authentic and relevant, but it was consistent with the prosecution's as well as the defendant's story of how the fire started. In law, as in everyday life, people's knowledge of reality often remains incomplete and contested—perhaps especially in the law, because trials usually don't take place unless there are multiple accounts of what happened, each backed by at least plausible evidence. All of this is true when the visuals are clear and probative, but sometimes they are not; like any other method of communication, including ordinary speech, visuals can be used, inadvertently or deliberately, to obscure rather than to clarify. For instance, any jurors in *Murtha* who believed (contrary to the judge's instructions) that the animation component of the visual display depicted what had really happened, as opposed to what the defendant thought had happened, would have been misled.

Moreover, pictures, even or perhaps especially when they are probative, can trigger cognitive biases that impair rather than improve understanding of the facts. By increasing the number of pictures at trial, digital technologies could make these biases worse. We observed one such bias earlier, the *processing fluency* effect: Jurors may be more likely to think that a picture is truthful just because it's easier for them to process pictures than words. Pictures can also create a *visual hindsight bias.* The hindsight bias is people's tendency to overestimate the likelihood of a known outcome— "I knew it all along"—and the ability of decision makers to have foreseen that outcome.[126] Pictures can make people think, in effect, "I saw it all along."[127] That said, there is not enough research yet to gauge whether these or other[128] potentially adverse effects outweigh the benefits of digital visuals and multimedia for legal decision making.[129]

Second, whether or not digital media improve legal knowledge in an absolute sense, they certainly change *how* decision makers learn and think about the reality they are judging. Judges and jurors who get their information on screens, for instance, intuitively frame that information in terms of the features of the screen. This includes not only perceptible features such as the way in which the composition of visual elements on the screen affects their meaning[130] but also habits of viewing and interpretation that people have absorbed from watching television, movie, and computer screens. In addition, when digital tools are used to put sequences of pictures on the screen, judges and jurors learn about case-relevant reality through a medium that can evoke particular genres and stories from mass-mediated culture. Those narratives can subconsciously shape decision makers' understanding of how stories like that go, which in turn affects their thinking about whose story to prefer at trial.

Furthermore, the ever-increasing mobilization of information in the digital age and the seemingly limitless ability to combine pictures and words using digital media are changing what and how jurors *expect* to learn about the case. Television news and documentaries and video and audio clips that accompany news and blogs online lead people to think that those with reliable information should be able to convey it audiovisually. People expect to be able to see and hear for themselves what they need to know, not just to read or hear about it.[131] According to what some have called "the *CSI* effect," jurors increasingly expect prosecutors to present forensic evidence in criminal cases and, some lawyers believe, hold the absence of such evidence against the State even if no such evidence was available.[132] We believe that an even more general effect may be occurring as people become more accustomed to having audiovisual information at their fingertips. Far from appearing "too slick" when they use digital multimedia, lawyers who fail to meet jurors' expectations for audiovisually replete, integrated presentations may be judged harshly.[133] At the same time, as one trial judge has commented, this habituation to the visual may lead jurors to downplay or ignore those aspects of the law, such as states of mind, that cannot as readily be visualized.[134]

Interactive digital media are also changing people's expectations about how legal knowledge is acquired. The evidence presentation system in *Skakel* and the increasing use of programs like TrialDirector and Sanction reflect a new epistemological frame which has spread through digital culture in general: the idea of knowledge as interaction.[135] People today are less likely to conceive of themselves as passive learners, to whom information is funneled from a source, with the medium of communication being a kind of container or conduit for the message to be conveyed.[136] Rather, people expect to use digital media in a hands-on fashion to shape the knowledge they are acquiring and their experiences of acquiring it. New media are ushering a democratization of meaning making into legal proceedings, resembling that which is already taking place in digital culture as a whole.

Third, the digitization of law has the potential to change people's fundamental attitudes toward the nature of legal knowledge. Digitization invites us to reconsider the basic tension at which we hinted at the beginning of this chapter: How can lawyers be trustworthy teachers if they are also relentless advocates? Can rhetoric be reconciled with the search for truth? Specifically, how can more advocates using more digital mediations of legally relevant reality yield *more*, not less, reliable knowledge of that reality?

In many fields other than law, including the human sciences, the philosophy of science, the philosophy of language, and linguistics, it has been recognized for some time that meaning depends on context and that truth depends on the ways in which it is represented.[137] Recent studies of the physiology of perception indicate that even our most basic contacts with reality are socially mediated and constructed.[138] In short, scholars in many disciplines have sought to explain how knowledge is locally constructed through culturally embedded practices[139] and through techniques of investigation and representation.[140] This theory of knowledge and truth is sometimes called *constructivism* (although our argument does not depend on the label we use).[141]

While some legal academics have recognized that legal meaning is produced by the ways law is practiced[142] and that rhetoric in its many guises is constitutive of, not opposed to, truth,[143] many participants in and observers of the legal system continue to feel uneasy about constructivism. The competing pull of objectivism and naïve realism—the belief that reality is just out there to be seen or "seen through" our representations of it—remains strong for all of the reasons explained in chapters 1 and 2.[144] The fear seems to be that embracing constructivism would undercut confidence in the capacity of legal proceedings (paradigmatically, trials) to yield provable truths about the world.[145] From this perspective, acknowledging that what we can know about reality depends on how advocates present it puts the law's claims to legitimacy into the hands of those who, at least in the popular imagination,[146] are prepared to obscure or even to subvert the truth whenever it's in the client's interest to do so.

Concerns about law's relationship to truth may change as people come to accept and appreciate how digital tools are used to present and explain evidence. The very conspicuousness of digital representations of reality can help everyone interested in the legal system to understand that representations can thoroughly mediate knowledge without reducing that knowledge to the mere feints and posturing of advocates. We have seen in both chapters 2 and 3 that digital technologies can provide unprecedented access to knowledge about reality. At the same time, the display of audio-visual explanations on courtroom screens, especially ones that unfold in the real time of the court proceeding (like computer animations or the fire reconstruction sequence in *Bontatibus*), make the mediated basis of that knowledge evident to an unprecedented degree. When lawyers use digital technologies to represent reality visually, the fact of mediation—of fabrication—is just too plain to be ignored. In *Bontatibus*, jurors might not have understood and believed the defendant's expert's account of how the fire started had they not watched the series of digital illustrations unfold. They believed that they knew what happened because they had seen the digital visuals. In *Skakel*, it may well have been the juxtaposition of crime scene photos and diagrams that led jurors to understand and believe the prosecution's explanation for why the pieces of weapon and blood stains were found where they were. Knowledge in cases like this arises not from "seeing through" the mediations but from dwelling on them until understanding emerges. In short, in the digital age, legal knowledge may increasingly be perceived to be reliable *because* it is mediated.[147]

In proposing this kind of constructivism as a way to hold teaching and advocacy, truth and rhetoric, together, in contrast to a naïvely realist epistemology in which these paired terms are diametrically opposed, we must be careful not to slip into another form of naïveté. For one thing, naïve realism cannot simply be transcended. It is a fundamental part of our psychological makeup and hence a default mode of response to our mediated world. Digital media can be used to appeal to this habit of response, as they were in *Scott* and may have been in the multimedia sequence in *Bontatibus*: to invite jurors to see or at least imagine, as they listened and watched, the tragic events unfolding again—a reenactment of reality itself. And digital tools, like analog ones, can be used not to get at the truth but to mislead, whether inadvertently or deliberately. Throughout the book, we confront examples of digital displays whose accuracy, explanatory value, and even basic fairness may be questioned.

Legal decision makers should not presume that "Is it truthful *or* is it manipulated?" is the only question worth asking. Of course, any tangible evidence can be altered, unintentionally or deliberately. Courts correctly inquire about whether a videotape, say, has been edited or enhanced in a way that makes it a misleading representation of what it is offered to prove. But it is a mistake to stop there, as Justice Scalia did in *Scott* and as the trial judge in *Murtha* may have done. Instead, legal decision makers (like scientists)[148] should assume that every representation manipulates unmediated reality somehow, and ask: How does this representation construct meaning, and what features of it warrant greater or lesser credibility? These questions have always been asked, but there has also been the belief, or at least the pretense, that they could somehow be gotten past to reach a truth beyond manipulation. Lawyers, judges, jurors, and the public need instead to concentrate on how juxtaposition, sequencing, interaction, animation, and other aspects of digital displays represent and explain reality, without being somehow frustrated that there is no way to get at the truth that does not depend on these features. The close, contextualized studies of digital representations and explanations in this chapter and throughout the book are intended to help those interested in the legal system to address these questions and so to become more sophisticated and critical audiences for, and users of, legal digital media.

In the next chapter, we continue to study digital demonstrative evidence, but in a special context: expert scientific evidence. The use of digital tools to create and reveal what an expert witness claims to be scientific truth raises especially urgent questions about the reliability and persuasiveness of pictures in the digital age.

4

Picturing Scientific Evidence

When everyday knowledge runs out or is inconclusive, legal decision makers turn to scientific or other technical experts for the knowledge they seek. Scientific evidence has been a part of trials for centuries, but today it is perhaps more important than ever, as the range of lawsuits demanding such evidence has expanded (think of products liability and toxic tort cases, for instance) along with the breadth and depth of scientific knowledge. In many of these cases, scientific experts have themselves made and/or relied on pictures in forming the opinions they offer as witnesses in court. Judges and jurors may be invited to look at a blow-up of a latent fingerprint taken from the crime scene, juxtaposed with a known print from the defendant, as visual proof that the defendant was there. Or they may see a computer-generated scan of the defendant's brain, introduced to show that the defendant suffers from a mental abnormality that limits his responsibility for his actions. Though ultimately displayed in court and sometimes (especially in the case of forensic scientific pictures) made with that goal in mind, these are pictures that the scientists create for themselves and their colleagues in the course of learning about the facts.[1]

This chapter concerns these sorts of scientific pictures. "Visualization," writes sociologist of science Sheila Jasanoff, "is one of the techniques by which scientific evidence achieves credibility—and so gains, for purposes of legal decision making, the status of fact."[2] We've already seen in previous chapters that pictures can persuade legal audiences of the truth of all sorts of factual claims. What, if anything, is different about scientific pictures?

When scientific experts rely on their pictures to support their testimony about facts, it is, of course, important that those pictures represent reality accurately. Scientific pictures can resemble what they purport to depict (as in the photograph of a cell seen in a microscope), or they may be caused by the reality they purport to represent (as in an electrocardiogram); in either case, we very much care whether they give us reliable data about that reality. At the same time, though, most scientific pictures, unlike the documentary or photojournalistic pictures discussed in chapter 2, result from very complex interventions in the reality they depict and extensive manipulations during the process of picturing itself. Fingerprint comparisons and neurological activity are not just sitting out there waiting to be photographed or shot on video. Scientists employ complicated machinery and follow elaborate protocols to extract the meaningful data from messy reality, to make those data visible, and to craft pictures that explain as well as re-present them. In this deliberate constructedness, scientific pictures are more like the demonstrative evidence we studied in chapter 3. So, analyzing scientific pictures requires that we combine the concerns raised in chapters 2 and 3: questions about the reliability of pictures that seem to show us the "real" and questions about the kinds of knowledge that digital picturing tools can be used to construct.

Moreover, when scientific pictures are offered as evidence, the pictures and the testimony depend on each other to a greater extent than other sorts of testimony and pictures usually do. Because the scientific expert speaks about arcane, difficult matters beyond the scope of everyday perception and knowledge, judges and jurors often need the pictures to help them understand the testimony. Figuring out the pictures thus becomes all the more important in deciding how much weight to accord the expert's knowledge. From the expert's perspective, the pictures help to bolster his or her own authority and credibility. In effect, the expert tells the audience, "You don't have to take my word for it; see for yourselves what the science shows."[3] At the same time, because the subject matter and the significance of the picture are unfamiliar to lay audiences, judges and jurors need the expert to help them interpret the picture.[4] These interdependences—the audience needs the pictures to understand the expert and needs the expert to understand the pictures—create a unique rhetorical situation.

Expert witnesses may indeed teach judges and jurors what the pictures should mean, in the process enhancing their own credibility on the stand.[5] But they cannot constrain judges and jurors from bringing their own meaning-making habits to bear. So, while legal decision makers, craving the assurance that scientific expertise seems to offer, may invest experts and their pictures with great authority, they may also construe what they see in ways that go beyond or conflict with the experts' own interpretations. And this may lead to decisions at odds with precisely that more secure foundation that scientific knowledge was summoned to provide in the first place.

Scientific pictures, then, need to be tested for reliability before they are admitted into evidence, and they need to be scrutinized, like any other pictures, for the range of meanings they may provoke. How should judges determine what scientific knowledge, pictorial or other, is reliable enough to be put before jurors? This has long been an important question, but it has become even more pressing since the Supreme Court's 1993 decision in *Daubert v. Merrell Dow Pharmaceuticals* gave trial judges greater responsibility for vetting proffers of expert evidence.[6] *Daubert*, the two Supreme Court cases that elaborated it,[7] and the subsequently revised Federal Rule of Evidence 702 deal with the reliability of scientific and other expert evidence in general (we summarize the law in a note)[8] and have been the subject of many books and thousands of scholarly commentaries. Yet, relatively little attention has been paid to the courtroom use of scientific pictures in the post-*Daubert* era.[9] How does the question of the relationship between scientific and legal knowledge change when pictures, and not just words and numbers, are at issue?

We begin with a brief survey of the history of pictures of scientific evidence in court. We then frame a central issue for both science and law, or indeed any truth-seeking practice or discipline, in the digital age: Knowing how easily digital pictures can be manipulated and recognizing that honest scientists and lawyers may be strongly motivated to "clean up" their pictures in order to make the truth of the matter as they understand it as clear as possible, how should a community—of scientists, of legal decision makers, of the public—decide when a picture is truthful enough to be relied upon? And how can judges and jurors, who lack scientific expertise, know whether a scientific picture offers reliable knowledge? Then, assuming that the scientific picture is reliable enough, we confront the tension between lay and expert vision: between how laypeople read a scientific picture and how scientific experts want them to read it.[10] Nonscientists may not see what scientists see when they look at scientific pictures; perhaps more problematic, nonscientists may read into the pictures meanings that scientists would not.[11] How should judges decide whether even a sufficiently trustworthy scientific picture is so prone to mislead or prejudice lay viewers that it should not be admitted after all?

Scientific Visual Evidence in Court

People with specialized knowledge have long assisted fact-finding in court. As early as the fourteenth century, "special juries" consisting of people with relevant expertise were convened to decide cases (for instance, a jury of cooks and fishmongers was called to decide whether the defendant had sold bad food), and courts often appointed experts as advisers (for instance, a surgeon, to help decide whether a wound was fresh).[12] By the eighteenth century, parties began calling their own experts to testify as witnesses, not only physicians and others with distinctive medical knowledge but also engineers, surveyors, and others.[13] As the legal scholar Jennifer Mnookin has explained, expert scientific evidence became especially prominent as a category of evidentiary proof in the late nineteenth century, about the same time that visual evidence, especially photographs, also became significant.[14] Scientific experts and new forms of visual evidence each seemed to offer a solution to the uncertainties inherent in ordinary eyewitness testimony: Experts laid claim to superior knowledge and purported to be above the fray; visual evidence in the form of photographs seemed to convey objective proof of the facts of the matter. Several forensic sciences also arose during this period and shortly thereafter, producing expert witnesses who catered to the parties' needs for superior forms of proof, often supporting their opinion testimony with photographic or other demonstrative evidence.

So, for instance, handwriting analysis emerged as a recognized area of expert testimony in the last third of the nineteenth century, the first type of science developed specifically for use in court.[15] Experts brought photographic enlargements of handwriting exemplars to the courtroom so that jurors could compare for themselves examples of a defendant's handwriting and samples involved in the litigated events.[16] The early forensic handwriting expert Persifor Frazer measured a person's signature in every possible way and then averaged the measurements to yield a numerical expression of the person's "typical" handwriting; in court, he showed jurors a composite photograph made from photos of the many examples he had studied, allowing jurors to see at a glance the typical signature to which his quantitative analysis had led.[17]

X-rays made their way into court within months of their discovery, late in 1895.[18] In a medical malpractice case brought the following year against a surgeon for allegedly failing to diagnose and properly treat a fractured bone, the plaintiff's lawyers and their expert radiographer set up equipment in court so that the judge and jury could see X-rays of various familiar objects and then view the X-ray of the plaintiff's damaged femur. The trial judge admitted the X-ray into evidence, and the plaintiff won.[19] X-rays soon became a popular craze, adding cultural familiarity to scientific authority to enhance their credibility and persuasiveness in court.

Fingerprint evidence followed suit. Applying the methods for identifying ridge characteristics developed by Sir Francis Galton toward the end of the nineteenth century, expert testimony on fingerprint identification was first introduced in court in 1910.[20] The expert accompanied his testimony with photographs of prints taken at the crime scene and enlarged photographs of the defendant's prints.[21] Indeed, fingerprint examiners typically showed jurors blown-up pictures of the prints in question, annotated to indicate the points of resemblance.[22]

These early instances of scientific demonstrative evidence exemplify several issues that continue to arise in contemporary cases. The handwriting and fingerprint cases show expert witnesses using overtly manipulated pictures—enlarged, composited, annotated—thus posing the question whether enhancements designed to make the witness's point clearer might also mislead jurors or otherwise impair their judgment. The early X-ray case shows the lawyers provoking jurors' interest and promoting their confidence in the reliability of the expert's novel visual technology by demonstrating it in court.[23] By encouraging jurors to think that they could see the facts for themselves, experts may have made their opinions seem more credible, but they may also have led jurors to neglect the limits of their decidedly nonexpert understanding of what they saw. This tension was not resolved in these early cases, and it persists today whenever such pictures are introduced.

The promise of more accurate fact-finding offered by both experts and scientific pictures was called into question almost from the beginning. Nineteenth-century expert witnesses were already being castigated as hired guns, for proffering dubious science, and for eliciting undue deference from jurors.[24] Photographs, it was recognized, could lie,[25] while X-rays and other pictures requiring expert interpretation could mislead jurors who thought that they could see and understand for themselves.[26] These and other criticisms of expert witnesses are voiced just as loudly today,[27] as experts of all kinds routinely testify in courtrooms throughout the country.[28] And the rise of digital photography and photo editing has only heightened concerns about the pictures that scientific experts show in court.

Pictorial Reliability in the Digital Age

Photographers have always adjusted their pictures in the service of realism and comprehensibility.[29] What is new in the digital age is the widespread knowledge not only that photos can easily be edited but that they *are* edited, and how it is done.[30] This is changing viewers' beliefs about the relation between photographs and the reality they purport to show—about the reliability of scientific and other pictures.

Two important technical differences between digital and analog photography make seamless editing widely available. The first is that digital pictures are built out of *pixels*, not the silver grain of analog photos. Pixels are data readable by a computer. They are discontinuous individual imaging elements, each of which can be precisely numerically defined for size, shape, and location in the picture field.[31] And, because they are made of the same stuff as any other digital data, pixels, and hence the appearance of the picture, can be changed with the click of a mouse or the drag of a cursor. The second difference is that digital picture files, when brought into the editing windows of Adobe Photoshop or related imaging software, can be developed by working in data *layers* rather than on a continuous surface. Layers can be used to perform myriad changes, including "sandwiching" digital data by putting different pictures together, carrying out adjustments to parts of pictures, or making global changes to the entire picture. These layers can then be reintegrated into the whole picture so it looks seamlessly "right." The picture maker can then collapse all these changes, additions, and subtractions into a single layer which can no longer be separated into its component parts, so that the changes may not be discoverable.[32]

The upshot of digital photography and the software that is used to realize it is that it's much easier to make things that look like a photograph but do not correspond to the facts of the world in front of a lens. (We'll have more to say about this in chapter 6.) What's "real" in photographic depictions, therefore, is up for grabs as never before, because any photographic picture can be questioned for its accuracy and authenticity. "The referent has become unstuck," to quote again the architecture and media scholar William J. Mitchell.[33]

New digital picturing tools have made it easy—maybe too easy—for scientists (and others) to create just the pictures they want. Clearer and less noisy, these enhanced pictures can offer more emphatic support for the scientist's properly generated findings. But they also present with increasing frequency the risk that what is depicted no longer corresponds closely enough to "what's really there" to count as a reliably accurate representation of reality. At the extreme, digital picturing tools can facilitate not just exaggerated or misleading truth claims but outright fraud, as in the notorious recent case of the biomedical scientist Woo Suk Hwang, who gained worldwide attention by claiming, in articles published in the prestigious journal *Science* in 2004 and 2005, to have created human embryonic stem cells by cloning. Subsequent investigations revealed that Hwang and his team had falsified most of their data; the papers were ultimately withdrawn and Hwang was disgraced.[34] Parts of the fraud were uncovered by scrutinizing the photos accompanying the research: Some of the photos purporting to show cloned stem cells, for instance, turned out to be identical to photos published by another member of the team in a different journal and labeled as cells created without cloning.[35]

Scientific picture fraud of this sort is spectacular but rare. Much more common is the temptation to tidy up an essentially truthful picture so as to better represent reality as the scientist, after painstaking research, honestly believes it to be. As the editors of the journal *Nature* put it: "It is doubtful that scientists were more angelic [in bygone days] than now. It is more likely that, when it came to image manipulation, they wouldn't because they couldn't."[36] Now they can. In response, the editors of the *Journal of Cell Biology* and *Nature*, among others, have issued guidelines specifying permissible and prohibited techniques for taking, modifying, and publishing pictures.[37] Forensic imaging experts have promulgated their own sets of rules.[38]

Given scientists' own concerns about picturing in the digital age, how should trial judges go about deciding whether the expert's pictures are themselves good enough science to be shown to jurors? A murder case, and the visual evidence that the prosecution used to prove the killer's identity, lets us explore that question.

Forensic Scientific Pictures in Court: State v. Swinton

The strangled body of a twenty-eight-year-old woman was found in 1991 on an abandoned road in Hartford, Connecticut.[39] When the paramedics found the victim, they tried to revive her, took her to a local hospital, and cleaned her body, which possibly destroyed significant forensic evidence. There was no evidence connecting the suspect, Alfred Swinton, to the body except for bite marks on the victim's breast.[40] The State offered the testimony of Dr. Constantine (Gus) Karazulas, a "highly qualified" forensic odontologist, to prove that the bite marks were made by Swinton.[41] His testimony was illustrated with (among other things) two types of digital pictures: digitally enhanced photographs of the bite marks on the victim's body, produced using Lucis digital image processing software, and overlays of pictures of the defendant's teeth on the photos of the bite marks, created in Adobe Photoshop.

The defendant challenged the admission of both sorts of pictures.[42] The trial court admitted both.[43] The defendant was convicted of murder and sentenced to sixty years in prison.[44] On appeal, the Connecticut Supreme Court ruled that the trial court had correctly admitted the Lucis-enhanced photos but had erred in admitting the Photoshop overlays.[45]

Lucis. Lucis software, made by Image Content Technology, employs a patented image-processing algorithm, Differential Hysteresis Processing (DHP), to extract and highlight variations in pixel intensities within a digital picture.[46] This capability can be used to enhance and reveal image detail that would otherwise be undetectable to the human eye. Lucis is extremely simple to use, involving the operation of just two cursors or sliders. The program is standard in forensic sciences that utilize pattern identification, including the identification of bite marks, fingerprints, footwear, and tire impressions.[47] In addition to making visible and salient case-critical features of photographs that would otherwise remain invisible or doubtful, Lucis's main benefit to forensic experts and lawyers is that it does this without any loss of data,[48] making it easier to persuade judges and jurors that the enhanced picture has not been improperly manipulated. Furthermore, Lucis enhances pictures globally (the program affects the entire picture rather than pinpointing certain areas for enhancement), thereby adding to its reliability in producing a trustworthy picture.[49]

Adobe Photoshop. While Lucis provides an enhanced function for visualizing details within the picture, Photoshop is a comprehensive program for processing still images. We have already mentioned that Photoshop files often consist of multiple layers that have been flattened into a final picture, making the individual steps in the creation of the picture harder to detect.[50] It is also worth repeating that Photoshop, unlike Lucis, permits local as well as global changes to the picture. And, given its widespread use for artistic and other purposes that are not constrained by demands for truthful representation, judges and jurors might well be suspicious of using Photoshop to create probative visual evidence in law. That said, Photoshop is, according to forensic experts[51] and textbooks,[52] a standard program used by forensic odontologists to compare casts and overlays of a suspect's teeth to a bite mark. Photoshop has also been used in fingerprint identification[53] and handwriting examination.[54]

Lucis and Photoshop at the Swinton *trial.* To introduce the Lucis-enhanced pictures, the State offered the testimony of Major Timothy Palmbach, overseer of the division of scientific services in the state's Department of Public Safety. Palmbach testified that experts had used Lucis in forensic settings. Because his office did not possess the hardware and software required to produce the enhanced pictures, Palmbach personally made them at Lucis's manufacturer's offices. He testified generally about Lucis's image-enhancement capabilities. Then, using a laptop, Palmbach demonstrated to the judge and jury exactly how the original bite mark photograph had been modified.[55] Palmbach emphasized that Lucis neither adds data to nor takes data away from the original picture.[56] The enhanced photograph certainly looks different, though: With pixel intensity contrasts heightened throughout, the victim's breast looks mottled, and the bites and bruises appear much darker (Figure 4.1).

Karazulas, the forensic odontologist, introduced the Photoshop overlays. He explained how he created two types of overlays, one using tracings of the defendant's dentition and the other scans of his dental molds. For the first, Karazulas placed the upper and lower molds previously taken of the defendant's teeth (by Lester Luntz, another forensic odontologist, about two months after the crime)[57] on a photocopier and printed out a picture of the molds. He then placed a piece of paper over that picture and manually traced the biting edges of the teeth. The tracings were then photocopied onto clear acetate, yielding a transparent overlay depicting the edges of the defendant's dentition. These tracings, together with both enhanced and unenhanced bite mark photos, were then scanned into a computer so that they could be used in Photoshop.[58] For the second kind of overlay, the scanned dental molds were put into Photoshop and the upper layers of their occlusal edges (i.e., the biting surfaces) isolated. These images of the teeth were then made more transparent.[59]

Each final composite picture shows what appears to be a strip or sheet of something nearly transparent (like clear acetate) with the tracings of the biting edges of the defendant's teeth or the translucent teeth molds, respectively, superimposed on an unenhanced or enhanced bite mark photo in such a way that the tracings or dentition align with the bite marks. The overlays also feature scales (along one dimension for the tracings, two for the translucent molds), standard devices in forensic odontological imaging to facilitate measurement and to show that the picture has not been distorted. In the set of overlays using the tracings, the outlines of teeth are at first glance a little hard to pick out from the underlying bite mark photos, although the scales and the edge of the overlay strip itself cue us to look for the outlines.[60] In the other set of overlays, by contrast, the translucent teeth seem to lie directly and prominently on the victim's breast, just inside the ostensibly corresponding bite marks (Figure 4.2).[61]

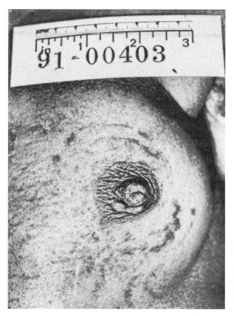

Figure 4.1. Lucis-enhanced autopsy photo in *Swinton* (courtesy of Barbara Williams, copyright © 2001 Dr. Gus Karazulas).

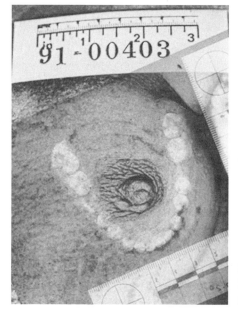

Figure 4.2. *Swinton* Photoshop overlay (courtesy of Barbara Williams, copyright © 2001 Dr. Gus Karazulas).

Karazulas also used other techniques to come to the conclusion that the defendant Swinton was the one who had left the bite marks on the victim, including a visual inspection of the defendant's dental molds, an examination of the unenhanced autopsy photos, and a comparison of the two,[62] but the Photoshop overlays were the pièce de résistance of his testimony. While jurors looked at each overlay on the courtroom screen, Karazulas pointed out each place at which the shape of the bite mark and characteristics of the teeth were "consistent" or "very consistent" or where the one "correspond[ed]" to the other.[63] As in cases of expert testimony regarding fingerprint identification and other pattern-matching forensic sciences going back a century or more, jurors did not have to rely on Karazulas' words; they could see for themselves that the defendant's dentition matched the victim's wounds.[64]

On the witness stand, however, Karazulas admitted that he himself did not use Photoshop to create the overlays. Instead, he had a colleague at Fairfield University, a chemistry professor who was more proficient in Photoshop, operate the program to create the superimpositions. Karazulas testified that, over the course of two days, he spent seven to eight hours watching his colleague make the overlays, instructing him not to alter the original pictures. Karazulas could not say whether Photoshop was accepted as a standard and competent imaging technology in the field of odontology.[65] Instead, Timothy Palmbach testified that he was "personally aware of uses [of Photoshop] within the odontology field" and that he had read "several papers" referring to the use of Photoshop in bite mark analysis.[66] But Palmbach also testified that Photoshop, unlike Lucis, "was capable of actually altering photographs."[67]

At the state supreme court: formulating an admissibility test. To be admissible, scientific (like any other) evidence must be both relevant and reliable.[68] In *Swinton*, the Connecticut Supreme Court's main concern was the reliability and hence the admissibility of the Lucis and Photoshop pictures, rather than that of the science underlying the bite mark expert testimony itself.[69] The court recognized at the outset that traditional approaches to visual evidence, such as the usual perfunctory treatment of demonstrative evidence as "merely illustrative," as opposed to substantive, were neither fully coherent nor appropriate for these new and potentially very persuasive forms of digital pictures.[70] Instead, the court opted to treat the Lucis and Photoshop pictures as substantive evidence, clearing the way for more rigorous scrutiny. But how much more? If the pictures were like enlargements or reproductions of photographs, they would be admissible if a witness testified simply that they were fair and accurate representations of what they purported to depict. The Lucis and Photoshop pictures seemed to be more than mere photographic enlargements— but what were they, exactly?[71]

Finding no clear guidance in the case law, the court decided to treat both sorts—the Lucis enhancements and the Photoshop overlays—as "computer-generated evidence" and, "let[ting] caution guide our decision," sought to formulate a single, broad, "fairly stringent" standard applicable to both and, indeed, to *all* computer-generated pictures.[72] To articulate that standard, the court turned to cases from other jurisdictions regarding the admissibility of enhancements of photos and videos, to Federal Rule of Evidence 901(b)(9), which addresses the authentication of machine-generated pictures,[73] and to secondary sources. Ultimately, the court decided that computer-generated pictures can ordinarily be authenticated "by evidence that

1. The computer equipment is accepted in the field as standard and competent and was in good working order,
2. Qualified computer operators were employed,
3. Proper procedures were followed in connection with the input and output of information,
4. A reliable software program was utilized,
5. The equipment was programmed correctly, and
6. The exhibit is properly identified as the output in question."[74]

"Reliability must be the watchword in determining the admissibility of computer generated evidence,"[75] wrote the court. The court's test encourages judges to achieve that goal by scrutinizing the *process* used to create the picture: acceptable equipment and software, competent operator, proper procedures. Of the various ways in which a scientific picture's trustworthiness might be established—for instance, the testimony of a witness that the picture corresponds to the reality that the witness observed, the absence of anything discrepant in the picture (e.g., inconsistent shadows cast by different objects), or satisfactory evidence of how the picture was made[76]—emphasizing process usually makes the most sense. After all, rarely will anyone be in a position to say that the picture corresponds to what he or she observed with the naked eye, because only by means of technology can what the picture shows be seen. This is plainly the case with regard to the Lucis and Photoshop pictures in *Swinton*. And, while other experts may sometimes be able to point to visual discrepancies that undermine a picture's claims to reliability (as in the Hwang case mentioned earlier), many picture manipulations don't leave such traces. Scientists' own standards for ensuring the reliability of digital pictures, therefore, tend to focus on process,[77] demanding that picture makers use certain techniques, refrain from others, and report any alterations that would not be obvious to or assumed by viewers.[78] *Swinton* adopts the same general approach.[79] Rigorously applied, the test promises to provide an antidote to what Norman Pattis, Alfred Swinton's defense lawyer, calls the "black-box phenomenon," whereby judges and jurors uncritically place their trust in computer-generated pictures.[80]

Applying the test. The court ruled that the testimony of the State's forensic expert witness, Timothy Palmbach, had laid an adequate foundation for the admission of the Lucis photo enhancements. First, Palmbach had testified that Lucis was used and relied upon in forensic pattern analysis, including bite marks (factors 1 and 4),[81] and had explained why Lucis was considered reliable and accurate for these purposes. Second, he had testified not only that he himself was a well-trained and highly experienced forensic analyst but also that he had knowledge of and experience in using Lucis to created digitally enhanced images of footprints, tire prints, and, on two occasions, dental imprints on breasts (factor 2).[82] Third, Palmbach had testified "accurately, clearly, and consistently" regarding the input and output of data (factor 3).[83] Crucially, Palmbach had used his laptop during trial to demonstrate Lucis to the jury, comparing the enhanced to the unenhanced photos in front of the jury.[84] He had been able to testify that there was nothing in the enhanced picture that was not present in the original photograph.[85]

In contrast, the court held that the prosecution had failed to offer a sufficient foundation for the Adobe Photoshop dental overlays (both those that used the tracings of the defendant's dentition and those that used the translucent dental molds). First, neither Palmbach nor the forensic odontology expert, Constantine Karazulas, had been able able to testify that Photoshop was sufficiently accepted in the field to be considered "competent" or "standard practice" (factor 1).[86] Second, Karazulas had not testified that a qualified computer operator had been employed; he could testify only that he had had someone else operate the program because he did not know enough to do it himself (factor 2).[87] Third, and for the same reason—he did not operate the program himself—Karazulas had not been able to assure the court that proper procedures had been followed in connection with the input and output of information (factor 3). Fourth, the State did not persuade the court that Photoshop was a sufficiently reliable program (factor 4).[88] And, while the court did not specifically address the remaining factors in its test, it explained at some length why Karazulas did not know enough about how Photoshop works to have been subject to meaningful cross-examination as to how the overlays were produced—including, most important, how the superimposition of the image of the defendant's translucent teeth over the bite mark was produced[89] and whether the exhibits had been altered or otherwise impermissibly manipulated in the Photoshop process.[90]

Reliability and beyond: the lessons of Swinton.[91] At a general level, *Swinton* fosters congruence between legal and scientific standards for ensuring the reliability of scientific pictures, because the court's multifactor test allows for the incorporation of scientific reliability norms. The first five of *Swinton's* six factors could well be read as a set of blanks to be filled in by the particular scientific practice involved in the making of the pictures. For instance, the baseline evidentiary foundation that the equipment and methodology be "accepted in the field as standard" (factor 1), followed by the general language of "proper procedures" (factor 3), invite the expert witness to explain just what procedures are proper in science for the production of the kind of picture being offered. Moreover, the expert witness Palmbach's *demonstration* of Lucis, although not required by the court's test, allowed the judge and jury to see those proper procedures and methods, something for which they would otherwise have had to rely on Palmbach's word. For a moment the courtroom became the laboratory, with legal decision makers in the role of fellow scientists, witnesses to the successful experiment.[92] As the lawyer and expert in the first trial involving X-rays recognized, there is no more convincing way of aligning the law's vision with that of science—of establishing the provenance that ensures the reliability of the scientific picture.

In contrast, the prosecution plainly failed to satisfy the court as to the Photoshop overlays' provenance, as we have already discussed. But, even if the person who actually made the overlays in Photoshop had testified as to the nature of the program and the procedures he had followed, the court might not have been satisfied that the overlays were trustworthy enough for jurors to see.[93] Was this cautious approach to the Photoshopped pictures justified?

We observed at the beginning of the chapter that when scientific pictures are offered into evidence, jurors need the expert's testimony to explain the picture and the picture to explain the testimony. In *Swinton*, pictures and testimony were intimately related: Karazulas walked the jurors through his interpretation of the overlays, explaining how he derived from his visual inspection of these pictures the conclusion that it was the defendant whose teeth had left the bite marks.[94] Because the credibility of his conclusion depended so directly on the pictures, it was, of course, important for the court to be assured that the pictures were trustworthy. This much is true, or ought to be, of every scientific picture offered as evidence.

The court's caution, however, may also have been grounded in a concern that, when jurors looked at the Photoshop overlays and their viewing habits "bump[ed] up against" those of trained forensic scientists,[95] lay vision was too likely to diverge from scientific—and so, to ensure that relevant scientific knowledge was not misapplied, the court was ready to keep the pictures out. The court might well have thought, for instance, that, when looking at the overlays, a lay audience *wouldn't see what other experts might*. In particular, lay viewers might fail to appreciate that, "[b]ecause odontological matching depends on millimeters, a [shift of a] millimeter or two either way [during the process of creating the overlays] could make the difference between a point of concordance and a point of discordance."[96] Experts in the field would likely be more critical viewers. Jurors, in contrast, might be too prone to having their vision framed by Karazulas's opinion, and, once they saw what Karazulas wanted them to see, it might be too difficult for cross-examination to lead them to see things differently.

The court might also have been concerned that the overlay would prompt jurors to *see what experts wouldn't*. Being conversant with neither forensic odontology nor the use of Photoshop to illustrate it, jurors might be less likely than forensic scientists to understand that, as an overt manipulation of visible reality, the overlay was not to be (mis)read as a *depiction* of that reality. Two of the overlays, for instance, show us the biting edges of the defendant's lower teeth superimposed on the bite marks supposedly made by those teeth. The teeth appear to be right on top of the victim's breast. But this means that we are looking simultaneously at the bite marks *and* the edges of the teeth that (according to the prosecution) made those marks, both seen from *above*, when in the act of biting those edges of the teeth must have been facing the other way, downward.[97] Jurors who saw the overlay's visual explanation of the expert's opinion as a kind of staged reenactment of the event would see what experts wouldn't.

We might think of this as a kind of naïve realism, except that it goes beyond what we saw in the readings of the videos in chapter 2; here, to see the overlay as a reenactment is to read past the overt signs (e.g., the edge of the overlay running diagonally across the top of the underlying picture of victim's breast or the ruler and scale on the overlay) that the overlay is an explanatory construction, not a re-creation of reality. And jurors who saw the overlay this way might have been more inclined to accept the prosecution's identification of the defendant as the biter.[98]

We can only speculate about the meanings that the *Swinton* jurors may have found in the Photoshop overlays. They may not have been conscious of those meanings themselves. Moreover, even if jurors are prone to interpret these pictures as we suggest, it does not follow that the best evidentiary practice would be to exclude them; it might be preferable to let the expert use the pictures but for the opposing attorney to respond by interrogating the pictures (analogous to the defense's visual strategy in the first Rodney King trial) or to come up with competing pictures of his own.[99] We take up these and related issues in more detail in chapter 7.

Scientists want to produce accurate pictures, but they also want to create persuasive ones. To command the attention of journal editors, colleagues, funding agencies, and the public, many scientists devote great care, sometimes enlisting the help of photographers and other visual professionals,[100] to making their pictures as attractive, striking, and laden with relevant meaning as possible.[101] When members of the relevant scientific communities are the primary audiences for these pictures, they can be counted on to identify and comprehend the pictures' intended meanings. They can also be counted upon to resolve ambiguities in the pictures in ways that are consistent with the training and traditions of professional practitioners.[102] When, however, scientific pictures are disseminated to wider audiences, such as scholars in distant disciplines or the public at large, possibilities abound for meanings to proliferate beyond and even contrary to those originally intended. This can happen because of not only the obvious differences in audience but also the differences in context. Scientific pictures in the mass media or on the Internet, for instance, may not be accompanied by the same kind of explanatory material as they are in their original journal contexts; they may instead be framed by words and other pictures whose creators either misunderstand the science or are driven by other agendas.[103]

Plainly, this proliferation of "unauthorized" meanings can happen when scientific expert witnesses show their pictures to lay decision makers in court. The legal system, therefore, must sort acceptable from unacceptable readings of reliable-enough pictures and then determine whether the latter pose such a risk to good judgment that the pictures should be excluded, even though the acceptable readings may help the jurors to understand the expert's testimony. Federal Rule of Evidence 403 allows trial judges to exclude even relevant evidence "if its probative value is substantially outweighed by the danger of unfair prejudice, confusion of the issues, or misleading the jury."[104] In *Swinton*, as we saw, the court expressed its disapproval of the Photoshop overlays in reliability terms, but some of the risks that the overlays posed—that jurors could be misled by reading the overlays in "unauthorized" ways—could also be thought of in terms of Rule 403.

In the rest of this chapter, we put these risks front and center. We discuss a cutting-edge scientific visualization tool—functional magnetic resonance imaging, or fMRI—which creates brain scan pictures with a plethora of visual effects and meanings. Jurors need the pictures to understand the testimony of neurologists, neuroscientists, and other experts, because the data on which these experts rely are extremely complex and subtle; the pictures help to make the crucial data salient. The pictures can do this only if they are intelligible to jurors. And they are intelligible in part because they seem to mesh with jurors' prior knowledge: Jurors think that they know what they're looking at when they're looking at something that looks like a brain. Of course, jurors also need the expert to understand the brain scans. And yet, the pictures' strength in making the fruits of arcane knowledge accessible is also their danger. If lay viewers find the pictures readable, it's partly because they can tap into a cultural reservoir of familiarity with brain scan images. But the meanings triggered by that broad cultural resonance may exceed the ones that the pictures' makers intended. In these respects, fMRIs are exemplary of many modern scientific pictures seen by the general public. The more lawyers, judges, and jurors understand about the multiple visual rhetorics of fMRIs and other scientific pictures, the better they can evaluate whether admitting them will serve or frustrate the goal of achieving accurate and just legal judgments.

fMRI Science as Legal Evidence

Brain imaging has become part of the popular imagination.[105] From the CT (computerized tomography) scans offered in the 1982 trial of John Hinckley, Ronald Reagan's would-be assassin, to persuade jurors to find Hinckley not guilty by reason of insanity,[106] to the pictures of Terri

Schiavo's CT scans, presented on television in 2005 and posted on the Internet as evidence that she was in a hopelessly vegetative state,[107] millions of people now know (or think they know) what human brains, or at least pictures of brains, look like.

Functional magnetic resonance imaging, or fMRI, is the latest and most advanced of brain imaging technologies. Using fMRI, scientists can map brain activity—that is, they can identify which areas of the brain (to a resolution of a few cubic millimeters) are relatively more active, in the sense that more neurons are firing, when people are in various mental states or performing various tasks: experiencing emotion, feeling violent impulses, engaging in moral reasoning, or lying as opposed to telling the truth. Because fMRI is functional (that is, it tracks real-time changes in brain activity) and has better spatial and temporal resolution than earlier functional brain-imaging tools, such as PET (positron emission tomography) and SPECT (single photon emission computed tomography), neuroscientists, psychologists, psychiatrists, and others increasingly prefer fMRI as an investigative and diagnostic technique.[108]

It now seems to be only a matter of time before expert testimony based on fMRI, just like testimony based on earlier forms of neuroimaging such as CT, PET, and SPECT scans, enters the law on a large scale.[109] Most likely, fMRI evidence will be offered to prove mental impairment in a wide range of situations where that is legally relevant.[110] Businesses and the government are already interested in using fMRI as a lie detection tool; someday, fMRI test results may be admitted as evidence for that purpose, and a growing literature is already debating the issue.[111] The prospect of fMRI science in court raises anew the question already posed by CT, PET, and SPECT evidence: Should jurors be allowed to see the scans themselves, pictures that the scientific community considers highly informative and probative but that lay audiences may be tempted to misinterpret?

What is fMRI? Functional neuroimaging (as opposed to *structural* imaging, as in computerized tomography [CT] scans or structural MRIs) can track the workings of the brain in real time. Functional MRI does this by measuring changes in local blood flow and blood oxygenation level (BOLD, or blood oxygen level dependent) that are associated with neuronal activity. When neurons are active, they demand energy, which is supplied by adenosine triphosphate (ATP), which in turn is produced by oxygen and glucose in the blood. Because more oxygen is supplied to the active brain region than is consumed, the ratio of oxygenated to deoxygenated blood in the active region increases. This results in changes in the blood's magnetic resonance (MR) signal intensity, as prompted and measured by an MR scanner, because oxygenated and deoxygenated blood have different magnetic susceptibilities.[112]

In a typical fMRI study, subjects' brain activity is measured first while they are at rest and/or performing a control task and then while they are engaged in the experimental task (looking at emotion-provoking stimuli, say, or lying). The tasks are repeated many times and the measurements averaged over the entire run to increase the reliability of the data.[113] The MR data are processed using various algorithms, and, after a very complex set of steps, statistically significant differences in brain activity between the baseline and experimental conditions are identified. Neuroscientists and other trained observers can look at the data and ascertain which portions of the brain are more or less active during which sorts of mental functions.

Figure 4.3 shows a typical fMRI scan. This is in fact a representation of a "slice" of the brain, looking down at the top of the head.[114] The grey and white areas are a structural brain image, much like what a CT scan would produce. The colored areas (which unfortunately can't be seen in the black and white reproduction) represent the functional data, indicating where the brain is significantly more or less active in the experimental or test condition versus the baseline. The particular colors depend on the level of statistical significance and, to some extent, on the experimenter's preference. Many different slices may be arrayed in a single figure or illustration, comparing different subjects' brain activity patterns during the same test, relative activity at different locations (slices) within the same subject's brain, and so on. Each fMRI picture may look like a brain, but it is really a *data map*, with quantitative information being plotted onto a picture of a brain slice.[115]

Admissibility of fMRI expert testimony. In American federal and most state courts, the law governing the admissibility of expert testimony based on fMRI, like any other expert testimony, starts (as noted earlier) with Federal Rule of Evidence 702 and *Daubert*. The gist of this law is that expert scientific evidence must be both relevant and reliable. Currently, fMRI science may not be a reliable enough source of scientific knowledge for the law.[116] The sensitivity of the scanning equipment and the dependence of fMRI research on methods and assumptions that vary from one lab to another mean that research findings on any given question may not yet be robust enough for courts to rely on.[117] Furthermore, the mapping of psychological functions onto brain anatomy—the goal of all fMRI brain

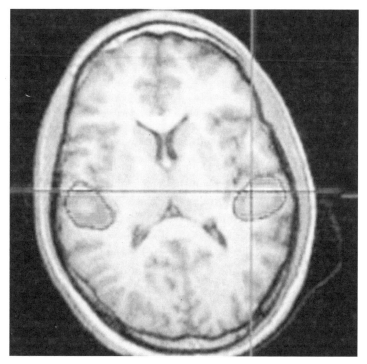

Figure 4.3. Typical fMRI picture (courtesy of R. Todd Constable).

research—crucially depends on how the researchers have specified the mental functions to be investigated and how they have operationalized them in their experiments. There is no general agreement among psychologists, cognitive scientists, and other researchers about most of these matters (as is only to be expected from a science in its early stages), which limits the ability of prudent experts to say that relative activity or inactivity in brain areas x, y, and z *means* that a person suffers from impulse control, is lying, or whatever the psychological fact at issue may be.[118] And whether results produced in experimental settings generalize to the real world with which the law is concerned seems to be an even bigger problem for fMRI research than it is for psychological research generally (as the widely reported example of fMRI lie detection exemplifies).[119]

As of this writing, then, fMRI may not be ready for prime time.[120] But it may well be soon. As fMRI science matures, as varying methods converge and important results are replicated, fMRI-based expert testimony will be offered more frequently—and judges will be increasingly likely to admit it, just as they have PET scan and other neuroimaging evidence in hundreds of cases over the past two decades.[121] If experts testify on the basis of fMRI findings, will they also be allowed to show jurors the pictures? We turn to this question next.

The Visual Rhetorics of fMRI: Should the Pictures Be Shown in Court?

The benefits of letting legal decision makers see fMRIs seem obvious: The pictures help to clarify and explain the results of fMRI studies. If they did not, they would not be used to illustrate those results in thousands upon thousands of peer-reviewed articles, textbooks, and conference and symposia presentations. Pick up any fMRI study, look at a table reporting differential brain activation levels, and then look at the figure the authors have included to display their findings. The table presents more data, but the picture makes immediately obvious the principal brain regions involved.

The risk side of the equation is more complicated. Some scholars, such as the sociologist of science Joseph Dumit, have argued that neuroimages (he writes about PET scans) should *not* be used in court, at least not in jury trials.[122] Dumit posits that PET scans are "expert images": They "require help in interpreting even though they may appear to be legible to a layperson."[123] As such, these pictures pose a paradox: "If [the pictures] are legible, then they should not need interpretation [by an expert], but if they need interpretation, then they probably should not be shown to juries."[124] The problem, Dumit asserts, is that jurors' cultural familiarity with brain scan pictures will lead them to misread the pictures and to draw from them dispositive inferences that the pictures, as understood by experts, do not support. A related problem is what the neuroscientist Dean Mobbs and his colleagues have referred to as the "Christmas tree phenomenon": Jurors will be so dazzled by the "pretty lights" in the fMRI picture that they will not pay sufficient attention to the expert's explanation of what they are seeing.[125] The risks that the pictures will confuse or mislead jurors, that is, are too great to justify admitting them.

What fMRIs may mean to lay viewers. Perhaps the most striking feature of fMRIs is that they seem to let us *look at the brain*—to see mental activity as it occurs. They seem to offer direct access to the real, to the psychological fact to be proven (say, mental impairment). Even experts may think this way: One experimental psychologist, writing of (and to) others, has observed that "[t]here is a real danger that pictures of blobs on brains seduce one into thinking that we can now directly observe psychological constructs."[126] But to understand fMRIs this way is a kind of naïve realism. The pictures don't show us what the subjects were thinking when scanned.[127] At best, they accurately report relative brain activity levels in different areas that may be generally (and, given the state of neuroscientific and psychological knowledge, more or less tentatively) associated with certain mental functions. And they do this only as the output of an exceptionally complicated aggregation of equipment, scientific knowledge, laboratory practices, and computing power, each of which mediates the information (neuron firings) that the pictures purport to represent. It's as far from looking at a brain in action as reading a data table is. But, if even experts may be tempted to think that the pictures offer unmediated access to the underlying reality, jurors are all the more likely to be confused.[128]

Second, and relatedly, jurors may think that the fMRI is a *picture* of someone's brain. This nicely captures what (in chapter 1) we called *remediation*, the way in which one representational medium invokes the forms and connotations of another.[129] That is, jurors may intuitively assimilate fMRIs to a more familiar medium like photographs[130] or radiographs from X-rays. Indeed, speaking of X-rays makes it clear that an awareness of the technology and expertise required to produce an fMRI need not be inconsistent with an appeal to naïve realism. A century of familiarity with X-rays has accustomed us to the idea that scientific and technological expertise can peel back or penetrate layers of obscurity to provide direct visual access to the underlying reality.[131] When people read fMRIs as if they were X-rays, they invoke this same conceptual template. In fact, when one looks at an fMRI, one is not seeing a picture of the brain in the way that one sees a picture of blood vessels in an angiogram. As noted earlier, fMRIs are statistical maps, visualizations of data sets, in the guise of representations of the brain.[132] Both of these ways of reading the fMRI—as providing either unmediated access to the subject's thoughts or at least a direct "read-off" of brain activity—may incline jurors to endow the picture, and hence the testimony that is based on it, with more credibility, authority, and certainty than it warrants.

Third, fMRI pictures are likely to be especially credible to lay audiences because of their status as prototypical scientific pictures. The fMRI visualizes brain function for the nonscientist audience as an instance of mechanized, computerized, and therefore objective scientific knowledge—and objectivity entails reliability and truthfulness.[133] As the psychologist Paul Bloom has remarked, fMRI research "has all the trappings" of scientific credibility: "big, expensive, and potentially dangerous machines, hospitals and medical centers, and a lot of people in white coats."[134] And the pictures that fMRI research produces possess another quintessentially scientific feature: They are mathematized objects, visual representations of a series of computerized measurements and computations, often explicitly including numbers and scales of various sorts.[135] In both respects, the persuasiveness of fMRI pictures may derive from their resonance with other representations of scientific truth in the culture at large, rather than from factors that scientists would consider relevant to their probative value.

Fourth, the contrasts between the bright colors on which fMRI scans typically rely to make salient their significant data (the "Christmas tree phenomenon") and the regions without such colors perceptually convert sometimes very subtle differences of degree (of blood oxygenation levels) into differences in kind: brain activity versus no brain activity. This may lead viewers to more readily infer, say, that the subject of the fMRI has condition X or fits into legally relevant category Y—say, is incapable of controlling his antisocial behavior—when the actual differences in neural activity between the subject and "normal" persons may be very small and, in the scientific sense, not very reliable.[136]

Fifth, the presumptive credibility of fMRIs may trigger in lay viewers' minds networks of common-sense psychological inferences that have consequences for legal judgments. Brain pictures tend to naturalize the psychological construct of interest (for instance, mental competence) by appearing to ground it in visible reality and to locate it in the person—specifically, in that person's brain.[137] This reduces psychosocial complexity to supposed features of the brain;[138] it confuses the part (brain) for the whole (person-in-situation).[139]

The upshot of all of these responses to fMRIs is that people may think that a scientific argument is better reasoned simply because it's accompanied by brain pictures, even if the pictures add no information.[140] By making psychological abstractions seem physically real, fMRIs can make expert claims about those abstractions unduly persuasive.[141]

Responding to the judgmental risks of fMRIs. Even though lay viewers may misconstrue fMRIs for any or all of the reasons discussed, proponents of the pictures can make several counterarguments. First, fMRIs may well be "expert images" in Dumit's sense, but this does not mean that lay audiences cannot understand them properly. That jurors need the expert to understand the pictures (and the pictures to understand the expert) doesn't mean that the pictures shouldn't be shown. Rather, the pictures and the expert testimony can *explain each other*. Dumit's "paradox" of expert images is illusory. We believe that judges and jurors can be taught to know what scientists already know: that fMRIs are not "snapshots" of the brain, not direct read-offs from reality, but, rather, highly mediated outputs of scientific investigation. They can also be taught that the probative value of the pictures (and the testimony) depends in part on the nature of those mediations—the validity of the underlying theories and concepts and of the principles that guide the multiple translations from experimental intervention to final visual representation.[142] Judges and jurors can also be instructed to interpret fMRIs in light of their context within relevant scientific discourse. In routine scientific practice, including conference presentations and publications, scientists use pictures along with words and notations to construct arguments about the reliability, validity, and importance of their work. Words and illustrations back each other up;[143] each explains the other. The same should be true in court. Here, the relative opacity of the fMRI—"If it's not a snapshot of the brain, then just what are we looking at?"—enlists the expert as the interpreter of the picture. As the anthropologist Charles Goodwin has explained,[144] the only-partly-legible picture provides an opportunity for the expert to *perform science* by modeling informed looking at the picture. Thus, when an expert's words explain the image in court, each makes the other more intelligible and persuasive. Allowing jurors (and judges) to hear expert testimony and to see expert images therefore actually brings courtroom scientific discourse into closer alignment with scientific practice.[145]

The real question is the extent to which jurors will recognize that they need the expert to understand fMRIs. Will the pictures trump the testimony, as Dumit, Mobbs, and others fear? Not necessarily. Expert testimony will frame the fMRI, from the authentication to the description to the interpretation of the picture. The foundation needed to authenticate the picture will prompt jurors to focus on the picture's mediated aspects, and competent cross-examination should help to ferret out the limitations of the data to prove the fact at issue.[146] (Of course, there remains the possibility that the opposing lawyer may not conduct cross-examination in a competent enough fashion to accomplish this.) Expert witnesses, moreover, are capable of setting forth the science clearly enough for laypeople to understand,[147] although, to be sure, they do not always do so. Research shows that when expert scientific evidence is clearly presented, jurors generally do a satisfactory job of understanding it and using it properly to inform their judgments.[148] More specifically, although jurors of course come to court with preconceived notions of every sort that may sometimes diverge from legal norms, when those preconceptions are explicitly identified and addressed, jurors are more likely to decide in accordance with the law rather than with the preconceptions.[149]

Second, although it is true that the multiple meanings of fMRIs allow for "unauthorized" readings, this is true of all pictures, expert or non-expert. Recognizing that visual displays may prompt decision makers to reach judgments on inappropriate grounds (e.g., animosity toward a party), Rule 403 subjects them to a balancing test: Admit them unless any risk of undue prejudice or confusion they pose substantially outweighs their probative value. Some visual displays pass this test; others do not. If the trial judge believes that in any given case there is too great a risk that fMRIs or other neuroimages will lead jurors to give undue credence or weight to the expert's testimony or otherwise be misled or confused, the pictures can be excluded.[150]

Third, even if not showing the fMRI scans in court would avoid certain judgmental biases (as described earlier), showing the scans can help to avoid others. For example, many lawyers and commentators claim to have observed what has been called "the *CSI* effect." They believe that jurors expect prosecutors to produce forensic DNA evidence in every case and tend to judge the prosecution more harshly when the proof disappoints these expectations.[151] More generally, exposure to television programs like *CSI* has shaped jurors' ideas of what scientific truth looks like: computerized, visually striking, and, above all, visible. In *Old Chief v. United States*, the U.S. Supreme Court recognized that parties have a right to present evidence in the form that they deem best suited to meet jurors' expectations of what convincing proof should be, even if that evidence is not logically necessary to the determination of guilt or innocence.[152] Thus, if the fMRI-based expert testimony itself is admissible, the proponent of the fMRI evidence ought to be permitted to show the pictures in order to avoid being unfairly prejudiced by having disappointed the jurors' expectations about what scientific proof looks like.[153]

Fourth and finally, to the extent that misconstruals or "unauthorized readings" of fMRIs are based in naïve realism, the cure may well be more, not fewer, pictures. Instead of keeping the pictures out, the law should confront decision makers' preconceptions head on and refocus the search for legal truth where it should be (as we argued in chapter 3)—on the ways in which legal knowledge is mediated. And the way to do that is to show more pictures—to multiply the styles of representation. If viewers see only the standard views of the functional data superimposed on the structural brain image, highlighted in the usual fashion, they may well remain captivated by the notion that they are "looking at the brain." But if they also see fMRI data represented on rotated 3-D views of a highly articulated cortex,[154] on "smoothed" brain pictures,[155] and/or on "glass brains" (outlines of brains mapped onto grids),[156] they are much more likely to understand that none of these are "snapshots" of the brain and that each is no more (and no less) than a particular visual representation of the scientific data, the product of deliberate (and sometimes debatable) choices by the research team.[157] It is the variety of representational styles itself that makes the point that different modes of imaging can convey the "same" information in very different ways, offering different signal-to-noise ratios, methods of visualizing statistical significance, and implications regarding neuronal activity in areas other than the regions of interest,[158] as well as other explicit and implicit differences in visual meaning.[159] The courtroom display of such pictures should not only assist jurors in understanding the fMRI expert testimony but also disabuse them of the tendency to view the data representations naïvely and hence uncritically. Ideally, legal decision makers will be able to appreciate that these and other scientific pictures gain rather than lose reliability by being so elaborately constructed. But appreciating this and getting the most out of scientific evidence depend on all participants becoming more aware of how the pictures are assembled and how they make meanings.

Scientific pictures are not like the pictures we've encountered in previous chapters. Like the videos discussed in chapter 2, they purport to be highly reliable evidence of the facts of the matter. As crafted explanations rather than purely photographic "read-offs" of reality, they also tend to resemble the digital illustrations and montages we examined in chapter 3. Their reliability is necessarily at issue, but so are the ways in which their construction and presentation shape the meanings that viewers find in them.

These questions, moreover, arise in a context in which viewers' desire to see and understand the pictures is most acute. Legal decision makers want the scientific pictures to help them grasp the expert knowledge that they need to decide the case. At the same time, they need the experts to help them understand the pictures. The pictures are offered to bridge the epistemic gap between those with expert knowledge and those without.

Yet, if the pictures achieve this goal, they do so in part by appealing to nonexpert habits of seeing. Indeed, the more intelligible the picture seems, the more lay audiences may think that they can depend on their intuitive viewing habits. And once those habits are invoked, who knows what readings of the picture they will prompt? Scientific pictures can help good legal judgment by making it more likely that jurors will understand and decide in accordance with the best available expert knowledge. But the same features that enable these pictures to make arcane knowledge intelligible and useful to lay decision makers can lead to perceptions, thoughts, and feelings that interfere with good judgment.

Our analysis of the reliability and rhetoric of scientific pictures leads to two recommendations. First, trial judges who make the threshold decision whether to admit scientific pictures and the lawyers who raise and frame the admissibility issue need to understand enough of the science and technology behind the pictures to determine whether the pictures meet relevant criteria for accuracy and reliability. Second, all participants in the legal system need to study scientific pictures, like any others, closely enough to identify and articulate the multiple meanings that the pictures yield. Judges must do this so that they can decide wisely whether a reliable enough scientific picture should nevertheless not be shown to jurors. Jurors must do this so that they can appropriately use the pictures they do see to improve rather than impair their judgments. And lawyers must do this so that they can help to educate both judges and jurors to do this aspect of their jobs as well as possible.

5

Multimedia Arguments

Almost all of the visual displays we have examined so far, from videos and digitally enhanced photographs to computer animations and multimedia montages, were offered in court as demonstrative evidence. These sorts of pictures may contribute powerfully to the lawyer's theory of the case, but they are constrained to do so only implicitly, because lawyers aren't supposed to deliver arguments during the evidentiary phase of trial. In contrast, during their closing arguments (also called *summations*), lawyers are free to advocate their clients' positions overtly.[1] They're not confined to the presentation of evidence; they can say and show things that wouldn't be allowed earlier in the trial. And that means that the persuasive power of digital technologies is on display during closing arguments as nowhere else. Taking advantage of their greatly enhanced ability to write with pictures, lawyers today are constructing multimedia presentations that integrate pictures, text, sound, and their own live performance to inform, entertain, and convince their audiences.

A lawyer's job is to be persuasive, but how far should lawyers be allowed to go? Should jurors' verdicts be influenced by arguments couched in the same visual vernacular and presented in the same media used in advertising and mass entertainment? Are the kinds of implicit inferences that these arguments encourage audiences to draw—inferences that the lawyers do not express and that the audiences may draw without being aware that they are doing so—a proper part of legal decision making? As more and more lawyers make high-tech, multimedia closing arguments, these questions become more urgent. They are especially pressing because the opposing attorneys are unlikely to have seen the presentations in advance and may not have the opportunity to respond before the jury deliberates.

We begin by outlining the law of opening statements and closing arguments and the use of visuals in both. We then briefly describe some notable early uses of multimedia advocacy. The remainder of the chapter focuses on the groundbreaking multimedia arguments in the *Skakel* case (which we encountered in chapter 3) and in two lawsuits brought against Merck, Inc. for harms allegedly caused by the painkiller Vioxx. We'll see that digitization doesn't merely add bells and whistles to traditional arguments. It fundamentally changes the possibilities for legal rhetoric.

Persuasion Outside of Trial: Visuals in Alternative Dispute Resolution and Video Settlement Brochures

Before we look at digital multimedia in courtroom arguments, we need to say a little about their use outside of court. Most cases do not go to trial,[2] and most legal arguments are presented not to judges or juries but to opposing counsel and to alternative dispute resolvers such as arbitrators. For at least a generation, lawyers have been using new media tools to persuade outside of court.[3] Perhaps the most widely used form of multimedia legal persuasion outside of court, and the most rhetorically complex, is the video settlement brochure. The basic purpose of the video settlement brochure is to summarize the client's case in the strongest possible fashion for the opposing party and lawyer before trial, giving the opponent a preview of what the judge and jury will see and hear and thus inducing the opponent to settle on terms favorable to the client.[4] Video settlement brochures are unconstrained by the rules of evidence or courtroom protocols that govern the use of visuals and multimedia in opening statements or closing arguments at trial. Consequently, they can include not only samples of what might be later offered into evidence, such as excerpts from day-in-the-life films, eyewitness depositions, expert opinion testimony, and selected demonstratives (including photographs, videos, and animations), but also a broad range of other materials: interviews with the family and friends of a party, excerpts from television news programs or other media sources relevant to the case, and voice-over narration, typically the lawyer's own,[5] none of which are subject to cross-examination or limited by rules excluding hearsay evidence. The brochures can knit these materials together using all of the techniques available to documentary filmmakers.[6] And, like the best expository documentaries,[7] the brochures persuade by expressing a clear theory of the case, supporting it with what appears to be factual evidence, and appealing to the audience's reason while also moving the audience to feel that the client's position is right (or, more precisely, persuading the opposing lawyer that the judge and/or jury will think and feel that the client is in the right).[8]

As we turn from alternative dispute resolution to formal adjudication, law goes on display in at least two new senses. If the case is tried to a jury, the presentation will be made to an audience of laypeople, whose responses will draw on knowledge and expectations that may differ from those of mediators, arbitrators, or opposing attorneys. And, when shown in open court, visuals and multimedia can become available to the public at large,[9] joining in the circulation of pictures and visual meanings that is so central to our digital visual culture and contributing more directly to the public's image of the law.

Persuasion at Trial: Opening Statements and Closing Arguments

Although jurors will have learned something about the case from both the judge and the lawyers during jury selection (voir dire), the opening statement offers lawyers their first opportunity to present jurors with a coherent *theory of the case*: a simple, plausible story, supported by the evidence and the law, that ideally will compel jurors to decide the case the way the advocate wants them to.[10] Counsel are constrained during opening statements to stating those facts that they have good reason to believe will be admitted into evidence, and most jurisdictions also allow advocates to mention briefly during opening statement the main legal principles involved in the case.[11] Explicit argument is prohibited.[12] But the way in which lawyers describe and arrange the facts, even if not overtly argumentative, may of course further their persuasive goals. The very purpose of permitting lawyers to summarize their cases at the outset is to give jurors a framework for understanding the detailed evidence to follow, and basic cognitive psychology indicates that jurors' ultimate decisions are likely to be influenced by what they first learn about the case and how they learn it.[13]

After all of the evidence has been presented and (in most jurisdictions) before the judge instructs the jury on the law and sends them off to deliberate, the lawyers present their closing arguments. The closing argument is when the lawyer brings the entire case together for the jurors, constructing as complete a story of the case as possible in light of the important evidence actually presented rather than (as in the opening statement) a preview based on the evidence the lawyer expected to be presented. After sitting through the entire trial, most jurors will already be strongly inclined toward one side of the case or the other, so it is unlikely that a lawyer's summation will change many jurors' minds; the summation, in the words of the trial advocacy expert J. Alexander Tanford, "is not for the purpose of recruiting new troops, but for arming those already on your side."[14] Closing arguments ideally offer jurors a comprehensive conception of the case, one to which the jurors may (if the lawyer has been successful) match the notions they have already, but perhaps still only vaguely and incompletely, developed. The closing argument is also the lawyer's last and best opportunity to suggest to jurors a shared discourse they can use when they deliberate en route to their verdict.[15]

During summation, lawyers may not only argue the facts in evidence, stating them fairly and accurately, but also make inferences from the facts, as long as those inferences are "based on some remotely plausible interpretation of the evidence."[16] They may also refer to facts that are matters of common knowledge, to fictions in the form of anecdotes, novels, television programs, or movies, and to Bible stories.[17] They may impute fictitious speech to persons involved in the litigated events as long as this is done for purposes of argument and does not distort the evidence. They may use words to "paint a picture" of the evidence that puts the client in the most favorable light and the opposing party in the least favorable. And advocates may both display emotion and make arguments that elicit emotional responses, as long as they do not too overtly appeal to the jury's sympathy toward or prejudice or anger against a party.[18]

Visual Displays in Opening Statements and Closing Arguments

Visual aids are allowed during both opening statements and closing arguments. As a general matter, these include not only exhibits that will be or have been admitted into evidence but also props, diagrams, charts, drawings, and other graphics that the judge believes will help the jury to understand the case it is about to hear or has just heard. During opening statement, visual displays, like words, cannot be overtly argumentative. During summation, by contrast, the visuals may argue explicitly (as long as they are not misleading or unfairly prejudicial), and advocates may use visual displays not previously introduced or authenticated.[19] Some courts, however, have urged greater caution in the admission of visual aids in closing argument.[20]

Over the past two decades, more and more attorneys have gone beyond props, flip charts, and previews or reprises of demonstrative evidence in their opening statements and closing arguments. They have been turning to new technologies that permit them to combine pictures and words as never before in the service of their arguments—to create smooth, even slick, audiovisual performances that give judges and jurors the impression that the lawyers are in complete control of the case. In designing some of these visual displays, advocates have drawn on the codes and content of modern visual storytelling, from television dramas and news shows to advertisements and feature films, to produce multimedia displays that inform and entertain in the service of persuasion—and that test the boundaries of what courts will permit.

An early example of this genre is the closing argument video prepared in 1989 by the plaintiff in *Standard Chartered PLC v. Price Waterhouse*.[21] Standard Chartered had sued the accounting firm, at the time of trial the largest in the world, for allegedly failing to spot faulty loan practices by a bank that the plaintiff had acquired. The trial judge invited the parties to use their imagination to make their summations of an eleven-and-a-half-month-long trial about accounting practices more intelligible to, and less boring for, the jurors. Standard Chartered responded with a video. The video began with documentary shots of the *Titanic* and then shifted to clips from *A Night to Remember*, the 1958 feature film about the *Titanic* in which indifferent officers and a preoccupied captain appear to recklessly disregard a telegram warning about the presence of icebergs in the ship's vicinity. The video then cross-cut those clips with a stream of re-enactments (e.g., of a bank officer perfunctorily stamping "approved" on loan applications) and other scenes describing how the defendant sank the plaintiff's takeover deal by carelessly failing to notice the target bank's faulty loan practices. The plaintiff's theory of the case was clear: Being the largest in the world is no safeguard against negligence. Although the trial judge had prescreened the video and found it appropriate, the appellate court disagreed, opining that the video "was designed to inflame the jurors' emotions, not assist their minds" and ruling that the video was not to be used when the case was retried. "The enterprise that we engage in is not show business," the appellate court concluded.[22]

The *Titanic* closing argument video invoked Hollywood fictions too overtly to survive appellate scrutiny. This made it easy for the reviewing court to assert that the video "dr[ew] irrelevant and inflammatory conclusions which ha[d] a decided tendency to prejudice the jury against the defendant."[23] But technology can be deployed in more sophisticated ways that more subtly link the advocate's theory of the case to moral themes that resonate deeply in popular culture.

In an insider trading case against the investment firm Kidder, Peabody and its former executive and corporate takeover wizard Martin Siegel, the plaintiff, Maxus Corporation, had to persuade jurors that Siegel had conspired with Ivan Boesky to drive up the target company's stock price, thus costing Maxus, which eventually purchased the target, millions of dollars.[24] The lawyers for Maxus faced the difficult rhetorical task of converting a complex commercial dispute involving massive amounts of circumstantial evidence into a simple, credible, compelling story line that would mesh with jurors' intuitive beliefs and point them to the desired verdict. So the lawyers and their trial consultants made a closing argument video that incorporated animated graphics, archival photographs, excerpts from videotaped depositions, and other materials to express their theory of the case in the most convincing manner possible.

The lawyers' strategy was to depict the case as a struggle between Us and Them—an archetypal conception of how conflict is structured and who should win that goes back to the biblical tale of David and Goliath. The video started by locating the parties on a map of the United States. Its disproportionate enlargement of Texas, shaped and colored to evoke the state's highly popular flag, encouraged the Texan jurors to identify with a home-grown plaintiff; conversely, drawing on implicit social stereotypes, it also encouraged them to distance themselves from the defendants, those "outsiders" from New York. To enhance the effect, at one point the state of Texas suddenly snapped out of the graphic display as if it were shooting a line (or a lasso?) around New York. This feature of the map graphic reflected the video makers' purposeful exploitation of a highly popular television commercial that had been receiving a good deal of air play at the time of the trial in Texas.[25] The video thus deployed a story frame that anyone familiar with our culture's core moral tales (or the local culture's implicit folk knowledge) could immediately recognize and understand. Marty Siegel, the unscrupulous outsider, was recognizably the "bad guy" in a visually narrated scenario that implicitly prompted the jury's sympathy and animosity along well-established lines.

Toward the end of the closing argument video, a climactic moment artfully exploited digital technology's visual and sound editing capabilities to draw on another popular cultural reference, constructing an implicit argument whose success depended upon its subtlety. At his deposition, Marty Siegel repeatedly refused to answer questions, taking the Fifth Amendment more than six hundred times. The video captured this by nine sequential clips of Siegel looking down at a prepared text. As one clip followed another on the screen, they took the shape of a three-by-three grid reminiscent of the popular TV game show *The Hollywood Squares*. When the grid was complete, the audience both saw and heard the simultaneous Siegels turning the Fifth Amendment right to refuse to testify into a self-protective mantra.

When the nine Siegels are seen and heard simultaneously "taking the Fifth," the effect is comical. The viewer laughs at the incongruous sight of a once esteemed Wall Street investment banker cast in a TV game show that typically featured celebrity has-beens desperate to revitalize their careers (or at least to make a buck). The visualization of the incanting Siegels diminishes him by implicitly portraying him as just another celebrity has-been and by converting him from a unique individual into a replicable unit. That the audience's response, and the normative associations that it carries, is being triggered by an iconic game show, however, remains implicit, unarticulated, and hence largely unavailable to critical reflection. The humor on display is disarming, but there is a more serious intent at work here. The humorous gloss of Siegel ensconced in all nine squares distracts decision makers from a suspicious (if not actually impermissible) inference that may also be taking place: the association of Siegel with other so-called Fifth Amendment criminals who hide the truth of their misdeeds behind a wall of silence.[26] Viewers get the message because they instantly recognize the visual code of a popular television game show icon, while the critical bite of the crucial inference remains hidden.[27]

Digital technologies now permit trial lawyers (and their consultants) not only to construct ever more persuasive combinations of pictures, words, and sounds but also to integrate these displays on the courtroom screen more effectively with their spoken arguments. We turn next to two cutting-edge and controversial examples of multimedia legal advocacy.

Interactive Multimedia in the Skakel Summation

As described in chapter 3, Michael Skakel was tried in 2002 for the murder of his Greenwich, Connecticut, neighbor Martha Moxley in 1975, when both were fifteen years old.[28] On June 7, 2002, Skakel was convicted.[29] The press proclaimed the verdict a "stunning" victory for the prosecution. The prosecution's diligent trial preparation and especially Chief State's Attorney Jonathan Benedict's experience as a prosecutor and oratorical skill were instrumental in the outcome. CNN's Jeffrey Toobin reported that Benedict gave "one of the best summations I've ever heard."[30] Dominick

Dunne wrote that "[h]is summation was as brilliant as anything I have ever heard in a courtroom. He was like Gregory Peck in *To Kill a Mockingbird*. It's too bad the speech wasn't televised because it should be shown to law students."[31]

In addition to his oratory, Benedict's closing argument featured the same customized, interactive multimedia presentation system that the prosecution had used during the evidentiary phase of the trial. The digital software allowed Benedict to "w[eave] dozens of disparate facts into a simple scenario as chilling as any thriller."[32] In particular, the graphics and audio with which Benedict accompanied his rebuttal helped him to "connect the dots for jurors," as *Newsweek* put it,[33] and thus marshal the evidence to convince the jury of Skakel's guilt beyond a reasonable doubt.

The prosecution's basic story was that Michael Skakel was infatuated with his neighbor and childhood friend Martha Moxley and that, while socializing and drinking with some friends and his older brother Thomas on the evening of October 30, 1975, he was driven to jealous anger when he watched Martha flirting with Thomas. Later that night, after the group had dispersed, Michael went to Martha's house and beat her to death with a golf club in or near her driveway, then dragged her body to a tree behind the house. The defense contended that Michael could not have been at the Moxley home when the crime was committed, having driven to another friend's house. Michael had indeed gone to Martha's house later but, being drunk and feeling rejected, had merely climbed a tree behind the house in order to spy on Martha through her bedroom window and masturbated while sitting in the tree.

In the first portion of the closing, Benedict described the facts and began to argue the evidence. As he spoke, key graphics that had been admitted into evidence appeared on a screen behind him, retrieved on cue from the CD-ROM by fellow prosecutor Christopher Morano. The jury saw the photograph of Martha Moxley, photographs of the trees in which Skakel allegedly masturbated, the crime scene diagram, and other pictures, synchronized with Benedict's summation. The persuasive benefits of this presentation were similar to the explanatory payoffs from the use of the interactive system during the evidentiary phase: Jurors and judge were able to focus their attention on important demonstratives exactly when those visuals were most pertinent to the prosecution's account, making that account easier to understand and to believe.

The use of the digital multimedia system during the rebuttal portion of closing argument, in contrast, did more than make the oral argument more understandable and vivid. Benedict replayed three crucial clips from the thirty-two-minute audiotape recording of Michael Skakel's 1997 conversation with the journalist Richard Hoffman, already in evidence and heard by the jury in its entirety. The first two clips tended to undermine Skakel's own alibi that he had left his home with his brother and some friends and could not have been at the scene of the crime when the murder was committed.[34] But it was the third audio clip that was the most critical. In it, Michael Skakel admitted to a "feeling of panic" on meeting Dorthy Moxley, Martha's mother, the next morning. As the jury heard and saw Skakel's words, they also saw photographs of Martha Moxley: one of her alive, juxtaposed with Dorthy Moxley's words to indicate what Mrs. Moxley was thinking about when she asked Michael Skakel where Martha was, and two of Martha's corpse where it was found under the tree, to indicate what Michael Skakel was thinking about when he said he had a feeling of panic (Figure 5.1):

- [Screen 1] "And then I woke up, went to sleep, then I woke up to Mrs. Moxley saying 'Michael, have, have you seen Martha?' [Photograph #1 of a smiling Martha Moxley is shown] I'm like, 'What?' And I was like still high from the night before, a little drunk, then I was like 'What?'"
- [Screen 2] "I was like 'Oh my God, did they see me last night?' And I'm like 'I don't know,' I'm like, and I remember just having a feeling of panic." [Photograph #2 of the corpse of Martha Moxley is shown]
- [Screen 3] "Like 'Oh shit.' You know. Like my worry of what I went to bed with, like may . . . , I don't know, you know what I mean I just had, I had a feeling of panic." [Photograph #3 of the corpse of Martha Moxley is shown]

According to reporters, those observing the trial collectively drew in their breath when Michael Skakel's voice described his "feeling of panic" and the picture of Martha Moxley's body appeared on the screen.[35] It was the trial's climactic moment. Benedict argued: "How could the sight of Dorthy Moxley possibly produce a feeling of panic in an innocent person, in a person who had gone to sleep knowing nothing of Martha Moxley's murder?"[36]

Without digital technology, the prosecution might have shown pictures of Martha Moxley, alive and then dead, while re-creating the scene using words like these: "Ladies and gentlemen, imagine how Michael must have felt when the doorbell rang the next morning and he heard Mrs. Moxley's

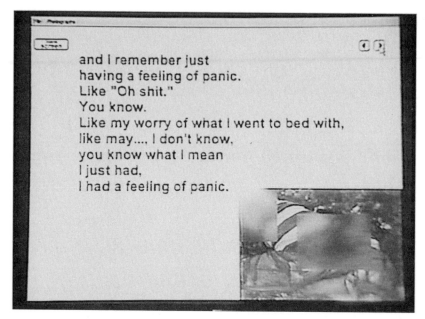

and I remember just
having a feeling of panic.
Like "Oh shit."
You know.
Like my worry of what I went to bed with,
like may..., I don't know,
you know what I mean
I just had,
I had a feeling of panic.

Figure 5.1. The climactic screen in the prosecution's multimedia summation in *Skakel* (courtesy of Brian Carney, WIN Interactive, Inc.).

voice—this is Martha's mother at the door—and he was hung over and surely burdened with thoughts of the night before. He said that he felt panic. How could the sight of Dorthy Moxley possibly produce a feeling of panic in an innocent person, in a person who had gone to sleep knowing nothing of Martha Moxley's murder?" So what difference do new media make?

Digital technology enabled the prosecution to present an implicit argument that *could not have been made* without it. Digital technology allowed the prosecution to draw together disparate representations of reality (audio recording, transcript, photo) created at different times and for different purposes, presenting them as a single, seamless representation—a *self-contained audiovisual narrative.*[37] As Skakel uttered the word "panic," jurors saw Martha Moxley's lifeless body appear on the screen as it lay at the crime scene (a picture that may also have reminded them of the gruesome autopsy photos they had seen during trial). This juxtaposition of Skakel saying "panic" with the picture of Martha's dead body was immediately repeated. Of course Skakel experienced a "feeling of panic" when Martha's mother asked him the next morning if he had seen Martha the night before. The picture of Martha's battered, lifeless body immediately explains, according to the prosecution, the implicit meaning of Skakel's words. Viewers instantly make the connection: Skakel, upon awakening, must have recalled with horror what he had done the night before. It's a story that everyone understands. The viewers' revulsion at what Skakel had done readily casts an image of guilt in their minds. And, because this understanding is immediate, credible, and seemingly complete, viewers experience little reason to question what they know.[38] This spatial and temporal concentration of dramatic meaning was made possible only by digital technology; an analog display of Martha's picture, accompanied perhaps by the sound of the defendant's voice emanating from a tape recorder (and perhaps the text of the crucial words displayed on a flip chart or overhead projector), would not have had the same effect.

The multimedia display thus enabled the prosecution to merge its version of historical truth with narrative truth,[39] providing jurors with the satisfying impression that the factually true account of events, verified by the component pieces of admitted evidence, was also a coherent, compelling story, and vice versa. By presenting the crucial part of its case on a screen with synchronous sound, the prosecution was better able to trigger the habits of thinking and feeling that the audience was accustomed to using when responding to film and video narratives outside of court. These habits did not replace those with which the jurors attended to the rest of the argument; the multimedia display was part of Benedict's rebuttal, not the entirety of it, and his words provided both the narrative spine and the context for the audiovisuals. Rather, those viewing habits accompanied and infused jurors' uptake of the rest of the argument.

The most important cultural reference point that the prosecution's digital multimedia closing exploited is the cinematic *confession*. Both the law and popular culture place a premium on the suspect's confession,[40] notwithstanding the psychological ambiguities with which confession is fraught and the many studies showing the surprising frequency of false confessions.[41] One of the most popular television dramas as of this writing, *The Closer*, is based on the ability of its heroine, a homicide detective, to elicit a (true) confession from the suspect in every episode.[42] The most widely watched dramatic show of all, *CSI*, typically ends with a confession that confirms the truth as already revealed by forensic science.[43] Indeed, dramatic confessions on the witness stand have been a hallmark of televised courtroom fictions since *Perry Mason*, regardless of their rarity in actual trials.[44]

Digital technology enabled the prosecution to combine pictures, text, and audio to create an integrated presentation of the evidence in a form that jurors would understand as a confession.[45] First there is the use of Michael Skakel's recorded voice. The sound evoked an intimacy that generated a powerful sensation of being privy to the defendant's innermost thoughts and feelings. Still more important, because the prosecution's multimedia CD-ROM combined the audio with the visuals, Skakel's voice seemed to arise from the same place as the rest of the story—on the screen.[46] The unified representation, in a single medium and within the same frame, made it easier for the audience to assume that all of the evidence was a unified story unfolding in the emotionally salient, temporally concentrated now as they watched the screen. In addition, the accompaniment of the visual transition (from the picture of Martha alive to Martha dead) by the sound of the defendant's voice—the first picture of Martha's lifeless body appeared precisely as the defendant was first heard to utter the word "panic"—cued the audience to understand that the speaker was not only the narrator but also the orchestrator of the depicted events. It implicitly conveyed that Skakel was both the person whose recorded voice described (in court, in 2002) the change from the live to the dead Martha and the person who (in Greenwich, in 1975) *brought about* that change.

Second, digital technology allowed the prosecution to create the impression of a "confession" in highly dramatic fashion. The visual transition from the picture of Martha smiling and alive to, moments later, the picture of her dead body was startling.[47] By locating and sequencing pictures and text as it did, the prosecution was able to take advantage of the audience's predisposition to pay attention to sudden visual change.[48] The dramatic shock was heightened by the accompanying sound of the defendant's word "panic." The visual and aural transitions thus recreated the melodramatic surprise confession beloved of the writers and directors of courtroom dramas.

Whether these ways of invoking jurors' intuitive habits of thought and feeling enhanced or impaired justice in the *Skakel* case cannot depend solely on whether the defendant really did kill Martha Moxley. Justice would not have been served if the verdict was improperly influenced by something fundamentally suspect in the prosecution's new rhetorical tools.[49] The Connecticut Supreme Court's opinion in the case appears to give the green light to such audiovisual arguments, at least when they are as grounded in already admitted evidence, as was the prosecution's here. As the court explained, every element of the presentation already was in evidence and had been seen by the jury in its entirety, and the visual argument was directly connected to that evidence.[50] Prosecutors did not "deceptively edit" Skakel's interview with journalist Hoffman just because the multimedia display did not include portions on which the *defendant* sought to rely; the court recognized that counsel in closing argument have "considerable leeway in deciding how best to highlight or to underscore the facts,"[51] although other courts have been more cautious about replaying defendants' audiotaped statements during closing argument.[52] The court also did not differentiate the prosecution's digital presentation from the use of more traditional visual aids, the admissibility of which remains within the discretion of the trial judge.[53] And the court correctly ignored the defendant's suggestion that the newfangled digital display persuaded improperly by somehow incorporating subliminal messaging.[54]

And yet the use of digital multimedia in *Skakel* to construct the semblance of a confession may deserve more careful scrutiny than the Connecticut Supreme Court gave it. The prosecution's audiovisual summation may well have given jurors the impression that they were *hearing* the defendant confess, as if they had direct access to legally relevant reality, when in fact they were *inferring* a confession from the prosecution's digital reconfiguration of the evidence. The appeal to jurors' naïve realism was effective precisely because it was so thoroughly mediated: The prosecution used the tools of digital technology to integrate selected forms of popular cultural storytelling with the audience's perceptual habits, thus bringing the audience that much closer to a feeling of direct experience— and hence the truth of the matter.[55] Regulating implicit inferences is a difficult task, and courts should be especially vigilant when the state invites jurors in a criminal case to draw arguably misguided inferences against a defendant.[56]

PowerPoint in the Vioxx Cases: Introduction

On May 21, 1999, the pharmaceutical giant Merck obtained approval from the Food and Drug Administration (FDA) to market Vioxx, a prescription medication for the relief of arthritis pain.[57] Other drugs commonly taken for this pain, such as aspirin and ibuprofen, have the frequent side effect of causing gastrointestinal bleeding, sometimes severe enough to cause death. Vioxx belonged to a new class of drug called COX-2 inhibitors, which were designed to relieve arthritis pain while reducing the risk to the gastrointestinal tract. It was hailed as a tremendous breakthrough in arthritis pain relief and became a classic "blockbuster" drug. Merck aggressively marketed its blockbuster via direct-to-consumer advertising on television and elsewhere and through sales campaigns addressed to physicians. Between 1999 and 2004, more than 20 million people took Vioxx, earning Merck billions of dollars in sales.

Like all drugs, however, Vioxx posed risks of side effects, the most serious of which were cardiovascular: heart attacks and strokes. The large-scale clinical trial on which the FDA relied when it approved Vioxx, known as the VIGOR (Vioxx Gastrointestinal Outcomes Research) study, showed that patients on Vioxx suffered about four times as many heart attacks as patients in the control group, who were taking naproxen, a common, over-the-counter pain medicine.[58] Merck attributed these results to the fact that naproxen protects the cardiovascular system (an assertion for which there was some, albeit ambiguous, support), not that Vioxx harms it, and pointed to other, earlier studies that had not shown that Vioxx significantly increased the risk of heart attacks. Merck continued to market Vioxx aggressively, touting what the company called Vioxx's "positive safety profile" and arguably downplaying the drug's cardiovascular risks. The FDA sent warning letters to Merck concerning what the FDA called "false and misleading" claims about Vioxx's cardiovascular safety. In April 2002, pursuant to FDA request, Merck revised the Vioxx package insert to mention the VIGOR findings.

Merck, like other drug companies, sought to expand the market for its patented products, so, in 2001, the company launched a second large-scale clinical trial to test whether Vioxx might also be prescribed for another medical condition. This study had to be stopped in September 2004 because nearly twice as many of the patients on Vioxx as in the control group (who were taking a placebo) were suffering heart attacks. As a consequence, Merck pulled Vioxx from the market on September 30, 2004, and, at the time of this writing, the FDA has not allowed the company to start selling it again.[59] One leading scientist, extrapolating from the clinical data, estimated that as many as 160,000 people in the United States may have had heart attacks or other adverse cardiovascular events attributable to Vioxx.[60]

Nearly 30,000 lawsuits were filed against Merck, in which approximately 45,000 people claimed that they or their family members suffered heart attacks as a consequence of taking Vioxx.[61] About twenty cases have reached verdicts, with divided results: Plaintiffs did better earlier on, but Merck has won eight of the last ten.[62] (In November 2007, Merck announced a proposed settlement with lawyers representing many of the plaintiffs, capping its potential liability and limiting future suits.)[63] The first Vioxx case to go to trial was *Ernst v. Merck*, brought by the widow of Robert Ernst, who took Vioxx for about seven months before dying of arrhythmia on May 6, 2001, at the age of fifty-nine. The products liability trial began in Texas state court in the summer of 2005. On August 19, 2005, the jury voted 10-2 in favor of the plaintiff and awarded her a total of $253 million, including a $229 million punitive damages award, which was reduced to $26.1 million pursuant to Texas law.[64] The jury's verdict was later overturned on appeal.[65] Less than eight months after the verdict in *Ernst*, trial began in the case of *Cona and McDarby v. Merck* in New Jersey state court. Tom Cona and John McDarby, both of whom suffered nonfatal heart attacks after taking Vioxx, claimed failure to warn and consumer fraud as bases for liability. On April 5, 2006, the jury found for both plaintiffs. Cona received no compensatory damages (he had taken Vioxx for only a few months), but the jury awarded McDarby and his wife a total of $4.5 million in compensatory damages and $9 million in punitives.[66] On appeal, the verdict on the failure-to-warn claim was upheld, but the consumer fraud claim and the punitive damages award were overturned.[67]

These trials (like other Vioxx cases) presented two major issues. The first was whether the plaintiffs could persuade their respective juries by a preponderance of the evidence that Vioxx was not reasonably safe. Although the details of the applicable law (the Texas law of products liability in *Ernst*; the New Jersey law on failure to warn in *Cona and McDarby*) differed, in both cases the plaintiffs had to prove, on the basis of the findings that emerged from the VIGOR and other clinical trials and other evidence, that Merck knew or should have known of Vioxx's cardiovascular risks yet culpably failed to provide prescribing doctors and/or their patients with adequate warnings of those risks.[68] Merck could be expected to respond with evidence indicating that it had acted responsibly in repeatedly testing Vioxx for safety before obtaining FDA approval; that the clinical studies did not clearly indicate that the drug posed significant cardiovascular risks; and that Merck adequately disclosed all relevant information to the FDA prior to approval and to doctors thereafter.

The second, even more contested issue was whether taking Vioxx was a "producing or contributing cause" (*Ernst*) or a "substantial contributing factor" (*Cona and McDarby*) of the plaintiffs' injuries.[69] Each man took Vioxx and later suffered serious heart problems, but that alone doesn't mean that Vioxx caused those problems; the men might have had heart attacks anyway. Plaintiffs faced a variety of challenges here. The clinical trial evidence on which the association between Vioxx and heart attacks rested was complex and far from clear. For instance, the published scientific studies available at the time of the *Ernst* case seemed to show that Vioxx put users at a statistically significant increased risk only after at least eighteen months of use.[70] Bob Ernst, however, had taken Vioxx for just eight months before his death.[71] The coroner, moreover, found that Ernst had died of arrhythmia, but no clinical trials had linked Vioxx to arrhythmias as opposed to heart attacks.[72] In addition, at least some cardiovascular failures could be attributed to preexisting health conditions. John McDarby was seventy-five years old at the time of his heart attack and was a diabetic with a history of high cholesterol and other problems that had resulted in multiple arterial blockages of up to 95 percent—all well-established risk factors that might have led to a heart attack with or without Vioxx.[73]

In such factually complex and closely contested cases, it was especially important for plaintiffs' lawyers to give jurors ways of interpreting the evidence that would incline them to hold Merck responsible, indeed to maximize Merck's culpability and thus be inspired to award greater damages.[74] To construct opening statements and closing arguments that would achieve this goal, the lawyers turned to digital technology.

PowerPoint in the Vioxx cases:
Digital Rhetoric and Courtroom Performance

The lead lawyer for the plaintiffs in both cases, W. Mark Lanier, is a renowned trial lawyer based in Houston. A preacher with a speaking style that puts jurors at ease, Lanier is also a self-proclaimed "communication theory wonk" who is interested in innovative trial techniques. For each case, he likes "to take his skills to the next level."[75] He liked PowerPoint, had used it in his preaching, and was looking to make the most effective use of it in his trial work. A week before the *Ernst* trial began, Lanier invited Cliff Atkinson, a communications consultant who had written about PowerPoint,[76] to help with the opening statement. Lanier had already started what Atkinson calls a "story template" for his case; Atkinson took this and turned it into a storyboard and then slides for the opening argument. The two then worked together to modify the slides, a collaboration that Lanier described as "synergistic."[77] They repeated this process for the closing argument and again in *Cona and McDarby.*

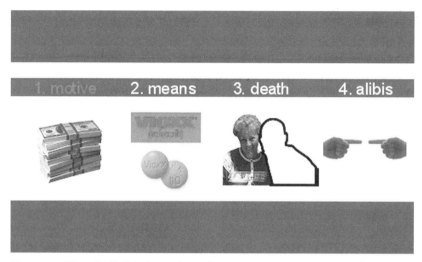

Figure 5.2. "Framing" slide from plaintiff's opening statement in *Ernst* (courtesy of Cliff Atkinson, BBP Media, and attorney Mark Lanier).

The results were PowerPoint slide shows that went well beyond any previously admitted in court.[78] Six features of the opening statements and closing arguments in the Vioxx cases illustrate the unprecedented rhetorical potential of multimedia displays built with digital technologies.

Framing the case.[79] A few minutes into his opening statement in *Ernst*, after showing a series of pictures of Bob and Carol Ernst, Mark Lanier told the jurors, "What you've got to do is basically be the detectives here. . . . [I]f we were going to put it into a TV show, this would be '*CSI* Angleton.'"[80] Lanier knew from voir dire that he was addressing jurors who thought of themselves as tough on crime, and he knew that they watched crime shows.[81] The reference to *CSI* invited them to conceive of their task in terms that they would find both familiar and heroic (because the detectives on *CSI* always solve the mystery). It also implied that they should think about the case against Merck as a *criminal* case.

Moments later Lanier developed the idea: "First of all, I'm going to show you a motive. I'm going to show you the means. I'm going to show you the death. And I'm going to show you ultimately the alibis and how the alibis don't fly."[82] As Lanier spoke, he displayed an animated Power-Point slide (Figure 5.2).[83] Words indicating each of the four elements—motive, means, death, alibi—appear in sequence, from left to right, in a banner across the screen, each followed by an iconic picture: "Motive," for instance, is illustrated by a stock photo of a stack of $100 bills; "means," by the Vioxx logo above two Vioxx pills. In the next slide, the navigation bar with the four elements moves to the bottom of the screen, where it serves as a running table of contents for the rest of the slide show.[84]

Ernst wasn't a criminal case: Proof of a civil defendant's motive is unnecessary in a products liability case (and irrelevant to determining the defendant's liability).[85] And defendants in such lawsuits have to show only that the plaintiffs' evidence is insufficient to prove defectiveness or causation.[86] But "motive," "means," and perhaps especially "alibi" are parts of people's common-sense prototype of a criminal case, and jurors who think about a case of accidental death as if it were a criminal case are primed to interpret the evidence to the plaintiff's benefit. The criminal case template inclines them to look for a "bad guy" and to believe that the unfortunate, accidental outcome occurred *because the bad guy brought it about*. So the more blameworthy jurors find Merck's behavior (say, in concealing or misrepresenting the cardiovascular risks Vioxx posed), the more likely they are to find the requisite causal connection between the bad acts (concealment or misrepresentation) and the bad outcome (heart attacks).[87] The framing of the case, that is, creates cognitive expectations about who caused what, and jurors are inclined to resolve conflicts and ambiguities in the evidence in accord with those expectations.[88] In addition, depicting Merck as if it were the defendant in a criminal case, the villain in a melodrama, appealed to jurors' emotions, making them more likely to *want* to decide the case in the plaintiff's favor—and to punish Merck by assessing a large damage award.[89]

The visual features of this keynote slide reinforced the verbal message and established a pictorial language that was relied on to organize the entire presentation. Cliff Atkinson designed the layout, color, and text of this and subsequent slides in a consistent graphical style that made clear the *cognitive hierarchy* of the opening statement, from the main themes of motive-means-death-alibi to more detailed segments to supporting evidence. The slide show segment for each major theme begins and ends with a split-screen layout: on the left, a brief text (e.g., "1. Merck had the motive"); on the right, the associated icon (e.g., a stack of $100 bills). This visual rhythm helped to shape the audience's expectations about the information they were about to receive and to signal when those expectations had been satisfied. The repetition of the stock photos that announced each theme and subtheme (the stack of $100 bills, the Vioxx logo and pills, and so on) gave jurors visual anchors for each concept. And running across the bottom of every slide was the navigation bar from the keynote slide, with the four enumerated themes in order and the label of the theme currently in play highlighted in red. This navigation bar continuously cued the audience to its current location in the presentation, orienting them and reiterating the elements of the theory of the case without distracting them from Mark Lanier's spoken words.

Digital technologies made this visual display possible. PowerPoint, as we saw in chapter 3, lets the lawyer construct a sequence of visuals so that the audience can be carried along as it might be when watching a television program or movie. The slide shows in *Ernst* provided complete visual continuity for what might otherwise have been an attention-taxing speech of more than two hours. In addition, digital technologies make it much easier to combine and manipulate the pictures and words on each slide to suit the advocate's needs.[90]

Telling stories with pictures (and words). We argued earlier that Lanier wanted jurors to think about *Ernst* as a melodrama in which the good guy, Bob Ernst, died at the hands of the bad guy, Merck. Lanier asserted, for instance, that "Merck had the motive [and] the motive was money," illustrating this with a slide showing "1. Merck had the motive" on the left and a stack of $100 bills on the right.[91] But Lanier couldn't rely just on blunt assertions; he also needed to tell a *story* about Merck that made its bad conduct—rushing Vioxx to market[92] and putting profits over safety[93]—appear to be the logical and natural fruit of its bad character.

According to the complete-sentence headlines on the slides, "[o]ld family-run Merck was a good drug company run by scientists."[94] Jurors see a stock photograph of a doctor's black bag, the sort carried by physicians who once upon a time made house calls, and a stethoscope.[95] But, in 1994, "Merck breaks tradition and hires new CEO Raymond Gilmartin, a Harvard-trained businessman, not a scientist, [who] turns a good drug company into a business-first company."[96] For three consecutive slides, pictures of $100 bills—in one animated slide, accumulating in ever-taller stacks—show what Gilmartin (whose name appears in red) and the new Merck are all about.[97] The principle of "sales at all costs"[98] leads Merck to "add marketing people to science teams,"[99] as represented by a stock photo of an old-fashioned microscope, next to which a red plus sign and a photo of a black briefcase with an open laptop on top of it are faded in.[100] While these words and pictures are being projected, Lanier elaborates: The "family-run" company, in which Merck "had always brought the guy running the company up through the ranks so he understood the company values,"[101] changes into a "big international concern" run by a businessman.[102] "[T]he good company run by scientists"[103] is turned over to "the briefcases and laptop people and a PR-type guy and a sales-type guy" who "turn the company upside down."[104]

Lanier tells a simple, familiar tale of stark contrasts: the family-run business supplanted by the corporate giant, traditional values replaced by greed, pure science polluted by salesmanship—all converging on the most basic opposition of all, good versus evil. There may be nothing explicitly false in what Lanier or the PowerPoint slide headlines say, although surely Merck was a "big international concern" long before 1994, and the development and marketing of pharmaceuticals was a multibillion-dollar affair—and therefore had something to do with business and salesmanship—long before Gilmartin became Merck's CEO. Yet, by dividing the "good old Merck" run by scientists from the "bad new Merck" personified by Gilmartin, Lanier deftly prepared jurors to hold the new Merck responsible for the harms Vioxx (allegedly) caused while retaining their prior belief in the many good things that the company had done before.

The design of the slide show as a whole enhanced the emotional appeal of the plaintiff's story of the case. Consider, for instance, the manipulation of color. Stock photos representing science and scientists, doctors and medicine, tend to be cast in cool, clean blues and light greens.[105] In contrast, when "sales at all costs" becomes the "key" to the company,[106] ultimately driving Merck to "go 'all in' on Vioxx,"[107] the dominant tonality shifts to harsher hues, such as yellow and ochre.[108] A particularly striking picture shows a descending airplane under the caption "Without more money coming in fast, Merck will nose dive," in a fireball of orange-red (Figure 5.3), colors universally recognized as a symbol for warning and danger.[109] Although it is impossible to prove, this use of color may have led jurors unconsciously to associate anxiety and danger with the subject matter of the case, Vioxx; if they did, they may have been more inclined to perceive Vioxx, and Merck, as a threat—to Bob Ernst, to doctors and the community, and even to themselves—and to be motivated to repel that threat by holding Merck liable.[110]

The virtues of simplicity. The PowerPoints used in the *Ernst* opening statement are striking in their visual simplicity. Most slides present only a single picture or a very small number of closely related pictures forming a single, unambiguous visual proposition (e.g., the Vioxx label-and-pills icon, an equal sign, and the iconic stack of $100 bills),[111] accompanied by a succinct caption or headline. Moreover, the vast majority of the pictures

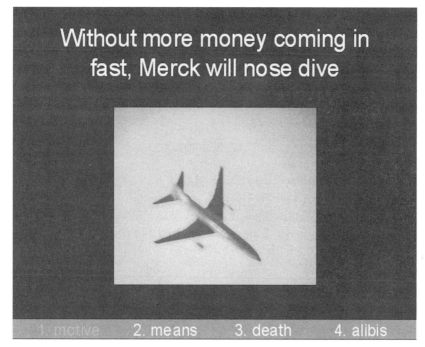

Figure 5.3. Iconic pictures and simple text: a slide from plaintiff's opening statement in *Ernst* (courtesy of Cliff Atkinson, BBP Media, and attorney Mark Lanier).

(roughly three-quarters) are generic, stock photographs that do not purport to describe actual facts at issue in any specific way. What rhetorical purposes does this simple and largely nonprobative visual style serve?

The main purpose of an opening statement, as discussed earlier, is to give the jury a framework for understanding the vast amount of information to come—to set out the theory of the case at a very general level. Too many specifics, perhaps especially in a case involving complex and contested issues of drug development and regulation and medical causation, might distract and confuse the jurors.[112] The *Ernst* slide show's condensed visual style serves this goal very well, giving jurors readily understandable visuals and concise texts and thus allowing them to conserve their cognitive resources for other stimuli—most important, for the attorney's spoken words and performance.

This visual style also has other, more interesting virtues. It gives visible form to the plaintiff's effort to convince jurors that this is a *simple case.* When Lanier introduces the "means" portion of the opening, just before the first of fifteen slides featuring extremely basic illustrations of a heart or blood vessel, he tells jurors: "Now here is some technical science. I won't get into a lot of detail [now] because there are good people who are going to come explain the science to you."[113] He continues: "[T]his is where a simple case is going to try to become very complicated by these folks. And they're going to do all they can to complicate the picture. But it's really not that hard."[114] Lanier's rhetorical strategy is to persuade jurors that the medical proof, and hence the difficult question of causation, is a *simple picture* that the defendant will gratuitously try to complicate. And the more strongly jurors believe that deciding the case is simple, the more confident and unconflicted they will be in their judgment.[115] The graphical style of the PowerPoint pictures is a fitting visual metaphor for the judgmental simplicity in which Lanier encourages the jurors to believe.[116]

The reliance on stock photos, which make up more than two-thirds of the pictures in the opening slide show,[117] has rhetorical implications of its own. These photos, unlike the pictures discussed in previous chapters, are not really intended to teach or to prove facts. They are *visual metaphors*: the plane shown with the statement "Without more money coming in, Merck will nose dive"; a man's hands resting on a table on either side of stacks of poker chips, shown with the line "Merck goes 'all in' on Vioxx." Together with those catch phrases, the photos signify an underlying concept, part of the plaintiff's story and hence theory of the case, which is implied but not expressed at that moment.

The photos succeed as signifiers only to the extent that they direct viewers' attention to the underlying concepts and do not distract them with the particular reality of the objects depicted.[118] To do that, the photos have to be simple and generic. The photos that include human forms, for instance, are entirely impersonal: white adult males (sometimes females) in business attire or doctors or scientists in antiseptic costume, devoid of any quirks that would indicate ethnicity, personality, or history. In addition, most of the photos are severely cropped to eliminate any individuating details of location or atmosphere—anything that would really pique viewers' curiosity or divert them from recognizing the depicted object or scene as a visual symbol for the underlying claim.[119] The restrained aesthetic of the pictures evokes just enough meaning to cue the concepts, on which attorney Lanier then elaborates in his speech.

Yet, something about these pictures, their "found" or stock nature, resists capture by or reduction to the verbal argument, and this resistance helps to account for the overall "feel" of the visuals as used in court. This is a matter of what philosophers of language would label the *pragmatics* of the communication, the way in which the meaning of a word (or, in this case, picture) derives from how it is used.[120] These combinations of words and pictures are anomalous for a courtroom—surely not what the jurors expected—but they are so overtly anomalous that the audience, plainly, is in on the joke.[121] Jurors may be laypeople when it comes to the law, but they know as well as anyone that the stock photos here are not intended to represent anything in evidence. Throughout, the audience senses that Lanier is taking them into his confidence (because *they* know that *he* knows that they can recognize a stock photo when they see one), and this tends to put them at ease. Jurors also know that stock photos are the stuff of advertising, so they are likely to pick up on another implicit message—the lawyer's self-deprecating allusion to himself as "salesman" of the client's case—which may further endear the lawyer to them. Thus, far from being merely "hokey," as one journalist described them,[122] the stock photos and other "simplistic" aspects of these PowerPoint slides contribute in very sophisticated ways to the rhetoric of the argument.[123]

Remediation at trial. We explained in chapter 1 how digital technology promotes the creation of new and multiple meanings through *remediation*, the incorporation by a work in one medium of the forms and codes of another. In the closing argument in the *Cona and McDarby* trial, Lanier and Atkinson framed their entire story of the case in terms of a popular cultural narrative—the hit television program *Desperate Housewives*—while simultaneously visually and performatively framing the argument in terms of that narrative's medium, television. This implicitly gave jurors a model for how to understand the trial information that may well have bolstered the credibility of the plaintiffs' case while undermining the defendant's.

A few minutes into his summation, Lanier told jurors that the leading Merck executives and scientists were "people who in their job and in their capacity deviated from what, I believe, they should have done. And then as they did they kind of started saying some things to help cover their tracks. But the further they went down that road, the further they got from the truth. So I thought, what TV show has that? And it came to me: *Desperate Housewives*. But we have to make a change. This is 'Desperate Executives.' So that's what I give you for my closing argument."[124] As Lanier says "*Desperate Housewives*," a slide appears with the program's promotional still, its five protagonists under the program's familiar logo, placed inside a depiction of a flat-screen television monitor. Then the

Figure 5.4. Remediation: a slide from plaintiffs' closing argument in *Cona & Mc-Darby* (courtesy of Cliff Atkinson, BBP Media, and attorney Mark Lanier).

word "Executives" replaces "Housewives." And, as Lanier proceeds to introduce each of the five Merck personnel in question, a photo of each replaces the head of one of the television starlets.[125] All of the pictures throughout the rest of the PowerPoint show appear as if on the same flat-screen monitor, underneath the title of each slide. And, as in *Ernst*, the entire presentation is organized in the terms introduced by the "framing" slide. Here, the argument (or program) is divided into four "episodes" ("Shoot for the Moon," "Trouble in Paradise," "The Cover Up," and "Game Over"; see Figure 5.4); the name of the episode being argued at any given moment, along with the "Desperate Executives" logo, appears at the bottom of every slide.[126]

Describing the story of Merck and Vioxx in terms of the characters on *Desperate Housewives*, considered just as a verbal strategy, does two things. It gives jurors a popular cultural template for understanding Merck's conduct as a deviation from the norm of how a good company ought to behave and thus, as discussed earlier, for identifying that conduct as the cause of the plaintiffs' heart attacks.[127] It constructs Merck's personnel as, if not villainous, then at least deceitful, concealers of the truth, and thus bad enough guys to play the part of the plaintiffs' antagonists. At the same time, by invoking the catty, conniving women on the television program as analogies for Merck's executives and scientists, the "Desperate Executives" theme seems designed to amuse jurors and thus to deflect their attention from the questionable relevance of these character sketches of the defendant's personnel—sketches tied to fictional television characters—to the legal claims which the plaintiff bears the burden of proving.[128]

As a visual strategy, the slide show remediates jurors' experience in court in terms of the familiar activity of *watching television*.[129] Lanier ended the first "episode" of "Desperate Executives" by recapping a story similar to the one he told in *Ernst*: Merck desperately needed a new blockbuster drug to replace the ones going off patent, so the company rushed Vioxx to market, downplaying the cardiovascular risks it knew or should have known that Vioxx posed. Then he said: "Now, as appropriate for any TV, we're going to pause for a commercial break. As you listen to this commercial, listen for the warning, please."[130] Jurors saw the words "commercial break" on the television monitor depicted in the PowerPoint slide. Then the courtroom screen switched from the monitor interface to full-screen video, and jurors watched one of Merck's direct-to-consumer television advertisements for Vioxx. The ad shows an elderly man walking his dog in the park and happily meeting his friends, while the narrator says that with Vioxx, you can "plan your day around your life, instead of your pain." The narrator mentions some of the drug's risks and side effects, but nothing about cardiovascular events—the omission for which Lanier had primed the jurors.

The brilliant stroke of adding the televised Vioxx ad to the PowerPoint show remediates the multimedia summation as television in yet another way:[131] This "commercial break" implicitly asked jurors to equate Merck's *courtroom defense*, already very competently presented by Christy Jones, Merck's well-spoken lawyer, with the company's slick television advertising. Just as the ad with its high production values glosses over Vioxx's cardiovascular risks, instead using pictures, music, and a reassuring narrator's voice to offer a rosy picture of the drug's benefits, so jurors cannot now trust Merck to provide the "un-Madison-Avenued" truth in court. If jurors make this inference from the ad to Merck's defense of the lawsuit in general, they may be more inclined to view Merck as a huckster, deceptive in the events leading up to trial and now just as untrustworthy in the courtroom. The plaintiffs' theory of the case, that Merck rushed Vioxx to market in pursuit of the big bucks, giving scant regard to safety, becomes that much more plausible, because that's just what advertising is all about: packaging information in whatever way will most increase sales and therefore revenues. And what makes this implicit argument work (if it does) is precisely the contrast between the slickness of the ad, on the one hand, and what jurors recall of the sobriety of Merck's lawyer's representations of the company's conduct, on the other. The ad seems to burst into the courtroom like "real evidence," a bit of reality—the way Merck *really* went about its business, as opposed to the way its lawyer has described the company's conduct.

It is crucial that this contrast is brought home to jurors as part of the same "program" *displayed on the same screen* as the rest of Lanier's argument. Digital picturing and display technologies allow the jurors to attend to whatever audiovisual information the advocate wishes to put in front of them, whether that information originated as a television ad, a document, a videotape of a deposition, or a newly created PowerPoint slide, as if it all comes from a single (trustworthy) source, and to see all of it within a unified frame. By integrating the different explicit and especially implicit messages within a unified experience, the advocate helps the audience to take up those messages as mutually reinforcing aspects of a single argument.

Using digital technology responsively. One of the great virtues of digital picturing technologies, as we have discussed in chapter 3 and earlier in this chapter, is their flexibility. They allow people to manipulate more pictures more rapidly than was ever possible in an analog world. PowerPoint may be less flexible than some other programs, but skillful lawyers like Mark Lanier can use it to repurpose visual information, even on the fly in the courtroom, to fit their argumentative goals.

One important issue in *Ernst* was the adequacy of Merck's safety testing of Vioxx before the drug reached the market. Merck had prepared a PowerPoint slide to help its witnesses explain the plethora of tests supporting the company's judgment that Vioxx was reasonably safe. Merck's slide consisted of a combination of visual table plus timeline, with icons representing each of the dozens of clinical studies conducted before the FDA approved the drug. During cross-examination of Merck's witnesses, Mark Lanier sought to bring out that one study after another was flawed or irrelevant for various reasons. To help Lanier illustrate this, his associate Dara Hegar re-created Merck's slide and put it on a tablet PC. As Lanier elicited responses to his questions, he marked up the re-created graphic table, crossing out one icon after another and striking through

Merck's summary of the clinical trial data: not fifty-eight clinical studies including some 10,000 enrolled patients, for instance, but a mere four studies with less than a quarter of that number of patients. Lanier thus visually dismantled Merck's own display and (he hoped) undermined the credibility that Merck had tried to achieve with its own slide.[132] For closing argument, Cliff Atkinson rebuilt this performance into a new PowerPoint slide,[133] enabling Lanier to use animation to make icon after icon disappear on cue and, once again, to replace Merck's vision of the data with his own. Lanier and his team thus used digital technology in closing argument to remind jurors of what he had done during the evidentiary phase and thus to enhance the impact of his spoken summation.[134]

With several months to prepare for the trial in *Cona and McDarby*, Lanier and Atkinson used PowerPoint to repurpose many of the pictures used during the earlier trial, modifying and repositioning them to fit the different context of the new case. One important part of the new context that was not apparent until the trial itself, however, was Merck's own strategy, which differed from that used in *Ernst*. Throughout much of her summation, Christy Jones, Merck's lawyer, built a PowerPoint chart that, when complete, included nearly twenty events before and after April 11, 2002, the date on which Merck, pursuant to FDA request, changed the Vioxx label to include the warning of cardiovascular risks.[135] Jones argued that these events showed that Merck had behaved responsibly in testing Vioxx, uncovering risks, and communicating those risks to the FDA, doctors, and the medical community.[136] While Lanier sat at the counsel's table listening to Jones's summation, he re-created Merck's graphic in PowerPoint on his laptop and inserted it into his own prepared presentation.[137] Roughly midway through his own closing, he showed the slide, walking the jurors through the many events Merck had cited, counterarguing that in each instance Merck had not tested properly, had not accurately stated the risks, and/or had not communicated those risks adequately. By responding *in kind*, using the same digital medium that the opposing attorney had used to present her own visual display, Lanier much more effectively turned Merck's own arguments against it, just as he had done in the previous case with Merck's table of clinical trials.[138]

Humanizing the medium. The plaintiffs' PowerPoint slide shows, however extensive their rhetorical effects, were not designed to carry the entire burden of persuasion in these cases. Instead, they were part of *multimedia performances* in which Mark Lanier integrated high-tech and low-tech displays with his speech, body language, and use of the courtroom space.

Consider the range of visual displays Lanier utilized. Interrupting his PowerPoint show, he grasped a key document (for instance, the draft report of the main study showing the increased risk of heart attacks associated with Vioxx) and held it in front of the jury, then placed it on a document projector and used his finger to highlight a key feature of a statistical graphic.[139] He used a tablet PC to sketch over the very simple illustration of a blood vessel on the PowerPoint slide to show how plaque builds up in the artery.[140] He inserted video clips into the presentation, as we have already described. At other times, Lanier directed jurors' attention away from the courtroom screen. He strode over to a flip chart and wrote key words on it for emphasis.[141] When he explained the VIGOR clinical trial, which compared the effects of Vioxx and naproxen, he picked up a sample package of Vioxx in one hand and a box of Aleve in the other and held them up as he stood in front of the jury box, reminding jurors of what the study showed.[142] And, to dramatize the claim that for persons like Tom Cona and John McDarby, who were already at risk of suffering a heart attack, it was Vioxx that "pushed them over the edge," he stood a plastic cup near the edge of counsel's table and nudged it until it dropped onto the floor.[143]

The function of the PowerPoint slides themselves varied, depending on Lanier's broader argumentative goals. Many of the slides remained in the background of the jury's visual field, providing jurors with mental anchors for key concepts and enhancing their ability to remember them.[144] Other slides, including the diagrams of arteries used to help explain the basic science, the excerpts from trial or deposition testimony and documentary evidence, and certainly the "theory of the case" slides discussed in detail earlier, were intended to be the focus of the jurors' attention. They conveyed more information, both explicitly and implicitly, and carried more of the argumentative load. Lanier left these pictures on the screen for longer periods of time, referred to them more extensively in his speech, and walked over to stand by the jury box and join the jurors in looking at them on the screen.[145]

By varying not only his use of media but also the cadence and volume of his speech and his gestures and position in the courtroom, Mark Lanier (in the words of Cliff Atkinson) *humanized the medium.* He "broke the hypnotic effect of the gaze on the screen, focusing the jurors on himself—entertaining, engrossing, always moving—while PowerPoint provided the context."[146] Sometimes Lanier spoke as if he were unaware of what was being shown on the ten-foot-wide screen behind him; this made it appear to jurors as if Lanier was performing in front of a theatrical backdrop or even inside a television set.[147] At other times, as noted earlier, he turned around and watched the screen with the jurors, leaving the lawyer's "territory" in the space of the courtroom and entering the jurors'—giving the jurors, at carefully chosen moments, the feeling that he was one of them.[148] So, despite the extensive visual displays, the screen did not overwhelm Lanier as the jurors' source of information. Digital technology did not disrupt but instead enhanced the rapport Lanier had built with jurors through his speech, body language, and position in the courtroom—all of the other rhetorical tools he had at his disposal.

As we observed earlier, the Vioxx litigation has so far yielded mixed outcomes, with Merck winning most of the cases. Mark Lanier won both of these trials and did so with what many observers regarded as weak facts going to the crucial issue of causation.[149] Trials vary from each other in too many respects to permit the conclusion that lawyering, or digital technology in particular, made the difference. In the cases examined here, however, digital rhetoric exposed jurors to new kinds of arguments and thereby invited them to think and feel differently about the facts before them. But is it a good thing for the law if digital rhetoric significantly influences what legal decision makers think and how they decide? We conclude the chapter by taking up this question.

Legal rhetoric is being transformed in the digital age. Digital persuasion appeals differently from traditional arguments both to audiences' basic perceptual and cognitive capabilities and to their expectations, derived from their everyday reliance on television and computer screens, about what credible and convincing stories look and sound like. And, as Mark Lanier's summation in *Cona and McDarby* illustrates, trial lawyers can even use digital technology to parlay audiences' self-awareness of their media habits into an increased sense of comfort and familiarity with, and hence readiness to accept, the advocates' arguments.

For many observers of and participants in the legal system, however, the fact that multimedia rhetoric may be new, engrossing, and, above all, persuasive is precisely the problem. Some readers may be troubled or even outraged that a jury verdict obligating a company to pay millions of dollars in damages or sending a person to prison for many years could be based on the kinds of audiovisual arguments made in these cases. Why should jurors see pictures of descending planes, dripping pipes, hands with poker chips, and steamrollers that seemingly have nothing to do with the facts being tried? Unlike the demonstrative material discussed in previous chapters, these visuals seem gratuitous, not justified by any need to put admissible evidence before the trier.[150] What legitimate purpose is served by superimposing pictures of even admissible evidence—of documents with callouts, for instance—on the picture of a television monitor and encouraging jurors to imagine that they are watching a television program as they attend to the lawyer's argument? The thoughts and feelings that these digital pictures are designed to trigger may seem insufficiently tethered to the law and the evidence, which (according to prevalent legal norms) are supposed to be the exclusive bases for judgment.[151] Moreover, how could it possibly be a good thing to exacerbate cognitive biases that can divert jurors from following the law—for instance, the tendency for a strong belief in the blameworthiness of the defendant's conduct to compensate for the weakness of the causal link between that conduct and the plaintiff's injuries, which some claim is how the jurors in *Ernst* jurors found Merck liable?[152]

All of these concerns are heightened by the procedural context of closing argument. Multimedia displays seen and heard at the end of the trial may exert an undue influence on jurors' judgments because of what psychologists call the *recency effect*: When people are exposed to a sequence of messages, the last one is likely to be most influential.[153] In addition, visuals and multimedia used only in closing argument raise special fairness concerns because these displays, unlike those offered as demonstrative evidence, are typically not disclosed to the other side beforehand, which prevents opponents from adjusting their own presentations to anticipate those displays and undermines their ability to respond critically and effectively afterwards. And, if the display is presented during rebuttal (as in *Skakel*), the opponent may have no opportunity to respond at all.

Possibly the most fundamental concern about the new media displays is that they expand the role of *implicit processes* in legal argument and judgment and thereby increase the likelihood that factors other than the law and the evidence will improperly influence verdicts. For the reasons noted in chapter 1, visual and especially multimedia displays make it easier for advocates to communicate arguably inappropriate messages without saying them explicitly. At the same time, at least some of the thoughts and feelings that those messages trigger—the inferences and associations that the displays prompt audiences to draw, leading to the conclusions the advocates desire—are more likely to remain subconscious, hidden from the audiences themselves. This kind of persuasion may not be subliminal in a technical sense, but it seems surreptitious. And these are exactly the kinds of effects that our analyses of the *Hollywood Squares* graphic, the *Skakel* audiovisuals, and the "Desperate Executives" slide show found to be the most potentially powerful rhetorical moments in those cases. It would be difficult to contend that legal judgment, which is supposed to be governed by reasoned and critical reflection, is improved the more it relies upon influences and mental processes of which the decision makers are unaware.

Some implicit processing is inevitable in legal judgment; according to cognitive psychologists, that's just the way that people think.[154] And emotions, subconscious or not, are also unavoidably a part of legal (perhaps especially jurors') decision making.[155] Judgment at trial cannot be and never has been confined to rational, explicit thinking about legal rules and evidence. Trial lawyers have always been allowed to go beyond the evidence, using inferences, analogies, metaphoric language, and pictures to encourage judges and jurors to accept their preferred view of the case. They do this, as the evidence scholar Robert Burns explains, by offering *stories* that appeal to decision makers' notions of what's right and just while being consistent with the law and the evidence.[156] And jurors cannot help but draw on their perceptual, cognitive, and emotional habits, developed through their everyday experiences and built into their common sense, as they think about which story best accounts for the evidence and best comports with their sense of how stories like that are supposed to go.[157] So "outside influences" in the form of the broader culture's storehouse of narratives and their characters, plots, and morals are already a part of every trial.[158]

All of that said, the law must still strive to distinguish better from worse decision-making processes and hence appropriate from inappropriate modes of persuasion. Even if implicit thinking and emotional responses are unavoidable and even if traditional argument can prompt biased judgment, perhaps the new media tools foster too much of these things. So the question should be, using as a baseline the risks to judgment already posed by spoken arguments with only analog illustrations, whether the risks that digital technologies present so threaten to mislead, confuse, or prejudice jurors that they outweigh the new media's benefits. We assume that this question—what differences does digital picturing make?—can best be answered on a case-by-case basis.

We suspect that some of the concern with which some academics and other observers regard digital multimedia in law is grounded in distrust—of pictures and, more particularly, of jurors. High-tech visuals can be too persuasive, some think, because jurors are too easily persuaded. Stock photos of steamrollers, it is thought, can only distract jurors from their proper task; nonevidentiary pictures of plummeting planes and ATM machines can only inflame them against the opposing party. We think that such views tend to underestimate the visual and media literacy of ordinary citizens, for reasons that will be made clearer in chapter 7. But keeping in mind that legal judgments can be biased even by wholly probative and unquestionably admissible demonstrative pictures, not to mention by words alone, we contend that jurors are capable of approaching most high-tech (or low-tech) multimedia arguments with intelligence and discrimination—especially if they are provided with the information they need to view those displays critically.

This leads to a final point, and the concern about current digital rhetorical practice that we believe is most well founded. As judges and jurors become more aware of the implicit meanings and possible effects of multimedia arguments and subject them to more critical reflection, judges will make more informed decisions about whether to allow those arguments and jurors will make more productive (or less harmful) use of them in reaching verdicts. The analyses we have conducted in this chapter are exercises in bringing those meanings to the surface. The same goal makes it important for the opponents of displays to have effective opportunities for counterargument and/or counter-presentation. So, for instance, prior disclosure of multimedia arguments or at least the intent to use them should be required to the fullest extent consistent with the protection of attorneys' work product and the spirit of the adversarial system.[159] We explore this and other issues in chapter 7.

The multimedia arguments we've studied are at the cutting edge of legal advocacy today. But, even as we write, digital technologies are about to transform the practice of law at a deeper level. Dispute resolution, including adjudication, is going online; there are proposals for the entire trial and judgment process to be conducted on and through computer screens. In the next chapter we explore the present and the near future of law in the digital and multimedia age.

6

Into the Screen
Toward Virtual Judgment

In this chapter we go from law's high-tech present to its possible future—a future that may be closer than you think. The latest picturing and display technologies, from computational photography to virtual reality, are creating ever more complex relationships between representation and the real world, making it increasingly difficult for jurors and judges to assess the truthfulness of what they see. At the same time, negotiation, mediation, and even adjudication are moving online, so that the same computer screens (and the computing capacities behind them) on which lawyers rely to construct evidence and arguments may soon constitute a virtual justice system—one machine for courtroom, procedures, and judgment. The legal system's migration to cyberspace promises easier access to justice for more people and more efficient dispute resolution. These are laudable goals. The danger, however, is that not enough thought will be given to how technology will shape justice. We argue that, just as lawyers, judges, policy makers, and the general public need to know what is different about pixels in picturing, they must go behind the computer screen to understand better both the interfaces and the nature of computing itself, because that is what will drive the justice system of the future.

Different Kinds of Reality and Different Ways of Presenting It

The bricks-and-mortar courtroom is becoming increasingly mediated, as we've seen in preceding chapters. The technologies for carrying this trend much further already exist; some have even been used in legal proceedings. Here we survey the many different ways in which the latest media can convey reality to those in court, and we identify some of the evidentiary and rhetorical issues that are likely to arise.

Technology enables us to create pictures in five different layers of reality. First, we can make pictures like photos or videos that imitate what we can see with our own eyes in the real environment.[1] Second, these pictures can be augmented with information superimposed on them in real time, in a dynamic, interactive fashion; we call this *augmented reality*. Third, *virtual reality* refers to completely computer-generated pictures, offering a greater or lesser illusion of three-dimensionality.[2] This category includes still and moving pictures, as well as dynamic environments that can be explored interactively (video games are an example). In the fourth kind of environment, *augmented virtuality*, the virtual pictures are augmented by data drawn from the real world (photographs, for instance).[3] Finally, in an *immersive virtual environment*, people put on equipment, typically some sort of headpiece and gloves with sensing devices, in order to enter and interact in a three-dimensional simulation of an environment.[4]

Beyond photography. Since the 1800s, the standard way to capture pictures of the real environment has been the camera. Traditional photography is made up of a "box" of some kind, a lens of some kind, and a means of "fixing" the picture revealed under the lighting conditions at the time the picture is taken. Digital photography (as we discussed in chapter 4) has revolutionized how pictures are captured (by substituting sensors for film) and manipulated. The camera brings together sensations of light, color, form, and space into a unified picture. *Computational* photography disaggregates photography's basic elements so that each element and its relationship to a "lens" or defined point can be altered at will. The result is a picture that may look intensely "real" like a traditional photograph but is entirely virtual, with no basis in any reality outside of the computer.[5] Plainly, this exacerbates the potential confusion between the documentation of reality and visual invention that we explored in chapter 4. Conceivably, a computational photograph could be offered as demonstrative evidence (much as computer-generated event reconstructions have routinely been; see chapter 3), but its apparent realism and hence the immediacy of its impact demand that the proponent clearly label the picture and carefully document how it was constructed.

Holography, like computational photography, generates pictures without using a lens, but the hologram's compelling evocation of three-dimensionality is built from a recording of the scatter of light by and around objects in an actual three-dimensional space. Holographic video is also being developed. Holography has been used for forensic and other scientific purposes and to provide three-dimensional visualizations for teaching.[6] Some legal scholars have predicted that it will soon be used in courtrooms as well.[7]

Augmented reality. In earlier chapters, we studied still pictures with overlays (*Swinton*), video plus animation (*Murtha*), and digital files constructed from different media sources (*Bontatibus, Skakel*). In all of these examples, software was used to combine elements from different media *after* the underlying pictures or sounds had been made or recorded. With augmented reality technologies, data feeds from various sources are combined and displayed to people *while* they are viewing the actual world. In the Iraq war, for example, select troops have used helmet-mounted monocles that let them know their locations on a satellite-powered digital map while moving through the war zone.[8] Augmented reality users see words, graphics, numbers, and other pictures superimposed on views and sounds of the real environment.

Augmented reality equipment could be used to develop evidence as investigators, somewhat like the soldiers in Iraq, explore a crime or accident scene. It could also be used to generate new kinds of demonstrative evidence, dynamically combining information about the place with pictures of it; a video walk-through of a crime scene, for example, could feature not just time codes but information about persons known to have been present and a map of the neighborhood if relevant. The whole information flow could be projected onto a courtroom screen during trial. If so, judge and jurors would have to decode a mass of visual information—numerical read-outs, icons, maps, and so on—very rapidly, and the sheer amount of information might overwhelm them. The displays could also simultaneously trigger people's tendencies to defer unduly both to pictures that seem realistic and to those cloaked in technical or scientific authority. Moreover, the dynamic nature of augmented reality, responding as it does to its users' immediate needs, may make it harder for courtroom audiences to view the superimposed data critically, because those data may seem to arise from the depicted reality itself and not from a database whose origin and limitations may remain opaque. (We will have more to say about databases later in the chapter.) And if judge or jurors assume the point of view of the wearer of the equipment (recall our analysis of the video in *Scott* in chapter 2), their virtual participation in the depicted events may further bias their judgment. In short, careful foundations would have to be required before this kind of evidence could be used in a legally appropriate manner.

Augmented virtuality. Augmented virtuality was used to great effect in the second Bloody Sunday Tribunal.[9] On January 30, 1972, British forces killed thirteen people in the Northern Ireland city of Derry. The first tribunal of inquiry, although it used a great many pictures—maps, photographs, and a three-dimensional architectural model—failed to satisfy the public that the truth had been told. In 1998, a second tribunal was called to reassess the facts and provide a new report. To help witnesses testify now that more than a quarter-century had passed since the events, an interactive "virtual reality system" was created. The system allowed witnesses to walk virtually around the neighborhood in Derry where the events unfolded and, through touchscreen navigation, to show where they had been and what they would have been able to see from their locations. Where the urban environment had changed significantly since 1972 (buildings torn down or put up, for instance), contemporary photographs and maps augmented the virtual environment to recreate the past, inviting memories while anchoring the display in the present. Witnesses and lawyers could also mark up the screen with arrows to show where the witnesses had been, enhancing both the witnesses' and the audience's feeling of participation in the fact finding.

This interactive augmented virtuality system helped the tribunal's lawyers to prepare, organize, and deploy a vast amount of visual evidence. It may also have helped witnesses to testify as accurately as possible, although showing witnesses pictures that they could touch and move, while allowing them to correct mistaken memories of a previous experience, may sometimes have substituted newer, more powerful memories for somewhat dim but perhaps more accurate ones.[10]

Immersive virtual reality. Immersive virtual environments (IVEs) give users the sensation of "being there" in a digitally created environment.[11] They differ from even the most sophisticated screen-based simulations available in video and computer games and other media in that they can convincingly simulate three-dimensional experience for the user. To do this, IVEs typically require users to wear head-mounted eye goggles and wired clothing or similar hardware. The sense of presence that IVEs convey means that they may have the power to elicit from users cognitive and emotional responses approximating those that users would have to corresponding real-life phenomena, which is why the technology is being used in a variety of contexts—in cognitive science and social psychology experiments, pilot training, and clinical psychology treatments to help people overcome phobias.[12] Given current limitations on IVEs' capacity to generate realistic pictures in real time, however, we are still far away from an immersive environment that can truly fool users into believing that they are in a "real" place;[13] even if visually convincing, IVEs lack odor, weather, and other real-world sensory data.

One can readily imagine legal uses for IVEs: for instance, to provide a "virtual jury view," a good way for jurors to "visit" a crime or accident scene without leaving the courtroom.[14] The legal scholar Fredric Lederer[15] has described using an IVE to determine what a witness could have seen in an operating room in a hypothetical torts case involving a medical device malfunction. The witness was able to move around the virtual operating room while observers in the courtroom could see on a large screen what the witness was seeing.

The possible courtroom use of immersive virtual environments raises a number of evidentiary and other issues. As with nonimmersive, screen-based simulations and other high-tech demonstratives, the court would have to be assured that the IVE represents the real world accurately enough (see chapters 3 and 4). The court would also need to consider whether the IVE adds or subtracts information in a way that improperly influences judgment. That is, IVEs raise Rule 403 issues similar to those presented by two-dimensional simulations.[16] The virtual operating room just described, for instance, was constructed to avoid irrelevant and possibly prejudicial features; the same could be true of a virtual jury view. But courts would need to be alert to the risk.[17] Even if accurate and not misleading, however, would the sense of presence that IVEs offer turn jurors from neutral decision makers into active participants in the litigated events?[18] If judge, jurors, and parties have to take turns using the equipment to visit the virtual world, would some essential element of common experience be lost? And how would what transpires in the IVE have to be documented to create a complete trial record? The novelty and complexity of IVE technology will, for the foreseeable future, make these challenging questions.

New ways of presenting pictures. Like the variety of methods for generating pictures that we've just described, new devices for displaying pictures range from those located securely outside the body to ones that put the body in the center of the presentation.[19] Light Space Technologies offers a display consisting of twenty data slices projected onto a four-inch-deep screen inside a large box,[20] creating a strong illusion of three-dimensional solidity. With this technology, viewers do not have the data loss associated with the conversion of 3-D objects to 2-D pictures.[21] Using this box to display slices of the human brain, for example, would give fMRI data even greater reality, perhaps making it even more difficult for decision makers to view those images critically.

Toward the opposite end of the spectrum, a wall-sized version of PowerPoint has been created in which the slides seem to stand in a three-dimensional virtual space. Viewers can imagine themselves walking with the lawyer or witness through the data field, as the former's questions or the latter's responses may lead them.[22] This display makes quantity immediately visible and emotionally compelling; it also permits some information to be hidden on the backs of slides and revealed only when needed. Still more intriguing is technology that literally puts information at the user's fingertips, allowing the user to manipulate the data freely and directly. Some readers may have seen such movies as *Minority Report*[23] or *Ironman*,[24] in which characters maneuver transparent data seemingly located in midair. This kind of technology is already ubiquitous in screen form on touchscreen i-Phones and multitouch white boards[25] and may soon be available for courtroom use.[26] By freeing trial lawyers from the laptop, mouse, and other paraphernalia, the technology allows them to call up and display their pictures while maintaining a very direct relationship with their audience. It also lets the audience watch the lawyer command the information—perhaps turning the lawyer into a kind of magician. Whether these sorts of effects will lead jurors to think better or worse of the lawyers' presentations—to see their arguments as more directly grounded in the displayed facts or to dismiss their performances as all smoke and mirrors—is unclear.

These innovations in the display of evidence and argument suggest two implications. As witnesses, jurors, and lawyers increasingly interact with what's being shown, they will participate more in the presentation of trial information and use more of their experience, including the sense of touch, in thinking about that information.[27] And the modes of display—bigger, more powerful screens; boxes containing "solid" information; displays at the fingertips of gesturing speakers—will make courtroom pictures more "present" because of cues to three-dimensionality, movement, and scale. Will jurors who participate in the visualization of evidence be more likely to use in court the habits of thought and action they've developed using Nintendo's Wii or other interactive gaming systems? Will they be increasingly prone to confusion about the status of represented things that seem so present and therefore "real"? Lawyers and judges will have to craft ways to take advantage of what these new technologies have to offer. They will also have to help all participants in the proceedings to see past the magic of illusion and make critical judgments about the probative value of what is on display.

As digital displays on and beyond screens occupy more of the courtroom space and more of the attention of trial participants, a convergent trend is also taking place: Dispute resolution is migrating from courtrooms and other physical spaces to computer screens. We next examine this movement toward virtual judgment.

From Video to Virtual Reality: Dispute Resolution on the Screen

For some time, legal policy makers and the public have looked to audiovisual technologies to make justice easier to achieve and more accessible to more people. Technology can overcome time by making the presentation of evidence more efficient; it can overcome distance by replacing travel to and from court with mediated communications; it has been seen as a way to streamline decision making itself and even to prevent conflicts from requiring adjudication in the first place. Technology can also support the development of forms of law and dispute resolution not provided by the state, as desired by pluralists and libertarians.[28]

This quest to improve justice via technology begins with video: prerecorded video trials, cameras in court, and remote testimony. Recently, settlement negotiations, mediation, and even adjudication have begun to move online. The common thread is the screen: courtroom screens on which witnesses or other evidence appears, and now the computer screens through which disputants, cyberjurors, and, perhaps someday, all participants in the proceedings will interact. We know from earlier chapters how screens frame perception and judgment, and we should expect to encounter similar dynamics here. But, in addition, what will happen when legal disputes are presented and resolved on the same screens that people are accustomed to using for all of their personal computing? Will they carry over to legal decision making the habits of thought they've developed in their everyday experiences with computers?[29] On a screen with multiple windows, will seeking justice seem like just another task? And how will the software that promises to make dispute resolution more efficient and accessible invisibly shape the justice that emerges? We must pay close attention to what is on, and behind, the screen in order to understand the kinds of justice that technology offers.

Video in the justice system. In 1971, Judge James L. McCrystal of the Court of Common Pleas in Sandusky, Ohio, decided that "significant time

savings could be had with no loss of procedural justice"[30] by using videotaped depositions in lieu of all live witness testimony to be introduced
at trial. The result was the *prerecorded video trial* (PRVT), of which more
than two hundred were conducted before the practice was abandoned.[31]
Not only could the entire evidentiary phase of trial (i.e., all testimony,
but not opening statements or closing arguments) be prerecorded, but
so, too, could all demonstrative evidence, including demonstrations and
jury views.[32] The PRVT permitted lawyers to construct far more cohesive
narratives of the trial than would typically unfold in court, with its many
pauses in the action and other inefficiencies. The capacity to choreograph
the trial sequence positioned the attorneys as co-directors of the video.[33]
Judges, too, could acquire greater control over the trial: They could consider ruling on objections for as long as they liked, never needing to in-
terrupt witness examination, and they never had to advise the jury to disregard a lawyer's question or a witness's response.

Subsequent research inspired in part by the PRVT phenomenon
showed that jurors were not unduly influenced by videotaped as opposed
to live testimony; their judgments of witnesses' truthfulness, for instance,
were largely unaffected.[34] But did PRVTs undermine the notion of the
trial as a public event? Juries may well have watched more passively than
they would have a fully live trial. And they were certainly deprived of the
chance to observe and participate in a more completely public performance of justice—a live performance in which, as in the live performance
of music, meaning emerges from accidental and unintended effects and
from the responses of the audience and of the performers to each other,
and not just from the "scripts" that the lawyers have prepared.[35]

Prerecorded video trials, promoted by some legal scholars,[36] have fallen
from fashion, but videotape has become an integral part of legal practice.
Video thins the courtroom walls in three ways. It does so when proceedings are taped and made available to a broader viewing audience, as in
trials broadcast by Court TV.[37] Broadcasting trials serves the important
public function of making the justice system more transparent to the
citizens it is supposed to serve, and a number of states have expanded
coverage of trials for just this reason.[38] Video also makes the trial court's
walls more penetrable when it replaces stenography as the record of proceedings. This allows appellate judges to consider much more information than they could obtain from a paper record: They can, for example,
observe witnesses' demeanor. But whatever they see is shaped by where
the courtroom camera is placed and, hence, the angle and distance from

which trial participants are viewed; it is also shaped by the way that the camera frames the view and thus determines who is in the picture and who is left out (as well as the relationships between the persons seen, as we discussed in chapter 3).

The third way in which video thins the courtroom walls is by enabling persons not present in the courtroom at all to participate—for example, by the use of closed-circuit television for arraignments and other pretrial events involving incarcerated defendants, through videotaped witness depositions,[39] or through videoconferencing with remote witnesses. Video was first used in an arraignment in 1972, the same year that prerecorded video trials were first employed.[40] The advent of digital video ushered in videoconferencing, enabled by better software compression of video and audio data in real time and delivered along data lines like all other telephony.[41] Videoconferencing, unlike videotaping, is most often a real-time, present-moment, generally unedited experience, making it closer to direct physical presence.

The adequacy of videoconferencing depends on the quality of the audiovisual data and, in particular, its resolution and the fluidity of its transmission. Beyond this, the meaning of what is transmitted via videoconferencing is shaped by all of the perceptual effects created by videocameras mentioned earlier. Videoconferencing can create social effects as well. For instance, while multiple cameras may succeed in showing all of the participants in a proceeding, they do not show them all together; the entire group is effectively disaggregated into smaller units, so that distant viewers may perceive persons on the same screen to be allied—and alliances may in fact form between people who are together in the same room.[42] Another effect is the accidental intrusion of information about speakers that is normally excluded from legal proceedings. Singapore's Supreme Court Web site particularly touts videophone and videoconferencing because they allow lawyers to "participate in virtual hearings in the comfort of their offices, resulting in time and cost savings for parties and their counsel."[43] But, if the lawyer is being shown speaking from his or her own office, others in the videoconference will have access to personal information such as memorabilia, details of décor, and pictures of significant others that are normally not seen by the others when the lawyer goes to court.[44] In general, the appropriate environments and modes of communication for exchanges between lawyers, between lawyers and judges, or between litigants or witnesses and the court are still to be determined.

Alternative dispute resolution moves online. Prerecorded video trials were not the only innovation in American litigation in the 1970s. In the same decade, Alternative Dispute Resolution (ADR) emerged as a response to the increasingly expensive and time-consuming process of litigation.[45] Two branches of ADR appeared. One was "the multidoor courthouse," where professional judges, lawyers, and case workers, financed by municipal and state budgets, provided the staffing. In effect, this created expanded roles for both judges and lawyers as negotiators and dispute managers.[46] The other was the community mediation center, in which private actors, relying on private grants, federal funding, and local governmental funds, tried to resolve disputes referred by the courts. Both branches of ADR—the top-down, government-managed (but more dispersed than traditional litigation) one and the bottom-up, privately driven one—generated institutions and practices that have lent themselves to adaptation for the Internet.

Online dispute resolution (ODR) is, in the first instance, a species of ADR: a response to people's need for an efficient way to settle disputes, especially online disputes over issues that would normally fall within a small claims court's mandate. ODR also supports the global economy by enabling individuals who may be separated by half a globe and different legal systems to address their differences regardless of whether they arise from online or traditional transactions. Finally, there may be something about the technology itself—its seeming impersonality and promise of rapid results—that appeals to people who would just prefer not to deal with the courts. With roughly 20 percent of the world's population already online[47] and more joining every day, the demand for ODR will only increase.

Online dispute resolution takes many forms. Various sites on the World Wide Web that offer dispute resolution can be viewed as portals[48] for a variety of services, which run from simply bringing parties together to negotiate, to mediation, to arbitration resulting in legally binding decisions. One site may offer all of these services under different fee arrangements; prices increase as humans replace software in the transaction.

In 1998, a group of lawyers founded CyberSettle to speed up the settlement of insurance liability cases through "Automated Dispute Resolution."[49] CyberSettle operates efficiently in three countries because the asynchronous nature of Internet transactions makes time zones irrelevant, and none of the participating lawyers has to maintain multiple physical offices. Insurance liability cases are ideal for the kind of bidding for settlement that CyberSettle's software can easily handle, because claimants are looking only for monetary compensation and available datasets clearly define the range of the claims' values. Negotiations come down to naming amounts until some acceptable settlement is reached. Fast settlement serves everyone's interests: Lawyers can handle more clients, injured claimants can receive compensation faster, and the efficiencies allow insurers to lower premiums.[50]

This approach to ODR uses personal computing hardware; its accessibility and familiarity to computer users helps to make it effective. But CyberSettle is not highly interactive, nor is it especially responsive to diverse languages or local cultures, legal or otherwise. It is largely suited to disputes that are relatively simple and contained, capable of clear resolutions. A different approach is reflected by MARS (Mediation Arbitration Resolution Services),[51] which offers an online version of traditional mediation or arbitration conferences using videoconferencing technology (which they will provide, if necessary), combined with a computerized case management system for uploading and sharing documents. The conference software provides common space for disputants and mediator, as well as private "rooms" where the mediator can speak confidentially with the individual parties. On the MARS Web site, pictures of an office building, a home, and even the sandy beach of a proverbial island getaway illustrate the point that the company's services can be provided anywhere. Some disputants may find the wider bandwidth and personalization of the process attractive. As with the traditional videoconferencing discussed earlier, however, they risk exposing incidental information about themselves by revealing some of the ambience of whatever place they are dialing in from. Indeed, it could be that the relative anonymity and impersonality of the CyberSettle model, which relieves users of the demands of social interaction and any associated emotional stresses, may make some disputants feel safer.[52]

To be sure, ODR offers many benefits, including twenty-four-hour access, lower costs (which means more people can participate), and fast results. People may feel good about their ODR experiences, yet they may not fully understand important issues raised by the computing technology. Authentication of messages and the identity of their senders and receivers, protection of privacy, and security are all serious concerns. For instance, although encryption or other security measures can provide some degree of privacy, what is to prevent disputants from capturing all or part of their screens and sharing this material after messages are decrypted? What control do the disputants have over their case filings when (as is typical) the data are owned by the company that receives and stores them? Can they prevent the data from being turned over to information consolidators who will then sell them? In sum, while ODR can be faster, cheaper, and more convenient than justice in the bricks-and-mortar world[53] and may well be "good enough" justice for small disputes, it works in part because participants ignore the underlying software that makes it possible and thus fail to appreciate how little protection it affords if anyone involved fails to act in good faith.

Online courts. In November 2001, the Michigan state legislature passed House Bill 4140, establishing the first fully virtual court in the nation. Then-Governor John Engler hoped that it would attract business, especially high-tech business, to his state, which was in great need of economic development. He and the legislature clearly believed that a court specialized for business[54] and served by judges rather than juries would be attractive to startups and companies doing global business involving the Internet. They hoped that technology would make dispute resolution more efficient and smooth out problems of jurisdiction that often plague the adjudication of transactions involving businesses in different countries.

The Michigan Cyber Court was never realized; the legislature chose not to fund the plan. It is hard to know why: Perhaps not enough legislators thought that the court would serve the broad interests of the taxpayers who elected them, or perhaps their concerns about virtuality and the lack of physical presence, not to mention the underlying technology, were not adequately addressed. Maybe there is, in fact, not yet a market for this kind of court. Nevertheless, what was envisioned is instructive because, on paper, at least, it looks a lot like a bricks-and-mortar court put online.

This cyberspace-based court was to have all of the technology needed for fully electronic hearings, including videoconferencing screens and equipment, CD-ROMs for storing evidence, an automated court reporter, a voice-recognition system making real-time transcripts, and a digital audio and video recording system. All proceedings were to be carried out via audio, video, or Internet conferencing, whenever it might be convenient. The judge could sit anywhere that the technology permitted, with lawyers, witnesses, and parties appearing from remote locations. All of the proceedings, pictures and words, were to be publicly available on the Internet.[55] To attract litigants but avoid cluttering the court with minor matters, the proposal set a jurisdictional floor—only disputes valued at more than $25,000 would be heard—and conferred the subpoena powers necessary to bring parties and information together. The court was prepared to handle commercial matters of all sorts, including insurance, banking, and corporate disputes, while excluding landlord-tenant, criminal, and employment cases.[56]

The proposed court had many features that are recognizable as "court-like." One flaw, however, is that insufficient consideration was given to what should be public in a trial and what should remain private. This might in itself have given some legislators pause. Courts often deal in personally or professionally sensitive information, and they have developed ways of limiting public access to that information by sealing records, redacting parties' names, and so on. If information is contained in physical courthouses and law offices, it takes a lot of energy to access it even if it is, technically, public information. The Michigan plan, however, mandated that everything be made public and available on the Internet as the default, reserving to parties the opportunity to request permission to keep certain kinds of information private. While generous in its conception of the public nature of the trial, the proposal failed to appreciate the nature of the online world: "Public" on a searchable world stage means that anyone, anywhere, can access any trial information and republish it nearly instantaneously in contexts that neither the court nor the parties can control.

A real online court now exists—in virtual reality. Second Life is a virtual world accessed through the Internet. It is the co-creation of Linden Research, Inc. (aka Linden Labs), its originator and owner, and its many thousands of "residents," who are the users/members of the site.[57] Second Life is different from other online multiplayer games (e.g., Eve Online and World of Warcraft) because it lacks a specific meta-narrative deriving from role playing. Instead, time in Second Life is devoted to creating the virtual world itself using software tools provided by Linden Labs. Residents are able to earn "Linden dollars" when they participate in the virtual world's economy by making things and offering services. They can use their Linden cash to buy property and establish economic clout within the virtual environment. Residents are present in the form of avatars (graphic representations of themselves: man, woman, beast, or robot, whatever they choose); in fact, they can inhabit multiple avatars. They communicate with each other through either text or voice. Second Life offers a full life with cultural programming, entertainment, politics—and now law.

What about rules? Residents are constrained by the underlying program code that generates the virtual world and by their terms of service contracts (TOS). Linden Labs can change the governing code at any time. This doesn't mean that the owners can do anything they please—they would lose their business if they did—but it does limit users' ability to affect directly the policies that govern the virtual world. Because the main point of Second Life and other online virtual worlds is for users to have fun (and for owners to make a profit for sponsors), there are few formal restraints on behavior, although users have developed informal norms of conduct.[58] There is considerable pro-social expression and activity in Second Life but, with seemingly unlimited freedom of expression, it is no surprise that antisocial behavior also emerges,[59] including very violent conduct by avatars that would be inappropriate in real life.[60] As communities develop, some Second Life residents want to be able to legislate policy and so achieve some form of self-governance.[61] But, just as government fails to eliminate conflicts in actual life, so conflicts in Second Life, as real to residents as those in which they may be embroiled in regular life, require some way of being resolved. Slowly but surely, Second Life is getting lawyered up—with virtual law practices, adventuresome law schools holding courses and seminars, and even a branch of the American Bar Association.[62] An International Justice Center was founded in Second Life in March 2008 to increase public awareness of the real-life International Criminal Court; its opening was celebrated online with an address by an avatar of the Court's chief prosecutor, Luis Moreno-Ocampo.[63]

Enter the virtual court. As of July 2007, Second Life became home to a virtual E-Justice Center, founded by the Portuguese Ministry of Justice and the Lisbon Law School (see Figure 6.1). This court was created to deal with contractual disputes, rather than with reports of abuse by fellow residents.[64] The E-Justice Center "aims to promote the use of alternative means of dispute resolution as swift, informal and easy-to-use solutions via a channel accessible on a planetary scale, as well as emphasize the importance placed by the Portuguese government and the Presidency of the European Union on these resolution processes."[65] Its founders hope that the initiative will also be a laboratory in the use of informal and virtual methods of dispute resolution that might have applications in real life. The E-Justice Center has a ten-page "Arbitration and Mediation Rules" document[66] that outlines its system of justice. To increase the likelihood of compliance with its decisions, the rules require the deposit of real money for the proceedings to go forward. Every effort is being made to encourage participants to take the process seriously even though the financial stakes (at present) are low.[67]

Figure 6.1. E-Justice Center virtual courthouse, Second Life (with permission from The University of Lisbon Law School, Portugal).

If, however, Second Life grows as many expect it will, and as residents become accustomed to solving problems that arise there online, they will no doubt bring more compelling disputes to the E-Justice Center. That corporations are using Second Life as a venue for meetings as well as a place to market their products gives an appearance of real-world seriousness to this virtual world. As disparities of power in the real world—between individual persons and corporate persons, for instance—are moved into Second Life, it would not be surprising if more serious conflicts need resolution. Consider copyright problems, for instance: What if an avatar wants to customize her Prius in pixels? Will she be guilty of a contract violation or a theft of intellectual property?[68] And, as people invest more of themselves in their online personae, will their avatars be accorded the kinds of rights that will enable them (or the Second Life government) to bring criminal charges against those who violate those rights? Perhaps residents will choose to resolve conflicts that arise in actual life in virtual court because they like it better, for whatever reason. And what about the procedures for litigating in this online environment? For instance, will litigants appear as avatars (their customary in-world appearance) or through video conferencing (to link parties to more stable real-world identities)?

As the E-Justice Center and other virtual courts become more like actual courts, they will have to confront all of the questions about privacy and confidentiality of data, data access, data ownership, and data preservation that we have identified, as well as the questions about the role of pictures in just decision making that we have discussed throughout the book.

Readers familiar with the American legal system may wonder why, in this survey of justice and digital technologies, we have had so little to say about juries. The simple answer is that neither the various forms of ODR nor the virtual courts proposed thus far include a role for jurors. That said, if the adoption of online technology for conflict resolution continues, jurors are bound to play a part. We will look first at how two juries in traditional courts may have used their media habits in deliberations.[69] We then consider online juries.

The Role of Juries in the Court of the (Near) Future

Two juries. We outlined earlier several different intersections of technology with dispute resolution. As these and other technologies are incorporated into trials, how might jurors' conception of their task change? That jurors use their habits of thought and feeling, their common sense, in reaching judgments is well recognized,[70] but changing media sensibilities mean different kinds of common sense (as we have discussed in previous chapters). How differently might jurors who routinely use digital data respond to new courtroom media, and with what effects on their decisions?

In the 2001 *Bontatibus* arson-murder trial (see chapter 3), there was so much demonstrative evidence that the jury had to deliberate in the courtroom because the jury room couldn't accommodate both the evidence (including a large-scale model of the store) and the jurors. Deliberations were long, and the jury was divided.[71] At one point, the jury foreman suggested that each member give a "final argument" using the evidence to substantiate his or her own theory of the case, which the jurors did. Jurors thus enacted the role of the lawyer (some adopting the prosecutor's point of view, arguing for guilt, and others, the defense lawyer's perspective, arguing for innocence). They had all seen and heard the lawyers from each side give final arguments; it was a form that they knew from their own experience in court and, without a doubt, from watching television. The strategy guaranteed that each juror would have a chance to express to the others, without interruption, how that juror put the case together for himself or herself. Each juror had to use words and point to pictures and other pieces of evidence as they existed in analog space, including the digital pictures that we discussed in chapter 3.

In contrast, the jury that sat in Soham, England, in 2003, to deliberate on the guilt or innocence of Ian Huntley and his girlfriend, Maxine Carr, for the murder of two young girls displayed a different set of media habits. Before trial, the prosecution's case was entirely circumstantial; at trial, the defendant confessed that the girls had died while they were with him but claimed that the deaths were accidental. The jury had made visits to the scene of the murders (passing the victims' homes along the way), and they had also visited the site where the bodies had been found. The direct experience of the places in question must have heightened their sense of personal involvement, although the trial was compelling enough.

Before leaving to deliberate, jurors were given a DVD containing all the demonstrative evidence to take with them into the jury room. The evidence disk had a front-page menu with red ribbons connecting evidentiary folders (each containing some category of circumstantial evidence: a room, articles of clothing, fiber evidence, and so on) to the central image of a little girl's sweater (one of the items of circumstantial evidence); the ribbons met in a kind of red pool over the belly of the implied body. Jurors were able to explore the material on the disk at will, just as, sitting at home, they might select chapters or features of a movie on DVD or enter a video game. Ultimately, the jury found the defendants guilty of murder. We can only speculate that the jurors' active relationship to the evidentiary materials and their exposure to any implicit arguments the materials presented (e.g., the suggestion by the arrangement of red ribbons over the belly of the red sweater that blood had been spilled) may have influenced their judgment.[72]

As multimediated adjudication becomes the norm, lawyers will have to factor these new ways of thinking into how they strategize and present their cases. When jurors think about trial information, they will always use the modes of perception and communication with which they are most familiar. Some will be more traditional, as when the *Bontatibus* jury foreperson invented an "assignment" based on jurors' recent common experience in the trial to help advance the deliberations. Some will be new to the legal system (and yet already familiar from everyday life), as when the Soham jury was given the media disk designed with cultural cues that made it "user friendly" and easily explored. Both of these kinds of experiences await juries in increasingly high-tech courtrooms and in cyberspace.

Cyberjuries. In chapter 2, we discussed *Scott v. Harris*, which turned on questions of perception of and judgment about the risks to the public posed by a speeding car. In the end, the Supreme Court substituted its own viewing of the police dashboard camera videotape for that of a jury. The large pool of jury-eligible adults used by the legal scholars Dan Kahan, David Hoffman, and Donald Braman to study how the public might assess the videotapes at issue in *Scott*[73] was convened by an online firm, Knowledge Networks.[74] The proprietary sampling methods Knowledge Networks used yielded a statistically valid "virtual jury pool" for the purposes of Kahan's and his colleagues' experiment—to ascertain whether interpretations of the videotape correlated with demographic, attitudinal, political, or other characteristics of individual jurors.[75] These online jurors responded to some of the specific questions that actual jurors would have had to confront in order to render a verdict (e.g., whether Harris's driving posed a great enough danger to the public to justify Officer Scott's use of life-threatening force to end the chase), but they did not deliberate, nor were they obligated to try to reach a common verdict.

A different model for constituting online "juries" is offered by iCourthouse (see Figure 6.2).[76] Anyone can post a case on the iCourthouse site. Once a case is posted, anyone who wishes can, for any reason, sign up to be a "juror" and offer comment. A lawyer who posts a case can, for a fee, receive a written report "certifying the official results including verdicts, comments, juror questions, and a jury profile."[77] iCourthouse claims that the report helps lawyers to estimate the strengths and values of their cases more accurately. Lawyers can thus use iCourthouse as a way of obtaining an anonymous focus group for their cases. The lawyers do not help to choose the "juries." The number of respondents, which can be in the hundreds, varies from case to case and moment to moment. Like deliberating jurors in bricks-and-mortar courts, iCourthouse "jurors" can exchange views, but, unlike traditional juries, they are not bound to come to a decision as a group; all each juror does is to offer an opinion. The software offers no way of reducing juror bias—the nature of the case may disproportionately attract certain kinds of people, for instance, and those with predispositions toward one side or the other are as free to register their comments as anyone else. However these potential biases may color the input that the lawyers receive, they would surely undermine the legitimacy of any actual adjudication or other legally binding resolution that depended on a similar process.[78]

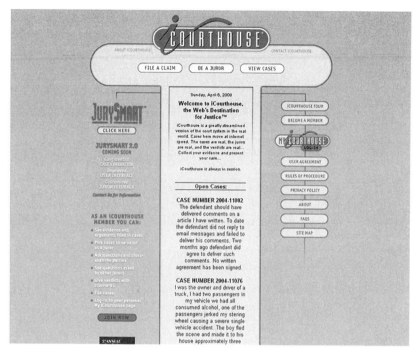

Figure 6.2. iCourthouse home page (reprinted with permission from Percepticon, Inc.).

Between Knowledge Networks' statistically valid sample selected by quantitative criteria and iCourthouse's self-selected pool of people interested in offering their own opinions and biases lie the jurors in actual life. People are called to serve as jurors because they are eligible adults and are identified because they are registered voters, are on tax roles, or have driver's licenses that show them to be in the right geographical area and old enough to vote. From these pools of eligible jurors, panels are composed at random from those who show up at the courthouse when summoned; from these panels, the opposing lawyers during the voir dire process may strike some potential jurors for cause (e.g., close relationship to a party) and others for any reason at all (other than a provably discriminatory one; these are called peremptory challenges). The software used to gather cyberjuries could provide lawyers with at least as much demographic information about potential jurors as the lawyers would have when exercising their peremptories, and perhaps much more, but it cannot as yet replace the personal observation of potential jurors that face-to-face scrutiny allows—at least, not until the bandwidth widens to permit something more like videoconferencing, assuming that participants in the program desire it. On the other hand, software and databases could facilitate the creation of specialized cyberjuries appropriate to the case (just as in premodern England; see chapter 4)—financial experts to resolve complex commercial disputes, for instance—if, once again, that is what the disputants prefer. Yet, we must also ask whether the possible proliferation of "designer juries," in cyberspace or in bricks-and-mortar courtrooms, would tend to undermine the popular notion of legal justice as an aspect and activity of the community as a whole, one that represents the community's interests and not only those of the parties.

The legal scholar Nancy Marder has raised other issues regarding online juries.[79] Perhaps more people will be willing to serve as jurors when service is made so convenient that they can participate from their homes (and do so anonymously), but will they participate with the same seriousness when the ceremony and formality of courthouse spaces are missing? The content and dynamics of jury deliberations will no doubt also change. Cyberjurors will lack the group identity forged by having watched the trial in a shared space and then being confined to a small room to talk their way to a verdict. Dispersed in their various homes and offices, they will also be subject to the distraction of other household or office members and the temptation to discuss the case with them.

In addition, how will the fact that serving on a cyberjury means working with just another open window on a multitasked computer desktop affect jurors' perceptions, attention, and judgment and the quality of the justice they render? It is not possible to have an interactive screen and to lock it at the same time. Jurors cannot be prevented from cutting and pasting information from a court window into another or from using a "print screen" command (or a camera) to record the whole screen at any moment in time.[80] Locking documents can cause the computer to malfunction.[81] How can jurors be stopped from looking up words they don't know, surfing for information relevant to the case, or even reading press coverage?[82] Furthermore, both privacy and copyright implications may arise when evidence files and PowerPoint arguments are posted to a cybercourt's Web site, because all of the picturing used in the cyber trial will be vulnerable to downloading and copying. If, to overcome the problems of information seepage and copying, jurors are required to submit to electronic surveillance, might jurors also become subject to unforeseen invasions of their privacy?[83] How can a system of justice function in such an environment?

Any use of cyberjuries to decide real cases will have to confront these and other questions about community, security, and privacy that become far more salient in the digital world. The law has traditionally respected the secrecy of jury deliberations, allowing them to be recorded on only a few occasions[84] and generally forbidding postverdict impeachment by jurors of their own verdicts.[85] How will the need to back up cyberjury communications threaten that privacy, since the backup data will be preserved on a server somewhere? Who might have access to the data? On the other hand, if the deliberations are not backed up or are kept only as long as the deliberations are taking place, then all jurors will have to be present for all of the discussions and some of the advantages of asynchronicity offered by the Internet courthouse, open all the time every day, will be lost.

A common theme runs throughout our discussions of new picturing and display technologies and then new forms of dispute resolution and adjudication: Jurors, judges, and other trial participants and observers will be looking at and responding to digitally produced information on screens. What they see on those screens will powerfully influence what and how they think and decide. What will not be seen are the underlying technologies that generate these pictures on screens. For most people, it is probably as hard to imagine what is happening inside the computer as it is to imagine that, when they look at the world, they are seeing something their own brain has constructed on the basis of perceptual stimuli and neurally encoded prior experience. We have tried to call attention to some of the ways in which the software behind the screen can shape the judgment and decision making that emerges. We now pursue the inquiry, and the underlying questions, one step further: from decision making by cyberjuries to a form of law on the screen where the computer itself makes the judgments.

Judging Machines

More than thirty years ago, Anthony D'Amato, a law professor, wrote that using computers to decide cases would bring people under a rule of law and not persons, furthering the goals of fairness and equality.[86] But could legal judgment itself really be turned over to computers? And, even if it could, would it be a good idea?

Consider that machine-made judgments with direct legal effects are already a reality in American life. In administrative law, computer programs make decisions about our social benefits, whether we are deadbeat parents, whether we pose a threat to air travel safety, and whether we are on voter rolls. These programs "seamlessly combine rulemaking and individual adjudications without the critical procedural protections owed to either of them."[87] This is accomplished by simple database management, which lacks what the legal scholar Danielle Citron calls "technological due process."[88] Those who define the administrative programs' goals (and the legislators and administrators who approve them) tend not to understand what goes on, and with what consequences, when those goals are translated by technical people into the software that actually runs the system, so that the system acquires a life of its own.[89] Even when citizens are provided the means to seek redress for what they believe to be erroneous decisions, many lack the information and skills needed to pursue their claims.[90]

Elsewhere, legally binding decisions of the most momentous sort are being made by computer—electronic voting machines—without any means of redress at all. After the problems of the 2000 presidential election, technology seemed to offer the means to simplify voting methods and to make them more consistent across the country. Touchscreen voting would be friendly and easy to use. (It is.) Computers could speak to voters in different languages and allow voters with disabilities of various kinds to vote independently and privately. These were, and are, worthwhile goals. The 2002 Help America Vote Act (HAVA)[91] banned the use of punchcard and lever voting systems for federal elections, essentially creating a market for electronic voting machines. The Direct Electronic Recording (DRE) machines, certified by the government, offered barebones screens reminiscent of the screens of early personal computing, implying honesty (nothing up our sleeves), as well as the reliability of computer-processed data. Yet, a DRE machine can tabulate a vote for a candidate other than the one a citizen has voted for; honest votes can be tallied incorrectly along the way or at the end of the day.[92] And voters have no way of knowing whether any of this has occurred because the machines are essentially black boxes: opaque to their users, and running on proprietary software not readily available for public examination. In turning to computer technology to replace flawed, inefficient personal judgments with rational, machine-generated ones, the designers of the system failed to appreciate, or at least to acknowledge, that the machines are, in fact, subject to all of the problems involved in using computers for making judgments. We will return to this theme shortly.

A true judging machine, as opposed to one that simply counts votes or administers a program in which determining the fit between an individual case and the decision rule is relatively simple (e.g., people can draw Social Security benefits only when they are of a certain age), would have to match complex fact patterns to often ambiguous legal rules. Can this be done by algorithm—that is, a set of instructions for accomplishing a task that, when converted to computer code, becomes a software program? The systems used for the bidding phases in ODR practices like CyberSettle, discussed earlier, use algorithms. Users submit information about what they believe to be the value of the case to computers through menu screens that prestructure the information. The computers analyze the information and calculate "offers" so that the parties can try to settle their disputes quickly. The "expertise" in the system lies in how it puts the elements of information together and weights them for degrees of importance.[93]

A judging machine would have to do more than this; it would have to be, among other things, linked to a legal expert system. A true expert system is a piece of software that incorporates both a base of knowledge and the ways of thinking that an expert in a field would deploy so that software users can see and learn from how the program analyzes a problem. That is, the system does not just generate an answer; it displays how it reached that answer[94] (in contrast, e.g., to research databases and search engines). Designers of any expert system have to consider how knowledge will be acquired, how it will be represented, and how it will be utilized.

A legal expert system has to address "three functions of legal reasoning: justification, prediction, and persuasion."[95] Any such system, of course, embodies assumptions about how the law and legal decision making should be conceptualized. For instance, an expert legal system for common law jurisdictions, in which precedents are fundamental, ought to encompass both case-based and rule-based reasoning, as well as be sensitive to different kinds of rules: statutes and regulations, on the one hand, versus judges' holdings in particular cases, on the other. Lawyers have to deal with the problems their clients bring to them in all their narrative detail, but they also need to find ways of harmonizing those messy, individualized situations with the framework of generally applicable rules; judges, too, must reconcile stories and rules, albeit from a different perspective. And while case- and rule-based analysis may very broadly be described as reflecting inductive and deductive reasoning, respectively, programming methods cut across this distinction: either case- or rule-based expert systems can be programmed inductively or deductively. So creating an expert legal system is no simple task.

SHYSTER is a case-based expert system for lawyers. Designed by James Popple, a lawyer and a computer scientist,[96] SHYSTER uses artificial intelligence techniques to solve legal problems by linking facts with their legal ramifications.[97] Popple sought to create an expert system that purports to "perform at a level expected of a lawyer,"[98] engaging in lawyerly pragmatic reasoning and working back and forth between rules, principles, and cases. According to Popple, users enter the case that they wish to analyze by entering their facts one at a time in response to questions asked by the program.[99] These discrete pieces of information can be "tagged" (permitting indexing) so that they relate to attributes predefined by the software.[100] This enables the program to locate the case in relation to the most relevant other cases in the database.[101] Once those associations are made, the software generates a report that sets forth the decisions in the related cases and other pertinent rules of law, explains how the user's case is more similar or dissimilar to each precedent, and predicts how a court would likely decide the case. Further, it allows the user to pose hypothetical questions in which variations in the fact pattern can be analyzed and alternative predictions offered.

It is important to emphasize that legal expert systems like SHYSTER, just like those used in medicine, are meant to be advisory.[102] They can help practitioners to gauge the soundness of their own judgments; they are not intended to be fully automated decision makers. But might our familiarity with computers join forces with pressures from an overburdened legal system to incline us to use computers at least for lower-level, but still binding, legal decisions?

Consider some of the issues that a judging machine based on the model of expert legal systems would present. If the system is not updated, it becomes petrified, frozen at the time when it was first set up. But, even assuming that there is a way to enter into the knowledge base all cases as they are decided and all new statutes and other rules as they are enacted or amended, the system would need to account for changes in the relationships among all of the materials, newer and older. Inevitably, the system would leave out information for which creative lawyers might look when seeking answers to their own legal analysis questions.[103] The capacity of expert systems to "remember" what might seem to be an endless amount of detailed knowledge that we ourselves cannot imagine retaining and recalling may lead users to attribute far more power and authority to them than the systems warrant. This perception would only be amplified should the computers be used for actual judging. Or users may find that the collapse of meaning needed to reduce naturally ambiguous and changing legal language to raw material for algorithmic justice is a reasonable trade-off for the judging machine's perceived efficiencies.

Perhaps the most important issue is, again, that the allure of impartial, rational decision making will conceal from users what's inside the black box of the judgment machine. Just as the expertise implemented in the CyberSettle software reflects particular judgments about the relative importance of the information entered into the system, so the much more complex legal expert system, although it may seem to represent an impersonal template for "pragmatic legal reasoning," in fact reflects the particular jurisprudential views and biases of its creator. The same would necessarily be true of a judgment machine with adjudicatory authority. To believe that a judgment machine could do a better job than human judges requires that we believe, among other things, that rules of law are absolutes, that the principles that should guide their applications to the facts of particular situations are transparent, that the language through which those principles are expressed can be unambiguous, and that all of these aspects of law are not reasonably open to dispute. One enthusiast of using artificial intelligence for the parsing of legal texts foresees that, once rules and regulations are processed through expert systems, "[w]ords will always have the same meaning, which will reduce the frequent possibilities of misunderstanding and different interpretation. . . . [T]he software will 'understand' the contents of the words," ultimately enabling "simulation of individual cases, calculation of greater possibilities for a more correct decision and even preparation of draft reasons of judgments and decisions."[104] Even if this seems plausible for a rule-driven and bureaucratized Continental legal system or some domestic administrative benefit schemes, few first-year law students would find it to be a credible vision of Anglo-American adjudication.

But the problem goes still deeper. We love our computers, and we rely on them for an increasing number of tasks and services: communication, travel, information, entertainment, and, as we've seen, more and more aspects of law. The flexibility of computers makes them powerful tools across a wide range of domains. Yet, the same qualities that make them desirable also introduce problems of privacy, security, and information imbalance between participants. These issues take on special urgency as law continues its migration to cyberspace. For a legal system to flourish, people must believe that it is basically fair and tethered to what people can believe is real. In a democracy, we have always believed in reasonable transparency as one of the pillars on which our legal system rests: publication of statutes, judicial opinions, and other public documents; public trials; and the rights of citizens to raise challenges to the law, among other things.[105] Computer technology promises all of these things at one level, yet threatens them at another. This is our next topic.

Behind the Computer Screen: Problems and Hopes for Law's Digital Future

Three features of computing technology are both fundamental and problematic for using computers to carry out legal judgments: first, systems managers who are technical staff, not legal staff, are always at the top of the hierarchy; second, computers are not like human brains; and third, computers are limited in ways that most people do not see.

The wizard.[106] There is always a "wizard," also known as the systems manager, at the top of the hierarchy of skilled persons who supervise computer systems. This person (or persons) has access to everything. The honesty of the system depends upon the wizards.[107] An intruder who has access to the passwords of the systems managers can act like them relative to the system. The system itself, algorithms running on hardware, won't know the difference; it won't even know whether the intruder is human or virtual (a bot, virus, or worm).

Computers versus brains. Human brains are highly dynamic. Different regions of the active brain are physically connected in multiple ways, and both our thinking and our underlying neural material change through both deliberate training and experience. Human memory in particular is highly malleable, affected by physical deterioration in the brain, by information acquired after a perception or event is initially encoded, and, perhaps most important, by the individual's needs and desires to remember (or forget).

Computers don't (yet) have needs and desires, but digital memory is also malleable, perhaps much more so than most people realize. Digital information, whether the data refers to words, numbers, pictures, mathematical equations, sounds, or what have you, is all made out of strings of bits (1s and 0s), the binary code that tells the machine what is there and what to do with it. That is both its strength and its weakness. Binary encoding makes computerized information strong because all things become comparable and transmissible. Yet, binary encoding also means that all data are easily corruptible through accident or deliberate interference.

The loss of the smallest amount of data, a single bit, can bring a whole system to a standstill (as anyone who has experienced the "blue screen of death" or frozen desktop will recognize). Human brains, by contrast, do not stop because of data loss (unless it is quite massive). The biological systems that embody human memory are both more fungible and more stable than machine memory because they feature redundant storage and ways of generating memories.

In another respect, though, computer memory, despite (or perhaps because of) its malleability, can be enduring indeed. Data that are saved go into nonvolatile memory and are recorded.[108] Putting files in the metaphorical trash doesn't eliminate them; it just makes it possible for the computer to reuse the space they occupied by overwriting them with new data. Unless deleted files are overwritten with random bits seven times (according to current thinking), readable data can be recovered; they have even been recovered from the dust of pulverized hard drives. So, even without backing up, data can be retrieved, at least in theory. But, because of the vulnerability of computer memory noted earlier, system security measures usually entail that all data are backed up and redundantly stored, with copies kept elsewhere. So, if you put files in the trash on your own computer and empty it, it is quite possible that you, or someone else, would be able to retrieve them—and, if your computer is attached to a local network or to the Internet, anything you have sent out will also reside elsewhere, and you probably won't know where that elsewhere is.

The limits of computer "intelligence." Our computers seem very powerful because we attribute intelligence to them[109] and because they can do tasks we cannot. One of the most common things we do with computers is to maintain databases to organize information for us.[110] These databases can contain information vastly exceeding what any person or any readily searchable analog source can offer. Through our purposeful access to these immensities of data, databases can show us pictures of the world—changing patterns of financial transactions, dynamic weather maps, and so on—that we can see in no other way. Their capacity for revealing these patterns on demand may lead us to treat databases with a kind of abstract reverence.

When an individual decides what data need to be collected and what the relevant searches will be, the system may be reasonably transparent to its maker and errors may be easily corrected. Magistrate Judge Morton Denlow, for instance, created a database of case settlements so that he and other judges could better advise litigants.[111] Automated data collection and compilation, the sorts of databases that currently make decisions or advise governments, are different in both magnitude and kind. These databases can be full of errors that will never be corrected. Simple decision errors about the definition of the item being entered or even typing errors can lead to the recording of bad information. Information accurately and honestly entered can be based on bad sources. In particular, when the data being entered are gathered from people's responses, it may be that the people who provided those data were lying, for any number of reasons. So, even the most well made database has to be corrected for errors and constantly updated. A database is only as good as the data it contains. But rarely is each datum in a vast database scrutinized for accuracy, especially in the case of the automated systems in wide use by both government and industry. And identity-theft victims have discovered how hard it is to find and correct every copy of bad information in one database or another.[112]

The implications of these essential aspects of computing for any part of any legal process dependent on computers, from augmented reality evidence to online dispute resolution to judging machines, are obvious but profound. Let's review them. First, the systems manager—or a hacker who impersonates one—has complete access to all system data: its accuracy, its privacy, its very existence. The reliability of computer-generated evidence and computer-guided judgments depends entirely on the integrity of the wizard behind the screen. Second, the vulnerability of computer memory and the security measures sure to be taken in response create a dilemma. On the one hand, the proper functioning of the algorithms through which CyberSettle, iCourthouse, or the judging machine of the future do their work is always at risk due to accidental or intentional corruption of data memory. On the other, computer security leads to the dissemination and preservation of data that participants in the legal process might prefer remain confidential, threatening them with costly losses of privacy. Third, although errors in databases may be merely noise if the picture desired is large enough (like those used for weather tracking, market behavior analysis, or management of the modern battlefield), they can make huge differences in individual cases—just ask anyone mistakenly put on a "no-fly" list, stricken from a voter registration list, or denied credit.[113] If erroneous information about one or two previous settlements enters CyberSettle's database, they may scarcely affect the range of recommended values in a given negotiation. By contrast, one or two incorrectly entered facts or precedents in a judging machine's database could change the verdict in a case. So it is an illusion that, just because computers can handle more data than we can, they are always more rational,[114] more objective, and more correct than human decision makers.

Moreover, people must disentangle their everyday experiences of communication *through* computers—e-mail contacts, warm Skype conversations with distant friends, game play, and comments posted to blogs on the issues of the day—from *how* computers actually work when being used for these purposes. When someone correctly responds to an e-mail that we have sent, we believe that we are using a trusted medium. This effect is even stronger because we are often sitting at our desks or using Wi-Fi sitting on a bench in a park, contexts that are somehow reassuring. In fact, we have no way of knowing exactly where the data we are sending are going. If we get a response to e-mail, for instance, we know that it was received, but we have no idea how it may have been diverted along the way. Think of sending and receiving information in an online game of poker.[115] There is something on the screen that looks like play, but you have no way of knowing what the connection is between what you are seeing and what is actually being recorded. You do not know whether information about what is in your hand is known to the "dealer" or has been passed to another player.[116] You have no way to know whether your winning streak has been artificially brought to a fast halt by dealers' "decisions." In fact, you have little control over anything once the electrical impulse has been passed from your keyboard (over which you have full control) to the computer, yours or someone else's.

These aspects of computing tell us that there simply is no such thing as a trusted platform.[117] Here, again, the problem of the black box of the electronic voting machine provides a concrete example. As the Help America Vote Act was being implemented, computer scientists started to educate the public that DRE machines are no more reliable than electronic poker and probably less so. There simply was (and is) no way for an all-electronic system to authenticate all of the information—to connect votes to the voters' intent, providing the ability to recount not just the computer tallies but the ballots themselves. Moreover, the private companies that manufacture the voting equipment have created proprietary computer code, all protected under patents and trade secrets and thus kept from public inspection. Neither members of the public nor the government can check to ensure that the machines are working properly because they do not have the necessary information. This same opacity could characterize a fully electronic, fully digitized court—if the software is designed as a product for purchase. That it need not be is suggested by the example of

CyberSettle: Although its algorithms are proprietary, the parties, unlike voters using DREs, remain in control of the process. They can check to see that their information has been correctly recorded; they can reject offers that they regard as inadequate or insensitive.

Adjudication and other forms of legal dispute resolution, at least as much as voting, are cornerstones of good social ordering in a democracy. The justice system represents one of society's most important ways of responding to real human problems. To serve the public interest, the public must by and large believe that the system has integrity and that it exhibits the kinds of values that inspire obedience to law. As the justice system moves on screen and online, ever more dependent on computers, the public must recognize that the same technologies that make digital displays and cyberspace possible pose critical risks to that integrity and to those values. We cannot forget that there is always a wizard, neither elected nor appointed through public process, with extraordinary privileges over the system. We cannot miss the fact that computer systems are always in a fluid state, with data constantly subject to loss, corruption, and leakage. And we must resist the illusion that the system is more intelligent and rational than we are.

For a legal system in the digital age to deserve the public's allegiance, the public must take and maintain responsibility for what's on and behind the screens on which justice is conducted. We suggest that these considerations be taken into account:

1. Both the underlying software and what's visible on the screen will influence the kind of justice that emerges online, so the design of both should be a reasonably open process, including experts from all relevant domains—not just law and computer science, but also sociology, visual and media studies, ergonomics, and so on—along with input from the general public. Interface design is crucial not only because it will affect the usability of the system but also because it will communicate values, evoking emotional as well as cognitive responses. Unlike the more complex and diverse sensory experience of a bricks-and-mortar courthouse, the interface will carry the entire burden of communication and expression. So every aspect of design matters.[118]

2. To promote transparency, the software on which any truly public legal system runs should be open-source code—code that results from a community effort and that reflects community, not proprietary, values. (There is an inherent conflict of interest between enterprises convened to make a profit and those devoted to other goals. We cannot afford a legal

system subject to trade-secrets laws and similar protections that are designed to help businesses enhance profits and manage competition.) This will allow computer professionals who are able to understand the code to check its important functions for accuracy. Open-source coding also harnesses the collective wisdom of many people, so bugs are more likely to be found.[119] The shift to open-source code will also encourage citizens to think of electronic adjudication as a public good for which they bear some responsibility and that should be accountable to them, and not just as a profit center.

3. While the subject of electronic data security is far too vast for us to survey here, we can suggest a few obvious parameters. Users of the system—claimants, defendants, and their lawyers (if any)—should be fully informed of the system's security and privacy features: how long communications and other records will be retained, who else will have access to them and under what conditions, and so on. Determining what should be public and what should remain private is crucial when a democracy creates a legal system in cyberspace. Full disclosure is needed before participants give their informed consent to the process and will be at least a partial answer to the asymmetries of information that can plague the underfunded and underrepresented in our current legal system. Likewise, as a public agency, responsible parties should be listed by name on all the sites or electronic filing system headers in question.

4. The justice system in a democracy should retain ownership of all data the system generates. The profit orientation of third parties represents an inherent conflict of interest here as well; the privacy and dignity interests of the system's users should have precedence, so data should not be provided to information consolidators or available for data mining. Moreover, data managers must be required to provide a forensic trail of the names of their employees who have had access, as well as logs of any actions taken. For citizens to believe that they have a fighting chance with a justice system, they must be able to believe that it functions neutrally and independently from the other systems to which they are subject.

5. If our legal system is to remain grounded in precedent, past decisions and other records must remain readily accessible and freely available without payment of unreasonable fees. Care must be taken, therefore, to ensure that, as system software evolves, it remains backwardly compatible and stored on archival-quality memory. And it should go without saying that systems also need to be in place to prevent, insofar as possible, the wholesale destruction of public information because of politics or

incompetence. Legal accountability is needed to protect the public's access to government decision making.[120]

The flourishing of law in a digital multimedia age will require the careful thought and vigilance of many persons: judges, lawyers, policy makers, and the public at large. In our final chapter, we discuss the kinds of good practices and ethical obligations that could improve the prospects for justice.

7

Ethics and Justice in the Digital Visual Age

Throughout this book, we have illustrated the challenges posed by law's digital visual revolution: to the nature of reliable legal knowledge, the bounds of permissible legal argument, and the distribution of meaning-making authority. As we tracked the changes in legal persuasion and judgment, we argued that justice today is more likely to be achieved if judges, jurors, lawyers, and the public encounter the new courtroom media with open eyes, as knowledgeably as possible. The figure of Justice is typically depicted holding scales and wearing a blindfold.[1] But what exactly does it mean to take the blindfold off? How should law be ethically practiced and judgments justly rendered in a world of digital visuals and multimedia?

In this concluding chapter, we reflect broadly on these changes in law and suggest what can be done to enhance the quality of justice in a world increasingly dependent on visual displays. First, we ask whether the expanding use of digital pictures and multimedia is a good thing for the law in general. We discuss how courtroom rules and procedures might be framed and judges and jurors educated to enhance the judgmental benefits of the new media while reducing their risks and thus to promote accuracy and fairness. We offer several recommendations for improving the visual literacy of all participants in the trial.

Next, we address the ethical obligations of those who make and display legal visuals and multimedia. Professional ethics codes obligate lawyers not to knowingly make false statements of fact to tribunals or to falsify evidence,[2] and presumably this applies to pictures as it does to words. But such simple directives offer little help to lawyers, judges, jurors, and the public when they are forced to navigate through the vast range of possibilities of visual representation. We propose and defend a set of ethical guidelines or best practices for legal visual communication and persuasion that takes account of the power and complexity of pictures.

Finally, we place law's digital visual transformation in a wider social context. Good legal practices with respect to picturing can be a model for informed, critical judgments in the culture at large. More important, looking ahead (as we did in chapter 6) to law's technologically mediated future, we urge that the public take responsibility for the design and control of online adjudication if the legal system is to maintain its legitimacy in a democratic society.

Are Digital Pictures Good for Law?

The examples of new courtroom media discussed throughout the book have probably prompted a variety of responses in our readers—some favorable, some not. These and other digital displays seem capable of offering both advantages and disadvantages for legal judgment. So are they, on balance, good for law, and, if not, can they be made better? To address this, we identify four criteria for good and just decision making: *accurate outcomes, good thinking, fair process,* and *expressive value*. We discuss each criterion and evaluate the use of digital visuals and multimedia in light of it. We then outline what the legal system can and should do to maximize the benefits that the new media can provide to legal judgment while reducing some of their drawbacks.

Accurate Outcomes. Are digital visuals and multimedia leading to more or fewer accurate verdicts? It's impossible to say for sure.[3] Visual representations can provide more information about and improve decision makers' understanding of the subject matter of the case. They can also make the information that they depict more salient and help decision makers to pay attention to and retain that information.[4] And, by increasing jurors' level of engagement, visuals may also motivate jurors to decide accurately, which should lead them to pay more attention to the content of the incoming information—which should, in turn, lead to more accurate decisions.[5] Yet, visual and multimedia displays may also decrease the accuracy of factual judgments. For instance, to the extent that visual and multimedia displays are more cognitively and emotionally engaging than purely verbal representations, those displays might well reduce viewers' ability and/or willingness to process information critically.[6] This, in turn, should make the message conveyed by the visuals more persuasive, even if the legally relevant content of the message does not warrant that effect.[7]

That said, there are reasons why the net effect of courtroom visuals and multimedia may well be greater accuracy of outcomes. Experimental studies have repeatedly shown that the strength of the evidence is, as it should be, the best predictor of outcomes;[8] visual and multimedia displays that make the evidence clearer, as most do, should enhance this effect. Lawyers, moreover, have strong incentives to represent the world accurately in court. Rules of procedure and professional responsibility obligate them to do so,[9] but, beyond that, it's also generally the best strategy. In addition, the lawyer who is caught deliberately misrepresenting facts risks losing all credibility before the jurors and the judge. Finally, visual displays can constrain both lawyers' and witnesses' ability to get away with *verbal* obfuscations and distortions.

Trial judges' decisions to admit or exclude individual pictures will, of course, shape the aggregate effect of new media on judgmental accuracy. By rigorously applying to digital displays the same basic admissibility rules to which other evidence is subject, the legal system makes it more likely that the only pictures jurors will see are relevant and reliable ones, which (all things being equal) should make it more likely that jurors, to the extent that their judgments are influenced by those pictures, will get those judgments right. Federal Rules of Evidence 401–402 and their state law equivalents should ensure that irrelevant pictures, which can undermine judgmental accuracy by confusing or distracting decision makers or leading them to decide on the basis of improper information, will be excluded. The rules governing the authentication of tangible evidence (Federal Rule of Evidence 901 and its state law equivalents) aim to ensure both relevance and reliability. They do this by requiring that the proponent offer evidence sufficient to support a finding that the matter in question—photograph, animation, or whatever it may be—is what its proponent claims it is. The authentication requirement permits the opponent to cross-examine the witness whose testimony the picture illustrates (and, especially in the case of digital visuals offered as substantive evidence, the person or persons responsible for the creation of the display). Effective cross-examination can expose any weaknesses in the display as a representation of what it purports to depict as well as any mischaracterizations (i.e., "miscaptioning") of the display by the witness.[10]

Any reliance on these evidentiary rules to enhance the justice of legal visual persuasion must, however, be qualified in three ways. First, relevance and reliability rules, like any others, don't always work perfectly to accomplish their intended purposes; some irrelevant or unreliable pictorial evidence will get through.[11] Second, judges who consider demonstrative displays to be "merely illustrative," as opposed to substantive, tend to subject them to less rigorous authentication requirements.[12] By doing so, they may be more likely to let inaccurate or misleading pictorial material be shown to jurors. One response to this would be for courts to subject all digital displays offered as depictions of reality to the stricter authentication standards used for substantive evidence, as the Connecticut Supreme Court did in *Swinton*, discussed in chapter 4.

Third, these rules address only the truthfulness or trustworthiness of pictorial evidence and hence the accuracy of the resulting decisions. That is an important part of people's concerns about the increasing role of digital visuals and multimedia in law. Just as urgent, however, are concerns that pictures, not only those offered as demonstrative evidence but also those used explicitly as argument, are adversely affecting *how* judges and jurors reach their decisions. Throughout the book, we have shown how new media provide decision makers with new kinds of information in new contexts, leading them to think, feel, and judge differently than they otherwise would. We turn next to whether these new ways of presenting evidence and argument conflict with ideals of good decision making and, to the extent that they do, what the legal system can and should do about it.

Good Thinking. Good legal decision making should feature careful, deliberative judgment. Decision makers should have access to all[13] (and, insofar as possible, only) relevant and probative evidence in readily understandable formats, and they should have adequate time and resources to think carefully about (and, where there is more than one decision maker, to discuss) the facts and the law before reaching their verdict. Will law in an increasingly visual, digital, and interactive environment be less likely than before to conform to these ideals of good decision making?

Threats to good thinking. We noted briefly how new media can improve legal thinking—for instance, by providing more relevant information and heightening decision makers' attention to the facts—but the same displays may also threaten good thinking in several interrelated ways. The first has to do with the decreased corrigibility of intuitive responses. Evidence from psychology and neurobiology indicates that when people think about matters of right and wrong, they tend to form quick, intuitive judgments and only later to reason more carefully and deliberately; most important, the intuitive judgments tend to govern or at least anchor the ultimate decision.[14] The norm of good decision making requires that those intuitive responses be made as amenable as possible to conscious scrutiny and, where warranted, revision. Visual displays, however, can convert complex cognitive judgments into perceptual ones, which, like moral judgments, tend to lead people to decide intuitively, and their (over)confidence in the accuracy of their perceptual judgments[15] may decrease their motivation to rethink them. Because visuals tend to be so cognitively and emotionally absorbing, moreover, they may make audiences even less willing and/or able to subject their initial responses to critical scrutiny.[16] (On the other hand, through the very process of discussing pictures, jurors may be able to bring to consciousness aspects of their reactions to the pictures and to the case as a whole that might otherwise have remained hidden,[17] improving legal judgment.)

Relatedly, digital visual and multimedia communication is often criticized on the ground that it makes it easier for legal advocates to manipulate or deceive their audiences (especially jurors). We should examine this criticism very carefully. If it means something like "presenting improperly altered evidence" and thereby leading viewers to believe what's not true, it indeed raises concerns—digital video and photos *can* easily be altered, as we saw in chapters 2 and 4. The answer is the requirement of authentication discussed earlier, including cross-examination of the witness who lays the foundation for the picture. The increasing availability of software for detecting alterations[18] and the prospect of losing face (not to mention disciplinary sanctions) may further discourage lawyers from engaging in this blatant sort of manipulation or deception.

To some, "manipulation" means "taking in the audience unawares," that is, concealing from them how they are actually being persuaded. To be sure, this observation could apply to any effective persuasion in any modality, because all rhetoric succeeds in part by concealing its own mechanisms, through a kind of seduction.[19] But maybe pictures are even more seductive than words. Perhaps pictures in law, like the visual rhetorics of advertising and political campaign films, are especially capable of inducing belief independently of the substance of the message, by appealing to peripheral cues rather than message content.[20] At the extreme, some fear that lawyers can use digital media to send audiences subliminal messages.[21] That threat may be greatly overstated,[22] but the broader point is not. We have shown throughout the book how legal visual rhetoric is especially well suited to communicating implicitly. And, when the persuasive appeal remains implicit, it cannot be effectively cross-examined, which is the primary aid that the trial offers judges and jurors to help them evaluate the trustworthiness and persuasiveness of evidence.[23]

A third threat that legal visual rhetoric may pose to good decision making is to trigger emotional reactions that overwhelm reasoned consideration of the evidence and arguments. Pictures that purport to describe reality re-semble unmediated reality more than words do[24] and therefore tend to elicit stronger emotional responses, similar to those aroused by the real thing depicted. At the same time, the associational logic through which pictures make meaning operates in large part subconsciously, so people often remain unaware of the true sources of the emotional associations that pictures pro-voke and the effects of those emotions on their judgments.[25] Although legal scholars debate to what extent jurors and judges actually do and/or should use their emotions in deciding cases,[26] the law, for the most part, formally discourages it, and everyone agrees that strong emotions can impair good thinking. For example, one study has shown (perhaps unsurprisingly) that gruesome crime scene photos make mock jurors angrier at and therefore more likely to convict the defendant.[27] The broader concern is that colorful fMRIs, vivid animations, and the many other kinds of pictures that judges and jurors are seeing will similarly lead to decision making that is overly influenced by emotional responses.

The threats reconsidered. Some expressions of concern about the effects of new media on legal thinking seem to be exaggerated. For instance, the oft-mentioned fear that legal discourse in a digital visual world will de-volve into something like advertising or political campaign films, where persuasion often depends on subconscious and emotional appeals and misleading representations of fact, is largely misplaced. To begin with, anyone who equates even the most adventurous courtroom multimedia to contemporary television or Internet advertising simply hasn't been paying very close attention to the ads. Thirty-second or shorter spots often con-tain far more features likely to distract audiences from message content: rapid cuts, pop music, dramatic camera angles, fantastical animations, celebrity endorsements, and so on, all of which clearly identify ads as a genre of entertainment far removed from demonstrative or argumenta-tive visuals in court. Indeed, as we saw in chapter 5, one of the plaintiffs' most effective maneuvers in *Cona and McDarby* was precisely to contrast the defendant Merck's slick television ads with the demeanor of the rest of the information presented at trial. Furthermore, unlike advertisements, aspects and implications of legal visual displays are subject to challenge by the opposing attorney, close judicial scrutiny, and later deliberation by decision makers. And, unlike most audiences for most political and prod-uct advertising, judges and jurors can test their responses to most court-room visuals against independent sources of information—the rest of the trial evidence, including that put forward by the opposing attorney.

We suspect that concerns about the threats that new media may pose to good legal thinking are partly driven by broader anxieties. After all, every medium of communication, including the spoken and the written word, may be used to persuade implicitly, through appeals to the emotions, and in ways of which the audience is not aware.[28] First impressions, for instance, can exert an undue influence on later judgments regardless of whether those impressions are prompted by visual or verbal stimuli.[29] Every new medium, moreover, provokes new concerns about improper influence and deception,[30] at least until the culture becomes acclimated to the medium and thus more savvy about its expressive and rhetorical capacities. Digital visuals and multimedia happen to be the new media in law, and the legal system has not yet adjusted to them.

A further anxiety arises from the perceived blurring or even dissolution of what many both inside and outside the profession like to believe have always been clear boundaries between the law and the culture at large.[31] Some legal professionals in particular may be anxious about the loss of control over the interpretation of meaning that seems inevitably to accompany the use of visuals and that digitization and the Internet are accelerating. They are anxious, too, about the demand for new professional competencies—in pictures, not words alone—and the suspicion that the skills that earned them success in law school and hence admission to the bar may no longer suffice for successful practice.[32] It is already difficult enough to master the practice of law. The prospect of having to cope with online adjudication and other dimensions of practice in virtual environments, discussed in chapter 6, only exacerbates these anxieties.

So, the threats to good legal thinking that the new media pose should be kept in perspective. Still, they have a real basis. The legal system, however, can take steps to reduce these threats to good thinking while retaining or increasing the judgmental benefits that the new media offer.

Judges, juries, and visual evidence. The critical moment for regulating legal decision makers' use of visual evidence, like any other kind, occurs when the trial judge decides whether to admit or exclude the evidence. In addition to the relevance and reliability rules discussed earlier, all jurisdictions have a very broad rule—in federal courts, Rule 403—which which allows judges to exclude any item of evidence if, despite being relevant and reliable, the item poses enough of a threat to good thinking.[33] This rule gives the trial judge discretion to keep out evidence whose probative value is substantially outweighed by its potential for creating unfair prejudice or confusion or for misleading the jury.[34] How should judges go about applying this vague balancing test to digital visual and multimedia evidence?

We propose that, in jury trials, judges should exercise their considerable discretion by letting jurors see all but the most incorrigibly prejudicial, misleading, or confusing displays. Given the fragmentary state of knowledge about the effects of visual and multimedia displays on thinking and judgment, any generalizations must be tentative. We believe, however, that decision making is more likely to be improved than impaired when properly informed jurors see the displays and deliberate about them together—and that when it's a close call, jurors thinking together are more likely to use displays in a way that improves judgment than the trial judge, thinking alone, might predict.[35]

Our position is based on two claims. First, at least for the near future, jurors in general are likely to be better than judges at "reading" visuals, precisely because jurors in general are more likely to be active participants in the digital visual culture described in chapter 1. They are at least as likely to have developed digital visual sophistication through their everyday practices of making, editing, comparing, and commenting on digital pictures.[36] They are, therefore, also in a better position to gauge the judgmental benefits that the visuals provide—to realize how much visuals and multimedia, over and above spoken words alone, add to their understanding of the facts and the respective parties' theories of the case.[37] Given the multiplicity of implicit meanings that a picture can generate, recognition of those meanings is likely to be dispersed among the picture's viewers, making this a situation in which, to borrow the legal scholar Cass Sunstein's language,[38] the knowledge possessed by "many minds" is superior to that possessed by a single person and in which the goal should be to elicit as much of that dispersed knowledge as possible. This leads to the second claim: When it comes to getting the most out of visuals and multimedia, jurors will have the benefit of discussing the displays during deliberation, sharing their multiple perspectives with one another and adding to their collective store of wisdom about how the visuals' multiple implications may help or impair their thinking.

We are, in short, advocating a bottom-up approach to the question of how digital visual and multimedia displays can best promote good legal thinking and judgment. This approach is consonant with the letter and spirit of the American Bar Association's recommendations for the conduct of jury trials, which provide, among other things, that "[p]arties and courts should be open to a variety of trial techniques to enhance juror comprehension of the issues," including "computer simulations . . . and other aids."[39] It recognizes and respects the knowledge about digital visuals and multimedia that jurors increasingly bring with them to court and trusts that letting jurors draw on that knowledge in reaching their decisions is more, not less, likely to yield good outcomes and good thinking.[40] Placing on jurors more of the responsibility for thinking about visual evidence and argument is consistent with both the ethos of the adversarial system and the general democratization of visual and multimedia meaning making that is taking place in the culture at large.

Improving legal visual literacy. We have argued that jurors who are *properly informed* can generally use new media in a way that improves their legal thinking and decision making. Jurors' ability to knowledgeably evaluate the visuals and multimedia they encounter derives from four sources: the judge, the lawyers, expert witnesses, and the jurors themselves. The legal system can and should improve each of these sources of digital visual literacy.[41]

Judges can be educated to make better admissibility rulings and, where the decision is to admit the evidence, to help jurors make better visual legal judgments. One way to enhance judges' visual literacy is through manuals like the Federal Judicial Center/National Institute for Trial Advocacy's *Effective Use of Courtroom Technology: A Judge's Guide to Pretrial and Trial,* which (among other things) alerts judges to particular features of visual displays that may mislead or distort jurors' judgments and advises judges about how to deal with them.[42] Another way is to offer judges continuing legal education in new media techniques.[43] This would help them to understand better the effects that the visual displays being offered in their courtrooms may create, to ask appropriate questions during any pretrial screenings of those displays, and to decide which displays the jurors should be prevented from seeing—or, in appropriate circumstances, to recommend modifications in the displays that would reduce risks of prejudice or confusion while retaining their probative value.

Judges who better appreciate the psychological and rhetorical effects of visual and multimedia displays will also be able to craft better instructions to guide jurors' consideration of those displays. One step is already being taken by the Oklahoma Criminal Court of Appeals, which has formulated model jury instructions to guide jurors in evaluating particular kinds of digital evidence. These instructions can spell out for jurors that a computer animation, for instance, is merely an illustration of one expert witness's testimony and is not itself evidence; that it is based on disputed facts and should be regarded as no more persuasive than the assumptions on which it is based; and that there may be specified differences (e.g., in scale, color, duration) between the animation and the facts it is offered to illustrate.[44]

We recommend that, in any case in which any visual or multimedia display is shown, jurors be instructed to think about and discuss the kinds of features that might affect their judgments about the display or the case as a whole, such as color, composition, iconography, or sequence. In addition, with respect to digital displays, jurors' attention should be called generally to how the technology and the medium may shape their perceptions and thinking. We have in mind, for instance, the kinds of effects that may have been produced by the use of multimedia in *Bontatibus* and *Skakel* and by the animation-video montage in *Murtha*.[45]

To be sure, psychological research[46] and some of the case studies of visual displays we have examined cast doubt on whether jurors can consistently adhere to all elements of such instructions—especially whether they can distinguish "merely illustrative" from "substantive" evidence, as the instructions some courts have used in connection with computer animations require. The research does suggest, however, that instructions that aim to bring to the surface jurors' preconceptions about the law can succeed in making them aware of beliefs that would otherwise remain implicit and thus help jurors to avoid the improper influence that those beliefs would otherwise exert on their decision making.[47] Similarly here, the main objective of instructions regarding the possible effects of visual displays is to get jurors to pay attention to and talk about aspects of the displays that might otherwise influence them without their noticing. We recommend that the instructions explicitly alert jurors to the likelihood that their responses to visual and multimedia displays may differ and encourage them to talk about their various reactions, to obtain the greatest benefit of their "many minds."[48]

In addition to crafting more thorough and effective instructions, judges could collectively assemble and share a library of visual explanations of basic, essentially uncontested, but complex and therefore potentially confusing subjects, not only for their own edification but also, with the parties' consent, for use as demonstrative evidence at trial. For example, the Federal Judicial Center has produced an educational video on the patent system for use by jurors.[49] And medico-legal and scientific animators have created visual explanations of complex subjects like DNA replication that courts may find useful as background information for jurors in relevant cases.[50]

Lawyers, in the course of direct and cross-examination and in closing arguments, can also help to educate jurors about the possible meanings of visual displays, but they themselves need to be sufficiently educated about the uses and effects of digital visuals and multimedia. Law schools are only beginning to introduce students to new media technologies and, in a few instances, to incorporate these technologies into courses on trial practice.[51] Continuing education programs sponsored by trial lawyers' groups can teach practitioners about persuasion in the digital age.[52]

Expert witnesses can also help educate jurors. First, where demonstratives are used to illustrate expert testimony about the facts of the case, the experts can take the time to teach the visuals to the jurors. As we discussed in chapter 4, experts can do this by carefully analyzing what particular visual features mean, as in the case of fMRIs; they might also helpfully address and correct jurors' likely misconceptions about those features. Forensic experts can also, where appropriate, demonstrate to the judge and jurors exactly how the visuals they use were created, as we saw in *Swinton*. This should not only assure decision makers about the reliability of the demonstrative (increasing good thinking) but also reduce the threats of confusion and unfair prejudice (reducing bad thinking).[53]

Second, in appropriate cases, judges may allow parties to introduce (or, using their authority under Rule 706 or state law equivalents, appoint) expert witnesses to explain the psychological effects of visual and multimedia displays. Just as some courts, concerned that jurors may give eyewitness testimony too much weight, allow expert testimony on the factors that extensive psychological research has shown affect the reliability of that testimony,[54] so courts may welcome expert explanations of possible cognitive and emotional effects of visual displays of which jurors would otherwise remain unaware. The proponent of such expert evidence would have to show (under Rule 702) that the testimony has adequate scientific support, and the opponent could attempt to show (under Rule 403) that it would so confuse jurors or delay the proceedings as to (substantially) outweigh the testimony's probative value. For this reason, expert testimony on visual and multimedia effects should probably be allowed only where the judge believes that a given display may be very important to the judgment (for instance, the video evidence in *Scott* or perhaps the Photoshop overlay in *Swinton*).

As for the jurors, their ability to respond intelligently and critically to visual and multimedia displays and to share their responses with each other would also be greatly enhanced if displays were permitted in the jury room during deliberations. Currently, visual displays treated as substantive evidence are admitted as full evidentiary exhibits that ordinarily go to the jury room, but "pure demonstratives" are not admitted as evidence and are generally not sent to the jury room.[55] Thus, some of the visual displays discussed in the book, such as the Lucis-enhanced photos in *Swinton*, would be reviewable during deliberations, but many others, including the photos and diagrams in *Skakel*, would not. The more courts follow the lead of the Connecticut Supreme Court in *Swinton* and subject all digitally processed pictures to more extensive authentication requirements, the more it makes sense for jurors to have access to all such pictures during deliberations in the same way that they have always had to pictures admitted as substantive evidence.[56]

There are several possible objections to allowing jurors freer access to courtroom visuals during deliberations. One is that, if the visual displays are taken into the jury room, the jurors may accord them too much importance relative to other trial information. This concern, however, must be balanced against another consideration: If the display is relevant and reliable enough to be shown to the jurors in the first place, jurors should be able to get the full advantage of looking at (and listening to) it carefully, as many times as they need to, instead of relying solely on their memories of it, which by the time the jury retires to deliberate may be weeks old.[57]

A second and related concern is that letting jurors review visual displays without the accompanying testimony that the displays were offered to illustrate may mislead or confuse them. This point applies with particular force to visual displays offered to illustrate expert evidence, such as the brain scans discussed in chapter 4, where at least part of the justification for admitting the pictures is that the expert's words help to explain the picture to the jurors. Our response is twofold: When reviewing the display in the jury room, jurors may rely on their notes on the testimony that an increasing number of judges allow them to take during trial.[58] And, as with any trial testimony, jurors may request that the judge read back to them the portions of the testimony, lay or expert, that they feel they need to understand the picture.[59]

A third set of concerns focuses on giving jurors the freedom to use interactive digital materials such as those used in the evidentiary phase of *Skakel* or the Soham case, discussed in chapter 6. It has been argued that jurors may not be technologically savvy enough to navigate interactive materials as well as the proponents did at trial, causing confusion and frustration, and that they may treat those materials as they would a computer game, trivializing and demeaning the trial process.[60] The latter criticism seems to us to place too little faith in jurors and the jury process. Most scholars have found that jurors take their obligations very seriously,[61] and we see no reason to believe that jurors who are even more engaged in the decision-making process (as interactive materials may prompt them to be) would do otherwise.[62] And both concerns could, if necessary, be adequately addressed by giving jurors access to interactive displays, not on their own in the jury room but by having them return to the courtroom, where court personnel could play back the portions they want to review.[63]

In sum, letting jurors see lawyers' visual and multimedia displays, not only during the evidentiary phase but again during deliberations, will maximize the benefits of those displays. It will increase the chance that the explanatory value of the displays will be appreciated and that the displays' implicit meanings will be noticed, made visible to the deliberating group, and subjected to the critical scrutiny of all. It is consistent with the spirit of the recent ABA *Principles for Juries and Jury Trials*, which encourage judges to promote the use of technology to enhance jurors' understanding of the case.[64] And it is the best way to keep the law in step with the digital age—to permit legal judgments to be made using the visual and multimedia tools on which our society at large increasingly depends and which people increasingly understand.

Fair Process. An ideal legal system provides fair procedures, which include equal opportunities for all parties to present their evidence and arguments to decision makers and sufficient transparency so that all parties know in advance what the rules and procedures governing evidence and arguments will be. Perhaps the most commonly expressed concern about the law's embrace of new visual and multimedia technologies is that parties' unequal access to the resources needed to use those technologies undermines this ideal of fairness. This is especially worrisome in the context of criminal trials, in which most defendants rely on underfunded (and overworked) public defenders to confront the generally superior (albeit hardly unlimited) resources of the prosecutor's office. In *Commonwealth v. Serge*, for instance, the Pennsylvania Supreme Court opined that "the relative monetary positions of the parties are relevant for the trial court to consider when ruling on whether or not to admit a [computer generated animation] into evidence" and that a disparity of resources that prevents a defendant from countering the prosecution's animation with one of his own could lead the court not to allow the prosecution's animation to be shown.[65]

Some preliminary research suggests that unequal use of new media may affect legal judgments: When one lawyer uses digital visuals and the opponent does not, the lawyer using them sometimes has an advantage.[66] Unequal use, however, does not imply unequal access. And we believe that concerns about unequal access, although real and perhaps especially compelling for criminal defendants whose liberty and even lives may be on the line, are generally overstated.[67] First, although the costs of high-end digital productions may be significant—computer animations, for instance, may cost tens of thousands of dollars—and will likely always be costly in the early stages of a technology's adoption, the costs of many legal visual and multimedia technologies are less substantial and in general are coming down.[68] Moreover, access to the hardware, software, and, most important, skills to create effective digital displays is increasing among lawyers, just as it is in society as a whole. Inequalities in access, then, are shrinking. Second, the very presumption that digital visual and multimedia technologies are a net cost of litigation may be mistaken. In return for the upfront investment in the visual displays, advocates may actually save time and money in preparing for and conducting the proceedings at which the displays are used—for instance, because using effective visual displays can result in more efficient witness examinations.[69] Third, aside from the cost of the continuing legal education we recommended earlier, there will sometimes be no out-of-pocket cost and so no resource inequality involved in being prepared to critique the other side's displays, which (as we argued) is an essential aspect of good lawyering in the digital visual age. In other instances, however, effective critique of an opposing display—for example, an accident or crime simulation—may require not only substantial preparation time but possibly also the cost of hiring one's own expert.

To the extent that unequal access to the means of making and presenting digital visual and multimedia displays remains a problem, legal and other public policy makers should be encouraged to consider providing funding and other resources so that all litigants can take advantage of the new media. The first step is already well under way: Federal court administrators and many of their state court counterparts have undertaken the task of equipping courtrooms with digital presentation systems.[70] States should also be encouraged to provide legal visual production technology and services to both state's attorneys' and public defenders' offices. In federal courts and some state courts, indigent defendants may apply to the court for funds to assist in the creation of visual displays.[71] Another possibility is for judges in particular cases to require, in appropriate circumstances, that any party that wants to create and use certain kinds of audiovisual displays provide sufficient funds to an opponent who demonstrates the need to produce its own displays.[72]

Fair process also requires that all parties have an adequate opportunity to examine and respond to opponents' visual and multimedia displays. Pretrial disclosure and discovery and in camera review of proposed visual displays serve this purpose and reduce some of the potential negative effects of unequal access.[73] Notice and disclosure requirements—for instance, an obligation to give the opposing lawyer most visuals and multimedia no fewer than thirty days before trial[74]—enhance fairness by giving the opponent an adequate opportunity to object (and, if possible, obtain a pretrial ruling on admissibility) and to prepare to meet the adversary's visual evidence if admitted.[75] At least one judge has proposed that any party wishing to introduce a computer animation or simulation be required to seek a pretrial ruling from the court on its admissibility.[76] We think, however, that the better rule is to leave the requirement of a pretrial motion and ruling to the discretion of the trial judge.[77] As digital visual and multimedia displays become increasingly common, trial judges should be permitted to perform triage and to demand pretrial hearings on only the more important ones. In any event, early disclosure and discovery of displays is not only good policy but generally good strategy; it helps proponents ensure that they are themselves well prepared for trial and puts them in a better position to overcome objections if the opponent waits until trial to raise them.[78] In the case of visuals and multimedia to be used solely for purposes of impeaching a witness's credibility or for closing argument, however, the general policy of openness should yield to the rule that protects an attorney from having to divulge his or her work product to the adversary.[79] Courts might, however, require (or lawyers may seek) prior in camera review of any visuals or multimedia to be used in closing that incorporate new audiovisual material in addition to what was previously displayed in court during the evidentiary phase.[80]

As legal proceedings increasingly rely on videoconferencing technology, ensuring that all videography and transmissions meet appropriate standards also becomes a matter of basic fairness.[81] As we observed in chapter 6, camera placement, angle, and lighting can all influence how viewers evaluate the remote witness (for example, a camera shot from above, looking down at the witness, can suggest lesser status), as can the presence of objects in the background of the frame. As yet, there are no clearly articulated standards for representation and transmission, but here are a few suggestions. In the case of incarcerated individuals being arraigned at a distance, for instance, the court needs to be satisfied that others in the remote room (but off camera) are not improperly influencing the proceedings.[82] At least as important, in two-way videoconferencing, cameras need to be arranged so that the view in the monitor implies appropriate eye contact, allowing viewers to make reasonably accurate judgments about whether the remote witness is being evasive or not. Standards should also take account of cultural differences that can contribute to the meaning of the interchanges, such as the appropriate perceived distance between speaker and audience.[83] Any of these effects, as well as transmission and other technical glitches that can degrade and thus diminish the witness's virtual presence in the courtroom, could be unfairly prejudicial to the witness and hence the party whose version of the facts the witness's testimony might otherwise support.[84] Although individual attorneys bear some responsibility for being familiar with courtroom technology (as we will discuss later), we believe that only the court is in a position to make sure that videoconferencing works adequately for everyone and therefore that courts ought to formulate the standards and provide the videoconferencing equipment to be used at trial. These standards could then inform the work of lawyers as well.[85]

A final step for ensuring that digital visuals and multimedia are used consistently with norms not only of fair process but also of judgmental accuracy and good thinking is to require that the displays be preserved so that appellate courts can adequately review their use. In most cases today, demonstratives not admitted as full trial exhibits do not even become part of the trial record; many are discarded or lost, thus becoming unavailable not only to judges but also to lawyers and legal scholars. Maryland's requirement that the proponent "preserve [all] computer-generated evidence, furnish it to the court clerk in a manner suitable for transmittal as part of the record on appeal, and present the . . . evidence to an appellate court if the court so requests,"[86] is a better practice. Finally, because so much of the meaning and effect of a display depends on how it is used, not only the display itself but also a video or other reasonably complete record of the moment in time when it was used should be preserved.[87] Ultimately, the legal system will have to change the way in which cases are reported so that at least those visual and multimedia displays that are addressed in the opinions become available to judges and lawyers in other cases.[88] Only then will meaningful comparative judgments and, eventually, a jurisprudence of new media be possible.[89]

Expressive Value. Expressive theories of law maintain that at least part of the justification for legal rules and practices is that they symbolize and publicly reaffirm and promote important societal values.[90] Given the criticisms of and concerns about digital visuals and multimedia already discussed, one might argue that this expressive value of law is also being threatened in the digital age. What kind of reasoned and just decision making do trials exhibit when jurors are inundated with slick PowerPoints, seemingly realistic but tendentious animations, and ever more ambitious multimedia displays? If only one side of the case uses high-tech visuals, the public may believe that fairness is undermined; if both sides use them, the trial may appear to be a competition of production values, rather than of evidentiary strength and cogency of argument. What valued social meaning is being expressed amid this extensive use of digital media?

Digital visuals and multimedia can enhance rather than impair both the theory and practice of justice—especially if lawyers take seriously the ethical obligations we recommend later regarding the use of pictures and if sound procedures enable all trial participants to engage in constructive conversations about those pictures.[91] The legal scholar Charles Nesson has written that the legitimacy of verdicts depends on the public's acceptance of them as true (enough) accounts of a real reality.[92] If that's so, a legal system in which the connections between pictures and reality are openly and critically contested holds forth at least the promise of making those connections, and the verdicts that depend on them, better understood and hence more widely accepted. Indeed, by fostering an informed and ethically responsible engagement with pictures, the legal system can express another positive value: exemplifying for the broader culture how the credibility and meanings of digital displays ought to be scrutinized and talked about, wherever those displays matter to people's beliefs and judgments.

The Ethical Use of Pictures

As we discussed in chapter 4, the trustworthiness of digital pictures is today a central concern for every discipline in which truth matters, including science, photojournalism, and law. Other fields, recognizing that gatekeepers (e.g., scientific journal editors or newspaper photo editors) cannot carry the entire load of ensuring the reliability of published pictures, have adopted best practices guidelines for those who make the pictures.[93] We believe that the law should do the same. But, developing guidelines for honest legal picturing is a more complicated affair, because legal advocacy involves making a case not just for what's true but for what's right. Lawyers choose and arrange their visual (and other) media to represent reality fairly and accurately but also to define issues, set agendas, and convey points of view. Every picture, like every word, is (or should be) part of an argument, so appropriate constraints on legal picture making have to take account of concerns that go beyond truthfulness or accuracy.

Moreover, in asking about the ethical use of pictures in law, we face a basic tension. On the one hand, the lawyer always sits behind any picture he or she shows and must remain ethically responsible for its use. On the other hand, any picture, perhaps especially a photo or video, seems to have an existence independent from that of the lawyer who deploys it. The picture itself seems to offer viewers access to legally relevant reality; it may even come to take the place of that reality in people's memories and imaginations.[94] The lawyer who uses the picture then seems to be merely a conduit for that visual truth, and the picture takes on a life of its own, generating responses that exceed the lawyer's control—and possibly the lawyer's and/or the audience's awareness.

We have argued throughout the book that pictures are ubiquitous and powerful, carriers of important information and not merely reflections of a preexisting reality. They are constitutive elements in a new visual and multimedia vernacular that connects what happens within the world of law with the common culture outside of it. As soon as the law allows these pictures to "speak," they acquire, as all speakers do, an ethical role. How much of the burden of ethically responsible picturing should be carried by the picture itself and how much by the lawyer (or legal visual consultant)?

Given these considerations, what might a norm of picture ethics for lawyers look like? It must address truthfulness in visual representation, but applied to a rhetorical situation in which truth is presented in the service of advocacy. The norm must be more permissive than the bounds of evidentiary admissibility, because lawyers must have room to advocate vigorously (and creatively) without having rejected proffers automatically impugned as unethical. Legal-picture ethics should also require transparency: Pictures that purport to depict reality must be open to scrutiny, and their makers must be prepared to document all stages of making, from pre- to postproduction. Legal-picture ethics should also require an awareness of the tools used to make, manipulate, and display pictures. Lawyers needn't acquire the skills of a graphics professional, but they must know enough about the technologies to ask their experts and their adversaries the right questions. Finally, picture ethics in law must be sensitive to the sociology of picture making and use: Any norm must apply to all phases of legal practice—not just courtroom advocacy, but also negotiation, mediation, and other situations in which neutral arbiters and detailed procedures are not available to protect against the use of misleading, unfair, or even flatly deceptive pictures.

With these thoughts in mind, we propose the following guidelines:

1. *Any picture that a lawyer uses to communicate with or persuade opposing counsel or third parties should reflect a reasonable effort to depict accurately or to explain or argue without misleading, distorting, or falsifying reality and may not have the overriding purpose of encouraging judgment on improper grounds.* The central duty not to use pictures to misrepresent, mislead, or falsify is consistent with lawyers' basic ethical obligation, expressed in the ABA *Model Rules of Professional Conduct,* not to knowingly make false statements of material fact or to falsify evidence.[95] It is also consistent with and serves the aims of the main rules governing the presentation and admissibility of demonstrative evidence: that each picture fairly and accurately represent what the witness claims it does and that any judgmental risks the picture poses (e.g., misleading viewers) not outweigh its probative value.[96]

The terms "misleading" and "distorting" must be construed in the context of the (potentially or actually) adversarial nature of law practice and the realization that, when parties dispute, key facts are usually contested. That is, mere partisanship does not make a picture "misleading." Advocates must be free to use pictures (and words) to express their views of the facts and the case, even though the opponents are likely to view things differently.[97] Relatedly, the need to allow advocates, when they are explicitly arguing, to go beyond the facts to present coherent and convincing theories of the case means that some manipulations of pictures that would arguably be unethical as demonstrative evidence because they distort reality might be ethically used in argument, so long as the creative depiction does not purport to be what it is not.[98]

Second, the norm imposes on lawyers a standard of reasonableness with regard to the accuracy of the pictures they use. Since lawyers' general ethics rules already prohibit knowing falsification, the issue is whether picture ethics should hold lawyers to any more rigorous standard than "don't lie." Although a good-faith standard would leave the greatest room for visual advocacy—and, given the underdeveloped state of professional knowledge about visuals and multimedia, would arguably be the fairest standard to adopt for the time being—the professional and popular concerns about the law's increasing use of new media indicate that lawyers should take the lead in assuming a higher standard of care. Lawyers should be expected to be sufficiently familiar not only with the facts represented in the picture but also with how the picture was made, and they should be reasonably conversant regarding the picture's likely cognitive and emotional effects. In short, they should be expected to possess sufficient visual literacy that they may properly be held accountable for using a picture that a reasonable lawyer should have known would pose a substantial risk of misleading its audience in some way that matters to the case.

Third, whether offered as evidence or in argument, lawyers have an ethical obligation not to use a picture for the overriding purpose of encouraging decision makers to decide on improper grounds, such as racial or other invidious bias, legally irrelevant or impermissible considerations, excessive emotionality, and other objectionable ways of reaching decisions. For instance, the *Hollywood Squares* portion of the closing argument video discussed in chapter 5 may well have had this kind of improper effect because it implicitly associated defendant Martin Siegel with "Fifth Amendment criminals" who, in the popular imagination, hide their guilt behind silence. Encouraging jurors in a civil case to draw an adverse inference from the defendant's claim of his Fifth Amendment privilege may not be prohibited, but it seems a less than honest strategy. In other cases, pictures might be so captivating that they distract jurors from (more reliable evidence of) the facts of the matter, leading to inaccurate judgments. However, since many pictures pose some risk of undermining the ideal of rational, deliberative judgment (as we explained in the preceding section), the proposed guideline does not make it unethical to create such improper effects, as long as producing those effects is not the advocate's overriding purpose in making and using the pictures.

2. *When a lawyer offers a picture as a depiction of reality, the picture and the lawyer should make the relationship between picture and reality transparent.* We have observed that, while lawyers use pictures to communicate and persuade, the pictures themselves "speak," sometimes in such a commanding voice that the pictures, and not the lawyers who offer them, seem to be the ones doing the communicating and persuading. For the very reason that viewers may be inclined to look to the picture to warrant its own credibility, the picture itself not only can but should bear some

of the burden of making clear how it mediates reality. This is especially so where there is any risk that viewers might otherwise be misled. We strongly recommend, therefore, that lawyers document how the final picture mediates reality. Who made the picture and how?

Adherence to this guideline entails several steps. First, the maker of the picture should be identifiable. If the picture is made by a visual consultant or other third person, that person should be prepared to stand behind the work—to be available to authenticate it if required by evidentiary rules (as discussed in chapter 4) and, at the very least, to provide the information needed for others to explain the picture's provenance when called upon.[99] Second, the original of an altered picture must be preserved unaltered for later comparison. This requires preservation of the raw data file in the case of a digital photo, of an archival print in the case of an analog photo, or of the unedited source tape(s) in the case of video. Third, every step between the original picture and the picture ultimately used should be properly documented.[100] And, fourth, where feasible, the process by which the original was transformed into the final version should be demonstrable, as it was in the case of the Lucis photo enhancement in *Swinton*, discussed in chapter 4.[101]

3. *A lawyer should know when to use pictures, be able to critique others' pictures, and have the visual and technological literacy to do both of these things well.* Lawyers need to use pictures in appropriate situations or at least be capable of using them. The *Model Rules of Professional Conduct* begin by requiring that lawyers shall provide clients with "competent representation," which is defined to include such "legal knowledge, skill, thoroughness, and preparation" as is reasonably necessary.[102] As the judges, jurors, and arbitrators who determine clients' rights and responsibilities increasingly expect and depend on visual and multimedia explanations and arguments, lawyers who cannot or do not use pictures, including new media, may at some point be seen as providing inadequate representation.[103]

A second, crucial affirmative responsibility is that lawyers who use pictures must open them up for critique and be prepared to explain and defend them. To the maximum extent consistent with other rules, lawyers must make their pictures available to opposing counsel and the court through early disclosure and discovery. This will provide adversaries with the greatest possible opportunities to see and think about the pictures and formulate their own verbal—or visual—responses, enhancing the depth and productivity of the ensuing dialogue about those pictures. As an

ethical habit, early disclosure will also help build a public image of lawyers in the digital age as forthright teachers and advocates, rather than as
concealers. And, when called upon to explain their pictures—for instance,
to the judge at a pretrial motion seeking permission to use digital media
at trial—lawyers must be able to talk about more than the relationship
between depictive pictures and the reality they purport to show. Lawyers
must also be ready to justify the full range of pictures they would use,
visual metaphors as well as "straight" documentation; they must be able
to persuade judges that their pictures fall within the range of permissible
advocacy and do not invite judgment on improper grounds.

A third obligation is to be able to respond to the pictures that opponents use, even with little or no preparation or preview of the other
side's visual materials. Lawyers need to respond on the fly to the opponents' pictures and reinterpret them in ways that help their client's
cause, for example, raising objections and then persuading the judge
that their interpretation supports the objection. During closing argument, they must be ready to try to correct any misimpressions which
the opponent's visuals may have created. Ideally, lawyers should be able
to respond to their opponents' visuals by designing their own counter-
visuals that would turn the opponents' displays against them (as, for
instance, we saw in Mark Lanier's use of PowerPoint in *Cona and Mc-
Darby* in chapter 5).

These affirmative obligations entail two others. Lawyers today should
have a responsibility to learn about the technologies of digital pictures
and multimedia. We do not expect that every lawyer will become an adept
in the use of every latest piece of picture making and presentation software; technologies change too quickly, and lawyers already have plenty of
work in keeping abreast of the law, mastering the facts of their cases, and
managing their practices. But, lawyers should know enough about how
pictures can be created and displayed that they can (i) make wise decisions about which aspects of their case to visualize, what kinds of pictures
to use, and which media to employ in making and displaying them; (ii)
make sure that the courtroom or other venue is properly equipped for the
intended presentation, provide their own equipment if desired and necessary, and be reasonably prepared to fix any technological difficulties that
may arise;[104] (iii) identify problems with the reliability or rhetorical effects
of their opponents' pictures and respond appropriately; and (iv) seek the
assistance of visual or communication consultants when it would be both
helpful and worth the expense.

For the same reasons, lawyers should be visually literate, which involves much more than knowing how to use PowerPoint or TrialDirector. It means being aware of the effects that pictures, as opposed to or in addition to words, can have on audiences. It means being alert to the multiple meanings that pictures can generate and the danger of concluding too soon that one has seen all there is to see. And it means having the mental flexibility to think visually as well as verbally: to recognize when a picture captures some crucial part of the theory of the case, making a thousand words unnecessary, or, when called upon, to be able to translate one's visual responses into words that colleagues, opponents, judges, and jurors can understand.

Taken together, these guidelines for picture ethics in law seek to promote good, responsible visual practices throughout the profession. Even though pictures do have a tendency to speak for themselves, so that decision makers may be drawn to the dummy rather than the ventriloquist, lawyers cannot abdicate to the pictures the ultimate responsibility for the meanings pictures make. The meanings of pictures are always constructions, the products of human design and picture-making technologies, and it is up to the lawyer to explain—to judges, jurors, other decision makers, and the public—how those pictures should be seen and understood. Moreover, by actively explaining their pictures and offering competing explanations for their opponents' pictures, lawyers (and the witnesses they put on the stand) can teach decision makers to make more informed judgments about the meanings of those pictures and their significance to the case. They can also keep their adversaries honest about their own uses of pictures. In these ways, good visual practices can improve the quality of legal decision making.

Digital Justice in a Democratic Society

Pictures are now a regular part of the practice of the law, and understanding and deploying them demands new skills on the part of lawyers, judges, and jurors. The burgeoning varieties of picturing that digital technologies make available complicate things still further: On the one hand, they promote fantasies of unprecedented access to truth (think, for example, of the fantastic voyages into data that the television show *CSI* regularly offers its viewers); on the other, they require ever more refined judgments about the actual reality those pictures depict (or, perhaps, falsify). If lawyers, judges, and jurors get smarter about making, using, and responding to pictures, it may help to counter what seems to be a growing public disillusionment with the legal system and the practice of law in general. Popular derogation of law and lawyers is nothing new, as indicated by the long history of lawyer jokes which foster as well as reflect public attitudes.[105] But, some of the contemporary criticism seems to come from a deep-seated suspicion and fear of pictures. If people believe that, in some important sense, all pictures can lie—that our visually mediated knowledge is unhinged from reality—then the more the law is infused with pictures, the more suspect it is. The more lawyers use pictures, the more opportunities they have to manipulate and the less they and the decisions to which they entice judges and juries should be trusted. The iconoclastic impulse on which this anxious view is based is just the flip side of naïve realism: Either pictures give us the truth, as the naïve realist assumes, or they're false, mischievous, and deceptive.

Our aim throughout the book has been to encourage the legal system and the public to replace both naïve realism and iconoclasm with a more rigorous and focused skepticism. Lawyers and judges need to understand and explain how pictures are constructed to make meanings and to help jurors and the public to do the same. This attitude is consistent with and, indeed, strengthens the belief that pictures can help us learn the truths we need to learn to do justice (albeit provisionally, partially, and subject to counterargument). Once naïve realism is transcended, retethering pictures to reality—insightfully debating how pictures represent reality, and with what effects for legal judgment—becomes possible. Legal decision makers need no longer be confined by the dichotomy of true versus false pictures.[106] And, as we have already said, lawyers working within a framework of ethical picturing obligations and appropriate procedures can model good, critical thinking and discourse about the credibility and meaning of pictures. Doing this and being recognized for it could help build the public image of lawyers as teachers as well as advocates, which we think would be a positive development.

Throughout the book we have emphasized new picturing practices that have arisen in the digital age: how people participate in making pictures, combine new and old data (that retain some "original" character due to digitization) to make new pictures, and circulate them freely (because the cost of "copies" is negligible), to suggest a few. We have also noted the presence of a new medium, cyberspace, and new habits of working on our computers with multiple windows open—and, through these windows, with many other people. Earlier in this chapter, in the context of jury decision making, we mentioned the power of many minds collaborating to parse the meaning of pictures shown in court. Cyberspace expands the possibilities for fruitful collaborations in every type of activity.[107] End users' experience of cyberspace, because of its webbed, laterally connected nature, tends to be empowering. Indeed, on the surface, cyberspace seems to be very democratic, letting a thousand flowers bloom a million times over.[108]

But the underlying software and hardware are not democratic in the same way.[109] Residents of virtual worlds are discovering the limits of virtual democracy. Linden Labs, asserting hierarchical management rights, closed down its Second Life forums, which had been a major site of news and community organizing, in favor of messaging from headquarters.[110] In contrast, when players of Eve Online accused employees of the owner, CCP Games, of intruding on the game in favor of certain players, CCP responded by forming a body of directors elected by the players to represent their interests; that group has now met face to face in Iceland (the home of CCP Games), a meeting that included a trip to the ancient seat of Icelandic democracy.[111] The corporate owners of the respective worlds, sharing the goal of keeping their player-members happy enough to maintain the revenue streams needed to preserve their worlds, thus dealt somewhat differently with the tension between lateral democracy and hierarchical control. The hardware on which any online system depends need not be democratically run, either, as the controversy involving telecommunication companies' compliance with government surveillance requests illustrates. A single room at AT&T's Internet and telephone hub in San Francisco allowed the company, at the government's request, to monitor and produce copies of all Internet traffic being carried by the company; had it not been for a whistleblower (who provided the documentation in connection with a class-action lawsuit years later), the public might never have learned about it.[112] The conduct was opaque; so are the consequences. This exemplifies the problem that the justice system faces in the digital age: How can there be enough transparency to avoid a Star Chamber?[113]

The migration of legal argument and judgment to cyberspace, which we sketched in chapter 6, demands that we ask what citizens can do to ensure that justice continues to flourish online. The faceless, seemingly automatic operations of judging machines, presaged by the algorithms employed by online settlement services today, may encourage users to think of adjudication less as a formal public event constituted through interpersonal relations among clients, lawyers, judge, and members of the public, and more in terms of a transaction for a fee—another commodity in a marketplace full of commodities. The consequence, according to the behavioral economist Dan Ariely, may well be to subsume the sense of justice under market norms, rather than social norms: a calculus oriented toward the costs and benefits of one's behavior to oneself, rather than a full consideration of the impact on others or the common good.[114]

Online adjudication may be understood as commodifying law in a second sense as well: by concealing from its users the conditions of its production, that is, the proprietary software that generates the outcomes. We recognize that the privatization of formerly public services is part of a larger sociopolitical trend and that different mixes of public and private can offer benefits that government services alone cannot.[115] But what if, in the justice system of the future, the habits of participation in self-governance that denizens of virtual worlds like Second Life have developed merely float on a surface constructed by proprietary code written and controlled by the system's owners?[116] In that event, online adjudication might well cut citizens loose from the sense of law as a public good established for the benefit of all citizens equally and responsive to the informed choices of the governed.

We believe that the continued legitimacy of online justice in a democratic society depends on transparency, public control, and informed consent. That is why we urged in chapter 6 that the public be involved in the design of the software and interface of the system of adjudication; that all software be open-source code, to promote visibility, accountability, and debugging; that all prospective users of the system be fully informed of the security and privacy implications of litigating online;[117] and that the government retain ownership of all data that pass through the system. In addition, procedures should be developed to ensure ongoing public participation in proposed revisions to the system, from changes in the appearance of the interface to the procedures for presenting evidence and argument and the methods of decision making. The particulars will very much depend on the sort of technologically mediated law we desire and where on the continuum from a "cyborg" court (i.e., a bricks-and-mortar courtroom with vastly enhanced information access and presentation capabilities) to a fully online and, perhaps, fully immersive online environment we want legal judgment to be located. The aim, in any event, will be to penetrate the opacity with which computing (for the reasons we discussed in chapter 6) is too often cloaked and thus to keep online justice open to democratic scrutiny and change.

Law in any culture, anthropologists tell us, is a complex of intersecting rules, norms, and practices for negotiating among conflicting needs and desires.[118] Recent neuroscientific research suggests that, at the level of brain biology, our sense of justice is also a complex thing, emerging from discrete brain areas responsive to fairness and efficiency.[119] The mixed system of law that our culture has evolved may well reflect this tension in our minds. Its strength, at a very general level, derives from its alternating currents: law as interplay between the making of rules and the crafting of fair procedures; justice as the equality of all under uniform rules and fairness as making complex judgments in thick factual contexts; dispute resolution as truth seeking through the application of reason and as persuasion on behalf of clients, in a "theater of justice."[120] Online justice may appeal to the efficiency-minded; as we saw in chapter 6, that has been its main selling point. Those who care more about the theater of justice may also find themselves attracted to online adjudication (especially when the bandwidth increases and fully immersive virtual proceedings become possible) because they can gather there with a wider community and be judged, if not by a jury of peers, then at least by a group among whom expressive power will be recognized and valued.[121] The problem with both of these types of desire for justice is that the technology itself narrows and "purifies" the muddy complexity of the human legal culture that has been constructed over a much longer period of time. We are not arguing against the technology; it is here to stay. We are, however, urging that the public overcome its credulity regarding the technology, just as it must overcome naïve realism about pictures, in order to resist fantasies of perfect justice that could leave our society without a rule of law deserving of a democratic citizenry's respect and allegiance.[122] By confronting with open eyes the potential perils of law in the digital age, we stand a better chance of realizing law's promise.

Notes

1. The tape can be viewed at http://www.youtube.com/watch?v=ROn_9302UHg (last accessed July 31, 2008).

2. California v. Powell, No. BA 035498 (Cal. Super. Ct., L.A. County, April 30, 1992) (first Rodney King trial); California v. Simpson, No. BA 097211, 1995 WL 704342 (Cal. Super. Ct. L.A. County, September 29, 1995) (Simpson criminal trial). Both trials inspired extensive commentary in the legal academy and the popular media.

3. Lawrence Lessig, *Free Culture* (New York: Penguin, 2004), 36. After we wrote early drafts of this chapter, we discovered Scott McCloud's *Making Comics* (New York: Harper, 2006), the first chapter of which is titled "Writing With Pictures." In a footnote, McCloud attributes the phrase to the renowned comic artists Will Eisner and Art Spiegelman (ibid., 54). McCloud's analyses of how comics combine words and pictures are highly relevant to our own concerns. We also note that Edward Tufte, in his *Beautiful Evidence* (Cheshire, CT: Graphics Press, 2006), the most recent (as of this writing) of his wonderful books on information design, seems to be getting at a similar notion, albeit in the limited context of graphic representations of quantitative data, when he describes *sparklines* as "wordlike" (ibid., 49).

4. See, e.g., Elizabeth Mertz and Jonathan Yovel, "The Role of Social Science in Legal Decisions," in *Handbook of Law and Society*, ed. Austin Sarat (London: Blackwell, 2004), 410–434 (discussing different epistemological aims and norms in social science and law).

5. There is a considerable scholarly tradition of reducing "thinking" to the verbal and mathematical. For a leading contemporary exposition of the anti-mental imagery position, see Zenon Pylyshyn, *Seeing and Visualizing: It's Not What You Think* (Cambridge, MA: MIT Press, 2003). For a leading exposition of the contrary position, see, e.g., George Lakoff and Mark Johnson, *Philosophy in the Flesh* (New York: Basic Books, 1999).

6. To illustrate: We might speak of the *image* of the *Mona Lisa* deployed in the Prince Spaghetti sauce ads in a campaign designed by M&R Hess in the mid-1980s (http://www.hessdesignworks.com/Mona's.html [last accessed July 31, 2008]). The ads presented a pair of *pictures*: on the left, the "regular" *Mona Lisa*, a reproduction of the famous painting; on the right, a "chunky" Mona (each holding an appropriately labeled jar of spaghetti sauce). The cover of the February 8, 1999, issue of the *New Yorker* featured a picture of Monica Lewinsky as Mona Lisa that must have been read by those who had seen the Prince ad as (among other things) a comment about the young woman's weight. The cover of the June 2005 *AARP Bulletin* similarly harks back both to Leonardo's masterpiece and the Prince campaign with a picture of an aged, heavy Mona Lisa in the style of Fernando Botero (who had made his own version of the painting in 1977). Following our terminology, the *pictures* are what appear on the magazine covers and in the Prince ad. The Leonardo reference is an *image* to which the pictures allude (or which the pictures evoke); the Botero reference evoked by the picture on the *AARP Bulletin* cover and the Prince ad campaign as evoked by the picture on the *New Yorker* cover are images, as well. (For the *New Yorker* cover, see http://www.studiolo.

org/Mona/MONA31.htm [last accessed July 31, 2008]; for the *AARP Bulletin* cover, see http://
www.aarp.org.mill1.sjlibrary.org/bulletin/toc/toc_aarp_bulletin_2005_all.html.) Many variant uses
of "image," "picture," "visual representation," and the like may be found in the literature; ours is
consistent with that of the visual theorist W. J. T. Mitchell. W. J. T. Mitchell, *Iconology* (Chicago:
University of Chicago Press, 1986); Mitchell, *Picture Theory* (Chicago: University of Chicago Press,
1994), 4 n. 5.

7. Models are not two-dimensional; neither are the immersive virtual environments that may
soon be used in court (see chapter 6). As external visual representations, however, both should
be considered "pictures" in our sense of the word.

8. In *The Domain of Images* (Ithaca: Cornell University Press, 1999), James Elkins somewhat
similarly maps visual representations into pictures, writings, and notations. We have learned
much from Elkins's outstanding work, but it's not our intention to adopt his taxonomy or to take
on any of the conceptual claims behind it.

9. As Steven Pinker, the cognitive linguistics scholar, has written, "the principle of the arbitrary sign is a powerful tool for getting thoughts from head to head." Steven Pinker, *The Blank
Slate* (New York: Penguin, 2002), 3.

10. Steven Pinker, *The Language Instinct* (New York: HarperCollins, 1994).

11. See Geoffrey R. Loftus, Walter W. Nelson, and Howard J. Kallman, "Differential Acquisition Rates for Different Types of Information From Pictures," *Quarterly Journal of Experimental
Psychology* 35A (1983): 187–98.

12. Stephen Kosslyn, *Image and Brain* (Cambridge, MA: MIT Press, 1994).

13. Joseph LeDoux, *The Emotional Brain* (New York: Simon & Schuster, 1996).

14. In Rudolf Arnheim's terminology, representational pictures are *isomorphic* with their referents, in contrast to the *conventional* relationship of words to their referents. Rudolf Arnheim,
Visual Thinking (Berkeley: University of California Press, 1971), 227.

15. The neurons involved in vision do not distinguish between visual representation and
reality.

16. We have in mind here what semioticians call *indexical* signs: The signifier is in some
sense contiguous with, although it need not resemble, the signified. The father of semiotics, the
philosopher Charles Sanders Pierce, gave as the prototypical indexical sign the footprint Robinson Crusoe found in the sand: The footprint meant that an animal had been there because the
animal had left (caused) the print. See Thomas A. Sebeok, *Signs* (Toronto: University of Toronto
Press, 1994), 31–32.

17. E.g., Richard Sherwin, Neal Feigenson, and Christina Spiesel, "Law in the Digital Age,"
Boston University Journal of Science and Technology Law 12, no. 2 (Summer 2006): 227–70.

18. Daniel T. Gilbert, "How Mental Systems Believe," *American Psychologist* 46, no. 2 (February 1991): 107–19.

19. Robert Robinson and others, "Actual Versus Assumed Differences in Construal: 'Naïve
Realism' in Intergroup Perception and Conflict," *Journal of Personality and Social Psychology* 68,
no. 3 (March 1995): 404–17.

20. These same frontal lobe regions take the longest to develop fully. E.g., Bruce Wexler,
Brain and Culture (Cambridge, MA: MIT Press, 2006), 105.

21. Daniel Kahneman, "Maps of Bounded Rationality: A Perspective on Intuitive Judgment
and Choice" (Nobel Prize Lecture, December 8, 2002), http://nobelprize.org/nobel_prizes/eco-
nomics/laureates/2002/kahnemann-lecture.pdf (last accessed July 31, 2008).

22. Indeed, according to research in what cognitive psychologists call *processing fluency*, the
easier it is for people to understand something, the more likely they are to believe that it's true.
(See Piotr Winkielman and others, "Cognitive and Affective Consequences of Visual Fluency:
When Seeing Is Easy on the Mind," in *Persuasive Imagery*, ed. Linda M. Scott and Rajeev Batra
[Mahwah, NJ: Erlbaum, 2003], 75–89.) Thus, one study shows that statements are more likely to

be judged true when they are easier to read (Rolf Reber and Norbert Schwarz, "Effects of Perceptual Fluency on Judgments of Truth," *Consciousness and Cognition* 8, no. 3 [September 1999]: 338–42). It follows that if people more readily think that they "get it" when they see a picture as opposed to reading or hearing words, they're more likely to think that what they're seeing is true. We refer to processing fluency in chapter 3 and elsewhere. For a highly readable popular treatment of intuitive judgment generally, see Malcolm Gladwell, *Blink* (New York: Little, Brown, 2005).

23. Robert Hopkins, *Picture, Image and Experience* (Cambridge: Cambridge University Press, 1998).

24. Visual and verbal representations of actual or imagined reality have long been in tension. The literary critic Erich Auerbach (*Mimesis: The Representation of Reality in Western Literature*, trans. Willard Task [Garden City, NY: Doubleday Anchor, 1953]) famously contrasted the picturing world of the ancient Greeks to the (largely) anti-iconic culture of the Hebrews. The visual theorist W. J. T. Mitchell (*Iconology*), among others, has described the dialectics of *ekphrasis* (the verbalization of the visual) and *ut pictura poesis* (the consonance of painting with poetry) since the Renaissance. The cultural historian Martin Jay (*Downcast Eyes: The Denigration of Vision in Twentieth-Century French Thought* [Berkeley: University of California Press, 1993], 594) has opposed what he sees as a felt need to reduce complexity and to establish hierarchy reflected in the denigration of vision in modern French thought with an appreciation for the irresolvable play of vision and visuality "in all their rich and contradictory variety."

25. On the critical role of visual perception and graphic representation of visual evidence in early modern science, see, e.g., Edward Tufte, *Beautiful Evidence* (Cheshire, CT: Graphics Press, 2006) (on Galileo's 1610 *Starry Messenger*); on "virtual witnessing," see Steven Shapin and Simon Schaffer, *Leviathan and the Air-Pump* (Princeton: Princeton University Press, 1985); on the dialectic between (analog) visual and quantitative technologies and representations of modern particle physics, see Peter Galison, *Image and Logic* (Chicago: University of Chicago Press, 1997). For good collections of readings on vision and visualization in the history of science, see, e.g., Michael Lynch and Steve Woolgar, eds., *Representation in Scientific Practice* (Cambridge, MA: MIT Press, 1988); Luc Pauwels, ed., *Visual Cultures of Science* (Hanover, NH: Dartmouth College Press, 2006). (We return to this topic in chapter 4.)

26. Among many excellent books that could serve as introductions to these topics, see Ann Marie Seward Barry, *Visual Intelligence* (Albany: SUNY Press, 1997); Donald Hoffman, *Visual Intelligence* (New York: Norton, 1998); Barbara Maria Stafford, *Visual Analogy* (Cambridge, MA: MIT Press, 1999); Elkins, *The Domain of Images*; James Elkins, *The Object Stares Back* (San Diego: Harcourt, 1996); Mitchell, *Picture Theory*; W. J. T. Mitchell, *What Do Pictures Want?* (Chicago: University of Chicago Press, 2006).

27. Malcolm McCullough, *Abstracting Craft* (Cambridge, MA: MIT Press, 1994), 42.

28. Annys Shin, "Newspaper Circulation Continues to Decline," *The Washington Post*, May 3, 2005, http://www.washingtonpost.com/wp-dyn/content/article/2005/05/02/AR2005050201457. html (last accessed July 31, 2008) ("The decline [in newspaper circulation in the six months ending March 31, 2005] continued a 20-year trend in the newspaper industry as people increasingly turn to other media such as the Internet and 24-hour cable news networks for information.").

29. Marshall McLuhan, *Understanding Media* (Cambridge, MA: MIT Press, 1964).

30. This and the next paragraph are adapted from Sherwin, Feigenson, and Spiesel, "Law in the Digital Age," 249–50.

31. Stephen McKenna, "Advertising as Epideictic Rhetoric," in *Rhetoric, the Polis, and the Global Village*, ed. C. Jan Swearingen and Dave Pruett (Mahwah, NJ: Erlbaum, 1999), 103–19.

32. It has been two generations since the historian Daniel Boorstin lamented the increasing dependence of politics on staged spectacles and photo opportunities. Daniel Boorstin, *The Image*

(New York: Atheneum, 1962). For other classic treatments of the topic, see Joe McGinniss, *The Selling of the President 1968* (New York: Trident Press, 1969); Joan Didion, "Insider Baseball," in *After Henry* (New York: Simon & Schuster, 1992), 47–86, on the packaging of the 1988 presidential race.

33. Robin Andersen, *Consumer Culture & TV Programming* (Boulder, CO: Westview Press, 1995), 211–24.

34. On *COPS*, see Elayne Rapping, *Law and Justice as Seen on TV* (New York: New York University Press, 2003); on *Profiles From the Front Lines*, see Neal Feigenson, Richard Sherwin, and Christina Spiesel, "Reality TV: The War on Terror" (paper on file with authors).

35. See Andersen, *Consumer Culture*, 29–32; David Barstow and Robin Stein, "Under Bush, A New Age of Prepackaged News," *New York Times*, March 13, 2005.

36. Stewart's reputation has continued to grow; in a 2007 poll, he ranked fourth among most admired journalists, tied with several network news anchors. Michiko Kakutani, "Is Jon Stewart the Most Trusted Man in America?," *New York Times*, August 15, 2008.

37. The concept of "visual literacy" dates at least to the 1960s and that of "media literacy" to the 1980s (see Kathleen Tyner, *Literacy in a Digital World* [Mahwah, NJ: Erlbaum, 1998], 104–6, 118), but both are still novel ideas in legal pedagogy. For an introduction to legal visual pedagogy, see Christina Spiesel, Richard Sherwin, and Neal Feigenson, "Law in the Age of Images: The Challenge of Visual Literacy," in *Contemporary Issues of the Semiotics of Law*, ed. Anne Wagner, Tracy Summerfield, and Farid Benavides (Oñati International Series in Law and Society) (Oxford: Hart, 2005), 231–55.

38. One way to think about the difference between words and pictures in what is now a "standard" legal culture is to think about how surprising it would be to search electronic databases like Lexis and Westlaw and find the visuals that were used as part of the case file, available for researchers to use. This may be changing, however, as we'll see in chapter 2: In *Scott v. Harris*, 127 S. Ct. 1769 (2007), for the first time, the U.S. Supreme Court posted on its Web site a link to the video evidence on which its opinion was based.

39. See http://www.npd.com/press/releases/press_060306.html (last accessed July 31, 2008).

40. See http://lyra.ecnext.com/coms2/summary_0290-521_ITM (last accessed July 31, 2008).

41. Ray Kurzweil, *The Singularity Is Near* (New York: Viking, 2005), 48–84. Paul Martin Lester, "Digital Hegemony: The Clash Between Words and Pictures" (1996), http://commfaculty.fullerton.edu/lester/writings/murspeech.html (last accessed July 31, 2008), offers a summary of the rate of technological change: "[I]f a generation is about 20 years, from cave drawings to writing is 1,275 generations; writing to the printing press is 250 generations; from the printing press to photography is 19 generations; from photography to desktop computing is seven generations; and from desktop computing to the Web is less than one half of one generation."

42. Digitally editing family photos to create a more ideal record of one's past, for instance, is becoming commonplace. Alex Williams, "I Was There. Just Ask Photoshop," *New York Times*, August 15, 2008.

43. And then they can try out three-dimension modeling with Google's Sketch-up software. See http://sketchup.google.com/ (last accessed July 31, 2008).

44. See http://en.wikipedia.org/wiki/Youtube (last accessed July 31, 2008). As of this writing, Facebook may have exceeded MySpace in number of users. Michael Arrington, "Facebook No Longer the Second Largest Social Network," June 12, 2008, http://techcrunch.com/2008/06/12/facebook-no-longer-the-second-largest-social-network/ (last accessed February 5, 2009) (both services attracting about 115 million people to their respective sites each month). It is difficult to compare YouTube usage directly with that of either Facebook or MySpace because the data aren't comensurate: number of video posts for YouTube versus "users" or "accounts" for the social networks.

On November 13, 2006, Google bought YouTube for $1.65 billion (http://en.wikipedia.org/wiki/Youtube). Since then, the site has continued to grow in cultural importance. For instance, in 2007, CNN televised debates among the candidates seeking to be nominated for president by the respective major parties, using questions submitted by the public via YouTube (Spencer A. Beckett II, "The YouTube Debates," http://bgeek.com/2007/07/23/the-youtube-debates/ [last accessed July 31, 2008]).

45. Bill Carter, "Thanks to YouTube Fans, 'Nobody's Watching' May Return From the Dead," *New York Times*, July 3, 2006.

46. These programs include Image Pro Plus (http://www.mediacy.com/index.aspx?page=IPP [last accessed July 31, 2008]); Mathematica (http://www.wolfram.com/ [last accessed July 31, 2008]); and Sigma Plot (http://www.systat.com/products/sigmaplot/ [last accessed July 31, 2008]).

47. For instance, architects use Autodesk's Autocad (http://usa.autodesk.com/adsk/servlet/index?siteID=123112&id=2704278 [last accessed July 31, 2008])for drafting and other graphics software, as well as more traditional drawing and 3-D models to plan buildings and display their proposals. Screenwriters and producers need no longer rely on hand-drawn storyboards; software such as FrameForge (http://www.frameforge3d.com/ [last accessed July 31, 2008]) allows them to create simple animations with manipulable lighting and camera angles so that they can decide in advance which shots are physically possible and aesthetically suitable.

48. See http://www.americasarmy.com (last accessed July 31, 2008).

49. Jay David Bolter and Richard Grusin, *Remediation* (Cambridge, MA: MIT Press, 1999).

50. Lev Manovich, *The Language of New Media* (Cambridge, MA: MIT Press, 2001), 83–86.

51. "Bluescreen" (the more general term is *chroma key*) is a video compositing technique for blending two images, in which a color (or a small color range) from one image is removed (or made transparent), revealing another image behind it. This technique is also referred to as color keying, color-separation overlay, and greenscreen. Readers may be most familiar with it from television weather forecasts, in which the presenter appears to be standing in front of various maps but is actually standing in front of a green or blue background. See "Chroma key," http://en.wikipedia.org/wiki/Bluescreen (last accessed July 31, 2008).

52. Wexler, *Brain and Culture*. Wexler argues that the neural interconnections whose interactivity characterizes the human brain depend on the nature of the sensory stimulation offered to the person and that, as adults act on their environments to preserve conformity between the external world and their (increasingly inflexible) internal world, they change the external world in which their children grow up, and hence the sensory stimulation available to the children, and hence their children's developing brains.

53. Robert Kenny, "Evaluating Cognitive Tempo in the Digital Age," *Educational Technology, Research, and Development* (2007), DOI 10.1007/s11423-007-0035-8 (online).

54. See, e.g., Roy D'Andrade, "Cultural Meaning Systems," in *Culture Theory: Essays on Mind, Self, and Emotion*, ed. Richard A. Shweder and Robert A. Le Vine (Cambridge: Cambridge University Press, 1986), 88–120; Clifford Geertz, *The Interpretation of Cultures* (New York: Basic Books, 1973); Claude Levi-Strauss, *The Savage Mind* (Chicago: University of Chicago Press, 1968); Richard Shweder, *Thinking Through Cultures* (Cambridge, MA: Harvard University Press, 1991).

55. Michael Cole and Jan Derry, "We Have Met Technology and It Is Us," in *Intelligence and Technology*, ed. Robert J. Sternberg and David D. Preiss (Mahwah, NJ: Erlbaum, 2005), 210.

56. Walter Ong, *Orality and Literacy* (London: Routledge, 1982), 78–116. Ong explains that, whereas thinking in an oral culture tends to be situational and in the moment and learning and knowing tend to be empathic and participatory, for instance, writing tends to separate the knower from the known, making possible more abstract and precise conceptual thought, a sense of objectivity, and an ability to be more articulately introspective (ibid., 36–49, 105).

57. For one thing, the new media and technologies are being introduced into a print-literate culture, and so we might expect that at first they would be closely bound to the purposes, and hence the mental habits, of literate verbal communication. See Tyner, *Literacy in a Digital World*, 13, 39–40. It could therefore take some time before a more distinctively "digital visual consciousness" emerges. (In a similar way, the introduction of the alphabet and writing into ancient Greece did not immediately transform an oral into a generally literate culture; what was needed was not only a critical mass of written texts but also a revaluation of the relative worth of oral and written communication in the transmission of the culture's most important traditions. Eric A. Havelock, "The Coming of Literate Communication to Western Culture," in *Perspectives on Literacy*, ed. Eugene R. Kintgen, Barry M. Kroll, and Mike Rose [Carbondale: Southern Illinois University Press, 1988], 130.) This partial containment of new media by older ones is precisely what Bolter and Grusin mean by "remediation."

58. Ian Hacking, *Representing and Intervening* (Cambridge: Cambridge University Press, 1983), 139.

59. William J. Mitchell, *The Reconfigured Eye* (Cambridge, MA: MIT Press,1994), 31.

60. See, e.g., Brad Hokanson, "Digital Image Creation and Analysis as a Means to Examine Learning and Cognition," *Lecture Notes in Computer Science—Cognitive Technology* (2001): 229 (reporting study showing that graphic design students using Adobe Photoshop "use[d] words *and* images in the creation of new images").

61. See http://urbanlegends.about.com/library/blphoto-wtc.htm (last accessed July 31, 2008). Viewers familiar with the observation deck of the World Trade Center should have realized that the initial "Tourist Guy" photo was impossible, because the deck was never open to the public at the time of day indicated in the mashup.

62. See Anne Friedberg, *The Virtual Window* (Cambridge, MA: MIT Press, 2006), 193–94; see also chapter 6.

63. Kevin LaGrandeur, "Digital Images and Classical Persuasion," in *Eloquent Images*, ed. Mary E. Hocks and Michelle R. Kendrick (Cambridge, MA: MIT Press, 2003), 117–36.

64. On the relationship between changing technologies of communication and increasing democratization of political expression in the eighteenth century, see, e.g., Nicholas Lemann, "Amateur Hour," *New Yorker* (August 7, 2006), 44–49; Simon Schama, *Citizens* (New York: Knopf, 1989).

65. Beaumont Newhall, *The History of Photography* (New York: Museum of Modern Art, 1982); John Szarkowsky, *Photography Until Now* (New York: Museum of Modern Art, 1989). For a critical discussion of why photographs can be understood only through context, see Mary Price, *The Photograph: A Strange Confined Space* (Stanford, CA: Stanford University Press, 1994).

66. Specialist Sabrina Harmon, who took the picture, has explained some of her various motivations for documenting what went on at Abu Ghraib. See Philip Gourevitch and Errol Morris, "Exposure: The Woman Behind the Camera at Abu Ghraib," *New Yorker* (March 24, 2008), http://www.newyorker.com/reporting/2008/03/24/080324fa_fact_gourevitch (last accessed July 31, 2008). Harmon was convicted by court-martial, in May 2005, of conspiracy to maltreat prisoners and other offenses.

67. E.g., James Allen and others, *Without Sanctuary: Lynching Photography in America* (Santa Fe, NM: Twin Palms, 2000).

68. Richard Serra's "Stop Bush" can be seen at www.artsjournal.com/man/2004/07/ (last accessed July 31, 2008). A major series of paintings was done by Fernando Botero (now presented to the Berkeley Arts Museum in Berkeley, California); see http://www.marlboroughgallery.com/artists/botero/artwork.html (last accessed July 31, 2008). On August 6, 2004, the comedian Bill Maher performed a segment on Abu Ghraib in which he stood on a box and delivered a monologue in the same pose, and the major studio film *Children of Men* (directed by Alfonso Cuarón [Universal Pictures, 2006]) references it almost casually as a prisoner is shown outside a bus

stop at a prison in the hooded costume (http://img233.imageshack.us/img233/718/016bp0.jpg [last accessed July 31, 2008]). The image even inspired a child's Halloween costume (http://www.thestranger.com/images/extra/special/halloween04_10.jpg [last accessed July 31, 2008]). The prisoner in the original photo, Ali Shalal Qaissi, later helped to start an advocacy group for former prisoners and torture victims and uses the iconic picture on his business card. Hassan Fattah, "Symbol of Abu Ghraib Seeks to Spare Others His Nightmare," *New York Times*, March 11, 2006.

69. The media scholar John Fiske first drew the distinction between a passively absorbed "mass" media culture and a participatory "popular" media culture. John Fiske, *Reading the Popular* (Boston: Unwin Hyman, 1989).

70. For extended discussions of this and other examples of popular participation in mediated entertainments, see Henry Jenkins, *Convergence Culture* (New York: New York University Press, 2006).

71. For Star Wars selections on YouTube, start with "Monty Python Star Wars," http://www.youtube.com/watch?v=2CLwxObfaNE (last accessed July 31, 2008); "Star Wars Help Desk," http://www.youtube.com/watch?v=oQ8DriPCX2o&feature=related (last accessed July 31, 2008); and "StarTrek vs. Star Wars," http://www.youtube.com/watch?v=hNxhrPaaCA4&feature=related (last accessed July 31, 2008). For a critical discussion, see Henry Jenkins, "Quentin Tarantino's Star Wars? Digital Cinema, Media Convergence, and Participatory Culture," in *Rethinking Media Change*, ed. David Thorburn and Henry Jenkins (Cambridge, MA: MIT Press, 2003), 281–341. For a discussion of the afterlife of the television series *Xena The Warrior Princess*, see Sharon Cumberland, "Private Uses of Cyberspace: Women, Desire, and Fan Culture," in ibid., 261–79.

72. See Neal Feigenson, "Digital Visual and Multimedia Software and the Reshaping of Legal Knowledge," in *Images in Law*, ed. Anne Wagner and William Pencak (Aldershot, UK: Ashgate, 2006), 97–98.

73. See Yochai Benkler, *The Wealth of Networks* (New Haven: Yale University Press, 2006), 212–72.

74. www.news.google.com; www.digg.com; www.reddit.com/ (all last accessed July 31, 2008).

75. Michael Lewis, *Next* (New York: Norton, 2001), 87–109.

76. See Gavriel Salomon, ed., *Distributed Cognitions* (Cambridge, UK: Cambridge University Press, 1993).

77. Cass Sunstein, *Infotopia* (Oxford: Oxford University Press, 2006).

78. For an insightful analysis of these and other ideas concerning the interpenetration of law and popular culture, see Richard Sherwin, *When Law Goes Pop* (Chicago: University of Chicago Press, 2000).

79. See Jennifer Mnookin, "The Image of Truth: Photographic Evidence and the Power of Analogy," *Yale Journal of Law and the Humanities* 10 (Winter 1998): 1–74. We discuss the law of demonstrative evidence in chapter 3.

80. Private communication from David Bolinsky, XVIVO Inc. (visual consultant in the case mentioned).

81. This is the Soham murder case, which we discuss briefly in chapter 6.

82. E.g., Gordon Bermant, "Courting the Virtual: Federal Courts in an Age of Complete Inter-Connectedness," *Ohio Northern University Law Review* 25 (1999): 527–62 (discussing virtual proceedings); Paul D. Carrington, "Virtual Civil Litigation: A Visit to John Bunyan's Celestial City," *Columbia Law Review* 98 (October 1998): 1516–37 (describing trials consisting entirely of previously prepared digital visual presentations, in which "trial advocacy will more closely resemble the work of the Hollywood film producer and less that of the Hollywood actor"); Nancy Marder, "Cyberjuries: The Next New Thing?," *Information and Communications Technology Law* 14, no. 2 (June 2005): 165–98 (discussing cyberjuries and their relationships to traditional juries); Henry H. Perritt, Jr., "Changing Litigation with Science and Technology: Video Depositions, Transcripts, and Trials," *Emory Law Journal* 43 (Summer 1994): 1071–93 (discussing possibility of entirely pre-recorded trials).

CHAPTER 2

1. The sociologist Kim Lane Scheppele calls the notion that the most reliable knowledge comes from the evidence that is closest to the event the "Ground Zero" theory of evidence. Kim Lane Scheppele, "The Ground-Zero Theory of Evidence," *Hastings Law Journal* 49, no. 2 (January 1998): 321–34.

2. 127 S. Ct. 1769 (2007).

3. *Scott*, Brief of Appellee-Respondent Victor Harris, 2007 U.S. S. Ct. Briefs LEXIS 16, at *3.

4. *Scott*, Petition for Writ of Certiorari, 2006 U.S. S. Ct. Briefs LEXIS 2948, at *3–4.

5. *Scott*, 2003 U.S. Dist. LEXIS 27348 at *2.

6. Ibid.

7. *Scott*, Brief of Appellant-Petitioner Timothy Scott, 2006 U.S. S. Ct. Briefs LEXIS 1229, at *4–5.

8. Victor Harris was not wearing a seatbelt. *Scott*, Brief for the United States as Amicus Curiae Supporting Petitioner, 2006 U.S. S. Ct. Briefs LEXIS 1246, at *3.

9. *Scott*, 2003 U.S. Dist. LEXIS 27348, at *8.

10. *Scott*, 127 S. Ct. 1769 (2009).

11. Harris's lawyer also submitted dashcam videos from the Peachtree City Police, but they seem not to be subject of discussion in the judgment of the Supreme Court, so we are not going to discuss them here. See *Scott*, Brief of Appellee-Respondent Victor Harris, 2007 U.S. S. Ct. Briefs LEXIS 16, at *4 n. 2.

12. See http://www.supremecourtus.gov/opinions/06slipopinion.html (last accessed July 15, 2008).

13. Geographical comments are based on Google Maps: http://maps.google.com/maps?tab=nl (last accessed January 11, 2007).

14. *Scott*, Brief of Appellee-Respondent Victor Harris, 2007 U.S. S. Ct. Briefs LEXIS 16, at *5.

15. In addition, it's not possible to tell from the tapes whether culverts and steep embankments were actually visible to the drivers. We can estimate the depth later, after the crash, when we see officers' bodies occluded by the angle of the hillside. Should this landscape have been known to the officers even though it was dark? Was this their local territory? Since, according to the rule the Court adopted at the end of its opinion, the officers were justified in using even deadly force to end the chase as long as the driver they were pursuing was "threaten[ing] the lives of innocent bystanders" (*Scott*, 127 S. Ct. at 1779), the officers' awareness of the danger that the culverts and steep embankments posed to Harris if the officers caused Harris to lose control of his car may be irrelevant. Nevertheless, the majority, earlier in its opinion, indicated that "we must consider the risk of bodily harm that Scott's actions posed to respondent" (ibid., 1778). It could well be that if jurors armed with local knowledge about the roads or other evidence had been permitted to see the videotapes and draw their own conclusions, the danger to Harris from the local landscape might well have entered into their calculation of the moral reasonableness of a verdict for the police.

16. The majority asserts that Harris "r[a]n multiple red lights" (*Scott*, 127 S. Ct. at 1775). Justice Stevens correctly observes that Harris and the officers "went through only two intersections with stop lights and in both cases all other vehicles in sight were stationary, presumably because they had been warned of the approaching speeders" (ibid., 1782). Justice Stevens continues: "Incidentally, the videos do show that the lights were red when the police cars passed through them but, because the cameras were farther away when [Harris] did so and it is difficult to discern the color of the signal at that point, it is not entirely clear that he ran either or both of the red lights" (ibid.).

17. Like other products that have wound up defining commonly performed actions, "Steadicam" is both a term and a trademarked name, Steadicam® of Tiffen.

18. The Entertainment Software Association reports that, as of 2007, "sixty-five percent of American households play computer or video games": http://www.theesa.com/facts/index.asp (last accessed September 9, 2008).

19. For comparison, think of narration in Renaissance European painting, where the story is told through visible emotion expressed by gestures and faces of *dramatis personnae*. See Svetlana Leontief Alpers, "Ekphrasis and Aesthetic Attitudes in Vasari's *Lives*," *Journal of the Courtauld Institutes* 23, no. 3/4 (July-December, 1960): 190-215.

20. Note also that while the officers may have been able to discern at least Harris's silhouette, viewers of the tape cannot see even that much, so that, perceptually, Harris becomes the car he is driving.

21. *Scott*, 127 S. Ct. at 1775-76.

22. See Robert Baird, "The Startle Effect: Implications for Spectator Cognition and Media Theory," *Film Quarterly* 53, no. 3 (Spring 2000), 12-24.

23. *Scott*, No. 05-1631, Transcript of Oral Argument (February 26, 2007): 28, line 3. Interestingly, the famous scene in *The French Connection* is not a "car chase" in the sense of one vehicle chasing another. Rather, "Popeye" Doyle (Gene Hackman) is racing underneath an elevated train to catch up to the drug ring member who is trying to escape him by riding on the speeding train above. In fact, there may be another reason to associate to *The French Connection* besides the excitement of its chase scene: It's a film about drug dealing. Officer Timothy Scott said that he assumed that Reynolds's pursuit of Harris was in connection with an undercover drug operation that he and Reynolds had been assigned to assist (*Scott*, Brief of Appellant-Petitioner Timothy Scott, 2006 U.S. S. Ct. Briefs LEXIS 1229, at *3). Perhaps, when it came time to write the opinion, Justice Scalia felt that the more generic reference to a "Hollywood-style car chase" would be clearer for an audience that might have not seen the movie.

24. Cf. *Old Chief v. United States*, 519 U.S. 172, 188 (1997).

25. Richard J. Gerrig and Deborah A. Prentice, "Notes on Audience Response," in *Post-Theory: Reconstructing Film Studies*, ed. David Bordwell and Noël Carroll (Madison: University of Wisconsin Press, 1996), 388–403.

26. Pointing out the obvious, Hollywood films use montage as their basic grammar, constructing their stories out of bits and pieces of film that are joined together after either hard stops (cuts) or conjunctions (transitions such as fades). The documentary filmmaker also uses montage but typically makes different truth-claims about the subject of the film. In contrast, the dashcam video at issue in Scott has no internal edits. Whatever is in front of the lens is recorded without prejudice or favor, but the dashboard camera has a narrow range of vision—when Harris's car leaves the road, for instance, it moves completely out of sight. This kind of discontinuity (in contrast to deliberate editing) is a hallmark of fixed cameras in general and surveillance cameras in particular. For the purposes of this litigation, the discontinuity in picturing the narrative is not a problem, but in other cases it may obscure crucial facts.

27. Of course, we would not argue that immediate response to a photographic picture (such as the videotape in this case) is not relevant; far from it. Instead, our argument is that it is necessary to have the response and then to parse it closely, observing how the immediate effect was achieved, what about the object under scrutiny caused it, and what more the object may have to tell us if we move past our initial response. David Freedberg expresses the ambivalence in the photographic image thus: "[T]he realism of the image supersedes all thought of mechanics. The tension between acknowledging the orchid [a metaphorical figure employed by Walter Benjamin] and realizing it is grown in the hothouse of technology, on the one hand, and the preceding suppression of all thought of technology, on the other, is precisely what constitutes the aura of verisimilitude." David Freedberg, *The Power of Images: Studies in the History and Theory of Response* (Chicago: University of Chicago Press, 1989), 235.

28. *Scott*, No. 05-1631, Transcript of Oral Argument (February 26, 2007): 41, lines 12–14.

29. Ibid., 45, lines 13–16.

30. Ibid., 54, lines 17–19.

31. *Scott*, 127 S. Ct. at 1775 n. 5.

32. Interestingly, Travis Yates, in "Police Driving, Safety Behind the Wheel," http://www.policeone.com/writers/columnists/TravisYates/articles/1242114/ (last accessed July 31, 2008), quotes Justice Scalia's assertion that the lower courts interpreted Harris's driving as "attempting to pass his driving test." Justice Scalia's comment criticizes the lower courts' failure to "see the tapes" as showing that Harris was driving recklessly, but, again, he does not tie his observation to anything in particular that is visible on the tape itself.

33. *Scott*, 127 S. Ct. at 1781 n. 1.

34. Sometimes those sound files are stand-alone documents (we discuss this in connection with the *Skakel* case in chapter 5); other times they accompany video files as soundtracks (as we'll discuss in connection with citizens' surveillance tapes later in this chapter).

35. Sounds are audibly "salient ways in which events affect their environment." R. Murray Schafer, *The Tuning of the World* (New York: Knopf, 1977), 161.

36. Ibid., 155–57.

37. We asked Daniel Kiecza of Bolt, Beranek, and Newman, a software engineer specializing in some aspects of sound, how difficult it would be to put in a person's mouth words that the person hadn't spoken. Even for a sound-only file (as opposed to an audiovisual video file), a great deal of acoustic data are needed to construct new words not actually spoken by a speaker. Voice timbre, word inflection, rhythm and emphasis, accent, and ambient sound all need to be considered. Kiecza estimated that the audio technician would need at least four hours of a person's recorded speech in order to digitally fabricate a person's words. Daniel Kiecza, interview by author Spiesel (December 6, 2007). In contrast to inventing words not spoken and putting them in a person's mouth in this way, sampling sounds and working with them is quite easy. Sounds of any kind, once digitized, are just as easy to copy, transform, and mix together as digital pictures. (We discuss the editing of digital pictures in more detail in chapter 4.) Suffice it to say that this ease has engendered new kinds of music (which can range from the DJ as composer, cutting between vinyl on turntables, to sound-sampling and "quoting," as the rap group 2Live Crew did in its cut "Oh Pretty Woman." A case involving this use of existing audio material for parody made it all the way to the Supreme Court (*Campbell v. Acuff-Rose Music*, 510 U.S. 569 (1994))). The recording industry's anxiety over the slipperiness of digital sound is reflected in its many efforts to protect its products—through threats, lawsuits, and digital rights management (DRM) schemes. The bottom line is that digital technologies have now made it possible to write with sound in a manner comparable to "writing with pictures," which we discuss in chapter 1.

38. We suspect but do not know that, when the police radios were in operation, other sound recording was overridden. This would allow clear records to be made of police radio communications.

39. See http://lyricsfire.com/viewlyrics/Smash-Mouth/Then-The-Morning-Comes-lyrics.html (last accessed July 31, 2008).

40. Because these two sound tracks are different, they might have influenced how a jury would construct the respective characters of the two sheriff's deputies (two different kinds of excitement) and thus influenced the jury's perceptions and judgments had the case gone to trial (even though the audio should have been irrelevant to any legal issues in the case).

41. As the legal scholar Richard Sherwin writes regarding televised trials, litigation public relations, and other legal efforts to use pictures to shape public opinion about matters of justice: "Once you enter the realm of appearances it may be difficult to control how the image spins." Richard Sherwin, *When Law Goes Pop* (Chicago: University of Chicago Press, 2000), 141.

42. Dan M. Kahan, David A. Hoffman, and Donald Braman, "Whose Eyes Are You Going to Believe? An Empirical (and Normative) Assessment of Scott v. Harris," *Harvard Law Review* 122, no. 3 (January 2009): 837–906.

43. Ibid., 866.

44. Ibid., 867–70.

45. Harris's lawyer, Craig T. Jones, provided to Dan Kahan and his colleagues for their study copies of the dashboard camera videotape submitted by Officer Scott. They, in turn, made the video available to us. We would like to thank Jones, Kahan, David Hoffman, and Donald Braman for sharing this material.

46. The changes we discuss are independent of the technical problem of preparing a videotape of that length for public downloading, that is, creating a streaming video file for posting on the Web. Those preparations could involve changing the file size and changing the file format. The tape was posted as a file for use with Real Player.

47. *Scott*, Reply Brief of Appellant-Petitioner Timothy Scott, 2007 U.S. S. Ct. Briefs LEXIS 100, at *12. The Supreme Court, however, stated that "[i]t is . . . clear that Scott's actions posed a high likelihood of serious injury or death to [Harris]" (*Scott*, 127 S. Ct. at 1778).

48. The image might be disturbing to those who recall seeing a similar "thumbs-up" given in so many of the notorious pictures from Abu Ghraib prison in Iraq. (See chapter 1 for a brief discussion.)

49. In response to a question from us, Harris's attorney confirmed that his client, Victor Harris, is an African American. There is no evidence in court documents that Scott was aware of Harris's race during the chase. Craig T. Jones, e-mail communication to authors, September 10, 2008.

50. Ironically, Justice Scalia refers to Harris's version of events, reflected in the written record of the case (and acknowledged as a reasonable possibility by the Court of Appeals), as a "visible fiction" (*Scott*, 127 S. Ct. at 1776). Did he mean that the (visible) video made the fictitiousness of Harris's (verbal) account "visible," that is to say, obvious for all to "see"?

51. Ibid., 1784. Justice Stevens is referring to the three justices on the appellate court and the original trial court judge, all of whom thought that there were triable issues and that a jury should have a chance to judge. (Including all of the judges who heard the case, including those on the Supreme Court, the "decision" was actually split eight to five.)

52. The legal ramifications of *Scott* are explored in depth by Howard M. Wasserman, "Orwell's Vision: Video and the Future of Civil Rights Enforcement," *Maryland Law Review* 68 (forthcoming spring 2009). As lower courts more frequently confront dashcam video evidence, they are, naturally, turning to *Scott* as the leading precedent. See, e.g., *Sharp v. Fisher*, 2007 WL 2177123 (S.D. Ga., July 26, 2007), aff'd, no. 07-13978 (11th Cir., July 2, 2008) (on basis of dashcam video evidence, granting summary judgment to police officers who used deadly force to end high-speed highway chase); *Green v. New Jersey State Police*, 2006 U.S. Dist. LEXIS 55334 (D.N.J., August 9, 2006), aff'd, 246 Fed. Appx. 158 (3rd Cir. 2007) (dashcam video evidence did not conclusively show that defendant police officers did not use unreasonable force in subduing suspect; summary judgment denied). More recently, in *Buckley v. Haddock*, no. 07-10988 (11th Cir., September 9, 2008), the Eleventh Circuit overturned the district court and granted summary judgment to the police on the ground that the officer's repeated tasing of a handcuffed motorist seated unresisting by the side of the road after a traffic stop did not, as a matter of law, constitute the use of unreasonable force. The majority, citing *Scott*, claimed to base its statement of the facts on the police dashcam videotape of the incident and to have construed the evidence in the plaintiff's favor (ibid., 2 n. 1), as it is supposed to do in ruling on a defendant's motion for summary judgment; the dissenting judge, however, having watched the same tape, described the officer's conduct in

very different terms. The dissenting judge, taking a page from the *Scott* majority, also suggested that the court publish the video along with the opinion (ibid., 21). The court did not do so, but the plaintiff's attorney, possibly prodded by a posting on a legal blog the following day (http://howappealing.law.com/ [last accessed September 19, 2008]), took up the suggestion and posted the video on YouTube (http://www.youtube.com/watch?v=SWC7iSGCk-s [last accessed September 19, 2008]).

As the *Scott* opinion has become part of legal culture, so the video itself is spreading into popular culture. A search of YouTube using "Scott v. Harris" as the search term returned 958 possible video clips, each posted by someone who apparently thought that it was relevant. This puts the *Scott* video ahead of the George Holliday video of the Rodney King beating, at 775 clips (as of September 5, 2008) (although that case arose before the advent of YouTube).

53. For another discussion of the need to interpret video evidence, see Jessica Silbey, "Judges as Film Critics: New Approaches to Filmic Evidence," *University of Michigan Journal of Law Reform* 37, no. 2 (Winter 2004): 493–571.

54. Modern digital recording systems offer more options; one of them is recording what is happening inside the vehicle. Our assumption, based on viewing the tapes, is that the police cruisers involved in *Scott* were using relatively old equipment. Newer systems are expensive, and, as with all equipment purchases, it takes time to upgrade. Interested readers can find a detailed discussion of digital video for police cars in Larry Sharp, "Digital Technology Advances Police and Law Enforcement In-Car Video Capabilities," http://www.policetechnologies.com/digital/whitepaper.html (last accessed February 9, 2009).

55. Between Chicago 1968 and New York 2004 lay antiglobalization demonstrations around the world. The demonstrations at the WTO meeting in Seattle in 2000, while planned to be peaceful, erupted in violence. This must have been on the minds of those organizing for public security in New York City during the convention; activists planning for the convention must have been aware of it, as well. The Seattle demonstrations were widely covered by the news. See, e.g., Geov Parrish, "Is This What Failure Looks Like?," *Seattle Weekly*, November 24, 2004, http://www.seattleweekly.com/2004-11-24/news/is-this-what-failure-looks-like/ (last accessed July 30, 2008).

56. See http://www.nyclu.org/rncdocs (last accessed July 30, 2008). Just reading the list of documents available through the NYCLU (many are no longer posted on the government site) will give the reader some sense of how extensive the law enforcement planning was. On its Web site (when accessed in May 2007; document no longer available), the NYPD chose to contextualize the RNC in terms of all the foiled terrorist events before and after 9/11. Jim Dwyer, writing in the *New York Times*, tells us that "[f]or at least a year before the 2004 Republican National Convention, teams of undercover New York City police officers traveled to cities across the country, Canada and Europe to conduct covert observations of people who planned to protest at the convention, according to police records and interviews." Jim Dwyer, "City Police Spied Broadly Before G.O.P. Convention," *New York Times*, March 25, 2007.

57. Michael B. Farrell, "Who's Taping Whom?," *Christian Science Monitor*, September 15, 2004.

58. Rocco Parascandola, "Ready for a 'Doomsday' Protest," *Newsday*, February 26, 2007.

59. The *New York Times*, that is, reported a crowd half the size claimed by the NYPD on its Web site, where the NYPD asserted that "[t]he demonstrators played out as expected. United for Peace and Justice attracted 800,000 to its march and rally for what the Times described as the largest protest in the history of American political conventions": http://www.nyc.gov/html/nypd/html/dcpi/nypd_rnc_overview.html (last accessed May 29, 2007; as noted, some information is no longer available on this site). Why double the numbers unless the desire was to magnify the threat? Another source, by contrast, wrote: "The protest organizer, United for Peace and Justice, estimated the crowd at 500,000, rivaling a 1982 antinuclear rally in Central Park, and double

the number it had predicted. It was, at best, a rough estimate. The Police Department, as is customary, offered no official estimate, but one officer in touch with the police command center at Madison Square Garden agreed that the crowd appeared to be close to a half-million." Robert D. McFadden, "Vast Anti-Bush Rally Greets Republicans in New York," *New York Times*, August 30, 2004. (Note the difference between the official NYPD comment and the claims on its Web site.)

60. Jim Dwyer, "Videos Challenge Accounts of Convention Unrest," *New York Times*, April 12, 2005.

61. News coverage on the use of video by the police department has this to say: "But police, too, are attempting to protect their rights. They use video in the event protests turn violent, to investigate crimes afterward, and to transmit images through wireless cameras to police command centers. They use it for training and, they say, to investigate groups that may have links to terrorist organizations." Farrell, "Who's Taping Whom?" See also Jim Dwyer's video report, http://video.on.nytimes.com/index.jsp?auto_band=x&rf=sv&fr_story= 8be43bbe911fe4027477fad-3f56017ec4672d86c , showing a police officer with a camera (at 3:38 on the clip) (last accessed August 29, 2007); see also http://iwitnessvideo.info/blog/14.html (last accessed August 28, 2007) for Judge Charles Haight's decision on the Handshu guidelines regarding police surveillance of people at public gatherings.

62. The journalist Wes Allison referred to demonstrations as a "wild card" at the 2004 convention: "In New York, Republicans hope a ruckus works in their favor. Convention chairman Ed Gillespie said protesters will be linked to the Kerry campaign and Democrats will be held responsible for any disrespect the protesters show toward the presidency or the convention. Many have ties to Democrat-leaning causes, including organized labor, environmentalists and peace activists." Wes Allison, "Protests a Wild Card at GOP Convention," *St. Petersburg Times* (Florida), August 29, 2004. (These words were published two days after Dunlop was arrested.)

63. Both law enforcement and political demonstrators may have wanted to enact a "conversation" in a public place in order to send their messages to their respective constituents (other government agencies for the one, citizens sharing political views for the other), both addressing undecided members of the public as well. The law provides few guideposts for understanding speech rights in this context because it has typically conceived of "place" as mere property, making it difficult to incorporate into that conception ideas about the rights of citizens in public places. See Timothy Zick, "Space, Place, and Speech: The Expressive Topography," *George Washington Law Review* 74, no. 3 (April 2006): 439–505.

64. For an overview, see Nat Parry, "NYPD's Homegrown Hysteria," August 20, 2007, http://www.consortiumnews.com/2007/082007.html (last accessed July 31, 2008).

65. This kind of preemptive policing also took place more recently, before the opening of the 2008 Republican National Convention in St. Paul, Minnesota. Glenn Greenwald, "Scenes From St. Paul—*Democracy Now*'s Amy Goodman Arrested," September 1, 2008, http://www.salon.com/opinion/greenwald/ (last accessed September 3, 2008). For a description of the ongoing tension the police felt toward Critical Mass riders, see Jim Dwyer, "Aggressiveness of Bike Chases Stirs Questions for the Police," *New York Times*, February 24, 2006.

66. This and other quotes from Dunlop in this paragraph are from his first-person account during a radio interview on *Democracy Now*, available at http://www.democracynow.org/2005/4/14/ny_law_enforcement_caught_doctoring_video (last accessed July 31, 2008).

67. For another description of conditions, see Drew Poe, "Documents Show Pier 57 Contained Asbestos, Lead Contamination and Fire Hazards; HRPT Aware of Contamination Prior to Use of Pier to Detain Protestors," November 26, 2004, http://dc.indymedia.org/newswire/display/109884/index.php (last accessed July 31, 2008).

68. See http://www.democracynow.org/2005/4/14/ny_law_enforcement_caught_doctoring_video (last accessed July 31, 2008).

69. Michael Conroy, interview by authors, February 12, 2007, New York City (notes on file with authors).

70. With thanks to Eileen Clancy of I-Witness Video, we were able to view the tapes in question and take notes on them. Jim Lehrer of the Media Arts Center, Orange, Connecticut, gave helpful technical insights on the basis of a verbal description of what we saw.

71. Other tapes of police made by citizens at the demonstrations show officers using digital cameras. See the picture gallery at http://www.2600.com/rnc2004/index.html (last accessed July 25, 2008). The digital data would have had to be exported to VHS tape. Once on VHS, the originally digital files could be successively copied, which produces generational degrading because, unlike digital media, each analog copy of an analog copy is further removed from the original data. Photocopies of photocopies on paper suffer from the same problems.

72. This training is mentioned in the Intelligence Documents, http://iwitnessvideo.info/documents/index.html#doc-rnc-intel (last accessed July 31, 2008), and other sites.

73. See http://www.democracynow.org/2005/4/14/ny_law_enforcement_caught_doctoring_video (last accessed July 31, 2008).

74. The *New York Times* lays out the differences between the cut and the uncut versions. Uncut we see a crowd generally and Dunlop just standing with his bicycle; we see him walking calmly by some police offers, not looking at them; we then see him close up, clearly not resisting arrest. In the tape submitted by the district attorney, we do not see him in the crowd, do not see him being arrested, and see him only from the back after arrest. See the inserted visuals "Cut and Uncut," http://www.nytimes.com/2005/04/12/nyregion/12video.html? pagewanted=1&ei= 5090&en=46f3604d0befb92f&ex=1270958400&partner=rssuserland (last accessed July 30, 2008) (link to the right of the story).

75. We would need to know if the cameras were even set for time/date metadata recording; the camera operator can choose whether to do this. Had the cameras ever been reset since coming from the factory? Were they set to record the time/date stamps on that occasion? When the tape was copied to VHS, if the time/date stamp was not visible in the original digital recording, it would not be embedded in the picture that viewers can see. If the time/date stamp had not been set, then it is unclear whether the videography was ever intended to be used as evidence. In fact, the other copy of the police tape that was compared to the one supplied to Conroy did have time/date stamps visible when it was played, so these data on the tape given to Conroy had to have been deliberately suppressed.

76. See Dwyer, "Videos Challenge Accounts."

77. Michael Conroy interview.

78. On cultural diffusion, see generally Jack Balkin, *Cultural Software* (New Haven: Yale University Press, 1998). For a discussion of the legal dimensions of this phenomenon, see Wasserman, "Orwell's Vision."

A sequel, of sorts, to the Alexander Dunlop story: On July 25, 2008, a tourist filmed bicyclists on another Critical Mass ride. The tape shows a police officer deliberately knocking down a rider who was not doing anything but riding and who appears to have been trying to avoid the officer. On the basis of the officer's sworn complaint, the rider was arrested and charged with attempted assault and disorderly conduct. But the officer's story "b[ears] no resemblance to the events seen on the videotape." The tape was posted on YouTube; within five days, nearly a million people had viewed it. "The availability of cheap digital technology—video cameras, digital cameras, cell phone cameras—has ended a monopoly on the history of public gatherings that was limited to the official narratives, like the sworn documents created by police officers and prosecutors. The digital age has brought in free-range history." Jim Dwyer, "When Official Truth Collides With Cheap Digital Technology," *New York Times*, July 30, 2008. The officer who body-slammed the cyclist was charged with assault, harassment, and filing a false arrest report; all charges against the rider were dropped. John Eligon and Colin Moynihan, "Office Is Indicted in Toppling of Cyclist," *New York Times*, December 15, 2009, http://cityroom.blogs.nytimes.com/2008/12/15/officer-to-be-indicted-in-toppling-of-cyclist/ (last accessed February 5,2009).

79. For the wars on and with photography, see http://nycphotorights.com/wordpress/ (last accessed July 31, 2008). Confrontations between would-be citizen videographers and the police have occurred, for instance, in the days preceding the 2008 Republican National Convention in St. Paul, Minnesota. The police, while claiming they were looking for weapons, seized computers and cameras from journalists, especially members of the alternative press. See J. D. Tuccile, "St. Paul Preemptive Raid Caught on Video," *Civil Liberties Examiner*, August 31, 2008, http://www.examiner.com/x-536-Civil-Liberties-Examiner~y2008m8d31-St-Paul-preemptive-raid-caught-on-video (last accessed September 3, 2008). Incidentally, comparing this to another account from the print media (http://www.startribune.com/politics/27695244.html?elr=KArksLckD8EQDUoa EyqyP4O:DW3ckUiD3aPc:_Yyc:aULPQL7PQLanchO7DiUs) makes clear how much the medium contributes to the message. The same arrested lawyer appears in both stories. The video version just shows her arrest. The print version leads with her picture (from the back) but defers her story until after describing a cache of homemade weaponry, including a bucket of urine seized at a different location not involving her at all. This way of framing the lawyer's story, of course, could create an impression of guilt by association.

80. November 11, 2007.

81. "Caught on Tape: LAPD Beating," http://video.google.com/videoplay?docid=7263747123 967851446&vt=lf&hl=en (last accessed September 9, 2008). There are several different postings of this video on different sites. While the underlying video remains the same, the presentation varies. The example we discuss has video text that names the officers and suspect and includes an article about the event that can be found at http://panafricannews.blogspot.com/20 (last accessed September 9, 2008).

82. The spokesperson's comment is no longer posted. We retain the quotation in the text because it underscores the fluidity of information on the Internet and the difficulty of making firm connections between the various elements of any posted video. The article cited in n. 81 from Pan African News quotes Los Angeles Police Chief William Bratton as saying at a news conference: "There's no denying that the video is disturbing. But as to whether the actions of the officers were appropriate in light of what they were experiencing and the totality of the circumstances is what the investigation will determine."

83. "UCLA Student Tasered by Police in Library," http://www.youtube.com/watch?v=5g7zlJx9u2E (last accessed July 31, 2008).

84. See http://www.thenewspaper.com/news/19/1961.asp (last accessed July 31, 2008). This description of events (unsigned) provides both a link to the video and a transcript of the audio, provided by Mr. Darrow. The subtitle of the publication is "A Journal of the Politics of Driving." Patrick M. O'Connell and Georgina Gustin, "Officer in Trouble Over Motorist's Video in South County," *St. Louis Post-Dispatch*, September 11, 2007, http://www.stltoday.com/stltoday/news/special/srlinks.nsf/story/9AA8B7F1CC9DD78986257353007A90C6? OpenDocument (last accessed July 31, 2008).

85. "Police Officer Taped Ranting at Driver Fired," September 21, 2007, http://www.cnn.com/2007/US/09/21/madcop.video.ap/index.html (last accessed July 31, 2008). There is a strong implication that the police department is relying on video surveillance for both the protection and the evaluation of its personnel, because one of the reasons that the officer was fired was that he hadn't turned on his own dashboard camera. For other sides to the discussion, see the editorial suggestion by the *St. Louis Post-Dispatch* (September 19, 2007) that "[t]hanks to Internet sites like YouTube.com, the videotape of the ugly confrontation between motorist Brett Darrow and St. George Police Sgt. James Kuehnlein in the wee hours of Sept. 7 now has been viewed more than half a million times and has raised almost that many questions: Did Mr. Darrow, who had a video camera mounted in his car and a reputation for baiting police officers,

deliberately provoke the sergeant? Did the sergeant play into his hands by losing his temper and over-reacting?," http://nl.newsbank.com/nl-search/we/Archives? (last accessed July 31, 2008). For a discussion of the problems exemplified by this encounter as understood by law enforcement personnel, see http://forums.officer.com/forums/showthread.php?p=975286 (last accessed July 31, 2008).

86. For example, on July 13, 2007, a married, pregnant, African American school principal in Independence, Missouri, Yvette Hayes, was arrested on felony charges because she had been mistaken for a car thief in a J. C. Penney parking lot. J. C. Penney security personnel had been following up on their suspicion that someone driving a green Jeep Cherokee had been stealing cars from the store's parking lot. Hayes was in her car, also a green Jeep Cherokee, parked in the lot with her two children (one sleeping, one drawing), while her sister shopped. The security personnel notified the Independence police of what they believed to be a suspicious car. When Hayes's sister was ready to leave, Hayes left as well. Police officers in two cars tracked her and caught up with her on the interstate. Even though they knew that she was driving a properly registered vehicle and not a stolen car, they conducted a felony stop. They made the obviously pregnant Hayes lie on her belly on the side of a busy highway; they approached the car, which contained the two children, with their guns drawn; and then they arrested Hayes. Toriano L. Porter, "Hayes Files Lawsuit," *The Examiner,* http://www.examiner.net/stories/103007/new_213525910.shtml (last accessed October 30, 2007).

Two police cars meant that the incident should have been recorded on two dashcam videos. Unfortunately, the tape from the lead car's camera is missing approximately four hours of material, including the portion that would have recorded this incident. The tape from the following car is complete. Among other things, it captures the police saying that they have to "cover their ass."

Hayes sued to obtain a copy of the police video. Adam Torres, "Woman Sues Over Request for Video," *The Examiner,* http://examiner.net/stories/072607/new_174061523.shtml, July 26, 2007 (last accessed October 30, 2007). The police department eventually gave it to her; the department also posted a portion of the recording on the World Wide Web, where it received national attention. The video seems to show the officers treating an obviously pregnant woman in ways that not only caused her embarrassment but also could have damaged her unborn child. Later, the police posted an edited version of the video, in which, while we see and hear them ordering Hayes to lie down in front of their vehicles, we also hear their voices moderate when they see that there are children in the car, and we do not hear them saying they have to cover anything. In an evocation of the majority opinion in *Scott,* the Independence Police Department released a copy of the dashcam video "so the public can see for themselves what happened during the police stop Friday night": http://www.myfoxkc.com/myfox/pages/Home/Detail;jsessionid=E379EE12FBA7580101231CE4F1E632A2?contentId=3814079&version=2&locale=EN-US&layoutCode=VSTY&pageId=1.1.1&sflg=1 (last accessed September 14, 2008).

Like most such stores, J. C. Penney conducts video surveillance of its parking lots, so it, too, had a record of (some of) the incident. After more than a month of public pressure and threats of boycott, the store turned over its tapes, which, according to a Hayes family spokesperson, "will show that Hayes never left her vehicle and support that she was a victim of racial profiling." Hayes sued both J. C. Penney and the Independence police, alleging an array of claims, including racial discrimination. At some point, a trial judge and possibly also a jury may have to decide what two very different videotapes mean.

The situation is about to get even more complicated. Police departments are urging citizens to report evidence related to criminal activity from their cell phones (Al Baker, "Police Urge Citizen Crimefighters to Text Their Tips," August 6, 2008, http://cityroom.blogs.nytimes.com/2008/08/06/police-urge-crimefighters-to-text-their-tips/?scp=1&sq=citizens'%20tips%20topolice&st=cse [last accessed September 14, 2008]). This was followed a few days later by the suggestion that citizens also send cell phone videos (Christina Hauser, "911 to Accept Cellphone Videos," September 9, 2008, http://cityroom.blogs.nytimes.com/2008/09/09/911-to-accept-cell-phone-videos/?scp=1&sq=citizens'%20pictures%20to%20police&st=c [last accessed September 14, 2008]). More recently, however, members of another police department took the opposite approach by confiscating cell phones and cameras from members of the public who had witnessed a very troubling event (Carlos Miller, "Do Police Have the Right to Confiscate Your Camera?," January 2, 2009, http://www.indybay.org/newsitems/2009/01/22/18565104.php [last accessed February 4, 2009]). A group of police officers had pulled a young man off a BART (Bay Area Rapid Transit) train at a station in Oakland when they were investigating a fight. While down and restrained, the young man, Oscar Grant, was shot and killed by one of the officers. The officer was later arrested and charged with murder. (For an account, see Demian Bulwa, Leslie Fulbright, and Henry K. Lee, "BART Officer Arrested on Murder Warrant in NY Day Shooting," January 14, 2009, http://www.sfgate.com/cgi-bin/article.cgi?f=/c/a/2009/01/13/BAM615A08A.DTL [last accessed February 4, 2009].) Prosecutors may well have been motivated to act not only by local community pressure, but also by the broader public attention created when a cell phone video of the event from a phone that the officers had failed to confiscate was posted on YouTube (http://www.youtube.com/watch?v=ZKKQ-gzc_Yw [last accessed February 4, 2009]). If this case goes to trial, there may well be bits of video evidence from more than one phone as well as video from surveillance cameras mounted on the transit platforms. Potential problems of authenticating these kinds of video fragments and then relating them to one another, as decision makers must in order to construct coherent narratives of the events, abound.

87. For a slideshow history of events on the Great Lawn, see http://www.nytimes.com/2008/07/23/nyregion/23about.html?ref=nyregion (last accessed July 31, 2008).

88. For a somewhat similar problem, see Randall C. Archibald, "Los Angeles Police Chief Notes Failures of Command at Rally," *New York Times*, May 30, 2007. Certainly the publication (before the convention) of an article in the *New York Post* quoting the Police Department as saying that members of the Weather Underground were planning to show up might have scared some people, but, for anyone who pays attention, this was just absurd; the Weather Underground had been disbanded many years earlier. Perhaps the name was being evoked as a kind of brand, instantly recognizable as standing for people who would make bombs, use guns, and not obey government (or other) authority. The name "Weather Underground," like the color-coded security warnings put out by the Department of Homeland Security, would serve both to scare noncombatants and reassure them that someone was looking out for their security.

89. Erwin Panofsky, *Perspective as Symbolic Form* (New York: Zone Books, 1991).

90. Anne Friedberg, *The Virtual Window: From Alberti to Microsoft* (Cambridge, MA: MIT Press, 2006), 194.

CHAPTER 3

1. See, e.g., American Bar Association, ABA *Model Rules of Professional Conduct*, "Preamble: A Lawyer's Responsibilities" (2007): "As advocate, a lawyer zealously asserts the client's position under the rules of the adversary system."

2. The conception of persuasion as diametrically opposed to education—the contest of rhetoric and truth—goes back at least to classical Greece, as illustrated in Plato's *Gorgias*. The argument in this chapter, which we and our colleague Richard Sherwin have made elsewhere (Richard Sherwin, Neal Feigenson, and Christina Spiesel, "Law in the Digital Age," *Boston University Journal of Science and Technology Law* 12, no. 2 [Summer 2006]: 227–70), promotes a different, partly Aristotelian conception of rhetoric, in which rhetoric is not inconsistent with but rather is *constitutive* of the imparting and acquisition of knowledge.

3. See, e.g., G. Christopher Ritter, *Creating Winning Trial Strategies and Graphics* (Chicago: American Bar Association, 2004), 5: "[H]ighly persuasive advocates spend their time at trial educating jurors. These advocates are teachers, not fighters; yet by taking the time to educate jurors, these lawyers are usually much more effective fighters than most of their more openly hostile counterparts."

4. Of course, diagrammatic pictures may contain descriptive components (as in an annotated photo), and diagrams, like descriptive pictures, may convey some of their meaning through visual elements such as color and composition. So there may be considerable overlap between the communicative and rhetorical functions of descriptive pictures and diagrams. (Indeed, we will conclude this chapter with a form of digital display—the computer animation or simulation—that can be thought of as a diagram in the guise of a descriptive picture. And many diagrams of course also depend heavily on *notations*, the third kind of picturing we mentioned in the introductory chapter.) But, at least at a general level, we can make an important distinction. The fact that evidentiary photos and videos remain anchored in observable reality is both a rhetorical strength (as we saw in chapter 2, they are generally taken up as credible representations of that reality, even as seeming to bring a bit of that reality into the viewer's presence) and a limitation (they are less well suited to the unambiguous expression of abstractions, although words may help to clarify and disambiguate the picture's meanings). Diagrams (as we noted in chapter 1), by contrast, tend to make meaning in a more top-down fashion; generally speaking, more of their important content can be translated without remainder into propositional form.

5. We will revisit the evidentiary presentation of complex quantitative data in chapter 4.

6. *Securities and Exchange Commission v. Koenig*, 2007 U.S. Dist. LEXIS 26088 (N.D. Ill.) (denying defendant's posttrial motions for judgment as a matter of law and a new trial).

7. Waste Management was later sold to another company, USA Waste; according to the conservative estimate of Koenig's own expert, the total shareholder loss resulting from the bad accounting was $1.45 billion. *Securities and Exchange Commission v. Koenig*, 2007 WL 4277439, at *4 (N.D. Ill. Dec. 3, 2007).

8. These included violations of sections 10(b) and 13(a) of the Securities and Exchange Act of 1934 and Rules 10b-5 12b-20, 13a-1, and 13a-13 thereunder, and of section 17(a) of the Securities Act of 1933.

9. *SEC v. Koenig*, 2007 U.S. Dist. LEXIS 26088 (N.D. Ill.) at *3–*4. In December 2007, the trial judge issued an opinion on remedies. *SEC v. Koenig*, 532 F. Supp.2d 987 (N.D. Ill. Dec. 3, 2007). As of this writing, SEC lawyers have submitted a final judgment pursuant to that opinion.

10. In addition to the public records of the case, we rely on interviews with Chris Ritter on September 19, 2007, and with Ritter and Bob Pommer on October 2, 2007 (notes on file with authors). Ritter, Pommer, and Jack Worland also reviewed this portion of the chapter for factual accuracy. We would like to thank all of them for making the visuals available to us.

11. As readers no doubt know, PowerPoint can be used as a design tool to craft and arrange text, shapes, drawings, and other visual elements within the frame of the slide. It can also be used as a presentation tool to show on computer or larger screens audiovisual materials originating from any source whatsoever, so long as the material has been digitized. (We will have more to say about PowerPoint in chapter 5.) Chris Ritter uses Adobe Illustrator to design his slides and prefers TrialDirector to PowerPoint as a display software (Chris Ritter, interview by authors, September 19, 2007), but the slides used in *Koenig* could have been created (although perhaps not as artfully) in PowerPoint as well as Illustrator.

12. See *SEC v. Koenig*, opening statement, slides 1–5, 26–35, 41–47, 77–83, 92–95, 96–105, 109–119, 120–122, 123–129, 130–135, 136–139, 143–152, 154–155, 158–159, 160–163, 168–170.

13. E.g., ibid., slide 76 (salvage valuations).

14. Ibid., slides 160–163.

15. Later in the chapter we will refer to research on temporal sequence and cognitive load that supports this point.

16. Bob Pommer and Chris Ritter, interview by authors, October 2, 2007.

17. From this point on, Koenig's picture appears twenty-seven times (in about 150 slides). Two-thirds of the time (eighteen of twenty-seven), the black box accompanies his picture. Whenever it does, photo and black box are placed within a rectangle with a slightly darker blue fill than the rest of the slide background, further linking picture and icon and setting them off from the rest of the slide. In three other slides, the black box appears in the same slide as Koenig's picture but in a different part of the slide.

18. Think of the common reference to jury decision making as a black box and jury research as an attempt to get "inside the black box" (e.g., Robert MacCoun, "Inside the Black Box: What Empirical Research Tells Us About Decisionmaking by Civil Juries," in *Verdict: Assessing the Civil Jury System*, ed. Robert E. Litan [Washington, DC: Brookings Institution, 1993], 137–80); see also the notion of "black boxing" in science and technology studies (e.g., Bruno Latour, *Science in Action* [Cambridge, MA: Harvard University Press, 1997]).

19. Another connotation for "black box" is the device that automatically records communications between airplane pilots and air traffic controllers; after an accident, the black box often becomes crucial, objective evidence about what happened. Jurors who drew this association might also have thought that just as Koenig's accounting practices hid the truth about the company from the SEC and hence from the public, so Koenig the witness was concealing from *them* the truth about what happened. Their job at trial, just as it was the job of the SEC's investigators, was to recover the truth from inside the black box. By implicitly aligning the jurors with its side of the case, the SEC would further dispose them to decide in its favor.

20. See *SEC v. Koenig*, 2007 U.S. Dist. LEXIS 26088 at *15; slide 39.

21. See *SEC v. Koenig*, No. 02 C 2180 (N.D. Ill. 2006), opening statement transcript, April 19, 2006, p. 87, line 23–p. 88, line 1.

22. Although what follows immediately in the opening statement describes other things that Koenig said and did in response to the memo, the "!?," as commonly understood, arguably attributes to Koenig words, or kinds of words, for which there is no evidence. This might have been considered both inflammatory and unfairly prejudicial; perhaps it escaped the notice of defense counsel (and the judge) because it seemed de minimis and/or mildly humorous and, in either event, within the bounds of acceptable description of the evidence during opening statement.

23. *SEC v. Koenig*, No. 02 C 2180 (N.D. Ill. 2006), opening statement transcript, April 19, 2006, p. 88, lines 2–10.

24. Bob Pommer and Chris Ritter, interview by authors, October 2, 2007.

25. *SEC v. Koenig*, No. 02 C 2180 (N.D. Ill. 2006), opening statement transcript, April 19, 2006, p. 88, lines 10–13.

26. Media sources for the Bontatibus story include "Building Owner Charged in Firefighter's Death," *New York Times*, March 9, 1997; WTNH.com, "Mistrial in Bontatibus Arson-Murder Trial," www.wtnh.com/Global/story.asp?S=274187 (last accessed July 31, 2008); WTNH.com, "Bontatibus Trial History," www.wtnh.com/Global/story.asp?S=274295 (last accessed July 31, 2008); Michelle Tuccitto, "Judge Tosses Suit Against Branford, Cop," *New Haven Register*, August 31, 2005.

27. State of Connecticut, Department of Public Safety, Investigation Report, case no. P-96-01611-3 (December 10, 1996), 17.

28. WTNH.com, "Bontatibus Trial History."

29. "Building Owner Charged in Firefighter's Death."

30. Report of Richard L. P. Custer, Custer Powell, Inc., (February 28, 2000), 9–10; Report of Richard L. P. Custer, Custer Powell, Inc., (March 9, 2000), 2.

31. In addition to news coverage and public records of the case, we rely in this account on

interviews with Thomas Ullmann on June 27, 2006, April 24, 2007, and December 5, 2007 (notes on file with authors).

32. For (2) and (3), see State of Connecticut, Department of Public Safety, Investigation Report, case no. P96-01611-3 (December 10, 1996), 6–7.

33. For a standard explanation of the common view of demonstrative evidence in general, see Kenneth S. Broun, gen. ed., *McCormick on Evidence*, 3rd ed. (St. Paul, MN: Thomson West, 1999), 373–76; for a somewhat different overview, see Christopher B. Mueller and Laird C. Kirkpatrick, *Evidence*, 3rd ed. (New York: Aspen, 2003), 1049–52. For the sometimes confusing overlap between the illustrative and substantive treatment of particular items of audiovisual evidence, see Broun, *McCormick on Evidence*, 376–86. On the origin of this confusion in the creation of the category of demonstrative evidence in the late nineteenth century, see Jennifer L. Mnookin, "The Image of Truth: Photographic Evidence and the Power of Analogy," *Yale Journal of Law and the Humanities* 10, no. 1 (Winter 1998): 1–74. For more detailed discussions of the law governing the admissibility of video and computer generated visual and audiovisual evidence, see, e.g., Gregory P. Joseph, *Modern Visual Evidence* (New York: Law Journal Seminars-Press, 1997); Fred Galves, "Where the Not-So-Wild Things Are: Computers in the Courtroom, the Federal Rules of Evidence, and the Need for Institutional Reform and More Judicial Acceptance," *Harvard Journal of Law and Technology* 13, no. 2 (Winter 2000): 161–301.

34. See, e.g., Broun, *McCormick on Evidence*, 374. This rule may be understood as analogous to the basic authentication requirement applied to proffered items of "real" evidence, such as alleged weapons or contraband involved in a crime, that a witness with knowledge offer testimony sufficient to show that the item is what its proponent claims it is (Federal Rule of Evidence 901(a), 901(b)(1) [2008]). An alternative, arguably even more permissive test is that demonstrative evidence will be admitted if the judge believes that it will help the jury to understand the testimony it illustrates. See, e.g., *State of Connecticut v. Swinton*, 268 Conn. 781, 802 n. 20 (2004) (quoting *Dontigney*, 215 Conn. 646, 652 (1990)).

35. At least one commentator has written that, whatever the formal rules may be, the practice is that the level of judicial scrutiny of courtroom displays goes up as the technology used becomes more sophisticated. Ritter, *Trial Strategies and Graphics*, 176–77. See also Federal Judicial Center/National Institute for Trial Advocacy, *Effective Use of Courtroom Technology* (Washington, DC: Authors, 2001) (arguing that all highly persuasive forms of digital evidence should be subject to the more strenuous admissibility standards applicable to substantive evidence). For further discussion of the law governing the admissibility of computer generated visual evidence, see the discussion of the *Swinton* case in chapter 4.

36. Connecticut judges, however, often do send demonstratives to the jury room, at least in criminal cases (Thomas Ullmann, interview by authors, December 5, 2007; notes on file with authors). In chapter 7 we revisit the question whether demonstratives should be allowed to go to the jury room.

37. If the demonstrative is treated as substantive evidence, then under Federal Rule of Evidence 401 (2008) or the state law equivalent, the proponent must establish its relevance by showing that it makes some fact of consequence to the case more probable or less probable than that fact would be without the evidence.

38. Federal Rule of Evidence 403 (2008). In many states, the balance is struck differently, permitting the judge to exclude evidence where the judgmental risks outweigh, rather than "substantially" outweigh, the probative value (see, e.g., Connecticut Rule of Evidence 4–3 [2008]), referred to in the discussion of *Murtha* later in this chapter).

39. The basic rule is that evidentiary rulings are committed to the trial judge's discretion and are reversible only for abuse of discretion; see, e.g., Mueller and Kirkpatrick, *Evidence*, 24–25.

40. In addition, to make analog versions of these illustrations would have required paint, paste, colored pencil—all time-consuming media to produce by hand, especially on the large

scale required for the illustrations to be seen by jurors in court, thus entailing expenditures of time and resources that could well have been prohibitive for a public defender.

41. We borrow the phrase "reconstructing reality" from W. Lance Bennett and Martha S. Feldman's classic, *Reconstructing Reality in the Courtroom* (New Brunswick, NJ: Rutgers University Press, 1981).

42. There do not appear to have been any challenges to the admission of the multimedia display. The photographs and audio had been separately authenticated and admitted. A possible issue raised by their juxtaposition (including the transcript and time codes) is that the moments in the fire captured by still photographs, each of which remains on the screen for some time, could never be matched precisely to the times indicated by the time codes; however, an approximate matching seems to have sufficed, given that the photos appear in correct sequence and that the audio recording is continuous.

43. According to Deputy Fire Chief William Pepe, one of the principal eyewitnesses, this was the one-and-three-quarter-inch hose, which had not yet been "charged," that is, there was no water in it. (Statement of William Pepe, Sr. to Branford, CT Police Department, incident no. 96-20506 [December 3, 1996], 3–4.) The pictures of the empty hose function as a kind of "Chekhov's gun." According to the playwright Anton Chekhov, if a gun is hung on the wall in the first act of a play, the audience expects it to go off in the third act. Regardless of whether the lack of water in the hose at the beginning of the sequence had anything to do with where and when the roof collapsed, it seems to foreshadow a related bad outcome later. And "lack of water" is closely enough related to "spread of fire" at a general level for viewers to link the two, even if subconsciously. See John B. Black, James A. Galambos, and Stephen J. Read, "Comprehending Stories and Social Situations," in *Handbook of Social Cognition*, ed. Robert Wyer and Thomas Srull (Hillsdale, NJ: Erlbaum, 1984), 3:45–86 (readers who find deviations from ordinary conduct or events earlier and later in a story tend to find a causal link between the two).

44. Half of the photos in the entire sequence appear in the last two and a half minutes (the entire sequence lasts 10 minutes, 17.39 seconds).

45. Statement of William Pepe, Sr. to Branford, Connecticut, Police Department, incident no. 96-20506 (December 3, 1996), 7.

46. This may be an appropriate place to mention another form of visual evidence more familiar to at least some lawyers and other readers—the *day-in-the-life* movie. This is a video documentary of the daily activities of a plaintiff in an accident or malpractice case, offered to show jurors the effects of the accident or malpractice on the plaintiff (see, e.g., Joseph, *Modern Visual Evidence*, §4.06; Jacob A. Stein, *Stein on Personal Injury Damages*, 2nd ed. [Deerfield, IL: Clark Boardman Callaghan, 1991], §22:35). Although these are videos, we mention them in this chapter rather than in chapter 2 because they are produced and edited exclusively for purposes of litigation (settlement negotiations or trial), and so more closely resemble the other demonstrative explanations of facts discussed in this chapter than they do the ostensibly unedited photographic pictures, made before any litigation, discussed in chapter 2. The aim of the day-in-the-life movie is to demonstrate to jurors in a clear and compelling manner just what the injury means to the plaintiff, in terms of both the plaintiff's physical and mental suffering and its effects on the plaintiff's family and other persons, all of which is relevant to the jury's determination of "general" or pain and suffering damages. The best such films—for instance, those made by the documentary filmmaker and legal videographer Bill Buckley of B & B Productions in Westport, Connecticut—are plainly rhetorical. They must represent reality faithfully enough to be admitted as evidence, but they also show the plaintiff as a noble or even heroic character in a daily drama, struggling not just to deal with terrible injuries but to overcome them and be the best person he or she can be under the circumstances. The editing of the footage shot in the field (typically several hours' worth) down to the fifteen to twenty minutes shown at trial is thus done not only to condense the presentation to a length that

judges and jurors can tolerate (see earlier discussion) but also to tell a clear and emotionally engaging story about the victim.

A related form of visual display that straddles the line between evidence and argument is the *video profile*. This is a montage of photographs and video depicting the life of the deceased victim in a wrongful death case, accompanied by a tasteful musical soundtrack. The video profiled is offered, like the day-in-the-life movie, as evidence on the issue of damages. In terms of the media used, the video profile is even closer to the multimedia display in *Bontatibus*. (The Bill Buckley Legal Video Archive at the Quinnipiac University School of Law, established in 2007, contains a large collection of Buckley's day-in-the-life movies, video profiles, video settlement brochures [on which, see chapter 5], and video statements.)

The emotional appeal of the video profile has been adapted by victims' advocates in capital cases. After the defendant has been convicted and during the sentencing phase, when jurors must decide whether the defendant will be sentenced to death or life in prison, the victim's family members and others are permitted to testify about the effects of the victim's death on their own lives. These are known as victim impact statements. In recent years, these statements have sometimes been presented in the form of *victim impact videos*—montages of photos of the victim's life, sometimes set to music. See, e.g., *Hicks v. Arkansas*, 327 Ark. 727 (1997); *Salazar v. Texas*, 90 S.W.3d 330 (Texas 2002); Christine Kennedy, "Victim Impact Videos: The New Wave of Evidence in Capital Sentencing Hearings," *Quinnipiac Law Review* 26, n. 4(2008): 1069–1105.

47. See Richard K. Sherwin, "Law Frames," *Stanford Law Review* 47, no. 1 (November 1994): 39–83.

48. For this and other facts not apparent from the visual display itself, see Statement of William Pepe, Sr. to Branford, Connecticut, Police Department, incident no. 96-20506 (December 3, 1996).

49. Black, Galambos, and Read, "Comprehending Stories."

50. On sympathy, anger, and attributions of blame, see Neal Feigenson, Jaihyun Park, and Peter Salovey, "The Role of Emotions in Comparative Negligence Judgments," *Journal of Applied Social Psychology* 31, no. 3 (2001): 576–603.

51. On March 20, 2001, Bontatibus's third trial, like his first, ended in a hung jury (WTNH. com, "Mistrial in Bontatibus Arson-Murder Trial"). The state decided not to prosecute him a fourth time.

Bontatibus also sued his store's insurer, the Hartford Fire Insurance Company, when it refused to pay on his claim for the destruction of the store on the ground that he had set the fire deliberately to collect the insurance proceeds. In 2004, this case also ended in a hung jury. The parties later settled for an undisclosed amount (Tuccitto, "Judge Tosses Suit Against Branford, Cop"). In 2003, Bontatibus filed a lawsuit in federal district court against the town of Branford and one of its police officers, alleging malicious prosecution. The case was dismissed on summary judgment in August, 2005 (ibid.). The administrator of Edward Ramos's estate sued the town of Branford and its fire chief in state court, alleging that he knew or should have known that his reckless conduct (in failing to promulgate adequate firefighting protocols and in other respects) was substantially certain to cause Ramos's death. (The "substantially certain" claim was intended to avoid the exclusive remedy provision of the state workers' compensation statute.) The trial judge granted summary judgment to the defendants and the Connecticut Appellate Court affirmed (*Ramos v. Town of Branford*, AC 20449 (June 12, 2001)).

Today, Bontatibus owns and operates another flooring store, in Guilford, Connecticut.

52. Paivio calls his model *dual coding* theory; see, e.g., Allan Paivio, *Imagery and Verbal Processes* (New York: Holt, Rinehart & Winston, 1971); *Mental Representations: A Dual Coding Approach* (Oxford: Oxford University Press, 1986). Mayer's work follows this model. Richard E. Mayer, *Multimedia Learning* (Cambridge: Cambridge University Press, 2001).

53. Information (or, to be precise, mental representations of information, embodied in neural correlates) can move from one channel to the other. For instance, printed words are initially processed by the visual channel (because they are visual stimuli) but are processed mainly in the auditory/verbal channel (Mayer, *Multimedia Learning*, 61).

54. Ibid., 63–80.

55. This does not mean that advocates should necessarily prefer digital technologies to analog ones. As we stress in our own teaching, advocates in any given situation may be able to teach and persuade more effectively using traditional visual tools; following Aristotle's definition of rhetoric, the advocate needs to choose the tools best suited to the task. See also Sam Guiberson, "Digital Media as Evidence and Evidence as Media," *Criminal Justice* 19, no. 1 (Spring 2004): 59; Ritter, *Trial Strategies and Graphics*, 181–86. Moreover, with the exception of studies of computer animations (which we discuss later in this chapter), there has been very little research so far on the effects of digital visual technologies on legal judgment (see, e.g., Neal Feigenson and Meghan A. Dunn, "New Visual Technologies in Court: Directions for Research," *Law and Human Behavior* 27, no. 1 [February 2003]: 109–26), so our discussion of these effects in the text, although it draws where possible on other bodies of psychological and other research, necessarily remains speculative.

It is also worth noting that courts thus far have acknowledged that PowerPoint, Sanction presentation software, and other programs may be "useful" and "engaging" ways of conveying information but have refused to consider them "reasonably necessary" for purposes of being taxable as costs to the losing party in a civil case under Federal Rule of Civil Procedure 54(d) (2007) and 28 U.S.C. § 1920 (2007); see, e.g., *American Color Graphics, Inc. v. Travelers Property Cas. Inc.*, 2007 U.S. Dist. LEXIS 22641 at *7–9 (N.D. Cal. 2007) (Sanction used to display sixty-one documents at trial); *Affymetrix, Inc. v. Multilyte Ltd.*, 2005 U.S. Dist. LEXIS 41177 at *11–12 (N.D. Cal. 2005) (animated PowerPoint presentation prepared for pretrial hearing).

56. Of course, digitally produced pictures can be printed and displayed as prints or on poster board or indeed in any way that analog pictures can. Conversely, analog pictures can be placed on a document projector and thus (digitally) displayed on a courtroom screen. For the most part, however, digital and only digital pictures are seen on screens.

57. In the not-too-distant future, legal digital multimedia may be experienced not on 2-D screens but in more fully immersive virtual environments (IVEs). We address this in chapter 6.

58. This is what the anthropologist Edward T. Hall, *The Hidden Dimension* (Garden City, NY: Doubleday, 1966), calls "cultural" space, as opposed to intimate or conversational space.

59. Susan Sontag, "Regarding the Torture of Others," *New York Times Sunday Magazine*, May 23, 2004; Mark Benjamin, "The Abu Ghraib Files," *Salon*, February 16, 2006, http://www.salon.com/news/feature/2006/02/16/abu_ghraib/index.html (last accessed July 31, 2008). The *Salon* article identifies the American in the second version of the picture (it is unclear whether this is an uncropped or differently cropped version of the same photo or a separate photo taken from a similar position) as Staff Sergeant Ivan "Chip" Frederick, who was court-martialed for his conduct at Abu Ghraib. Frederick pled guilty to other charges in October, 2004 and was sentenced to eight years in prison and other penalties (http://en.wikipedia.org/wiki/Ivan_Frederick [last accessed July 31, 2008]).

60. Thus, digitization can sacrifice some of the impact of real evidence: the sense of being in the presence of a three-dimensional piece of reality that bears the marks of its own unique history. People skilled in the use of visual software, however, can increase the visual sense of tactility if the proponent thinks that that is important.

61. The psychological and rhetorical effects might well be different when judge and jurors each watch their own small monitors, as they do in some high-tech courtrooms, as opposed to looking together at the same large screen. That experience would seem to resemble personal computing more closely than it does being at the movies. As yet there is no published

research testing the effects of courtroom screen size on judges' or jurors' case-relevant judgments.

62. See, e.g., J. K. Burgoon and others, "Interactivity in Human-Computer Interaction: A Study of Credibility, Understanding, and Influence," *Computers in Human Behavior* 16, no. 6 (November 2000): 553–74.

63. Michael A. Shapiro and Daniel G. McDonald, "I'm Not a Real Doctor, But I Play One in Virtual Reality: Implications of Virtual Reality for Judgments About Reality," *Journal of Communication* 42, no. 4 (Autumn 1992): 94–114.

64. See Federal Judicial Center/National Institute for Trial Advocacy, *Effective Use of Courtroom Technology*, 51–52 (observing that jurors are comfortable with courtroom technology because they can analogize from their own experiences with large-screen televisions and computers at home). We suggest that jurors may be especially likely to crave the familiarity and comfort that digital displays on the screen offer because the rest of trial—in particular, the task of putting together a coherent version of reality from the purely oral testimony of multiple witnesses, interrupted and undermined by cross-examination—can be so unfamiliar, disconcerting, and stressful.

65. See, e.g., Sherwin, Feigenson, and Spiesel, "Law in the Digital Age," and see discussion of multimedia arguments in chapter 5. Some who are accustomed to accepting television (at least, ostensibly factual programming such as news) as a "magic window" onto reality may adopt the same default interpretation of courtroom evidence and explanation offered in what appears to be a very similar medium. Others, especially younger persons, who are more used to interacting with what they see on screens—using TiVo to reorganize their television viewing, or digital editing software to remix video and audio captured from the Internet—may approach courtroom screens more critically, as we observe later.

66. For an anecdote, see Ritter, *Trial Strategies and Graphics*, 235–36. For the contrary view that "[j]urors are not particularly affected by technology failures unless the court and lawyers are anxious about it," see Federal Judicial Center/National Institute for Trial Advocacy, *Effective Use of Courtroom Technology*, 55.

67. For research showing that people respond similarly to computers and to television and other media in that they treat all media as social actors, see Byron Reeves and Clifford Nass, *The Media Equation* (Cambridge: Cambridge University Press, 1996); see also Burgoon et al., "Interactivity in Human-Computer Interaction."

68. Stephen W. Harmon, "Novice Use of a Dimensional Scale for the Evaluation of the Hypermedia User Interface: *Caveat Emptor*," *Computers in Human Behavior* 11, nos. 3–4 (Autumn-Winter 1995): 429–37. People might find computer-generated or computer-presented information to be especially credible because they believe that it is more objective, impersonal, and scientific, or (at least if they are inexperienced computer users) they may simply be wowed by the multimedia experience, believing that they have learned more from the computer than they actually have (ibid.). Other researchers dispute the general claim that people automatically assume that computers are credible. See B. J. Fogg and Hsiang Tseng, "The Elements of Computer Credibility," *CHI 99 ACM* (1999): 80. For a model and discussion of the complexities of credibility judgments as applied to information obtained via the Internet, see C. Nadine Wathen and Jacquelyn Burkell, "Believe It or Not: Factors Influencing Credibility on the Web," *Journal of the American Society for Information Science and Technology* 53, no. 2 (January 15, 2002): 134–44.

69. Brian Carney and Neal Feigenson, "Visual Persuasion in the Michael Skakel Trial," *Criminal Justice* 19, no. 1 (Spring 2004): 22–35. There may, of course, be good rhetorical reasons not to smooth out certain items of evidence in this way; for instance, the lawyer may want to emphasize the degraded nature of a given item.

70. *SEC v. Koenig*, opening statement transcript of April 19, 2006, pp. 94, line 17—p. 105, line 5. Part of the SEC's contention was that, under Koenig's direction, Waste Management changed

its method of accounting with regard to these payments without reporting it in the public filings required by securities law.

71. *SEC v. Koenig*, opening statement, slides 107–108. According to the SEC lawyer, Bob Pommer, the idea for the cookie graphic came from Jack Worland (Bob Pommer and Chris Ritter, interview by authors, October 2, 2007).

72. If editing is needed, video and audio clips have to be edited using other software, and then they have to be converted to file formats compatible with PowerPoint.

73. For various recommendations about good information design, see Mayer, *Multimedia Learning*; Stephen M. Kosslyn, *Elements of Graphic Design* (New York: Freeman, 1994); Edward R. Tufte, *The Visual Display of Quantitative Information* (Cheshire, CT: Graphics Press, 1983); Tufte, *Envisioning Information* (Cheshire, CT: Graphics Press, 1990); Tufte, *Visual Explanations* (Cheshire, CT: Graphics Press, 1997); Tufte, *Beautiful Evidence* (Cheshire, CT: Graphics Press, 2006).

74. If lawyers are attentive, simply using the software will teach them new design possibilities.

75. Ritter, *Trial Strategies and Graphics*, favors this style; it appears in many of his sample graphics.

76. See, e.g., Kosslyn, *Elements of Graphic Design*, 112–15. Edward Tufte's books (see note 73) also include many examples of this.

77. By repeatedly arranging these recognizable elements as they did, the creators of this visual display wordlessly communicated several messages at once, including that Koenig's methods diverged from accepted accounting norms; that Koenig concealed the truth; that he did this for improper reasons; and that each instance of his behavior was part of a common pattern or scheme of deception.

78. The classic article on the limitations of working memory is George A. Miller, "The Magical Number Seven Plus or Minus Two: Some Limits on Our Capacity for Processing Information," *Psychological Review* 63, no. 2 (March 1956): 81–97. More recent research indicates that adults are able to form and retain precise representations of no more than three or four items at a time—about the same capacity as infants. Lisa Feigenson, "A Double-Dissociation in Infants' Representations of Object Arrays," *Cognition* 95, no. 3 (April 2005): B37–B48. Psychologists use the phrase *cognitive load* to describe the demands on short-term mental processing; on cognitive loads and learning, see, e.g., John Sweller, "Cognitive Load Theory, Learning Difficulty, and Instruction," *Learning and Instruction* 4 (1994): 295–312. Ritter, *Trial Strategies and Graphics*, 136–51, explains and illustrates the benefits to lawyers of *pacing* the presentation of visual information. Ritter's examples use the analog medium of a poster board to which the lawyer adds each new item as desired, but digital technologies like PowerPoint make this process much easier.

79. The dimensions of a given PowerPoint or other presentation software slide and the minimum font size readable at ordinary viewing distances constrain the amount of information that can (or ought to) be fit into any one slide, especially in comparison to graphics in print media, but lawyers can turn this limitation into a strength by distributing the data over several slides.

80. That the previous slide disappears is also a potential disadvantage of the slide show, because the lawyer may want to keep a particular picture in front of the audience even as he or she proceeds with the explanation or argument. PowerPoint and other programs allow lawyers to avoid or at least mitigate this problem, though, as illustrated in the *Koenig* graphics discussed earlier. The same graphical elements can be carried over from one slide to another (e.g., the same color schemes can be used to indicate the same underlying point or level of analysis; cf. discussion of PowerPoints in the Vioxx cases in chapter 5), and pictures can be repeated as desired in new slides.

81. See Barbara Tversky, "Spatial Schemas in Depictions," in *Spatial Schemas and Abstract Thought*, ed. Merideth Gattis (Cambridge, MA: MIT Press, 2001), 104–5.

82. Paul S. Cowen, "Manipulating Montage: Effects on Film Comprehension, Recall, Person Perception, and Aesthetic Responses," *Empirical Studies of the Arts* 6, no. 2 (1988): 97–115.

83. See Jonathan Miller, "Moving Pictures," in *Images and Understanding*, ed. Horace Barlow, Colin Blakemore, and Miranda Weston-Smith (Cambridge: Cambridge University Press, 1990), 180–194. For a classic source on how readers and listeners "fill in the blanks" in verbal narratives with knowledge derived from familiar scripts about how events of that sort go, see Roger Schank and Robert Abelson, *Scripts Plans Goals and Understanding* (Hillsdale, NJ: Erlbaum, 1977).

84. Yet viewers also find movies with cuts (the cuts of which they are not consciously aware) more interesting and more active than movies without them. Robert N. Kraft, "The Role of Cutting in the Evaluation and Retention of Film," *Journal of Experimental Psychology: Learning, Memory, and Cognition* 12, no. 1 (January 1986): 155–63.

85. See Robert N. Kraft, "Light and Mind: Understanding the Structure of Film," in *Cognition and the Symbolic Processes: Applied and Ecological Perspectives*, ed. Robert R. Hoffman and David S. Palermo (Hillsdale, NJ: Erlbaum, 1991), 351.

86. Of course, movie and television audiences do not believe that they are *actually* participating in the depicted events. Rather, they can become what the psychologists Richard Gerrig and Deborah Prentice call "side-participants," cognitively and emotionally involved in the depicted events even though unable to influence the outcomes (just like those who overhear ordinary conversations). Richard J. Gerrig and Deborah A. Prentice, "Notes on Audience Response," in *Post-Theory*, ed. David Bordwell and Noël Carroll (Madison: University of Wisconsin Press, 1996), 388–403.

87. Gerrig and Prentice, "Notes on Audience Response"; see also Neal Feigenson, "Too Real? The Future of Virtual Reality Evidence," *Law and Policy* 28, no. 2 (April 2006): 271–93.

88. Michael A. Shapiro and T. Makana Chock, "Psychological Processes in Perceiving Reality," *Media Psychology* 5, no. 2 (2003): 163–98 (viewers of television shows use typicality of story elements as a heuristic for judging the perceived reality of what they are viewing; moment-to-moment reality judgments are strongly related to typicality). Video and computer gaming may frame viewers' expectations differently; we touch upon this in chapters 2 (with regard to *Scott*) and 6.

89. See http://www.indatacorp.com/About/history.aspx (last accessed July 31, 2008) (Trial-Director); Verdict Systems LLC (2002) (CD-ROM) (Sanction).

90. A brief history of the technology will help explain how we got to PowerPoint and beyond, to more interactive presentation software. Before PowerPoint, presenters who needed to show pictures in professional contexts had to use a slide projector or an opaque projector. Both required advance preparation that could be both time-consuming and costly. If the presenter wanted to be at all recursive, it was necessary, for smooth public presentation, to make more than one physical copy of the slides or transparencies in question, increasing the cost and also locking the presenter into prior decisions about what needed repeating. In addition, to achieve a truly professional appearance, slides or transparencies most often had to be designed by others. Presenters who wanted to use sound or film would have to coordinate several different machines for outputs, each with its own controls.

These and other problems were solved by the creation of presentation software. PowerPoint was created as a Macintosh product in 1987, purchased by Microsoft later that year, and released for the Windows market in 1990, when it became a part of the Microsoft Office Suite (http://en.wikipedia.org/wiki/Microsoft_PowerPoint [last accessed July 31, 2008]). At that point, it became a consumer tool, available to anyone making a presentation. More or less at the same time, a mass market for laptop computers began with the introduction of Mac Powerbooks in 1991, followed shortly by the IBM Thinkpad series equipped with Windows 95 (http://en.wikipedia.org/wiki/Laptop_computers#History [last accessed July 31, 2008]). Laptops enabled presentation software to go on the road, cementing its place in our increasingly mediated lives. Today, PowerPoint is nearly ubiquitous in educational settings from elementary schools to universities; it is standard in business and scientific presentations; and it is now being used more and more often by lawyers. (For data on the widespread use of PowerPoint, see David G. Levasseur and Kanan Sawyer, "Pedagogy Meets PowerPoint: A Research Review of the Effects of Computer-Generated Slides in the Classroom," *Review of Communication* 6, nos. 1-2 [January-April 2006]: 101–23.)

The creation of PowerPoint (and the comparable program for Macs, Apple Computer's Keynote) predated the widespread use of the Internet and the World Wide Web. Both the Internet and the Web were long in development, but their explosion as a publicly available medium that would transform the culture can be dated to 1993 (http://en.wikipedia.org/wiki/History_of_Internet#Networks_that_led_to_the_Internet [last accessed July 31, 2008]). After the Internet and the World Wide Web came into being, people became familiar with a different way of constructing relationships between elements of knowledge: through lateral connections and layered relationships. This is a fundamentally different way of thinking from the hierarchical outline form that PowerPoint's defaults encourage. (More recent versions of PowerPoint, however, include action buttons which permit some nonlinear movement within the presentation.) It also more closely reflects the associational logic of pictures.

While the Web was developing, so were new storage media. Compact disks (CDs) were "originally thought of as an evolution of the gramophone record, rather than primarily as a data storage medium. Only later did the concept of an 'audio file' arise, and the generalizing of this to any data file" (http://en.wikipedia.org/wiki/Compact_Disc [last accessed July 31, 2008]). As people began to use recordable CDs in the 1990s to record digital data files of all kinds, Macromedia (now owned by Adobe) produced a piece of authoring software, Director, to help people put together CDs containing content for presentations and not just file storage. Director permits the creation of menu-driven content, which lets users pick and choose what they want to show and in what order. Thus, PowerPoint, the laptop, the Internet and the World Wide Web, and CD authoring software converged to make multimedia expression the kind of widely available, everyday practice it has become for just about everyone with access to computers.

Media and presentation software continued to converge. PowerPoint added built-in tools that made it easy for end users to create sophisticated graphics and to add animations and transition effects between slides. A timed PowerPoint presentation can become almost like a little movie as it changes slides on a prearranged schedule, with visual effects that act as conjunctions between the slides' content. At the same time, films began to be published on DVDs, allowing viewers to do whatever they want with the movie—go directly to a favorite part of the movie, skip other parts, or watch one of the extra bonus features added to make purchase attractive. As people are being accustomed to having more control over what is presented to them, interactive trial presentation software like TrialDirector and Sanction caters to these expectations, drawing on all of the technologies mentioned earlier and facilitating habits of mind more suited to the Internet than to the older world of analog media.

91. Several handbooks for practitioners describe the basic capabilities of these programs. See, e.g., Sheldon E. Friedman, *The Litigator's Guide to Electronic Evidence and Technology* (Denver: Bradford, 2005); Mike Rogers, *Litigation Technology: Becoming a High-Tech Trial Lawyer* (New York: Aspen, 2006).

92. These files may include documents, photos and videos of the scenes at issue, and videotaped depositions and transcripts, as well as any other sort of evidentiary material (other than real evidence and live testimony). Logging and labeling the materials can be time-consuming and is often outsourced; in addition, video files can be quite large and can take some time to load during presentations (interview with Thomas Ullmann and his investigator, Matt Whalen, June 27, 2006).

93. In addition, from the first stages of case preparation before trial, the software helps the advocate to identify and organize the evidentiary material he or she intends to use at trial. All of the potential evidence is logged into the program and arranged in multiple hierarchies, so that the lawyer can easily and quickly retrieve it—putting before the fact finders the evidence they most need (and not burdening them with information they don't need) even as those needs shift with the changing events at trial. See Friedman, *Litigator's Guide*, 131; see also Carney and Feigenson, "Visual Persuasion."

94. For the facts of the case, see *State of Connecticut v. Skakel*, 276 Conn. 633 (2006). This section is adapted from Carney and Feigenson, "Visual Persuasion."

95. *Skakel*, 276 Conn. at 663–93.

96. Although the customized software used in this case had some features not then available in Sanction or TrialDirector, most of the digital capabilities we discuss in this chapter are applicable to these more widely used programs.

97. Observe that this is a kind of remediation: Carney imported this organizational tool from hyperlinking on the Internet.

98. Carney and Feigenson, "Visual Persuasion." On the most important benefits of trial presentation software generally (organization, speed, and flexibility), see also Paul J. Johns, "Technology-Augmented Advocacy: Raising the Trial Lawyer's Standard of Care; Changing Traditional Legal Education; and Creating New Judicial Responsibilities," *Ohio Northern University Law Review* 25, no. 4 (1999): 574.

99. See Jerome Bruner, *Actual Minds, Possible Worlds* (Cambridge, MA: Harvard University Press, 1986), 11–14.

100. On the other hand, if the goal is to teach the discrete steps of a process, animations may be less useful than static diagrams because the individual pictures of which the animation is comprised are transient and not readily inspected or reinspected, as viewers may need to do to confirm their understanding. See Tversky, "Spatial Schemas in Depictions," 104–5.

101. Meghan A. Dunn, Peter Salovey, and Neal Feigenson, "The Jury Persuaded (and Not): Computer Animation in the Courtroom," *Law and Policy* 28, no. 2 (April 2006): 228–48 (comparing animation effects in plane crash and car crash scenarios); see also Robert B. Bennett, Jr., Jordan H. Leibman, and Richard E. Fetter, "Seeing Is Believing; Or Is It? An Empirical Study of Computer Simulations as Evidence," *Wake Forest Law Review* 34, no. 2 (Summer 1999): 257–94 (finding animation had no effect on judgments in car crash scenario).

102. Dunn, Salovey, and Feigenson, "The Jury Persuaded (and Not)"; Bennett, Leibman, and Fetter, "Seeing Is Believing."

103. Saul M. Kassin and Meghan A. Dunn, "Computer-Animated Displays and the Jury: Facilitative and Prejudicial Effects," *Law and Human Behavior* 21, no. 3 (June 1997): 269–81.

104. Dunn, Salovey, and Feigenson, "The Jury Persuaded (and Not)": 241. This should provide a cautionary note for lawyers who rely on asking themselves (or focus groups) about what they think the effect of an animation or simulation will be, in order to determine whether it's worth creating one for an upcoming trial.

105. Brad E. Bell and Elizabeth Loftus, "Vivid Persuasion in the Courtroom," *Journal of Personality Assessment* 49, no. 6 (December 1985): 659–64.

106. Researchers have found that ease of mental processing can affect judgments of truth due to either (or both) *perceptual* fluency or *conceptual* fluency. Perceptual fluency refers to any features that increase ease of perceptual processing, including visual priming, figure-ground contrast, and presentation duration. Conceptual fluency refers to any factors that increase ease of semantic processing, such as verbal priming with words semantically related to the target picture. For a review, see Piotr Winkielman and others, "Cognitive and Affective Consequences of Visual Fluency: When Seeing Is Easy on the Mind," in *Persuasive Imagery*, ed. Linda M. Scott and Rajeev Batra (Mahwah, NJ: Erlbaum, 2003), 75–89.

107. Vicki L. Fishfader and others, "Evidential and Extralegal Factors in Juror Decisions: Presentation Mode, Retention, and Level of Emotionality," *Law and Human Behavior* 20, no. 5 (October 1996): 565–72 (finding that mock jurors who saw videotaped reenactment of accidental drowning of girl in swimming pool experienced more negative emotional responses and assigned less responsibility to the plaintiff).

108. *State v. Murtha*, CR03-0568598T (Conn. Super. Ct., J.D. Hartford, 2006).

109. Murtha's reasonable belief that the suspect was using or about to use deadly physical force against him or was about to inflict great bodily harm would be a complete justification to the shooting. Conn. Gen. Stat. § 53a-19 (2008).

110. *State v. Murtha*, CR 03 0568598 S, Hartford Superior Court, transcript of October 16, 2006, 2, lines 3–4; 4, lines 14–17.

111. Ibid., 7, line 1–9, line 4.

112. Ibid., 9, line 16–10, line 5. See also Matt Burgard, "Yet Another Connecticut Trigger Happy Cop? Jury Gets Another View of Shooting," *Hartford Courant*, October 17, 2006; Hugh Keefe, interview by authors, November 22, 2006 (notes on file with authors); Michael Georgetti, interview by author Feigenson, November 29, 2006 (notes on file with authors). According to attorney Keefe, the judge probably reasoned that if a witness can describe a subjective perception verbally and illustrate it with a drawing, why not allow an animation as a similarly simple demonstrative?

113. We do not know whether the animation influenced the jury's verdict. The jury may well have acquitted Officer Murtha or at least hung even without it: Murtha was a highly sympathetic defendant, a respected police officer who had worked his way through law school, while his victim was a drug dealer already in prison at the time of the trial on unrelated drug and weapons charges. See, e.g., Heather Collins, "Ex-Hartford Officer Acquitted in Shooting; Wants Job Back," *Journal Inquirer*, October 20, 2006.

114. The expert witness on how stress affects police officers' perception and memory was William Lewinsky, a professor in the Minnesota State University Law Enforcement program.

115. *State v. Murtha*, CR 03 0568598 S, Hartford Superior Court, transcript of October 16, 2006, 28, line 3–37, line 20; the video is available on Daniel J. Simons, *Surprising Studies of Visual Awareness* 2003 [DVD].

116. *State v. Murtha*, CR 03 0568598 S, Hartford Superior Court, transcript of October 16, 2006, 33, lines 12–16.

117. Hugh Keefe interview.

118. Seeing the video may also have empowered the jurors to think that they should decide the case by seeing for themselves, as the animation invited them to do. Perhaps ironically, the point of the "gorilla" video is precisely that visual perception can be deeply flawed, which might seem to undercut some of the implicit meanings of the video that we suggest. The explicit and implicit meanings of the video can be reconciled, however: The explicit meaning is that visual perception can be flawed due to inattentional blindness; the implicit meaning is that seeing is understanding, so that by paying attention to the defendant's video-animation hybrid, the jurors could learn what they needed to know to evaluate Murtha's self-defense claim.

119. The animation could have been understood to offer a kind of substantive proof that Murtha was at least partially blinded by the car's headlights at the crucial moment when he first confronted the suspect's car as it pulled back onto the road. He did not stress this point in his testimony, however, and his theory of the case did not depend on it.

120. The montage of animation and video, by associating Murtha's point of view with that of the video taken by the camera in the other police cruiser, also implicitly associates Murtha with those other "good" officers, embracing him in the group (rather than singling him out as the renegade shooter that, to the unprepared viewer of the surveillance video alone, he might well appear to be).

121. Under Conn. Code of Evidence § 4-3 (2008), "[r]elevant evidence may be excluded if its probative value is outweighed by the danger of unfair prejudice or surprise, confusion of the issues, or misleading the jury, or by considerations of undue delay, waste of time or needless presentation of cumulative evidence," a standard less favorable to admissibility than Federal Rule of Evidence 403 (2008) (admit unless probative value substantially outweighed by danger of unfair prejudice, etc.).

122. E.g., Joel Cooper, Elizabeth A. Bennett, and Holly L. Sukel, "Complex Scientific Testimony: How Do Jurors Make Decisions?," *Law and Human Behavior* 20, no. 4 (August 1996): 379–94 (mock jurors more persuaded by more highly credentialed expert when the testimony is highly complex); on factors influencing jurors' evaluations of expert testimony generally, see Sanja Kuntjak Ivoković and Valerie P. Hans, "Jurors' Evaluations of Expert Testimony: Judging the Messenger and the Message," *Law and Social Inquiry* 28, no. 2 (Spring 2003): 441–82.

123. Cognitive psychologists call this the *actor-observer bias*, and it's a "bias" because point of view ought to be irrelevant to judgments of responsibility. This actor-observer effect (Edward E. Jones and Richard E. Nisbett, "The Actor and the Observer: Divergent Perceptions of the Causes of Behavior," in *Attribution: Perceiving the Causes of Behavior*, ed. Edward E. Jones and others [Morristown, NJ: General Learning Press, 1971], 79–94) is well established in the social psychological literature. One experiment indicates that computer animations can induce this effect. In that study, an animation of an airline accident led mock jurors to assign less responsibility for the accident to the flight crew than did those who did not see the animation. The researchers speculated that this occurred not because the animation improved jurors' recall of case-relevant information (which it did not) but because showing the accident from the crew's point of view in the cockpit may have led jurors to make stronger situational attributions for the accident, deflecting responsibility from the actors. John M. Houston and others, "Computer Animation in Mock Juries' Decision Making," *Psychological Reports* 76, no. 3, pt. 1 (1995): 987–93.

124. Lawyers have long tried to do this with words, raising precisely these concerns; see Neal Feigenson, "Sympathy and Legal Judgment: A Psychological Analysis," *Tennessee Law Review* 65, no. 1 (Fall 1997): 1–78. Engrossing animations could well create even stronger effects.

125. This is the main reason why computer-generated accident or crime simulations are routinely subjected to a more searching authentication process. See, e.g., Federal Rule of Evidence 901(b)(9) (2008), which requires a vetting of inputs, program, and implementation to ensure that the animation is tethered closely enough to other indicia of external reality.

126. Baruch Fischhoff, "Hindsight ≠ Foresight: The Effect of Outcome Knowledge on Judgment Under Uncertainty," *Journal of Experimental Psychology: Human Perception and Performance* 1, no. 3 (August 1975): 288–99.

127. Thus, jurors who see an X-ray, knowing that the ambiguous spot on it turned out to be the tumor that killed the victim, may be more likely to believe that the radiologist, who of course didn't know when he read the X-ray that the spot indicated a tumor, should have seen it that way too. Erin M. Harley, Keri A. Carlsen, and Geoffrey R. Loftus, "The 'Saw-It-All-Along' Effect: Demonstrations of Visual Hindsight Bias," *Journal of Experimental Psychology: Learning, Memory, and Cognition* 30, no. 5 (September 2004): 960–68.

128. For instance, it has been suggested that pictures can exacerbate what psychologists call the *illusion of explanatory depth*, people's tendency to think that they understand things more fully than they do and to believe explanations because they find them satisfying rather than because they're correct (see Deena Skolnick Weisberg and others, "The Seductive Allure of Neuroscience Explanations," *Journal of Cognitive Neuroscience* 20, no. 3 [2008]: 470–77), and recent research has shown that people who saw brain scans illustrating the data reported in accounts of cognitive neuroscientific research found those accounts to be better reasoned than did people who read the articles but saw either bar graphs or no illustrations, even though the brain scans added no information to the data reported in the articles (David P. McCabe and Alan D. Castel,

"Seeing Is Believing: The Effect of Brain Images on Judgments of Scientific Reasoning," *Cognition* 107, no. 1 [April 2008]: 343–52). (We discuss this further in chapter 4.)

129. For a detailed, helpful summary of the persuasive and judgmental advantages and disadvantages of digital pictures in court, see Damian Schofield and Lorna Goodwin, "Using Graphical Technology to Present Evidence," in *Electronic Evidence: Discovery, Disclosure and Admissibility*, ed. Stephen Mason (Edinburgh: Lexis Nexis Butterworths, 2007), 107–11.

130. Cf. Anne Friedberg, *The Virtual Window* (Cambridge, MA: MIT Press, 2006), 183–84 (discussing the ideas of Paul Virilio and observing that screens change our experiences of space and time).

131. See Yochai Benkler, *The Wealth of Networks* (New Haven: Yale University Press, 2006), 218–19 (discussing how the Web, with its links to original materials, fosters a "see for yourself" culture).

132. See, e.g., Donald E. Shelton, Young S. Kim, and Gregg Barak, "A Study of Juror Expectations and Demands Concerning Scientific Evidence: Does the 'CSI Effect' Exist?," *Vanderbilt Journal of Entertainment and Technology Law* 9, no. 2 (Winter 2006): 331–68 (some evidence for a "tech effect" but not specifically a "*CSI* effect"); Kimberlianne Podlas, "'The *CSI* Effect': Exposing the Media Myth," *Fordham Intellectual Property, Media, and Entertainment Law Journal* 16, no. 2 (Winter 2006): 429–65 (experimental study finding no "*CSI* effect"); Tom Tyler, "Viewing *CSI* and the Threshold of Guilt: Managing Truth and Justice in Reality and Fiction," *Yale Law Journal* 115, no. 5 (March 2006): 1050–85 (2006) (discussion, based on general cognitive psychological theory, how any "*CSI* effect" might help as well as hurt prosecutors).

133. For anecdotal support for this speculation, see patent lawyer Matt Lowrie, presentation at symposium "The '*CSI* Effect': Litigation Strategies and Courtroom Dynamics," Suffolk University Law School, Boston, MA, May 10, 2007 (notes on file with authors).

134. Judge Raymond Brassard, Massachusetts Superior Court, presentation at symposium "The '*CSI* Effect': Litigation Strategies and Courtroom Dynamics," Suffolk University Law School, Boston, MA, May 10, 2007 (notes on file with authors). A possible implication is not that certain nuances of law cannot be visualized and so will remain less salient to jurors but rather that lawyers will try all the harder to put those nuances in visual form. (In chapter 4, for instance, we discuss the widespread perception that brain imaging allows viewers to "see" mental states.)

135. The idea of knowledge as interaction has taken hold in cognitive linguistics, cognitive neuroscience, and philosophy over the last twenty years or so. See, e.g., Patricia Churchland, *Brain-Wise* (Cambridge, MA: MIT Press, 2002); George Lakoff and Mark Johnson, *Philosophy in the Flesh* (New York: Basic Books, 1999); Alva Noë, *Action in Perception* (Cambridge, MA: MIT Press, 2004).

136. George Lakoff and Mark Johnson, *Metaphors We Live By* (Chicago: University of Chicago Press, 1980), 10–13 (the "conduit" metaphor: ideas are objects; linguistic expressions are containers; communication is sending).

137. E.g., Max Black, *Models and Metaphors* (Ithaca: Cornell University Press, 1962); Paul Ricoeur, *Hermeneutics and the Social Sciences*, trans. and ed. John B. Thompson (Cambridge: Cambridge University Press, 1981), 43 (noting that "hermeneutics itself puts us on guard against the illusion or pretension of neutrality" in the sense of being free from presuppositions) (human sciences); Bruno Latour, *Pandora's Hope* (Cambridge, MA: Harvard University Press, 1999) (philosophy of science); J. L. Austin, *How to Do Things With Words* (Cambridge, MA: Harvard University Press, 1962); Ludwig Wittgenstein, *Philosophical Investigations*, trans. G.E.M. Anscombe, 3rd ed. (New York: Macmillan, 1958) (philosophy of language); Eve Sweetser, *From Etymology to Pragmatics* (Cambridge: Cambridge University Press, 1990) (linguistics). This paragraph and the next are adapted from Sherwin, Feigenson, and Spiesel, "Law in the Digital Age," 227–28.

138. Gregory S. Berns and others, "Neurobiological Correlates of Social Conformity and Independence During Mental Rotation," *Biological Psychiatry* 58, no. 3 (August 2005): 245–53.

139. Clifford Geertz, *Local Knowledge* (New York: Basic Books, 1983); Bruno Latour, *Science in Action* (Cambridge, MA: Harvard University Press, 1987); Bruno Latour and Steve Woolgar, *Laboratory Life* (Princeton: Princeton University Press, 1986); Richard Shweder, *Thinking Through Cultures* (Cambridge, MA: Harvard University Press, 1991).

140. Peter Galison, *Image and Logic* (Chicago: University of Chicago Press, 1997); Ronald N. Giere, *Scientific Perspectivism* (Chicago: University of Chicago Press, 2006); Ian Hacking, *Representing and Intervening* (Cambridge: Cambridge University Press, 1983).

141. For instance, Giere, *Scientific Perspectivism*, uses the term "perspectivism" to denote a philosophy of scientific knowledge which, like our conception of legal knowledge, is opposed to both objectivism and relativism. He chooses "perspectivism" to distinguish his approach from what he sees as the excessive relativism of some philosophers and sociologists of science who have promoted the term "constructivism." Again, we do not attach too much importance to the particular label; we do not wish to enter into the "science wars" or any other such controversy here.

142. E.g., Karl Llewellyn, *The Common Law Tradition* (Boston: Little, Brown, 1962).

143. E.g., Richard K. Sherwin, "Dialects and Dominance: A Study of Rhetorical Fields in the Law of Confessions," *University of Pennsylvania Law Review* 136, no. 3 [January 1988]: 729–849; Sherwin, "Law Frames."

144. Objectivism, naïve realism, or both also seem to underlie what the sociologist Kim Lane Scheppele calls the "Ground Zero" theory of evidence (Kim Lane Scheppele, "The Ground-Zero Theory of Evidence," *Hastings Law Journal* 49, no. 2 [January 1998]: 321–34), the notion that the most reliable knowledge comes from the evidence that is closest to the event, the least "adulterated," the least mediated.

145. See, e.g., the "Received View" of trials in Robert P. Burns, *A Theory of the Trial* (Princeton: Princeton University Press, 1999); see also Charles Nesson, "The Evidence or the Event? On Judicial Proof and the Acceptability of Verdicts," *Harvard Law Review* 98, no. 7 (May 1985): 1357–92.

146. See Marc Galanter, *Lowering the Bar: Lawyer Jokes and Legal Culture* (Madison: University of Wisconsin Press, 2006).

147. This generalization elides distinctions between different representational technologies and over time. Specifically, as judges and jurors become increasingly familiar with a given technology, they may habituate to it, to the point of failing to notice its mediating status and instead "seeing through it" as a "window onto reality," as naïve audiences have tended to do (e.g.) with photographs and television (see Feigenson, "Too Real?").

148. See, e.g., Giere, *Scientific Perspectivism*, 14: Even when data are produced by the most "objective" scientific instrumentation, "no instrument is perfectly transparent. That is, the output is a function of both the input and the internal constitution of the instrument." What the output means and what is done with it, of course, involve further relationships among theory, instrumentation, observation, practice conventions, and so on.

CHAPTER 4

1. These pictures are thus to be distinguished from those discussed in chapter 3, some of which also accompanied expert testimony (e.g., the illustrations and multimedia sequence in *Bontatibus*, presented during the direct examination of the defendant's fire safety expert) but were offered to illustrate conclusions that the expert had already reached. The distinction maps roughly onto the traditional evidentiary one between demonstrative evidence (the kinds of pictures studied in chapter 3) and pictures that are themselves substantive evidence (but see chapter 3, as well as our discussion of *Swinton* later in this chapter, for problems with this distinction).

2. Sheila Jasanoff, "The Eye of Everyman: Witnessing DNA in the Simpson Trial," *Social Studies of Science* 28, nos. 5-6 (October-December 1998): 716.

3. This is one of the main themes of Jennifer Mnookin, *Envisioning Evidence: Expertise and Visual Proof in the American Courtroom* (forthcoming). In her history of the early reception of scientific and visual evidence in American law, Mnookin argues that courtrooms are "epistemological public spaces" in which science as well as law seeks validation. The law (with some equivocation) welcomed visual evidence to make sure that legal outcomes would conform to the best available scientific knowledge. But, in addition, scientific expert witnesses sought to visualize their opinions to make them more convincing. Battles of paid experts not only were unsettling to judges, jurors, and observers of the legal system but also tended to cast science itself into disrepute. Visual evidence—machine-made, objective, and self-evidently true—was promoted as a way to bolster the experts' credibility and authority in the court of public opinion (see ibid. at 14 [April 2006 draft]). Responding to Mnookin's thesis is beyond the scope of this book, but her insights into additional dimensions of the sociology of legal knowledge are well worth noting.

4. Joseph Dumit, *Picturing Personhood* (Princeton: Princeton University Press, 2004), 112, defines "expert images" as "objects produced with mechanical assistance that *require* help in interpreting even though they may appear to be legible to a layperson." This captures many but not all of the kinds of scientific pictures offered in court, because some scientific pictures would not even appear legible to laypeople (e.g., autoradiographs formerly offered to illustrate DNA expert testimony). Later in the chapter we argue against Dumit's conclusion that "if [expert images] are legible, then they should not need interpretation, but if they need interpretation, then they probably should not be shown to juries" (ibid.).

5. On the tension between expert witnesses as teachers of lay audiences and lay deference to their perceived expertise, see, e.g., David S. Caudill and Lewis H. LaRue, *No Magic Wand: The Idealization of Science in Law* (Lanham, MD: Rowan and Littlefield, 2006), 31–36; Jennifer L. Mnookin, "Scripting Expertise: The History of Handwriting Identification Evidence and the Judicial Construction of Reliability," *Virginia Law Review* 87, no. 8 (December 2001): 1729–33.

6. *Daubert v. Merrell Dow Pharmaceuticals*, Inc., 590 U.S. 579 (1993).

7. *General Electric Co. v. Joiner*, 522 U.S. 166 (1997); *Kumho Tire Co. Ltd. v. Carmichael*, 526 U.S. 137 (1998). The "*Daubert* trilogy" is the law in United States federal courts and in many state courts, although even those states that purport to adopt *Daubert* vary considerably in the extent to which they do so.

8. Under Rule 702, if "scientific, technical, or other specialized knowledge will help the trier of fact . . . , a witness qualified as an expert . . . may testify thereto in the form of an opinion or otherwise, if[:] (1) the testimony is based upon sufficient facts or data, (2) the testimony is the product of reliable principles and methods, and (3) the witness has applied the principles and methods reliably to the facts of the case." Both Rule 702 and *Daubert* require the proponent of the evidence to persuade the court that the evidence is sufficiently reliable and relevant to the matter to be proven for the trier of fact to consider it. *Daubert* proposes four factors for trial judges to use in gauging the reliability of proffered scientific evidence: whether the theory or technique on which the testimony rests can be or has been tested; whether the theory or technique has been subjected to peer review and publication; the known or potential error rate of the theory or technique when applied; and whether the theory or technique has been generally accepted in the relevant scientific community (*Daubert*, 509 U.S. at 593–95). Most courts that follow *Daubert* apply these factors with varying degrees of rigor (Mara L. Merlino, Colleen I. Murray, and James T. Richardson, "Judicial Gatekeeping and the Social Construction of the Admissibility of Expert Testimony," *Behavioral Sciences and the Law* 26, no. 2 [March 2008]: 187–206), while other courts have turned to additional or alternative tests (see Advisory Committee Note to Fed. R. Evid. 702; *Daubert v. Merrell Dow Pharmaceuticals*, 43 F.3d 1311 (9th Cir. 1995)). In states that do not follow *Daubert*, the admissibility of scientific evidence continues to be governed by the older *Frye*

test, which asks whether the proffered evidence is based on a theory or technique that is "generally accepted" in the relevant scientific community (*Frye v. United States*, 293 F. 1013 (D.C. Cir. 1923)); about one-third of the states follow *Frye* (see David E. Bernstein and Jeffrey D. Jackson, "The *Daubert* Trilogy in the States," *Jurimetrics* 44, no. 3 [Spring 2004]: 351–66). In any event, the decision whether to admit scientific evidence (like any other evidence) is within the trial judge's discretion and may be overturned only if the appellate court finds that the trial judge abused that discretion (see *Joiner v. General Electric*, 522 U.S. 166 (1997)).

We are simplifying the evidentiary issues somewhat. Some courts might consider at least some of the pictures we have in mind (e.g., the fingerprint comparisons) as illustrations of expert testimony but not as substantive evidence themselves, in which case the pictures would not have to pass *Daubert* or other applicable rules governing expert evidence and would be admissible if they help the trier of fact understand the evidence (see chapter 3 for more on the illustrative/substantive distinction). If considered substantive evidence on which the expert relied outside of court in coming to the opinions offered in court, the pictures would raise hearsay issues if viewed as the equivalent of statements about the world offered to prove the truth of what they "assert" (cf. Federal Rule of Evidence 801(c) [2008]). Functional magnetic resonance imaging (fMRI) pictures, for instance, might be treated as pictorial equivalents of statements that the subject had such-and-such level of neural activity in such-and-such a location under specified test conditions. Scientific pictures treated this way could then be shown in court only if they fit some hearsay exception (e.g., if made in the course of the fMRI lab's ordinary business activity; Federal Rule of Evidence 803(6)) or if, under Federal Rule of Evidence 703, the jury were instructed to consider the pictures *not* as substantive proof but only as helping them to understand the expert's testimony and only if their value for the latter purpose substantially outweighed the risk that the jury would misuse the pictures as substantive proof.

9. Exceptions include Jasanoff, "The Eye of Everyman," and Mnookin, *Envisioning Evidence*. Other leading writers on the subject of digital visuals generally have not really delved into the topic of scientific picturing. See, e.g., Fred Galves, "Where the Not-So-Wild Things Are: Computers in the Courtroom, the Federal Rules of Evidence, and the Need for Institutional Reform and More Judicial Acceptance," *Harvard Journal of Law and Technology* 13, no. 2 (Winter 2000): 252–61 (briefly discussing admissibility of certain computer generated visuals under *Daubert* and Rule 702); Edward J. Imwinkelried, "Can This Photo Be Trusted?," *Trial* 41, no. 10 (October 2005): 48–55 (discussing foundational requirements for digital and digitally enhanced photos but without reference to *Daubert* or scientific evidence per se); see also Andrew C. Wilson and others, "Tracking Spills and Releases: High Tech in the Courtroom," *Tulane Environmental Law Journal* 10, no. 2 (Summer 1997): 371–95 (briefly discussing admissibility under *Daubert* and Rule 702 of computer generated materials offered to illustrate accident reconstruction expert testimony).

10. Jasanoff, "The Eye of Everyman," 731.

11. Of course, the experts themselves may disagree about the proper way to "read" a picture within their field of expertise. See, e.g., Malcolm Gladwell, "The Picture Problem: Mammography, Air Power, and the Limits of Looking," *New Yorker* (December 13, 2004), http://www.newyorker.com/archive/2004/12/13/041213fa_fact?currentPage=1 (last accessed July 29, 2008).

12. See David H. Kaye, David E. Bernstein, and Jennifer L. Mnookin, *The New Wigmore: A Treatise on Evidence: Expert Evidence* (New York: Aspen, 2004), 331–32; Tal Golan, *Laws of Men and Laws of Nature* (Cambridge, MA: Harvard University Press, 2004), 18–21; Carol A. G. Jones, *Expert Witnesses: Science, Medicine and the Practice of Law* (Oxford: Clarendon Press, 1994).

13. Kaye et al., *The New Wigmore*, 333; Golan, *Laws of Men*, 21–22; Jones, *Expert Witnesses*, 57–60 (discussing landmark case of *Folkes v. Chadd* (1782), which involved engineering testimony); see Golan, *Laws of Men*, 5–51, for an extended discussion and analysis of *Folkes*.

14. Mnookin, *Envisioning Evidence*, 7–9 (March 2006 draft).

15. Mnookin, "Scripting Expertise," 1723, 1727, 1747.

16. The use of photographic enlargements as evidence dates to the 1860 case of *Marcy v. Barnes*, 82 Mass. 161 (1860), a suit on a note, in which the plaintiff offered magnified photographs to show that the defendant's signature on the note was genuine (ibid. at 163–64). See Charles C. Scott, *Photographic Evidence* (St. Paul, MN: West, 1969), 1:3.

17. Mnookin, "Scripting Expertise," 1792–94. These composite photographs followed the precedent set by Sir Francis Galton, who used ostensibly objective methods to create photographic composite portraits of types, such as murderers or violent robbers, with "mechanical precision." See Lorraine Daston and Peter Galison, *Objectivity* (Brooklyn, NY: Zone Books, 2007), 168–71.

18. Bettyann Holtzmann Kevles, *Naked to the Bone* (Reading, MA: Addison-Wesley, 1997), 30–32.

19. Ibid., 32; for a detailed discussion of the case, see Golan, *Laws of Men*, 177–95. It appears that the X-rays were highly persuasive evidence.

20. Simon Cole, *Suspect Identities: A History of Fingerprinting and Criminal Identification* (Cambridge, MA: Harvard University Press, 2001), 177–81. The case is *People v. Jennings*, 252 Ill. 534 (1911).

21. *People v. Jennings*, 252 Ill. at 546.

22. Jennifer L. Mnookin, "Fingerprint Evidence in an Age of DNA Profiling," *Brooklyn Law Review* 13, no. 1 (Fall 2001): 26–28; see Cole, *Suspect Identities*, 182. Firearms identification evidence was first introduced around the same time. In a 1902 homicide trial (*Commonwealth v. Best*, 180 Mass. 492 (1902)), the prosecution's expert "pushed" a bullet through the defendant's rifle and compared it to the bullets taken from the victim's body. Photographs of the test bullet and the fatal bullets were admitted to prove the similarity. Andre A. Moessens, Carol E. Henderson, and Sharon G. Portwood, *Scientific Evidence in Civil and Criminal Cases* (New York: Foundation Press, 2007), 469–70.

23. See Golan, *Laws of Nature*, 191–92.

24. Kaye et al., *The New Wigmore*, 333–39; Mnookin, *Envisioning Evidence*, 10–11 (March 2006 draft). For a good discussion of the crisis provoked by conflicting expert witnesses in nineteenth-century England, see Golan, *Laws of Men*, 52–106.

25. Jennifer L. Mnookin, "The Image of Truth: Photographic Evidence and the Power of Analogy," *Yale Journal of Law and the Humanities* 10, no. 1 (Winter 1998): 1–74.

26. Kevles, *Naked to the Bone*, 95.

27. Samuel R. Gross, "Expert Evidence," *Wisconsin Law Review* 1991, no. 6 (November-December 1991): 1113–1232; Kaye et al., *The New Wigmore*, 339–47.

28. In addition, some traditionally accepted forms of forensic expert evidence, including handwriting and fingerprint analysis, have been newly scrutinized in recent years. On handwriting experts, see, e.g., D. Michael Risinger, Mark P. Denbeaux, and Michael J. Saks, "Exorcism of Ignorance as a Proxy for Rational Knowledge: The Lessons of Handwriting Identification 'Expertise,'" *University of Pennsylvania Law Review* 137, no. 3 (January 1989): 731–88; on fingerprint analysis, see Mnookin, "Fingerprint Evidence." On the need to reexamine forensic evidence after *Daubert*, see generally Michael J. Saks and Jonathan J. Koehler, "The Coming Paradigm Shift in Forensic Identification Science," *Science* 309, no. 5736 (August 5, 2005): 892–95.

29. From the inception of photography, photographers have altered pictures in the process of developing and printing, aiming to produce pictures that are faithful to what the photographer saw. Routine adjustments, regarded as standard professional practices, include changing the balance of light and dark and the degree of contrast, cropping (taking just a part of the picture rather than all the information on the negative), enlarging, or sharpening the focus. No professional photographer would consider their use to be lying or inappropriate manipulation unless they changed the meaning of the picture and not just its readability.

All of these sorts of alterations concern what in the film industry would be called the "post-production" stage: editing the photo already taken. Pictures can also be manipulated during "preproduction" by staging the scene or during production through the photographer's choice of camera angle, distance from the object, type of lens, and so forth. Unsurprisingly, staging pictures is frowned upon in documentary photojournalism (see, e.g., David Schlesinger, "A Brief Guide to Reuters Values and Standards," http://blogs.reuters.com/blog/author/davidschlesinger/page/2/ [January 18, 2007] [last accessed July 29, 2008]). It is, by contrast, essential in most scientific picturing; as noted earlier in the chapter, many objects and events that scientists picture could not be visually represented (or would not even exist) but for the scientists' effortful preparations.

30. See, e.g., Hany Farid, "Photo Tampering Throughout History," http://www.cs.dartmouth.edu/farid/research/digitaltampering/ (last accessed July 28, 2008); Errol Morris, "Photography as a Weapon," http://morris.blogs.nytimes.com/2008/08/11/photograph-as-a-weapon/index.html (August 11, 2008) (last accessed August 25, 2008).

31. In addition, pixels carry information about color, such as saturation (how intense and where on the spectrum of light visible to human vision) and luminance (how dark or light).

32. For examples of how photographs can be altered layer by layer in Photoshop, see Sébastien Gaucher, http://www.seb4d.com/ (last accessed July 29, 2008) (click on "Tutorials" and choose the second thumbnail from the left [the house]).

33. William J. Mitchell, *The Reconfigured Eye* (Cambridge, MA: MIT Press, 1992), 31.

34. See, e.g., "Hwang Woo Suk," http://en.wikipedia.org/wiki/Hwang_Woo-Suk#Controversies (last accessed July 29, 2008); see also Jennifer Couzin, Constance Holden, and Sei Chong, "Hwang Aftereffects Reverberate at Journals," *Science* 311, no. 5759 (January 20, 2006): 321.

35. Gareth Cook, "Photos Cast New Doubt on Cloning," *Boston Globe*, December 20, 2005.

36. "Not Picture-Perfect," *Nature* 439, no. 7079 (February 23, 2006): 891–92.

37. Mike Rossner, "How to Guard Against Image Fraud," *The Scientist* 20, no. 3 (2006): 24–25; *Nature*, http://www.nature.com/authors/editorial_policies/image.html (2006) (last accessed July 29, 2008) (*Nature*); see generally Jennifer Couzin, "Don't Pretty Up That Picture Just Yet," *Science* 314, no. 5807 (December 22, 2006): 1866–68.

38. Scientific Working Group/Imaging Technology (SWGIT), "Overview of SWGIT and the Use of Imaging Technology in the Criminal Justice System," Version 3.0 2006.01.09, at 3 (2006); "Best Practices for Documenting Image Enhancement," Version 1.2 2004.03.04 (2004).

39. Parts of the following discussion are adapted from Lisa Podolski and Neal Feigenson, "Digitally Processed Images in Connecticut Courts After *Swinton*," *Connecticut Trial Lawyers Association Forum* 25, no. 1 (Winter 2007): 33–41.

40. See Dr. Constantine (Gus) Karazulas, Chief Forensic Odontologist, Connecticut State Police Forensic Science Lab, "New Forensic Odontology Tools" (paper, March 28, 2001) (on file with authors). The defendant also made several incriminating statements which the State offered against him at trial. *State of Connecticut v. Swinton*, 268 Conn. 781, 788–94 (2004).

41. *Swinton*, 268 Conn. at 787, 828 ("highly qualified").

42. Ibid., 794–95.

43. Ibid., 794 (Lucis), 826 (Photoshop).

44. Ibid., 794.

45. Ibid. The court also ruled that the error in admitting the overlays was harmless and therefore did not warrant reversal of Swinton's conviction.

46. Lucis enhances variations in image intensity by mathematically processing the image as a two-dimensional array of numeric data, selectively detecting and emphasizing certain aspects of the visual information, and converting the result back into an image (Image Content Technology LLC, "Lucis DHP Algorithm Technical Overview" [2003]: 4). Lucis processes color images

by first "reading" each pixel in a color image for its three values: hue, saturation, and luminance. ("Hue" represents the specific color of the pixel, "saturation" indicates how strong the color is, and "luminance" indicates how bright the picture is [ibid., 11].) Lucis then performs DHP on the luminance information in the image, as luminance represents the contrast information in the image. After DHP is done, Lucis recombines the original hue and saturation information for each pixel with the new luminance value and translates these values back into the original image format. Since Lucis does not alter the hue and saturation information, the output from Lucis contains the same color information as the original image. A change in color appears, however, because the intensity or brightness of the pixel has been shifted (ibid.). This change in pixel intensity makes visible details that would otherwise be undetectable or unclear.

47. See discussion of Palmbach's testimony at the *Swinton* trial; see also http://www.imagecontent.com/lucis/whitepaper.html (last accessed July 31, 2008). The program is potentially useful in any case in which bringing out image detail is important. For instance, Lucis can make faint handwriting or other inscriptions more legible, enhancing the usefulness of documentary evidence (Dr. Gregory S. Golden, DDS, Chief Odontologist, County of San Bernardino, CA, e-mail message to author Feigenson, March 10, 2006; Brian Matsumoto, Associate Adjunct Professor, University of California at Santa Barbara, Department of Molecular, Cellular, and Developmental Biology, interview by author Feigenson, March 10, 2006 [notes on file with authors]). It can be used to bring out details in X-rays and CT scans, which may be probative in medical malpractice cases or to prove injuries in any sort of case. Lucis is helpful in stress analysis, which may be relevant in products liability, construction, and environmental litigation. And it can bring out differences in particulate detail in the composition of materials, which may be relevant in patent or other litigation.

48. In any image-processing program, the visual data file on the sensor chip has to be read by software. A high-resolution file is very large, and so, to make the data file usable, it is often compressed through various algorithms, some of which involve data loss. Lucis shifts the relative emphasis of variations in pixel intensity without discarding whatever picture information is in the file before Lucis is used.

49. Of course, while Lucis can enhance variations in contrast in an image, if the variations are not present in the original version, Lucis cannot do anything about it. (Arguably, this is not a limitation of the program at all but rather a strength: It confirms that Lucis does not show viewers anything that was not in the original image.) A drawback is that Lucis is prone to create one visual artifact: a shadowing or highlighting at the edge of a sharp discontinuity that can obscure some of the information in a narrow band near the discontinuity. This artifact, however, is easy to identify, and other imaging-processing programs are prone to multiple artifacts (Barbara Williams, CEO, Image Content Technology LLC [makers of Lucis], interviews by author Feigenson, January 17, 2006 and February 27, 2006 [notes on file with authors]).

50. But not impossible. Hany Farid, a mathematician, has been developing specialized software for detecting subtle picture alterations (Hany Farid, "Digital Doctoring: How to Tell the Real from the Fake," *Significance* 3, no. 4 [2006]: 162–66), and Mike Rossner, Editor-in-Chief of the *Journal of Cell Biology*, has shown how to use Photoshop to detect some manipulations (Rossner, "How to Guard Against Image Fraud"); see also Nicholas Wade, "It May Look Authentic; Here's How to Tell It Isn't," *New York Times*, January 24, 2006 (discussing work of Rossner, Farid, and others). For a discussion of these issues from the perspective of the forensic professional preparing exhibits for courtroom use, see George Reis, *Forensics for Professionals* (Indianapolis, Indiana: Wiley, 2007).

51. Dr. Adam J. Freeman, DDS, Forensic Odontologist, interview by author Feigenson, March 4, 2006 (notes on file with authors). According to Freeman, Photoshop is generally more widely used because it is more affordable than Lucis, which is a more expensive software option and relatively new.

52. C. Michael Bowers, *Forensic Dental Evidence* (San Diego: Elsevier, 2004); Raymond J. Johansen and C. Michael Bowers, *Digital Analysis of Bite Mark Evidence Using Adobe Photoshop* (Santa Barbara, CA: Forensic Imaging Services, 2000).

53. Kasey Wertheim, "Adobe Photoshop for Demonstrating Latent Print Uniqueness," *Journal of Forensic Identification* 56, no. 6 (November-December 2003): 707–21.

54. Charles E. H. Berger and others, "Color Separation in Forensic Image Processing," *Journal of Forensic Sciences* 51, no. 1 (January 2006): 100–2; Alan Chaikovsky and others, "Color Separation of Signature and Stamp Inks to Facilitate Handwriting Examination," *Journal of Forensic Sciences* 48, no. 6 (November 2003): 1396–1405.

55. First, the photograph was scanned without enhancement into the computer. (Most scanners automatically enhance the image as it is scanned, which may make the image more visually appealing but removes data. The scanner used to create the images in *Swinton* was set to scan without enhancing the image. [We thank Barbara Williams for this observation.]) Next, a particular part of the picture was selected for enhancement; finally, "contrast ranges" were defined by manipulating a pair of cursors within the program. Once the cursors were set to particular values, the computer performed an algorithm and produced a picture in a "one-to-one" format (i.e., the same size as the unenhanced photograph).

56. *Swinton*, 268 Conn. at 799–800. Palmbach was not qualified, however, as an expert in computer programs and thus could not explain the Lucis algorithm itself or how it worked (ibid. at 801).

57. Ibid., 786–87 & n. 4.

58. Ibid., 822–23. Although the opinion is not entirely clear about this, it appears that Karazulas created some of the dentition tracings by placing the molds taken of the defendant's teeth directly on a scanner, scanning the image, and then creating the tracings as above (ibid., 822 n. 36, 823 n. 39).

59. Ibid., 823.

60. Karazulas, "New Forensic Odontology Tools," Figure 8 (corresponding to State's exhibit 117 at the *Swinton* trial; 268 Conn. at 823–24).

61. Karazulas, "New Forensic Odontology Tools," Figures 6–7, 9–10 (corresponding to State's exhibits 118–121).

62. *Swinton*, 268 Conn. at 821–22.

63. Ibid., 824–25.

64. Cf., e.g., Mnookin, "Fingerprint Evidence," 26–29. Karazulas later summed up his process: "I used Photoshop to created [*sic*] a semi-transparent impression of the teeth models. This was placed electronically on top of the image of the bitemark to clearly show the match. . . . To the best of my knowledge, no one had reduced the opacity of the teeth model and superimposed them on a bitemark in a court case. This process is the new gold standard for forensic odontology" (Karazulas, "New Forensic Odontology Tools," 3–4).

65. *Swinton*, 268 Conn. at 827–28.

66. Ibid., 827 n. 43.

67. Ibid., 828 & n. 46.

68. The law on this question, including Federal Rule of Evidence 702 (or the state law versions thereof), *Daubert*, and *Frye*, is summarized earlier in the chapter.

69. The court rejected the defendant's argument on appeal that bite mark evidence in general is unreliable, *Swinton*, 268 Conn. at 796–97 n. 14, and there does not appear to have been any challenge to Dr. Karazulas's qualifications to testify as an expert in this regard (cf. ibid., 820–21 [Karazulas's qualifications]). Bite mark evidence has often been admitted in American courts, but, like other forensic identification disciplines based on pattern analyses, it may well be subject to greater scrutiny as more courts adopt the letter or spirit of *Daubert*. For an overview of the law and the science, see "Identification from Bitemarks," in David L. Faigman,

David H. Kaye, Michael J. Saks, and Joseph Sanders, *Science in the Law: Forensic Science Issues* (St. Paul, MN: West Group, 2002), 231–93.

70. *Swinton*, 268 Conn. at 802–3 & nn. 20–21.

71. The State's use of Lucis, for instance, seemed to blur the difference between merely *presenting* (traditional photographic) evidence and *creating* new visual evidence, undermining the usefulness of that distinction in helping the court select the appropriate rule (ibid., 804–5).

72. Ibid., 804, 818. The court seemed especially concerned that "[d]igital images are easier to manipulate than traditional photographs and digital manipulation is more difficult to detect" (ibid., 805 n. 24, quoting Jill Witkowski, "Can Juries Really Believe What They See? New Foundational Requirements for the Authentication of Digital Images," *Washington University Journal of Law and Policy* 10 (2002): 267–94). On the detection of digital image manipulation, see Farid, "Digital Doctoring"; Wade, "It May Look Authentic." Note that although simple, unenhanced digital photographs (and videos) are literally "computer-generated evidence," it would seem that the court would not subject them to the more demanding foundational requirements of *Swinton* but only to the basic requirements applied to analog photographs. Such a conclusion might be justified on the ground that for the digital image to be manipulated, it has to be processed through some other program (which itself will be subject to the more stringent requirements) and/or that digital photography is already considered to have achieved sufficient "inherent reliability" to obviate a more demanding foundation (see *Swinton*, 268 Conn. at 831 n. 51).

73. Federal Rule of Evidence 901(b)(9) (2008) provides that a picture can be authenticated by evidence "describing [the] process or system used to produce [the picture] and showing that the process or system produces an accurate result." The idea that photographic and other similar evidence can be authenticated as substantive (not illustrative; see chapter 3) evidence by establishing the reliability of the process that generated it is known as the "silent witness" theory of admissibility; see Kenneth S. Broun, ed., *McCormick on Evidence*, 6th ed. [St. Paul, MN: Thomson West, 2006], 377–79). Fred Galves ("Where the Not-So-Wild Things Are," 259) has observed that the authentication requirements for ensuring the reliability of the process or system used to generate a picture also tend to satisfy the *Daubert* reliability test.

74. *Swinton*, 268 Conn. at 811–12 (quoting Christopher Mueller and Laird Kirkpatrick, *Evidence*, 2nd ed. [New York: Aspen, 1999]).

75. *Swinton*, 268 Conn. at 812 (quoting *Nooner v. State*, 322 Ark. 104 (1995)).

76. See Mitchell, *Reconfigured Eye*, 31–49.

77. E.g., Rossner, "How to Guard Against Image Fraud" (*Journal of Cell Biology*); *Nature*, http://www.nature.com/authors/editorial_policies/image.html (2006) (*Nature*).

78. Reis, *Forensics for Professionals*, 6, recommends that imaging professionals archive the original image; work only on copies of the original; use only valid forensic image processing procedures; and ensure that all processes are repeatedly and verifiable. We would add that taking meticulous notes to document all edits should also be a part of good picturing practices in forensic or basic science.

79. The sixth *Swinton* factor may seem to ask for verifying the accuracy of the picture by evidence of its correspondence to observed reality, but actually it's nothing more than a technical authentication rule, akin to establishing the chain of custody for a nonunique item of real evidence. For an historical precedent for the authentication of machine-made pictures based on the reliability of the process that produced them, see the discussion of early X-ray evidence in Golan, *Laws of Men*, 193–96.

80. *Swinton*, 268 Conn. at 825; Norman Pattis, interview with author Feigenson, July 7, 2008 (notes on file with author).

81. Ibid., 814–15.

82. Ibid., 815.

83. Ibid., 815–16.

84. Ibid., 816.

85. Ibid. And while Palmbach, not being a computer programmer or computer expert, was unable to testify, pursuant to the fifth factor of the court's test, that "the equipment was programmed correctly," the court appeared to find Palmbach's testimony on the first four factors sufficient to establish the reliability of Lucis and the visual evidence it was used to generate.

86. Ibid., 827–28 & n. 43.

87. Ibid., 828.

88. Even though the defendant's own expert testified that the American Board of Forensic Odontology considers Photoshop to be an "appropriate aid" in bite mark identification, the court found that this alone "does not satisfy our multifaceted standard." Ibid., 828 & n. 45.

89. Karazulas wrote that the "semi-transparent impression of the teeth models . . . was placed electronically on top of the image of the bitemark to clearly show the match" (Karazulas, "New Forensic Odontology Tools," 3–4). At trial, however, he was unable to describe clearly either the exact process by which the teeth were made to appear more transparent or the superimposition of the resulting translucent picture onto the bite mark photos (*Swinton*, 268 Conn. at 829–30). Among other things, he could not, according to the defense lawyer, Norman Pattis, give a satisfactory account of how a flat, two-dimensional picture (the acetate of the defendant's dentition) superimposed on another flat, two-dimensional picture (the bite mark photo) could accurately enough represent a curved, three-dimensional reality: the traces left by the biting of a woman's breast (Norm Pattis interview). As a result, the defendant was not able to cross-examine Karazulas effectively and was therefore not able to bring out for the jury the extent to which the visual evidence had been "created" (ibid., 830).

90. *Swinton*, 268 Conn. at 829–31.

91. As of this writing, *Swinton* has been favorably but not widely cited by other courts. See Catherine Guthrie and Brittan Mitchell, "The Swinton Six: The Impact of *State v. Swinton* on the Authentication of Digital Images," *Stetson Law Review* 36, no. 3 (Spring 2007): 706 (noting that ten cases had cited *Swinton* to that point).

92. See Steven Shapin and Simon Schaffer, *Leviathan and the Air-Pump* (Princeton: Princeton University Press, 1985).

93. The court stated that "[Gary] Weddle [the Fairfield University professor whom Karazulas had used to make the overlays], by the nature of his role in the actual creation of the overlays, is the most obvious choice to be the person qualified to testify regarding the Adobe Photoshop program, but we make no determination regarding whether his testimony, in and of itself, would have been enough to establish the reliability of this evidence" (*Swinton*, 268 Conn. at 831 n. 50).

94. Ibid., 821–25.

95. Jasanoff, "The Eye of Everyman," 731.

96. Ibid., 829 n. 47.

97. To align the biting edges of the semitranslucent teeth with the bite marks shown in the autopsy photo, the image of the teeth has been reversed left to right (as one can see by examining the reversed numbers on the scales on the overlay in Figure 4.2). Thus, the overlay accurately represents which teeth would have made which marks, but no camera could have captured the teeth from this angle (above) in the act of biting.

98. For instance, jurors who thought that the prosecution's visuals re-created the critical events for them (much as did the multimedia show in *Bontatibus* or a typical computer animation; see chapter 3) might have tended to downplay or ignore the absence of reliable population statistics (i.e., how many people in the population might be expected to display this dental pattern) or reliable testing of the expert's methodology, both of which ought to have been relevant to their judgment of the weight of the expert's opinion; instead, they might have thought that they had been presented with the forensic equivalent of a credible eyewitness to the crime.

99. We are not aware, however, that either tactic was tried.

100. See, *e.g.*, Felice Frankel, *Envisioning Science* (Cambridge, MA: MIT Press, 2002).

101. On visual rhetoric in science generally, see, e.g., Luc Pauwels, ed., *Visual Cultures of Science* (Hanover, NH: Dartmouth University Press, 2006); Michael Lynch and Steve Woolgar, eds., *Representation in Scientific Practice* (Cambridge, MA: MIT Press, 1988).

102. See Roald Hoffmann and Pierre Laszlo, "Representation in Chemistry," *Diogenes* 147 (Fall 1989): 23–51.

103. An example of this is the recent repurposing of a well-known educational animation, "The Inner Life of the Cell," by the intelligent design advocate William Dembski (interview with David Bolinsky, head of XVIVO, creators of the animation, December 20, 2007).

104. Federal Rule of Evidence 403 (2008).

105. This and the following section are adapted from Neal Feigenson, "Brain Imaging and Courtroom Evidence: On the Admissibility and Persuasiveness of fMRI," *International Journal of Law in Context* 2, no. 3 (2006): 233–55. We would also like to thank R. Todd Constable, Professor Diagnostic Radiology, Biomedical Engineering, and Neurosurgery, Director of MRI Research, Co-Director of the Yale MRRC, Yale University School of Medicine, for sharing his expertise in fMRI with us.

106. *United States v. Hinckley*, 525 F. Supp. 1342 (D.D.C. 1981). The case is discussed briefly in Dumit, *Picturing Personhood*.

107. See, e.g., "Terri Schiavo's 2002 CT Scan," March 29, 2005, http://www.msnbc.msn.com/id/7328639/ (last accessed July 29, 2008).

108. Its more precise functional brain mapping may facilitate planning for neurosurgery and allow for more effective development and administration of pain therapies (Columbia University functional MRI, "About Functional MRI: The Future Role of Functional MRI in Medical Applications" [2006], http://www.fmri.org/fmri.htm [last accessed July 29, 2008]). Functional MRI can detect abnormalities in brain function in persons at risk for Alzheimer's before the clinical presentation of symptoms characteristic of the disease (A. Parry and P. M. Matthews, "Functional Magnetic Resonance Imaging [fMRI]: A 'Window' Into the Brain" [2002], http://www.fmrib.ox.ac.uk/fmri_intro/fmri_intro.php [last accessed July 29, 2008]). And fMRI has already yielded unprecedented insights into the physiological bases for human cognitions, perceptions, and judgments (Joshua Greene, "From Neural 'Is' to Moral 'Ought': What Are the Moral Implications of Neuroscientific Moral Psychology?," *Nature Reviews: Neuroscience* 4, no. 10 [October 2003]: 846–50; Joshua Greene and others, "An fMRI Investigation of Emotional Engagement in Moral Judgment," *Science* 293, no. 5537 [September 14, 2001]: 2105–8).

109. See, e.g., Jeffrey Rosen, "Neurolaw," *New York Times Sunday Magazine* (March 11, 2007), 48–53, 70, 77, 82, 84.

110. The wide range of possible legal applications of fMRI is suggested in part by the previous and ongoing uses of CT, PET, SPECT, and other neuroimaging technologies in various legal proceedings. First, fMRI evidence may be offered to prove *adjudicative* facts, i.e., facts that are germane and limited to the particular case at hand (Kenneth Davis, "An Approach to Problems of Evidence in the Administrative Process," *Harvard Law Review* 55, no. 3 [January 1942]: 364–425). These include (i) determining the presence of brain injury due to trauma (e.g., *Green v. K-Mart*, 849 So. 2d 814 (La. App. 2003); cf. *Penney v. Praxair*, 116 F.3d 330 (8th Cir. 1997)); (ii) determining possible causes of brain injury (e.g., *Elam v. Lincoln Electric Co.*, 362 Ill. App. 3d 884 (2005); *Hose v. Chicago Northwestern Transp. Co.*, 70 F.3d 698 (8th Cir. 1995); *Rhilinger v. Jancsics*, 8 Mass. L. Rep. 373 (Super. Ct. 1998)); (iii) determining mental capacity for various purposes, including (a) the insanity defense (e.g., *United States v. Hinckley*, 525 F. Supp. 1324 (D.D.C. 1981); *People v. Weinstein*, 591 N.Y.S.2d 715 (Sup. Ct. 1992); see also President's Council on Bioethics, "An Overview of the Impact of Neuroscience Evidence in Criminal Law" [2004], http://www.bioethics.gov/background/neuroscience_evidence.html [last accessed July 29, 2008]; (b) *mens rea*, i.e., the specific intent required for proof of most

crimes (e.g., *People v. Williams*, 2004 Cal. App. Unpub. LEXIS 3213 (Ct. App. 2004); cf. *Jackson v. Calderon*, 211 F.3d 1148 (9th Cir. 2000)); and (c) competency, whether (A) to stand trial (e.g., *United States v. Gigante*, 982 F. Supp. 140 (E.D.N.Y. 1997), (B) to receive the death penalty or to be put to death (e.g., *State of Delaware v. Red Dog*, 1993 Del. Super. LEXIS 93), or (C) to execute a contract or a will or to give informed consent (Henry T. Greely, "Prediction, Litigation, Privacy, and Property: Some Possible Legal and Social Implications of Advances in Neuroscience," in *Neuroscience and the Law*, ed. Brent Garland [New York: Dana Press, 2004], 114–56; Lawrence Tancredi, "Neuroscience Developments and the Law," in *Neuroscience and the Law*, 71–113); (iv) declaring brain death, especially in cases where nonfunctional testing, such as CAT scans, yields ambiguous results (*In re Guardianship of Schiavo*, 2005 WL 465405 (Fla. Cir. Ct.)); and (v) determining racial or other bias (Greely, "Prediction, Litigation, Privacy, and Property"; see Jennifer L. Eberhardt, "Imaging Race," *American Psychologist* 60, no. 2 [February-March 2005]: 181-90).

Second, fMRI may also be offered to prove *legislative* facts, i.e., general facts relevant to legal reasoning and the lawmaking process, including the formulation of legal rules or principles by judges (Davis, "Problems of Evidence"). For instance, fMRI studies showing differences between adolescents' and adults' brain activity while participants were engaged in moral appraisal and reasoning tasks were cited in the briefs to the U.S. Supreme Court that successfully argued that executing juveniles is unconstitutional (*Roper v. Simmons*, 543 U.S. 551 (2005); *Roper v. Simmons*, Brief for Respondent, 2004 U.S. Supreme Court Briefs LEXIS 559, and Brief for Amicus Curiae of the American Bar Association, 2004 U.S. Supreme Court Briefs LEXIS 425; for a review of the research, see Mary Beckman, "Crime, Culpability, and the Adolescent Brain," *Science* 305, no. 5684 [July 30, 2004]: 596-99). In *Roper*, the Supreme Court alluded to "scientific and sociological studies" in finding that juveniles are in general less able than adults to control their behavior in a socially responsible fashion, and therefore, that juveniles cannot be among the "worst offenders" for whom the ultimate punishment of death is warranted (*Roper v. Simmons*, 543 U.S. at 569–70). The Court did not, however, specifically refer to neuroscientific research. In any event, the Court's prior finding of a "national consensus against the death penalty for juveniles" (ibid., 564) appears to have been a more important ground for its holding that executing juveniles is unconstitutional.

111. For a good popular introduction, see Margaret Talbot, "Duped," *New Yorker* (July 2, 2007), 52–61. For a sampling of the recent neurolegal literature, see Henry T. Greely and Judy Illes, "Neuroscience-Based Lie Detection: The Urgent Need for Regulation," *American Journal of Law and Medicine* 33, nos. 2–3 (2007): 377–431; Leo Kittay, "Admissibility of fMRI Lie Detection: The Cultural Bias Against Mind-Reading Devices," *Brooklyn Law Review* 72, no. 4 (Summer 2007): 1351–99; Michael S. Pardo, "Neuroscience Evidence, Legal Culture, and Criminal Procedure," *American Journal of Criminal Law* 33, no. 3 (Summer 2006): 301-37. A few of the leading scientific studies are F. Andrew Kozel and others, "Detection Deception Using Functional Magnetic Resonance Imaging," *Biological Psychiatry* 58, no. 8 (October 2005): 605-13; Frank Andrew Kozel, Tamara M. Padgett, and Mark S. George, "A Replication Study of the Neural Correlates of Deception," *Behavioral Neuroscience* 118, no. 4 (August 2004): 852–56; D. D. Langleben and others, "Brain Activity During Simulated Deception: An Event-related Functional Magnetic Resonance Study," *Neuroimage* 15, no. 3 (March 2002): 727–32; Tatia M. C. Lee and others, "Lie Detection by Functional Magnetic Resonance Imaging," *Human Brain Mapping* 15 (2002): 157–64; Sean A. Spence and others, "Cognitive Neurobiological Account of Deception: Evidence From Functional Neuroimaging," *Philosophical Transactions of the Royal Society of London* B:359 (2004): 1755–62.

112. E.g., Scott A. Huettel, Allen W. Song, and Gregory McCarthy, *Functional Magnetic Resonance Imaging* (Sunderland, MA: Sinauer Associates, 2004).

113. Ibid.

114. This is usually referred to as an *axial* view. FMRI data, when plotted onto a structural representation of the brain, are also depicted using sagittal (side) views or coronal views (from behind) and in various combinations.

115. E.g., Matthew Brett, Ingrid S. Johnsrude, and Adrian M. Owen, "The Problem of Functional Localization in the Brain," *Nature Reviews: Neuroscience* 3, no. 3 (March, 2002): 243, Figure 1.

116. For a more detailed analysis of the reliability and relevance of fMRI brain research as legal evidence and a brief discussion of the cases in which it has been presented, see Feigenson, "Brain Imaging and Courtroom Evidence."

117. Differences include the design of the experiments, the statistical algorithms used to synthesize the data, the protocols for reconciling data from different individuals' brains to a standardized "reference brain," and many other matters; see, e.g., Greely and Illes, "Neuroscience-Based Lie Detection."

118. For the argument that brain pictures may properly be used only to link structural abnormalities with specific cognitive deficits but should not be admitted to prove motivation, responsibility, or similar legal-psychological conclusions, see, e.g., Laura Stephens Khoshbin and Shahram Khoshbin, "Imaging the Mind, Minding the Image: An Historical Introduction to Brain Imaging and the Law," *American Journal of Law and Medicine*, 33, nos. 2-3 (2007): 171–92.

119. See, e.g., Talbot, "Duped"; Greely and Illes, "Neuroscience-Based Lie Detection."

120. Indeed, only a few reported cases (all arising from related litigation in different states) have mentioned its use in court. See, e.g., *Entertainment Software Association et al. v. Blagojevich*, 404 F. Supp. 2d 1051 (N.D. Ill. 2005), affirmed 469 F.3d 641 (7th Cir. 2006); *Entertainment Software Association et al. v. Granholm*, 404 F. Supp. 2d 978 (E.D. Mich. 2005) (preliminary injunction), 426 F. Supp. 2d 626 (E.D. Mich. 2006) (permanent injunction). In possibly a larger number of cases, medical testimony based in part on fMRIs has been offered to support private or administrative claims for disability, for instance, which have then been reviewed in court (e.g., *Torrado v. Kimberly-Clark Corp. Pension Plan*, 2007 U.S. Dist. LEXIS 23847 (E.D. Ark.)), although the fMRI evidence was not itself used in court.

121. See Feigenson, "Brain Imaging and Courtroom Evidence."

122. Dumit, *Picturing Personhood*. PET scanning involves the injection of a radioactive tracer into the bloodstream; by measuring electrical emissions, the process can, like fMRI, track brain activity in real time, but with lower spatial and temporal resolution.

123. Ibid., 112.

124. Ibid.

125. Dean Mobbs and others, "Law, Responsibility, and the Brain," *PLOS Biology, Public Library of Science* 5, no. 4 (2007), http://biology.plosjournals.org/perlserv/(last accessed July 29, 2008). Unless otherwise specified, references to fMRI images are to the most common mode of visualization in the scientific literature, the axial view of the "brain slice," produced by mapping the functional image onto a structural image and highlighting (coloring) voxels that meet the chosen significance threshold. Even a cursory review of the literature, however, reveals a variety of ways of presenting fMRI data (as we explain later in this chapter), and there do not appear to be any generally accepted standards.

126. Richard Henson, "What Can Functional Neuroimaging Tell the Experimental Psychologist?," *Quarterly Journal of Experimental Psychology* 58A, no. 2 (February, 2005): 228.

127. See, e.g., Mobbs et al., "Law, Responsibility, and the Brain."

128. For instance, the defense attorney in *People v. Weinstein*, 591 N.Y.S.2d 715 (Sup. Ct. 1992), was quoted as saying that PET "permits the defense to present to the jury, in highly effective color slide form, actual images of the defendant's brain" ("PET Scans Advance As Tool in Insanity Defense," *Journal of Nuclear Medicine* 34, no. 1 [1993]: 13N–16N, 25N–26N. Compare the title of a *New York Times* feature story: "Can Brain Scans See Depression?" (Benedict Carey,

"Can Brain Scans See Depression?," *New York Times* [October 18, 2005]). And, as one of the plaintiffs' lawyers in the *Entertainment Software Association* cases (*Entertainment Software Association et al. v. Blagojevich*, 404 F. Supp. 2d 1051 (N.D. Ill. 2005), affirmed 469 F.3d 641 (7th Cir. 2006); *Entertainment Software Association et al. v. Granholm*, 404 F. Supp. 2d 978 (E.D. Mich. 2005) [preliminary injunction], 426 F. Supp. 2d 626 (E.D. Mich. 2006) [permanent injunction]), the first case in which fMRI-based expert testimony was introduced, has observed: "Where do Illinois, California, and other states that have recently enacted this sort of anti-violent video game legislation get their findings that exposure to video games damages the frontal lobes? From 'new evidence' which [may lead some to believe that] you can look at the brain" (Katherine Fallow, attorney for plaintiffs in *Entertainment Software Association* cases, personal communication, December 23, 2005 [notes on file with authors]).

129. Jay David Bolter and Richard Grusin, *Remediation* (Cambridge, MA: MIT Press, 1999).

130. As one critic of the courtroom use of neuroimages has written, fMRIs "may appear to be deceptively similar to photographs of a person's brain." Jennifer Kulynych, "Psychiatric Neuroimaging Evidence: A High-tech Crystal Ball?" *Stanford Law Review* 49, no. 5 (May 1997): 1249–70.

131. E.g., Kevles, *Naked to the Bone.*

132. Judy Illes and Eric Racine, "Imaging or Imagining? A Neuroethics Challenge Informed by Genetics," *American Journal of Bioethics* 5, no. 2 (2005): 1–14.

133. See Mnookin, *Envisioning Evidence*, in which she explains the late-nineteenth-century recourse to scientific visual evidence as a desire for knowledge that, in its machine-made objectivity, would be superior to the partial and conflicting oral testimony of eyewitnesses (or even that of the expert witnesses themselves).

134. Quoted in Talbot, "Duped," 58.

135. See Michael Lynch, "The Externalized Retina: Selection and Mathematization in the Visual Documentation of Objects in the Life Sciences," in Lynch and Woolgar, *Representation in Scientific Practice*, 153–86.

136. This is assuming that the test yielding the fMRI picture was carefully designed to target exactly that psychological difference, which it may not have been (see earlier discussion of reliability and relevance issues in fMRI science).

137. Dumit, *Picturing Personhood.*

138. As Dean Mobbs and his colleagues have written: "[B]rain imaging provides only one window of many into the multiple influences on behavior that can be relevant to understanding why a person acted [as he or she did]. Such influences include the intricate interaction between genetic, prenatal, endocrinological, social, cultural, and economic factors" (Mobbs et al., "Law, Responsibility, and the Brain,").

139. Cf. M. R. Bennett and P. M. S. Hacker, *Philosophical Foundations of Neuroscience* (Malden, MA: Blackwell, 2003). For this reason, looking at fMRIs could also exacerbate jurors' general tendency to overattribute others' behavior to the kinds of people they are, rather than to the circumstances in which they find themselves—what psychologists call the fundamental attribution error—resulting in biased legal judgments. See Richard Nisbett and Lee Ross, *Human Inference: Strategies and Shortcomings of Social Judgment* (Englewood Cliffs, NJ: Prentice Hall, 1980). Note that, in many situations in which fMRI evidence is likely to be offered, the proponent may *want* to invite attributions of behavior to personal rather than situational factors—specifically, to aspects of the person (physiological brain impairments) for which the person should not be held legally responsible as opposed to aspects of the person (will) for which the person should. More invidiously, neuroimages of difference may exacerbate the effects of unconscious prejudice against outgroups (although they may also mitigate prejudice by showing people how their race-based perceptions are situation-dependent and amenable to change); see Eberhardt, "Imaging Race."

140. David P. McCabe and Alan D. Castel, "Seeing Is Believing: The Effect of Brain Images on Judgments of Scientific Reasoning," *Cognition* 107, no. 1 (April 2008): 343–52.

141. Ibid. McCabe and Castel's research is consistent with that of Deena Weisberg and her colleagues, who found that adding a bit of irrelevant neuroscience to explanations for various psychological phenomena made participants less able to differentiate good from bad explanations. Deena Skolnick Weisberg and others, "The Seductive Allure of Neuroscience Explanations," *Journal of Cognitive Neuroscience* 20, no. 3 (2008): 470–77.

142. See the discussion in chapter 3.

143. Françoise Bastide, "The Iconography of Scientific Texts: Principles of Analysis," in Lynch and Woolgar, *Representation in Scientific Practice*, 210.

144. Charles Goodwin, "Professional Vision," *American Anthropologist* 96, no. 3 (September 1994): 606–33.

145. Whether this sort of conformity or "strong link" between scientific knowledge and legal knowledge is the optimal relationship between law and science after *Daubert* is itself a matter of dispute. See David S. Caudill, "Law and Science: An Essay on Links and Socio-Natural Hybrids," *Syracuse Law Review* 51, no. 3 (2001): 841–62.

146. It should be noted that in the psychological research tending to show that participants are unduly influenced by neuroscience explanations (Weisberg and others, "Seductive Allure") or fMRI pictures (McCabe and Castel, "Seeing is Believing"), there was no equivalent to cross-examination.

147. Specifically, they can do this in the case of fMRI science, as exemplified by the cognitive psychologist Howard Nussbaum's testimony in *Entertainment Software v. Blagojevich*, case no. 05 C 4265 (N.D. Ill.) (transcript of hearing on preliminary injunction, November 14–15, 2005).

148. E.g., Neil Vidmar and Shari Diamond, "Juries and Expert Evidence," *Brooklyn Law Review* 66, no. 4 (Summer 2001): 1121–80.

149. See, e.g., Shari Diamond and Jonathan Casper, "Blindfolding the Jury to Verdict Consequences: Damages, Experts, and the Civil Jury," *Law and Society Review* 26, no. 3 (1992): 513–63; Vicki Smith, "Prototypes in the Courtroom: Lay Representations of Legal Concepts," *Journal of Personality and Social Psychology* 61, no. 6 (December 1991): 857–72; Vicki Smith, "When Prior Knowledge and Law Collide: Helping Jurors Use the Law," *Law and Human Behavior* 17, no. 5 (October 1993): 507–35.

150. More broadly, though, the proliferation of implicit meaning is not something that the law should strive to banish in order to conform to some naïve ideal of science as "free from rhetoric." Rather, it is inherent in all visual representation (see, e.g., Richard K. Sherwin, Neal Feigenson, and Christina Spiesel, "Law in the Digital Age: How Visual Communication Technologies are Transforming the Practice, Theory, and Teaching of Law," *Boston University Journal of Science and Technology Law* 12, no. 2 [Summer 2006]: 227–70), and it presents the law, like science, with occasions for elucidating those meanings and subjecting them to critical scrutiny.

151. E.g., Jamie Stockwell, "Defense, Prosecution Play to New "*CSI*" Savvy," *Washington Post*, May 22, 2005, but cf. Kimberlianne Podlas, "'The *CSI* Effect': Exposing the Media Myth," *Fordham Intellectual Property, Media, and Entertainment Law Journal* 16, no. 2 (Winter 2006): 429–65; Tom Tyler, "Viewing *CSI* and the Threshold of Guilt: Managing Truth and Justice in Reality and Fiction," *Yale Law Journal* 115, no. 5 (March 2006): 1050–85. Podlas and Tyler explain how the effect of *CSI* viewing on juror decision making may well differ from what is popularly supposed. For instance, contrary to the presumed pro-criminal defendant effect, viewing the show may incline jurors to give greater credence and weight to the prosecution's forensic evidence generally, which would lead to a pro-prosecution effect; and other basic social psychological principles (such as, according to Tyler, the need to see justice done) may incline jurors to convict the defendant despite any *CSI*-induced pro-defendant bias.

152. See D. Michael Risinger, "John Henry Wigmore, Johnny Lynn Old Chief, and 'Legitimate Moral Force': Keeping the Courtroom Safe for Heartstrings and Gore," *Hastings Law Journal* 49, no. 2 (January 1998): 439–40 (mentioning but not necessarily approving of this as one of several possible justifications for admitting real evidence lacking in strictly logical relevance).

153. Judges, too, may be prone to biases that displaying the fMRI images may help to counter. Recent research on trial court judges' efforts to implement *Daubert* and, in particular, the degree of scrutiny they give to different kinds of proffered evidence indicates that the more quantitative the expert evidence, the more likely judges applying *Daubert* are to exclude it (Merlino, Murray, and Richardson, "Judicial Gatekeeping"). It could well be that presenting the essentially quantitative data generated by fMRI technology in the nonquantitative form of a brain picture could help to counter this bias.

154. E.g., Brett, Johnsrude, and Owen, "The Problem of Functional Localization," 247, Figure 2.

155. E.g., Spence and others, "Cognitive Neurobiological Account of Deception: Evidence From Functional Neuroimaging," 17, Figure 4.

156. E.g., Huettel, Song, and McCarthy, *Functional Magnetic Resonance Imaging*, Figure 12.11; Spence and others, "Cognitive Neurobiological Account of Deception," 1759, Figure 3.

157. And, just as NIH has created an fMRI data center in which researchers who want to publish fMRI studies must deposit their raw data so that other researchers can reprocess that data (if they desire) using their own methodologies, it might be advisable to require parties that seek to introduce fMRI images into evidence to submit the raw data to their opponents (and to the court) so that the opponents can have their experts reprocess the data and show the court how different methodological choices and assumptions can yield different visual representations of the data. (We would like to thank Patrick LaRiviere of the University of Chicago for suggesting this.)

158. We would like to thank Todd Constable for pointing this out to us.

159. Finally, pictures can help explain how fMRIs mediate scientific knowledge of the brain in yet another way: by explicitly diagramming the stages of data generation (e.g., Huettel, Song, and McCarthy, *Functional Magnetic Resonance Imaging*, 186–88, Box 8.1) and/or image processing (e.g., Brett, Johnsrude, and Owen, "The Problem of Functional Localization," 244, Figure 1).

CHAPTER 5

1. Opening statements, as we'll see in a moment, occupy a kind of middle ground in which argument is officially forbidden but widely tolerated as long as it is not too explicit.

2. According to the Federal Judicial Center, for instance, in the twelve-month period ending March 31, 2007, the most recent period for which data are available, 1.4 percent of federal civil cases ended in trials, a little more than two-thirds of which were jury trials. The figure for criminal cases during the same period was 3.5 percent of criminal cases. *Federal Judicial Center Caseload Statistics, March 31, 2007*, http://www.uscourts.gov/caseload2007/contents.html (last accessed July 31, 2008). In state courts, for 2004 (the most recent year for which data are available), about 4 percent of civil cases ended in trials, including 0.5 percent jury trials. Richard Y. Schauffler, *Examining the Work of State Courts, 2005*, http://contentdm.ncsconline.org/cgi-bin/showfile.exe?CISOROOT=/ctadmin&CISOPTR=412 (last accessed July 31, 2005).

3. Nearly twenty years ago, one practitioner described his firm's use of digital multimedia to present demonstratives in informal and formal administrative proceedings; the administrative law judges he surveyed indicated that they did not often see lawyers using such tools, but doubtless their use has since increased (Richard J. Leighton, "The Use and Effectiveness of Demonstrative Evidence and Other Illustrative Materials in Federal Agency Proceedings," *Administrative Law Review* 42, no. 1 [Winter 1990]: 35). The National Institute for Trial Advocacy's

PowerPoint for Litigators, first published in 2000, is subtitled "How to Create Effective Illustrative Aids and Demonstrative Exhibits for Trial, Mediation, Arbitration, and Appeal" (Deanne C. Siemer and others, *PowerPoint for Litigators* [South Bend, IN: National Institute for Trial Advocacy, 2000]. Gregory Joseph, author of the treatise *Modern Visual Evidence*, recommends the use of video presentations at mini-trials, summary proceedings in which each lawyer presents his or her client's case to the principals for the other side (Gregory P. Joseph, *Modern Visual Evidence* [New York: Law Journal Seminars-Press, 1997], § 6.02[5], at 6–22, 23).

4. E.g., Joseph, *Modern Visual Evidence*, § 6.02[4], at 6–21; Bill Buckley, *How to Use Video Settlement Brochures* (DVD, available in the Bill Buckley Legal Video Archive [Series 1, Introductory Materials] at Quinnipiac University School of Law, Hamden, Connecticut).

5. Regina Austin, "The Next 'New Wave': Law-Genre Documentaries, Lawyering in Support of the Creative Process, and Visual Legal Advocacy," *Fordham Intellectual Property, Media, and Entertainment Law Journal* 16, no. 3 (Spring 2006): 850.

6. Ibid.

7. See, e.g., Bill Nichols, *Representing Reality* (Bloomington: University of Indiana Press, 1991), 34–38.

8. Video settlement brochures, like most legal visuals, are difficult for third parties to obtain and examine. An extensive (and, as of this writing, the only publicly accessible) collection of video settlement brochures and other legal video materials, the Bill Buckley Legal Video Archive, can be viewed at the Quinnipiac University School of Law in Hamden, Connecticut.

9. How available depends, of course, on whether the trial is televised or otherwise recorded and on whether particular visual displays become part of the publicly available record of the case. We do not address "cameras in the courtroom" in this book; for more on the latter issue, see chapters 6 and 7.

10. Robert P. Burns, *A Theory of the Trial* (Princeton: Princeton University Press, 1999), 37.

11. The American Bar Association has recently encouraged trial judges to pre-instruct jurors on the applicable substantive law, as well as more generally on trial procedures and the jury's role; see American Bar Association, *Principles for Juries and Jury Trials*, Principle 6.C.1 and Comment (n.p.: Thomson-West, 2005).

12. See, e.g., J. Alexander Tanford, *The Trial Process: Law, Tactics and Ethics*, 2nd ed. (Charlottesville, VA: Michie, 1993), 149.

13. See Paul Zwier and Thomas Galligan, "Technology and Opening Statements: A Bridge to the Virtual Trial of the Twenty-First Century," *Tennessee Law Review* 67, no. 3 (Spring 2000): 523–41. The basic psychological principles include *schema effects* (e.g., Shelley E. Taylor and Jennifer Crocker, "Schematic Bases of Social Information Processing," in *The Ontario Symposium on Personality and Social Psychology*, ed. E. Tory Higgins, C. P. Herman, and Mark Zanna [Hillsdale, NJ: Erlbaum, 1981], 1:89–134; Susan T. Fiske and Shelley E. Taylor, *Social Cognition*, 2nd ed. [New York: McGraw Hill, 1991], 124–41), the *"halo effect"* (Daniel T. Gilbert, "Ordinary Personology," in *The Handbook of Social Psychology*, ed. Daniel T. Gilbert, Susan T. Fiske, and Gardner Lindzey, 4th ed. [Boston: McGraw Hill, 1998], 2:89–150), the *primacy effect* (e.g., Murray Glanzer and Anita R. Cunitz, "Two Storage Mechanisms in Free Recall," *Journal of Verbal Learning and Verbal Behavior* 5, no. 4 [1966]: 531–60; Bennett B. Murdock, Jr., "The Serial Position Effect of Free Recall," *Journal of Experimental Psychology* 64, no. 5 [November 1962]: 482–88), and *priming effects* (e.g., Thomas K. Srull and Robert S. Wyer, "The Role of Category Accessibility in the Interpretation of Information About Persons: Some Determinants and Implications," *Journal of Personality and Social Psychology* 37, no. 10 [1979]: 1660–72). It has been claimed that "the vast majority" of jurors make up their minds during or immediately after the lawyers' opening statements (Donald E. Vinson, *Jury Persuasion* [Englewood Cliffs, NJ: Prentice Hall Law & Business, 1993], 161), and many trial lawyers believe that opening statements are crucial to jury persuasion (E. Allen Lind and Gina Y. Ke, "Opening and Closing Statements," in *The Psychology of Evidence*

and Trial Procedure, ed. Saul Kassin and Lawrence Wrightsman [Beverly Hills, CA: Sage, 1985], 232–52). The empirical research on the impact of opening statements, however, is more equivocal: Thomas Pyszczynski and Lawrence Wrightsman, "The Effects of Opening Statements on Mock Jurors' Verdicts in a Simulated Criminal Trial," *Journal of Applied Social Psychology* 11, no. 4 (1981): 301–13, found that the opening statements influenced mock jurors very early in the trial, predisposing them to favor one side or the other throughout the rest of the trial, while Paula L. Hannaford and others, "The Timing of Opinion Formation by Jurors in Civil Cases: An Empirical Examination," *Tennessee Law Review* 67, no. 3 (Spring 2000): 627–52, found through postverdict interviews with actual jurors that fewer than one in ten reported having begun to lean toward the plaintiff or the defendant during opening statements, whereas more than two-fifths reported beginning to lean during the presentation of evidence.

14. Tanford, *Trial Process*, 369.

15. Neal Feigenson, *Legal Blame* (Washington, DC: American Psychological Association, 2000), 114–15.

16. Tanford, *Trial Process*, 378.

17. A. Leo Levin and Robert J. Levy, "Persuading the Jury With Facts Not in Evidence: The Fiction-Science Spectrum," *University of Pennsylvania Law Review* 105, no. 2 (December 1956): 139–84. But not necessarily any Bible story: In New Jersey, e.g., and most other jurisdictions, "Golden Rule" arguments (based on the New Testament) are regarded as improper (see Neal Feigenson, "Sympathy and Legal Judgment," *Tennessee Law Review* 65, no. 1 [Fall 1997]: 1–78.

18. E.g., Tanford, *Trial Process*, 381–82.

19. As the Connecticut Supreme Court has stated (in language later quoted in its opinion in *Skakel*): "[C]ounsel is entitled to considerable leeway in deciding how best to highlight or underscore the facts, and the reasonable inferences to be drawn therefrom, for which there is adequate support in the record. We therefore have never categorically barred counsel's use of such rhetorical devices, be they linguistic or in the form of visual aids, as long as there is no reasonable likelihood that the particular device employed will confuse the jury or otherwise prejudice the opposing party. Indeed, to our knowledge, no court has erected a per se bar to the use of visual aids by counsel in closing arguments. On the contrary, the use of such aids is a matter entrusted to the sound discretion of the trial court" (*State v. Ancona*, 270 Conn. 568, 598 (2004) [in a trial of a police officer for fabricating evidence, approving the prosecutor's holding up a pair of blue tinted sunglasses during summation to symbolize what he referred to as the "blue code" of silence, "what he believed to be the unwillingness of some of the police officers to report and to testify truthfully" where that might implicate a fellow officer]).

20. See, e.g., *United States v. Crockett*, 49 F.3d 1357, 1360-61 (8th Cir. 1995) (trial court allowed prosecution during closing argument to project transparencies that characterized trial testimony argumentatively; appellate court found no abuse of discretion and affirmed, but commented in dicta on the situations in which the use of such devices could be restricted). For a review of the law on the display of visuals during opening statement, see Ray Moses, *Opening Statements in Criminal Cases* (Houston, TX: Center for Criminal Justice Advocacy, 2001).

21. *Standard Chartered PLC v. Price Waterhouse*, CV No. 88-34414 (Super. Ct., Maricopa Co., AZ, 1989), *rev'd*, 945 P.2d 317 (Ariz. Ct. App. 1996); see also Rorie Sherman, "And Now, the Power of Tape," *National Law Journal* (February 8, 1993); Richard K. Sherwin, *When Law Goes Pop* (Chicago: University of Chicago Press, 2000), 272 nn. 39–40.

22. *Standard Chartered PLC*, 945 P.2d at 359.

23. Ibid., 359 (quoting in part *People v. Thompson*, 555 N.Y.S.2d 266 (App. Div. 1990)).

24. The next four paragraphs are adapted from Richard K. Sherwin, Neal Feigenson, and Christina O. Spiesel, "Law in the Digital Age," *Boston University Journal of Science and Technology Law* 12, no. 2 (Summer 2006): 227–70. See Avi Stachenfeld and Christopher Nicholson, "Blurred Boundaries: An Analysis of the Close Relationship Between Popular Culture and the

Practice of Law," *University of San Francisco Law Review* 30, no. 4 (Summer 1996): 903–16; Kurt Eichenwald, "Kidder Will Pay Maxus $165 Million to Settle Insider Suit," *New York Times*, October 12, 1992.

25. In the ad, cowboys around a campfire learn—much to their distress—that the salsa that they have been eating with their dinner wasn't local (as was the advertised brand). "Hmmm, made in New York City," the hapless cook reads from the salsa jar label. "New York City?!!" cry the outraged cowboys in unison. "Get the rope!" In the final scene, we see the cook lying hogtied beside the campfire with the cowboys now happily consuming what is presumably the proper local brand—the advertiser's. According to the designers of the Maxis visuals, the map graphic was meant to resonate with the salsa ad: The image of Texas lassoing New York State invites a rapid, unconscious association to the TV ad's irate cowboys "lassoing" the hapless cook for importing a "foreign" and manifestly undesirable product from New York. See Stachenfeld and Nicholson, "Blurred Boundaries," 908–9.

26. Although "the Fifth Amendment does not forbid adverse inferences against parties to civil actions when they refuse to testify in response to probative evidence offered against them," *Baxter v. Palmigiano*, 425 U.S. 308, 318 (1976), the prohibition against judges and prosecutors suggesting that juries draw this inference against criminal defendants (recognized in *Griffin v. California*, 380 U.S. 609 (1965)) arguably taints its deployment in the civil context, as well.

27. After the video was shown but before the jurors began deliberations, Boesky and Kidder Peabody paid over $200 million to settle the case, a significantly higher amount than their earlier settlement positions; later, every juror asked to have his or her picture taken with the video graphics on the large courtroom screen. See Stachenfeld and Nicholson, "Blurred Boundaries," 912.

28. Some of the following discussion is adapted from Brian Carney and Neal Feigenson, "Visual Persuasion in the Michael Skakel Trial," *Criminal Justice* 19, no. 1 (Spring 2004): 22–35.

29. The verdict was affirmed by the Connecticut Supreme Court on January 24, 2006, *State v. Skakel*, 276 Conn. 633 (2006).

30. Jeffrey Toobin, interview on *Crossfire*, CNN, June 7, 2002, http://edition.cnn.com/TRANSCRIPTS/0206/04/ltm.11.html.

31. Dominick Dunne, "Triumph by Jury," *Vanity Fair* (August 2002), 123.

32. Lev Grossman and Simon Crittle, "Martha, RIP," *Time* (June 17, 2002), 34.

33. Suzanne Smalley and T. Trent Gegax, "At Long Last, 'Martha's Day,'" *Newsweek* (June 17, 2002), 36.

34. In the first clip, according to the prosecution, Skakel contradicted his own alibi. Referring to Andrea Shakespeare, a friend of the Skakels who had been at their house that evening, Skakel said: "And I remembered that Andrea had gone home." This statement was extremely important because every witness for both the prosecution and the defense had agreed that the alibi car—that is, the car in which Skakel claimed to have left his home well before the time of Martha Moxley's murder—left the area of the Skakel residence *before* the car that took Andrea Shakespeare home. Had Skakel been in the alibi car—the theory upon which his entire defense rested—he could not have seen, or later remembered, that Andrea had gone home. During the closing, the prosecution played this audio segment for the jury and simultaneously displayed a transcript of Skakel's words, just as the jury had previously heard and seen the words, except that the critical sentence in which Skakel contradicted his own alibi was highlighted in red. In the second audio clip, Skakel was heard discussing his latest alibi. In 1975, Skakel told the police that he had gone home after returning from his cousins' house, gone directly to bed, and not left his own house again that night. In 1997, however, Skakel related the following to Hoffman: "I said, 'Fuck this, you know why should I do this, you know, Martha likes me, I'll go, I'll go get a kiss from Martha. . . . I'll be bold tonight.' You know booze gave me, made me, gave me courage again." This statement established that Skakel changed his alibi and placed himself right at

the scene of the crime, looking for Martha Moxley at about the time she was being murdered. Again, the jury was able to hear Skakel's statement and simultaneously follow his words on the large courtroom screen.

35. Lynne Tuohy, "Remorseless Killer or Latest Scapegoat? After 27 Years, a Jury Will Decide Michael Skakel's Fate," *Hartford Courant*, June 4, 2002.

36. *State of Connecticut v. Skakel*, No. FST CR00-135792T, trial transcript, p. 138, lines 18–22 (June 3, 2002).

37. In addition, by leaving the discrete elements identifiable, the prosecution made clear that each had already been admitted into evidence, countering any possible charge that it had manipulated the evidence or misled the jury. See *State of Connecticut v. Skakel*, 276 Conn. 633, 769 & n. 106. The court there refers to both the photographs and the audiotape excerpts as "unaltered" when presented in the rebuttal. This, of course, overlooks the way in which the rhetorical significance of these audiovisual components is indeed changed by their being *excerpted*, *reframed* and *presented together* in an integrated multimedia show, as discussed in the text.

38. These observations are adapted from Sherwin, Feigenson, and Spiesel, "Law in the Digital Age," 245–46.

39. Cf. Donald P. Spence, *Narrative Truth and Historical Truth* (New York: Norton, 1982). Spence's book is devoted to unpacking the layers of narrative interpretation that lie between the psychoanalyst's case study of an analysand and whatever the factual truth of the matters of which the analysand spoke during therapy may be. He argues that the psychoanalyst's goal should not be so much to uncover that ground truth, to which the psychoanalyst is unlikely ever to have reliable access, as to help the analysand reinterpret his or her story of the truth in order to develop a functional self-narrative and self-image. In law, things stand a little differently, in that the legal system presumes that it often can have more or less reliable access to the truth of the matter. Nevertheless, from the trier of fact's point of view, it remains critical to integrate what seems knowable about the matters in dispute (historical truth) with, or into, a satisfying story that meshes with the trier's sense of how things go.

40. "[A] confession is universally treated as damning and compelling evidence of guilt" (Richard Leo and Richard Ofshe, "The Consequences of False Confessions: Deprivations of Liberty and Miscarriages of Justice in the Age of Psychological Interrogation," *Journal of Criminal Law and Criminology* 88, no. 2 [Winter 1998]: 429–96). The literary scholar Peter Brooks writes that "the law . . . today—as in medieval times—tends to accept confession as the 'queen of proofs.' Meanwhile, Western culture . . . has made confessional speech a prime mark of authenticity, par excellence the kind of speech in which the individual authenticates his inner truth" (Peter Brooks, *Troubling Confessions* [Chicago: University of Chicago, Press, 2000], 4).

41. See generally Saul M. Kassin and Gisli H. Gudjonsson, "The Psychology of Confessions," *Psychological Science in the Public Interest* 5, no. 2 (November 2004): 33–67.

42. Alessandra Stanley, "Hero, Hero: Tics, Flaws and Trouble at Home," *New York Times*, June 12, 2006.

43. Christina O. Spiesel, "The *CSI* Effect." Paper presented at symposium "The 'CSI' Effect': Litigation Strategies and Courtroom Dynamics," Suffolk University Law School, Boston, MA, May 10, 2007 (manuscript on file with authors).

44. See Steven D. Stark, "Perry Mason Meets Sonny Crockett: The History of Lawyers and Police as Television Heroes," *University of Miami Law Review* 42, no. 1 (September 1987): 249; see Tony Stein, "Real-Life Courtrooms Aren't Made for TV," *The Virginian-Pilot* (Norfolk, VA), November 13, 2003.

45. On appeal, the defendant recognized that this was the crux of the prosecution's strategy, complaining that "in the hands of the State's movie crew, an admission of masturbation literally [*sic*] became a confession to murder" (*State of Connecticut v. Skakel*, no. 16844, Brief of Defendant on Appeal, p. 78). Evidence offered by other witnesses at trial that Skakel had admitted to

the crime was scanty, arguably unreliable, and partly in conflict with other testimony. See Evelyn Marcus, "The New Razzle-Dazzle: Questioning the Propriety of High-Tech Audiovisual Displays in Closing Argument," *Vermont Law Review* 30, no. 2 (Winter 2006): 365.

46. A voice overheard or a voice from a tape recorder while pictures were on view might well have been perceived as merely a commentary upon other bits of reality (e.g., the photographic evidence) as opposed to part of that same reality. (See also discussion of sound in chapter 2.)

47. And, as if further emphasis were needed, the word "panic" in the transcript on the screen was enlarged and changed to red at that same moment.

48. Research on *change blindness* shows that people are surprisingly unaware of even large changes in their visual fields that occur gradually or outside their focus of attention (see Stephen E. Palmer, *Vision Science* [Cambridge, MA: MIT Press, 1999], 538; see also generally Daniel T. Levin, ed., *Thinking and Seeing* [Cambridge, MA: MIT Press, 2004]). Conversely, when the same changes occur suddenly, they become obvious (see Daniel J. Simons, *Surprising Studies of Visual Awareness* [2003] [DVD]). The changes on the screen in the *Skakel* argument were both sudden and within viewers' attentional focus.

49. See Marcus, "The New Razzle-Dazzle," 383.

50. Skakel, 276 Conn. at 769.

51. Ibid., 767, quoting State v. Ancona, 270 Conn. 568, 598 (2004).

52. See, e.g., People v. Ammons, 622 N.E.2d 58 (Ill. App. Ct. 1993).

53. Skakel, 276 Conn. at 767.

54. *Connecticut v. Skakel*, No. SC 16844, defendant's brief at 79 (filed Nov. 24, 2003).) If the charge of subliminal messaging had any basis in fact, upon investigation it would be verified and would indeed point to a risk of unfair prejudice that could substantially outweigh the presentation's considerable probative value. The claim, however, was entirely groundless. Subliminal messaging involves the display of an actual stimulus (for example, words) for such a short duration (say, one-twentieth of a second or less) or in such a masked way (for example, naked bodies subtly superimposed on ice cubes in a liquor advertisement) that the viewer is not consciously aware of having perceived the stimulus but is nevertheless affected by it. See, e.g., Ziva Kunda, *Social Cognition* (Cambridge, MA: MIT Press, 1999), 279–84. No subliminal content was concealed in the Skakel prosecution team's audiovisual presentation. All of the pictures, audio, and text that the prosecution put before the jurors in closing argument were properly admitted into evidence. All of the elements within the presentation, moreover, were disclosed to the defense lawyers well in advance of trial, so that they could be scrutinized for any objectionable aspects. (The uses of those elements in the closing argument, however, were not disclosed, in order to protect the attorneys' work product.) See Carney and Feigenson, "Visual Persuasion," 31.

55. We saw in chapter 4, in the case of fMRI, another example of technological mediation being deployed to create the impression of its absence, i.e., direct access to reality.

56. For instance, in an insightful critique of the prosecution's tactics, Evelyn Marcus argues that "[b]y repeatedly showing the victim's body as it was found beneath the tree at the same time he related Skakel's story about masturbating up *some* tree, the prosecutor visually reinforced for the jury what was, at best, a dubious connection—that the two trees were one and the same." Marcus, "The New Razzle-Dazzle," 388. Apart from whether the connection was "dubious" or not, Marcus correctly calls attention to an inference that the multimedia display triggered but left implicit and that jurors themselves, if they took the prosecution up on the implication, might not have been fully aware they were drawing. This is the sort of risk of misleading the jury that courts ought to scrutinize in any visual display.

57. Sources for the background material on Vioxx include: Marcia Angell, "Your Dangerous Drugstore," *New York Review of Books* (June 8, 2006): 38–40; Tamas Bartfai and Graham V. Lees, *Drug Discovery* (Amsterdam: Elsevier, 2006), 165–68; John E. Calfee, "The Vioxx Fallout,"

American Enterprise Institute for Public Policy Research (September-October 2005); Eric J. Topol, "Failing the Public Health—Rofecoxib, Merck, and the FDA," *New England Journal of Medicine* 351, no. 17 (October 21, 2004): 1707–9.

58. The results showed that 0.4 percent of patients on Vioxx and 0.1 percent of patients on naproxen suffered heart attacks. Claire Bombardier and others, "Comparison of Upper Gastrointestinal Toxicity of Rofecoxib and Naproxen in Patients With Rheumatoid Arthritis," *New England Journal of Medicine* 343, no. 21 (November 23, 2000): 1520–28. Thus, the VIGOR results were not published in a peer-review journal until roughly a year and a half after Merck received FDA approval to market Vioxx. Controversy later arose as to whether the percentage of patients taking Vioxx in the VIGOR study who suffered heart attacks was roughly 0.4 percent or 0.5 percent. This ambiguity resulted from a difference in how many heart attacks were included in the VIGOR data. See, e.g., Gregory D. Curfman, Stephen Morrissey, and Jeffrey M. Drazen, "Expression of Concern: Bombardier et al., 'Comparison of Upper Gastrointestinal Toxicity of Rofecoxib and Naproxen in Patients With Rheumatoid Arthritis,' N Engl J Med 2000; 343: 1520–8," *New England Journal of Medicine* 353, no. 26 (December 29, 2005): 2813–14; Sydney Z. Spiesel, "The Vioxx War," *Slate* (May 23, 2006), http://www.slate.com/id/2142160/ (last accessed July 31, 2008).

59. An FDA advisory panel appointed after Merck's voluntary withdrawal of Vioxx concluded, in February 2005, that the benefits of COX-2 inhibitors outweighed the risks and recommended that Celebrex and Bextra be allowed to stay on, and Vioxx to return to, the market. News reports subsequently revealed that many panel members had financial ties to Merck or Pfizer. On April 7, 2005, the FDA decided to allow Celebrex to continue to be sold, albeit with a stronger warning about cardiovascular risks on the label, but asked Pfizer to withdraw Bextra and, as noted in the text, did not allow Merck to bring back Vioxx. See Angell, "Your Dangerous Drugstore," 39.

60. Topol, "Failing the Public Health," 1708. Dr. Topol's videotaped deposition testimony was introduced into evidence and replayed during closing argument in the *McDarby* case.

61. Alex Berenson, "Plaintiffs Find Payday Elusive in Vioxx Cases," *New York Times*, August 21, 2007; Alex Berenson, "Analysts See Merck Victory in Vioxx Deal," *New York Times*, November 10, 2007.

62. Berenson, "Plaintiffs Find Payday Elusive" (twenty verdicts); Berenson, "Analysts See Merck Victory" (recent Merck victories).

63. Press Release, Merck Agreement to Resolve U.S. VIOXX Product Liability Lawsuits: Agreement Provides for $4.85 Billion Payment (Nov. 9, 2007), available at http://www.merck.com/newsroom/press_releases/corporate/2007_1109 print.html (last accessed July 31, 2008); Berenson, "Analysts See Merck Victory." As of this writing, the settlement had not yet been approved by all of the represented plaintiffs, but 95 percent had approved, and Merck was "nearly certain" that the settlement would go forward. Alex Berenson, "Courts Reject Two Major Vioxx Verdicts," *New York Times*, May 30, 2008.

64. Berenson, "Plaintiffs Find Payday Elusive."

65. Merck & Co., Inc. v. Ernst, 2008 Tex. App. LEXIS 3951.

66. Alex Berenson, "A 2nd Loss for Merck Over Vioxx," New York Times, April 6, 2006; Berenson, "Vioxx Jury Adds More in Damages," New York Times, April 12, 2006.

67. McDarby v. Merck & Co., Inc., 2008 N.J. Super. LEXIS 116 (App. Div.).

68. The law of products liability is generally premised on the notion that manufacturers have a duty not to make and sell defective products that cause harm. Under Texas law, the plaintiff in Ernst had to show that Vioxx was defective because of its marketing and/or its design. A "marketing defect" with respect to a product means the failure to give adequate warnings of the product's dangers that were known or by the application of reasonably developed human skill and foresight should have been known or the failure to give adequate instructions to avoid

such dangers, which failure rendered the product unreasonably dangerous as marketed (see "Products Liability," in *Texas Jurisprudence* 3d [St. Paul, MN: West Group, 2006] §55 [online]; *Sims v. Washex Machinery Corp.* 932 S.W.2d 559 (Tex. App. 1995)). An "unreasonably dangerous" product is one that is dangerous to an extent beyond that which would be contemplated by the ordinary physician with the ordinary knowledge common to the medical community as to the product's characteristics (*Otis Spunkmeyer, Inc. v. Blakely*, 30 S.W.3d 678, 682 (Tex. App. 2000)). A "design defect" is a condition of the product that renders it unreasonably dangerous as designed, "taking into consideration the utility of the product and the risk involved in its use" (*Hernandez v. Tokai Corp.*, 2 S.W.3d 251, 257 (Tex. 1998)). For a design defect to exist, there must have been a safer alternative design (ibid.).

The basis of the failure to warn claim in *Cona and McDarby* that, at least under applicable New Jersey law, manufacturers have a duty to provide adequate warnings about the dangers of their products (New Jersey Statutes Annotated 2A:58C-4 [2008]). "Adequate" warnings are those that a reasonably prudent manufacturer would have provided under the circumstances, taking into account reliable information generally available or reasonably obtainable in the scientific community (ibid.). So, although labeled differently, the failure-to-warn claim required essentially the same showing as did the products liability claim in the Texas case: that Merck knew or should have known of Vioxx's heart attack risks and failed to disclose those risks adequately to prescribing physicians and their patients.

69. Under the Texas law applicable in Ernst, a "producing" cause is "an efficient, exciting or contributing cause that, in a natural sequence, produces the injury. There may be more than one producing cause" (*Union Pump Company v. Allbritton*, 898 S.W.2d 773, 775 (Tex. 1995)). Texas case law also provides that only a defective product that is a "substantial factor" in bringing about the harm will render the defendant liable (ibid. at 776), but it is unclear whether there is any meaningful difference between the choice of terms. (The trial judge also instructed the jury that there may be more than one producing [or proximate] cause, and plaintiff's attorney Mark Lanier emphasized in his closing that the jury needed to find only that the Vioxx was "a" producing [or proximate] cause of Ernst's death [*Ernst v. Merck & Co., Inc.*, No. 19961*BH02 (Brazoria County, TX, 23rd Judicial District), closing argument transcript, August 17, 2005, 27, lines 12–18; 27, line 24–28, line 3].)

70. Merck's own reanalysis of the data from the APPROVe study (the study begun in 2001 to determine whether Vioxx reduced the incidence of precancerous colon polyps and discontinued in September, 2004) indicated that patients on Vioxx began to show increased rates of cardiovascular problems after as little as four months on the drug. The public release of this information triggered a firestorm in the press. See, e.g., Andrew Pollack and Reed Abelson, "Why the Data Diverge on the Dangers of Vioxx," *New York Times*, May 22, 2006.

71. *Ernst*, opening statement transcript, July 14, 2005, 105, line 25. Tom Cona may not have taken Vioxx continuously for *any* period of time: The record showed only one prescription in fifteen months preceding his heart attack and only three in all (*Cona and McDarby v. Merck Co., Inc.*, Nos. ATL-L-3553-05MT, ATL-L-1296-05MT (N.J. Sup. Ct., Atlantic County), opening statement transcript, March 6, 2006, 167, line 24–168, line 13 [argument of Christy Jones]).

72. See Alex Berenson, "Jury Calls Merck Liable in Death of Man on Vioxx," *New York Times*, August 20, 2005; Andrew Lawler, "Vioxx Verdict: Too Little or Too Much Science?," *Science* 309, no. 5740 (September 2, 2005): 1481. Lanier had to argue that Ernst suffered a heart attack because of a blood clot that was caused by the Vioxx, a heart attack that occurred so quickly that it left no muscle damage visible at the autopsy, and that the heart attack caused the arrhythmia (cf. *Ernst*, opening statement transcript, 50, line 25–53, line 4). The Texas Court of Appeals reversed the jury's verdict for the plaintiff on the ground that the plaintiff's expert witnesses failed to provide evidence sufficient for a reasonable jury to conclude that Vioxx had caused Ernst's death by clot or otherwise (*Merck & Co. v. Ernst*, 2008 Tex. App. LEXIS 3951).

73. E.g., *Cona and McDarby*, closing argument transcript, 4169, line 17–4170, line 9; 4172, lines 10–19 (closing argument of Christy Jones). Note that McDarby had also been taking aspirin, which (according to Merck's lawyer) would have countered any prothrombotic effect of Vioxx (ibid. at 4172, lines 3–9).

74. If jurors found Merck's behavior to be reckless or worse, they could award punitive damages as well as compensatory damages, as they in fact did to both Carol Ernst and John and Irma McDarby. While compensatory damages should not be affected by perceived culpability, if jurors (contrary to instructions) conflate responsibility and damage judgments, as some research indicates they do (see, e.g., Feigenson, *Legal Blame*, 106; Edie Greene and Brian H. Bornstein, *Determining Damages* [Washington, DC: American Psychological Association, 2003], 134–39), then attributing greater fault or blame to Merck could lead to larger compensatory awards as well.

75. For "communication theory wonk," Mark Lanier, interview by authors, September 6, 2006; for "take his skills to the next level," Cliff Atkinson, interview by authors, September 12, 2005 (all interview notes on file with authors).

76. Cliff Atkinson, *Beyond Bullet Points*, 2nd ed. (Redmond, WA: Microsoft Press, 2008).

77. Mark Lanier interview; Cliff Atkinson interviews, September 12, 2005, and September 28, 2005.

78. Anecdotal evidence suggests that thousands of lawyers are now using PowerPoint to augment their opening statements and closing arguments; its widespread use may also be inferred from the growing number of seminars and instructional materials for lawyers (e.g., Deanne C. Siemer and others, *PowerPoint for Litigators* [South Bend, IN: National Institute for Trial Advocacy, 2000]) and from passing references in dozens of cases to PowerPoint slide shows (e.g., *United States v. Honken*, 381 F. Supp. 2d 936 (N.D. Iowa 2005)). All of the appellate cases of which we are aware (e.g., *State v. Sucharew*, 205 Ariz. 16 (2003); *State of Hawai'i v. Smith*, 2006 Haw. LEXIS 163; *State of Missouri v. Wheeler*, 2007 Mo. App. LEXIS 624; *Browning v. State of Oklahoma*, 2006 Okla. Crim. App. LEXIS 17) that have specifically addressed the propriety of PowerPoint during opening statement or closing argument have upheld the trial courts' decisions to allow the presentations. They have done so primarily on two grounds. First, as noted earlier, trial judges have broad discretion to govern the conduct of trials, and their decisions to allow or prohibit the use of visual displays will be overturned only for abuse of that discretion. Second, the PowerPoint slides in these cases showed only pictures already admitted or to be admitted into evidence, and any textual labels on the slides "simply track[ed] the subject matter of the [lawyer's] statement" (*State v. Sucharew*, 205 Ariz. 16, 21). As with any other advocacy technique, the admissibility of PowerPoint in opening statements and closing arguments is within the broad discretion of the trial judge, and so it is unsurprising that there is so little case law on the topic, although the fact that most of the reported cases are so recent suggests that more challenges to and opinions dealing with these uses of PowerPoint may be forthcoming.

79. We discuss here only the opening statement in *Ernst*. For a discussion of the corresponding "framing" slide used in the *Ernst* closing, see Neal Feigenson and Richard K. Sherwin, "Thinking Beyond the Shown: Implicit Inferences in Evidence and Argument," *Law, Probability, and Risk* 6, nos. 1-4 (March-December, 2007): 295–310.

80. *Ernst*, opening statement transcript, 30, lines 17–18, 22–23. As Lanier speaks, a slide (11) appears with the logo of the popular television program *CSI*, except that the word "Angleton" (the Texas city in which the trial was being held) appears underneath. The popular cultural reference is very brief (in contrast, say, to the crucial audiovisual allusion to *The Hollywood Squares* in the Maxus case discussed earlier or to Lanier's use of *Desperate Housewives* as the central thematic in his closing argument in *Cona and McDarby*, discussed later), but, in addition to whatever entertainment value it provides, the mention of *CSI* cues jurors to expect that there will be a definitive answer to the mystery of what killed Bob Ernst and that the evidence will lead them to that answer by the end of the show—that is, the trial.

81. Mark Lanier interview.

82. *Ernst*, opening statement transcript, July 14, 2005, 32, lines 8–13.

83. *Ernst*, opening statement, slide 14.

84. Ibid., slides 15-151; see Atkinson, *Beyond Bullet Points*, 14–17.

85. In *Cona and McDarby*, during a colloquy with the trial judge before closing arguments, La-nier expressly disclaimed any intention to suggest to jurors that they were dealing with a criminal case (see *Cona & McDarby*, closing argument transcript, 4147, line 15–4148, line 11), and as we will see, he adopted instead a very different popular cultural model to frame the jurors' understanding.

86. The specific elements of a civil claim based in products liability—concepts like "defect," "failure to warn," and "causation"—are nowhere to be found in this slide or are at best left im-plicit, although, in his speech accompanying the slide, Lanier says, "The means [–] I'm going to show you Vioxx was a cause" (*Ernst*, opening statement transcript, 32, lines 20–21).

87. See Michael D. Green, Letter to the Editor, *Science* 310, no. 5750 (November 11, 2005): 973 (discussing *Ernst* and causation); see also Richard Nagareda, "Outrageous Fortune and the Criminalization of Mass Torts," *Michigan Law Review* 96, no. 5 (March 1998): 1121–98. Some of the postverdict remarks by the *Ernst* jurors seem to support this analysis. See Bill Dawson and Alex Berenson, "Working Through a Decision Cut in Shades of Deep Gray," *New York Times*, August 20, 2005.

88. See Feigenson, *Legal Blame*.

89. See Neal Feigenson, Jaihyun Park, and Peter Salovey, "The Role of Emotions in Compar-ative Negligence Judgments," *Journal of Applied Social Psychology* 31, no. 3 (2001): 576–603. Em-phasizing that Merck's executives were driven by the "bad" motive to maximize profit, although not relevant to the liability question, is relevant to the jury's decision whether, if they should find Merck liable, they should also assess punitive damages (as the trial judge recognized; see *Ernst*, opening statement transcript, 5, lines 13–16).

90. Cliff Atkinson obtained most of his illustrations for the *Ernst* PowerPoints from clip art available online and was able to find and incorporate the dozens of pictures he needed in a very short period of time. Then, having found the visuals he wanted, he used Photoshop to edit them so that they fit within the scheme of the particular slide and the presentation as a whole. With-out digital software and the Internet, all of this would have been much more laborious, indeed prohibitively so under the time pressure Atkinson faced on the eve of trial.

91. *Ernst*, opening statement transcript, 33, lines 6–7; opening statement, slide 16.

92. *Ernst*, opening statement, slide 55.

93. Ibid., slide 155; see *Ernst*, opening statement transcript, 33, lines 13–14.

94. *Ernst*, opening statement, slides 18–20.

95. Ibid., slide 19.

96. Ibid., slides 20, 22–23.

97. Ibid., slides 23–25.

98. Ibid., slide 28.

99. Ibid., slide 29.

100. Ibid.

101. *Ernst*, opening statement transcript, 35, lines 7–8.

102. Ibid., 35, line 14; 36, line 11.

103. Ibid., 34, lines 18–19.

104. Ibid., 38, lines 20–21, 25–p. 39, line 1; opening statement, slide 29.

105. Ibid., slides 21, 52, 91.

106. Ibid., slide 28.

107. Ibid., slide 46.

108. See, in addition to the slides already mentioned, ibid., slides 34 ("Key drugs are losing patents"), 36 ("Management is worried: key executives flee").

109. *Ernst* opening statement, slide 37.

110. As Lanier had told jurors at the outset of his opening statement, "[n]obody else can do it. . . . This is where you can make a difference in the world, absolutely can" (*Ernst*, opening statement transcript, 31, lines 5–7). The jurors know that they *can* take action, but will they want to? Visual persuasion, augmenting the verbal, may make the difference. For more on the interrelationships between perceived threats and blaming, see Neal Feigenson, "Emotions, Risk Perceptions, and Blaming in 9/11 Cases," *Brooklyn Law Review* 68, no. 4 (Summer 2003): 959–1001; Neal Feigenson, Daniel Bailis, and William Klein, "Perceptions of Terrorism and Disease Risks: A Cross-National Comparison," *University of Missouri Law Review* 69, no. 4 (Fall 2004): 991–1012.

111. *Ernst* opening statement, slide 51.

112. Lawyers may also avoid committing to particulars in their opening statements because at that point they cannot be sure exactly what evidence will be admitted at trial and they want to avoid appearing to have misrepresented the case to the jury or to have made promises they couldn't fulfill, either of which will undermine the jury's faith in the lawyer as a credible, trustworthy source. Moreover, lawyers may eschew detail in opening statements so as not to reveal too much of their trial strategy to the opponent—for instance, which witnesses' expected testimony will be critical to which aspects of the case. In all of these respects, opening statements are very different from closing arguments, by which point both the lawyers and the jurors know what evidence has and has not been admitted. The advocate's goal shifts from priming jurors to see and hear the evidence in a way that favors the client to referring back to that evidence in order to reinforce (what the advocate hopes is) the jurors' inclination to decide in the client's favor. Accordingly, the PowerPoint slide show that Lanier and Atkinson created for the *Ernst* closing argument, while maintaining a similarly consistent and simple visual style, includes many more probative pictures than the opening slide show does: For instance, the closing includes many more pictures of evidence (36 document slides, almost all with callouts, or 35 percent of the 103 closing slides, whereas only two documents, or 1.5 percent of the total, were shown in the opening) and more deposition video stills with transcript excerpts (11 slides, or 10.7 percent, but only one in the opening, or 0.6 percent). Fewer than a quarter (23 of 103, 22.3 percent) of the closing argument slides feature iconic stock photos or clip art illustrating verbal metaphors, whereas more than two-thirds (108 of 155, 69.6 percent) of the opening slides do so.

113. *Ernst*, opening statement transcript, 59, line 24–60, line 2; opening statement, slides 63–77.

114. *Ernst*, opening statement transcript, 60, lines 5–8.

115. See discussion of *processing fluency* in chapter 3; see also Feigenson, Park, and Salovey, "The Role of Emotions."

116. We find the same rhetorical contrast in the *Cona and McDarby* case. There Lanier tells jurors in his opening statement that "the truth is simple" (*Cona and McDarby*, opening statement transcript, 44, line 21), while Christy Jones, Merck's lawyer, begins her closing argument by telling them that "this is a difficult case" (closing argument transcript, 4159, line 3). In addition, in the *Ernst* opening, by using the *same* iconic illustration of the heart in four consecutive slides (*Ernst* opening statement, slides 69–72) as a backdrop to his list of the *different* problems caused when a COX-2 inhibitor like Vioxx "throws the cardiovascular system out of balance," Lanier also makes the entirely implicit visual argument that these problems—heart attacks (or myocardial infarctions), sudden cardiac death, and arrhythmias—are all of a piece, all related, all more or less the same thing. And getting the jurors to see these three problems as interrelated (e.g., *Ernst* opening statement transcript, 65, lines 3–7, 10–19) aids the plaintiff's case because (as noted in the text) clinical trials indicated that Vioxx posed an increased risk of heart attacks, but the coroner's report stated that Bob Ernst died of arrhythmia and there was (little or) no evidence that he suffered the kind of damage to heart muscle that is the signature of myocardial infarction (even though at least three expert witnesses testified that Vioxx was a contributing cause of Ernst's death).

117. 108 of 155 (69.6 percent).

118. The concepts of signifier, signified, and signification as used in the text are taken from the semiotician Roland Barthes, "Myth Today," in *Mythologies*, trans. Annette Lavers (New York: Hill and Wang, 1972), 117–19.

119. This is not to say that the stock photos Atkinson chose and modified are visually or rhetorically uninteresting in their own right; far from it. As noted in the text, for instance, the stock photos are often cropped so that only a portion of what must have been the original picture appears, leaving visible only a fragment of the scene or event. We see only hands shepherding chips or fingertips touching shells to indicate gambling (*Ernst* opening statement, slides 46, 96); only part of a hand, or even fingertips, grasping a pen to indicate the writing of prescriptions or checks (ibid., slides 126, 130). The edited picture now makes meaning through a kind of visual synecdoche, the part for the whole; the words on the screen then cue viewers as to how they should "complete the picture." So, for instance, the text of slide 126 reads, "Merck monitors every prescription Dr. Wallace writes" (ibid., slide 126), so we know that the closeup of a hand grasping a pen, poised above the prescription pad, is meant to exemplify the larger claim, "Merck goes after Dr. Wallace" (ibid., slides 123–35), which in turn stands for the more basic image of Merck as a money-hungry company pushing doctors to prescribe Vioxx while minimizing the drug's health risks. Note here how the *closeup* picture of the hand with the pen above a prescription pad creates a visual metaphor for Merck's intensive monitoring of prescribing physicians. At the same time, the pen is above the pad and the pad has not yet been written on, as if to signify that the good doctor is hesitating before bowing to pressure from Merck and writing the prescription.

120. E.g., Eve Sweetser, *From Etymology to Pragmatics* (Cambridge: Cambridge University Press, 1990).

121. In terms of the philosopher Paul Grice's well-known theory of *conversational implicature* (Paul Grice, "Logic and Conversation," in *Studies in the Way of Words* [Cambridge, MA: Harvard University Press, 1989], 22–40), Lanier and Atkinson have breached the "conversational norm" of the courtroom by offering these obviously nonevidentiary visual accompaniments to Lanier's speech, one after the other. But they have done so in such a way that the audience recognizes the breach of the norm.

122. Roger Parloff, "Stark Choices at the First Vioxx Trial," *Fortune* (July 15, 2005), http://www.sociablemedia.com/PDF/fortune_jul_15_05.pdf (last accessed July 31, 2008).

123. Finally, the consistently identifiable visual style *brands* the argument as a whole, allowing Lanier, and hence his client, to benefit from any positive associations that jurors may have developed in response to the visual displays: being entertained, having the impression that the lawyer was so well prepared for trial as to have constructed these displays, and believing that the lawyer cared enough about his client and the jurors themselves to go to the trouble of trying to present the case to them in this way. The visuals also brand the graphic designer Cliff Atkinson's work as distinctive, a style he can (and does) promote, through his book and speaking engagements as well as his legal work, to other potential clients.

124. *Cona and McDarby*, closing argument transcript, 4239, line 24–4240, line 10.

125. *Cona and McDarby* closing argument, slides 20–26.

126. In addition, the Merck logo appears on the TV screen, just like the CBS logo "bug" that appears on many stations/networks to identify them; this is another layer of irony in that the "show" Lanier is presenting appears to be on the "Merck network."

127. Social and cognitive psychologists have formulated and tested *norm theory* to explain the role of perceived norms in people's judgments of causal responsibility. See, e.g., Daniel Kahneman and Dale Miller, "Norm Theory: Comparing Reality to Its Alternatives," *Psychological Review* 93, no. 2 (April 1986): 136–53.

128. This rhetorical strategy is reminiscent of that in the *"Hollywood Squares"* video but differs in one respect: The PowerPoints here explicitly name the cultural reference point. This overt style is of a piece with the use of the stock photos as visual metaphors, discussed earlier. The brashness of replacing the heads of the television show's stars with head shots of Merck executives and scientists is so over the top that jurors know that on one level they are being kidded—which may make the other, implicit functions of the cultural reference more effective because jurors, amused and distracted, are less likely to question them.

129. The PowerPoints remediate the closing argument as television on three levels. The repeated display of the large "Desperate Executives" logo to introduce and conclude each "episode" and the smaller version of the logo on every slide continually invite jurors to imagine, as they listen to the lawyer and look at the pictures on the courtroom screen, that they are watching a television program. The constant presence of the television monitor depicted on the courtroom screen reinforces the implicit message that they should feel as comfortable taking in the information that the lawyer is displaying as they do absorbing images from television. And the navigation bar at the bottom of every slide (as we have already seen in the *Ernst* PowerPoints) assumes jurors' familiarity with not only their personal computer screens but also CNN, FOX News, ESPN, and other programming on which they are accustomed to relying for news and information about the world. All three aspects of the PowerPoints' design imply that jurors should listen to Mark Lanier's closing argument with the same mindset they use when watching television: Be ready to be informed while you're being entertained, but don't be too critical about how.

130. *Cona and McDarby*, closing argument transcript, 4248, lines 8–10.

131. According to Lanier, it was attorney Bob Leone who came up with the idea of showing the Vioxx ads as commercials within the context of Lanier's "Desperate Executives" closing argument (Mark Lanier interview).

132. Ibid.; Cliff Atkinson interview, September 28, 2005.

133. *Ernst* closing argument, slide 16 (repeated as slide 67).

134. Here is another example from *Ernst*. One of the plaintiff's assertions in support of the claim that Merck had deceived the FDA as to the risks of Vioxx was that Merck had communicated the results of an early clinical trial indicating those risks but had buried that information in a "document dump" of millions of items. To illustrate to the jury what millions of documents looks like, Mark Lanier had his staff bring box after box of documents into the front of the courtroom, until Merck's lawyers complained that they couldn't see the jury—to which Lanier responded, "Exactly!" (Cliff Atkinson interview, September 28, 2005). This was a rhetorically successful "demonstration": The real boxes had a tactile as well as visual appeal, and the body language of the staff carting them in reinforced their weight, which also underscored the seriousness of the trouble that had occasioned the trial. For closing argument, Cliff Atkinson designed a slide that reminded jurors of this amusing episode (*Ernst* closing argument, slide 41). Under the title, "Merck DECEIVED the FDA with a document dump," pictures of one document box after another appear every half-second, row piled upon row. The boxes seem to be accumulating at random, but, as the array reaches the top, the row of boxes fills in from right to left—leaving viewers' eyes just underneath the beginning of the slide title. The renowned trial lawyer Jeremiah Donovan once explained that he thinks of his relation to the jury during closing argument as if he has just seen a movie with them on a date, and he and the jury are now talking about the movie over coffee afterwards (Jeremiah Donovan, "Some Off-the-Cuff Remarks About Lawyers as Storytellers," *Vermont Law Review* 18, no. 3 [Spring 1994]: 756). By helping jurors to relive that entertaining (and telling) moment from the trial, Lanier and Atkinson used the digital medium in a way that acknowledged that they'd "seen the movie" too, increasing the jurors' empathy toward the lawyer, his client, and his cause.

135. *Cona and McDarby* closing argument, slides 4–6, 8–9, 16–17, 19, 25–27, 30–31, 33, 35, 37–39, 43–44, 46, 50–51, 53–56, 61, 65.

136. Jones also used this graphic to argue that Merck should not be held liable for any heart problems suffered by patients, like the plaintiffs in this case, who took Vioxx after the label had been changed to disclose the risks.

137. Mark Lanier interview; *Cona and McDarby* closing argument, slide 294.

138. Lanier says that he finds it very effective to take the opponent's PowerPoint slides and use them against the opponent (Mark Lanier interview).

139. *Cona and McDarby*, closing argument transcript, 4272, lines 5–13; closing argument, slide 323.

140. *Ernst*, opening statement transcript, 59, line 9–63, line 24. Both the tablet PC and Lanier's laptop were wired to the courtroom LCD projector, so that, with a flip of a switch, the screen could change from one to the other. The audience, therefore, did not need to shift its visual focus when Lanier shifted from the prepared PowerPoint slides to the tablet PC and indeed was unaware that any such shift had taken place (Mark Lanier interview).

141. For instance, the words "prostacyclin" and "thromboxane," anti- and pro-clotting substances in the body that Vioxx affects. *Cona and McDarby*, opening statement transcript, 32, line 17–33, line 1.

142. Ibid., 42, line 21–43, line 8.

143. Ibid., 28, lines 10–22; 46, line 23.

144. Mark Lanier interview. These slides can be thought of as providing the kind of "wallpaper" that often appears behind public speakers, especially at televised events, reiterating a two- or three-word slogan that proclaims the message of the speech (as we saw in the *Times* photograph of President Bush in chapter 1).

145. Ibid.

146. Cliff Atkinson interview, September 12, 2005.

147. Atkinson, *Beyond Bullet Points*, 7–8.

148. Mark Lanier interview.

149. See, e.g., Green, Letter to the Editor; Lawler, "Vioxx Verdict." As already noted, the Texas Court of Appeals reversed the jury's verdict in *Ernst* on the ground that the plaintiff's experts had not provided sufficient evidence from which a jury could reasonably conclude that Vioxx had caused Bob Ernst's death (*Merck & Co., Inc. v. Ernst*, 2008 Tex. App. LEXIS 3951).

150. In addition, because argument is not evidence, visual displays in closings are not, strictly speaking, governed by rules of evidence (although basic principles of relevance and fairness apply, at least by analogy). That gives advocates greater leeway in the words and pictures they use but, for that very reason, makes it more likely that they will overstep the bounds of whatever the law deems appropriate communication.

151. What Burns, in his *Theory of the Trial*, calls the "Received View" of the trial.

152. Green, Letter to the Editor.

153. E.g., E. Allan Lind, "The Psychology of Courtroom Procedure," in *The Psychology of the Courtroom*, ed. Norbert L. Kerr and Robert M. Bray (New York: Academic Press, 1982), 25–37. Psychologists have also observed *primacy* effects, in which earlier information is more influential (ibid. at 25–26). Accordingly, visual and other information presented during opening statements can also have strong effects on jurors' thinking. Because, however, opening statements are not permitted in some jurisdictions and because lawyers are allowed to argue overtly in closings as they are typically not during opening statements, it is always possible that jurors will be exposed in closing argument to words and pictures not previously encountered, heightening the potential impact of recency effects.

154. See, e.g., Shelly Chaiken and Yaacov Trope, eds., *Dual-Process Theories in Social Psychology* (New York: Guilford Press, 1999); see also discussion of intuitive thinking in chapter 1.

155. See, e.g., Neal Feigenson and Jaihyun Park, "Emotions and Attributions of Legal Responsibility and Blame: A Research Review," *Law and Human Behavior* 30, no. 2 (April 2006): 143–61.

156. Burns, *A Theory of the Trial*, 37. For a summary of the research showing that jurors tend to organize their understanding of trial evidence in story form, see Nancy Pennington and Reid Hastie, "The Story Model for Juror Decision Making," in *Inside the Juror*, ed. Reid Hastie (Cambridge: Cambridge University Press, 1993), 192–221.

157. Pennington and Hastie, "Story Model."

158. Sherwin, Feigenson, and Spiesel, "Law in the Digital Age," 247–48.

159. See, e.g., *United States v. Crockett*, 49 F.3d 1357, 1361 (8th Cir. 1995) ("[S]ome [trial judges] might limit use of visual aids in closing argument to those approved by the court well in advance").

CHAPTER 6

1. This includes macrophotographic (closeup) or telephoto pictures; it might also include pictures made with night vision goggles, depending upon any additional information such equipment might present. The basic nature of this category does not depend on its precise contours, which change with changing technology.

2. In addition to more technical definitions of "virtuality" or "virtual reality," there are more encompassing ones. According to Marie-Laure Ryan, "the meaning of virtuality stretches along an axis between two poles. At one end is the optical sense that carries the negative connotations to double and illusion (two ideas combined in the theme of the treacherous image); at the other end is the scholastic sense which suggests productivity, openness, and diversity . . . . [Virtuality] is simply thinking." Marie-Laure Ryan, *Narrative as Virtual Reality: Immersion and Interactivity in Literature and Electronic Media* (Baltimore: Johns Hopkins University Press, 2001), 27, 35.

3. See, for instance, "CyberOne: Law in the Court of Public Opinion," http://blogs.law. harvard.edu/cyberone (last accessed July 31, 2008). A video trailer for the course demonstrates augmented virtuality.

4. For a short explanation and pictures, see Klaus-Peter Beier, "Virtual Reality: A Short Introduction," http://www-vrl.umich.edu/intro/ (last accessed July 31, 2008). For more detail, see John Vince, *Introduction to Virtual Reality* (London: Springer, 2004).

5. For a discussion, see Ramesh Raskar and Jack Tumblin, "State of the Art Report: Computational Photography," *Eurographics* 2006, http://www.cg.tuwien.ac.at/events/EG06/program-STARs.php (last accessed July 31, 2008). For an example, see http://en.wikipedia.org/wiki/ Image:Glasses_800_edit.png (last accessed July 31, 2008). The software that enables the artist to make this is called ray-tracing (http://en.wikipedia.org/wiki/Ray_tracing) (last accessed July 31, 2008). While this software has been available to academia, industry, and, especially, the film industry, newer computers are sufficiently powerful to enable some real-time rendering of these effects, which will make the software marketable to consumers.

6. E.g., Constance Holden, "Handwriting Analysis Goes 3-D," *Science* 305, no. 5688 (August 27, 2004): 1236. For a general description of holography, see http://en.wikipedia.org/wiki/Holography (last accessed September 21, 2008). For new research and a good pictorial explanation, see Michael L. Huebschman, Bala Munjuluri, and Harold R. Garner, "Dynamic Holographic 3-D Image Projection," *Optics Express* 11, no. 5 (March 10, 2003): 437–45.

7. E.g., Fredric I. Lederer, "Potential Use of Courtroom Technology in Major Terrorism Cases," *William and Mary Bill of Rights Law Journal* 12, no. 3 (April 2004): 930 & n. 159 (describing use of holograms as demonstrative evidence in Courtroom 21 mock trial); Susan Nauss, "Internet Meets Obi-Wan Kenobi in the Court of Next Resort," *Boston University Journal of Science and Technology Law* 8, no. 1 (2002): 18, 35 (imagining that holography in cybercourt of future would allow jurors to perceive appearances and reactions of all parties and witnesses).

8. Noah Schachtman, "High-Tech Uniforms Finally Heading to War," http://www.noah-shachtman.com/archives/002872.html (last accessed August 1, 2008); see also http://www.af.mil/

news/story_media.asp?id=123077903 (last accessed August 1, 2008) (photos of augmented-reality goggles under consideration by U.S. Air Force).

9. This description is based on the account by Darius Whelan in "The Bloody Sunday Tribunal Video Simulation," in *Visual Practices Across the University*, James Elkins, ed. (Munich: Wilhelm Fink Verlag, 2007), 100–3; see also Damian Schofield and Lorna Goodwin, "Using Graphical Technology to Present Evidence," in *Electronic Evidence: Discovery, Disclosure and Admissibility*, ed. Stephen Mason (Edinburgh: Lexis Nexis Butterworths, 2007), 118–19.

10. Maryanne Garry and Matthew P. Gerrie, "When Photographs Create False Memories," *Current Directions in Psychological Science* 14, no. 6 (December 2005): 321–25 (both doctored and true photographs can create false memories for personal experiences).

11. Ralph Schroeder, "Social Interaction in Virtual Environments: Key Issues, Common Themes, and a Framework for Research," in *The Social Life of Avatars*, ed. Ralph Schroeder (London: Springer, 2002), 1–18; Jonathan Steuer, "Defining Virtual Reality: Dimensions Determining Telepresence," in *Communication in the Age of Virtual Reality*, ed. Frank Biocca and Mark R. Levy (Hillsdale, NJ: Erlbaum, 1995), 33–56.

12. For cognitive and social psychology experiments see, e.g., Jim Blascovich and others, "Immersive Virtual Environment Technology as a Methodological Tool for Social Psychology," *Psychological Inquiry* 13, no. 2 (2002): 103–24; for clinical psychology, where IVEs are being used in therapy to treat acrophobia and many other conditions, see, e.g., Jay David Bolter and Richard Grusin, *Remediation* (Cambridge, MA: MIT Press, 1999). IVEs are being used, for instance, to treat Iraq war veterans for posttraumatic stress disorder; see, e.g., "Virtual Iraq: VR Based Therapy for Post-Traumatic Stress Disorder," http://www.defense-update.com/products/v/VR-PTSD.htm (last accessed July 31, 2008).

13. As yet it is not possible to make an IVE that is the equivalent of Hollywood computer-generated special effects. Bear in mind that, when a user is moving through 3-D space, each new view (controlled by the user's movements) has to be rendered (generated) by the computer in real time. Looking at a picture of a boat in water with reflections, "[i]f we assume that this image took approximately 10 min to render on a workstation, we could produce six images an hour. But in a VR system we require something in the order of 20 per second! Which means that there is a speed factor of 12,000 between the two systems. Therefore, we will have to wait some time before it is possible to simulate such scenarios in real time." Vince, *Introduction to Virtual Reality*, 6. In more controlled situations, like flight simulators used by the military, the level of realism is greatly enhanced by a combination of highly focused tasks, kinesthetic feedback, and pilots' previous flying experience. E.g., Jack M. Loomis, James J. Blascovich, and Andrew C. Beall, "Immersive Virtual Environment Technology as a Basic Research Tool in Psychology," *Behavior Research Methods, Instruments, & Computers* 31, no. 4 (1999): 557–64.

14. E.g., Neal Feigenson, "Too Real? The Future of Virtual Reality Evidence," *Law and Policy* 28, no. 2 (April 2006): 271–93.

15. Fredric I. Lederer, "Courtroom Technology: A Status Report" 2005, http://www.legaltech-center.net/publications/articles/status.pdf (last accessed July 31, 2008); Fredric I. Lederer, telephone interview with author Spiesel, December 26, 2007 (notes on file with authors).

16. See Feigenson, "Too Real?," 276–79. Of course, the risk of improperly influencing viewers' judgments is not limited to virtual depictions; crime scene videos, too, may being excluded if they are too graphic. See Mark Curriden, "Crime Scene Videos: Dead Bodies on Videotape Worry Criminal Defense Lawyers," *American Bar Association Journal* 76, no. 5 (May 1990): 32.

17. Note, moreover, that IVEs' aspiration to provide complete fidelity to the "real" may get in the way of useful legal applications of the technology because, just as in the case of today's computer animations and simulations, lawyers will want to focus attention on the legally significant information and not necessarily present all of reality's visual (and other sensory) complexity.

18. Feigenson, "Too Real?," 284–87.

19. See Jonathan Grudin, "The Computer Reaches Out: The Historical Continuity of Interface Design," CHI Proceedings, Association for Computing Machinery (April 1990): 261–68.

20. http://www.lightspacetech.com/ (last accessed July 12, 2008).

21. Curious readers can use their scanners to capture a three-dimensional object and then use a camera to capture the same object. Differences in apparent three-dimensionality will be obvious.

22. Timothy Rogers, Sign Engine Theater, http://people.envision.purdue.edu/~tjrogers/ssa/video/index.html (last accessed July 10, 2008). This is not yet an off-the-shelf product, but the software exists for such displays to be created.

23. Directed by Steven Spielberg (Twentieth-Century Fox, 2002).

24. Directed by Jon Favreau (Dark Blades Films, 2008).

25. Jeff Han, "Unveiling the Genius of Multi-touch Interface Design," presentation at TED Conference, February 2006, at http://www.ted.com/index.php/talks/view/id/65 (last accessed July 31, 2008); Johnny Chung Lee, "Low-Cost Multi-touch Whiteboard Using the Wiimote," video demonstration, posted December 7, 2007, http://www.youtube.com/watch?v=5s5EvhHy7eQ (last accessed July 31, 2008).

26. A new product, Electric Rain's Stand Out, is a software package that combines the process of planning and organizing materials with the production of a polished multimedia presentation. It includes a function that allows users to post many kinds of files on "fly paper" and to use a mouse in very much the same way as the iPod Touch PDA. See http://erain.com/products/standout/. For a lecture and demonstration, see http://sessions.visitmix.com/ (last accessed July 31, 2008).

27. Haptic experience, our sense of touch, goes back to our earliest experience of exploring the world as babies. Whereas the sense of sight can carry us over great distances, touch is about what we can reach out and grab; it is closer, more intimate, and therefore especially powerful. People do differ, however, as to their need for touch. Consumer research has shown, for instance, that verbal descriptions of products can partially compensate people with a high need for touch, and pictures can partially compensate those with a low need for touch, for the frustration they feel when they are unable to touch the product. Both visual and verbal representations, of course, become increasingly important as more communication and persuasion occurs solely through computer and other screen interfaces. See Joann Peck and Terry Childers, "To Have and to Hold: The Influence of Haptic Information on Product Judgments," *Journal of Marketing* 67, no. 2 (April 2003): 35–48.

28. Bryan Caplan and Edward P. Stringham, "Privatizing the Adjudication of Disputes," *Theoretical Inquiries in Law* 9, no. 2 (July 2008), http://www.bepress.com.proxy.library.cornell.edu/til/default/vol9/iss2/ (last accessed July 29, 2008).

29. See, for example, Byron Reeves and Clifford Nass, *The Media Equation: How People Treat Computers, Television, and New Media Like Real People and Places* (Cambridge: CSLI Publications/Cambridge University Press, 1996).

30. Gordon Bermant, "Symposium: The Powers and Pitfalls of Technology: The Development and Significance of Courtroom Technology: A Thirty-Year Perspective in Fast Forward Mode," *New York University Annual Survey of American Law* 60, no. 4 (2005): 621.

31. Philip Auslander, *Liveness: Performance in a Mediatized Culture* (London: Routledge, 1999), 116–20.

32. For a detailed discussion of PRVTs, see John A. Shutkin, "Videotape Trials: Legal and Practical Implications," *Columbia Journal of Law and Social Problems* 9, no. 3 (Spring 1973): 363–93; see also Henry H. Perritt, Jr., "Changing Litigation with Science and Technology: Video Depositions, Transcripts, and Trials," *Emory Law Journal* 43 (Summer 1994): 1082–83.

33. For information on film editing, see Daniel Arijon, *The Grammar of Film Language* (Los Angeles: Sillman-James Press, 1991); James Monaco, *How to Read a Film* (New York: Oxford University Press, 2000).

34. Gerald R. Miller and Norman E. Fontes, *Videotape on Trial* (Beverly Hills, CA: Sage, 1979).

35. We would like to point out an additional problem with PRVTs: Recording all of the evidence, including demonstratives, turned those demonstratives into pictures within pictures. There is no research on how this may have affected the perceived credibility of the demonstratives. If PRVTs were to be conducted today, when at least some audiences are more sophisticated about this kind of multiplicity of representational layers, would people read the representation within the representation as governed by the overall realism of the events in question, or would they bring to their viewing and decision making habits of irony engendered by late-night television (see chapter 1)?

36. Paul D. Carrington, "Virtual Civil Litigation: A Visit to John Bunyan's Celestial City," *Columbia Law Review* 98 (October 1998): 1516–37; Perritt, "Changing Litigation."

37. CourtTV was founded in 1991. It is now the truTV network (http://en.wikipedia.org/wiki/CourtTV [last accessed July 31, 2008]).

38. In contrast to federal courts, state courts are quite hospitable to the use of camera recording; all fifty states allow it to some extent. See "Cameras in the Courtroom," Hearing Before the Senate Committee on the Judiciary, 109th Cong. 65 (2005) (statement of Seth Berlin, Partner, Levine, Sullivan, Koch & Schulz, LLP) ("All 50 states allow at least some camera coverage of judicial proceedings, including 37 states in which criminal proceedings may be televised in at least some circumstances"); Editorial, "For Courtroom Cameras," *Chicago Tribune*, November 27, 2005 ("All 50 states now allow cameras in at least some courts, and 39 permit TV coverage of criminal trials").

39. Of course everything we have said about the role of framing, screens, composition, and so on regarding the use of cameras for taping trials also applies to videotaped depositions of witnesses for the record (and possible appearance in court). For instance, according to one lawyer, "the optimum camera angle may depend on whether the person being deposed is your witness or an opposing witness." Another lawyer emphasizes that body language that might not attract attention in court may play very differently on tape. "Every lawyer who does video depositions can tell you about the times when he or she hands a document to a witness, he looks up at the camera and doesn't know what to say, then he looks over at his own counsel like, 'You didn't tell me about this.' . . . Even if the witness doesn't express confusion or surprise, the mere act of looking down may not come across well to a jury because it can look evasive on video." Dick Dahl, "Videotaped Deposition is Turning Point in Complex Insurance/med-mal Case Before Federal Court in LA," *Michigan Lawyers Weekly*, October 23, 2006.

40. "An Illinois court first used video technology to conduct videophone bail hearings in 1972. A Philadelphia court installed a closed-circuit television system for preliminary arraignments in 1974." National Center for State Courts, Briefing Papers, "Videoconferencing," http://www.ncsconline.org/WC/Publications/KIS_VidConBriefPub.pdf (last accessed July 31, 2008). Although first appearances and arraignments can be combined, they are ordinarily separate procedural stages. Remote arraignments have existed since at least 1982, when Dade County, Florida, began to use two-way television for misdemeanor cases. Jeffrey M. Silbert, Una Hutton Newman, and Laurel Kalser, "The Use of Closed Circuit Television for Conducting Misdemeanor Arraignments in Dade County, Florida," *University of Miami Law Review* 38, no. 4 (July 1984): 657–76.

41. For a brief history, see http://en.wikipedia.org/wiki/Digital_video (last accessed July 31, 2008). Consumer digital video became available in the early 1990s. Practically speaking, it was born with the Internet, but it took broadband Internet transmission to make possible the kinds of video exchange that we take for granted today.

42. See Gene D. Fowler and Marilyn E. Wackerbarth, "Audio Teleconferencing versus Face-to-Face Conferencing: A Synthesis of the Literature," *Western Journal of Speech*

Communication 44, no. 3 (Summer 1980): 236–52. That this could significantly complicate legal decision making has been observed in discussions of the use of videoconferencing in appearances and arraignments in criminal proceedings, where the defense lawyers have to choose whether to join their clients in a remote location, making possible consultation, advice, and support, or to remain in the courtroom, where the client may see the lawyer as part of the court and not as advocate but where the lawyer can confer in person with the judge. The benefits attributed to using videoconferencing in these contexts are savings in time and travel costs and easier management of security. Defendants have the right to refuse to appear or be arraigned in this fashion, although there are no doubt pressures toward accepting it. Poor technological arrangements can exacerbate the problems the defendants face; we discuss these briefly in chapter 7.

43. Singapore's Supreme Court Web site: http://app.supremecourt.gov.sg/default. aspx?pgID=361#10 (last accessed July 31, 2008).

44. For arguably analogous problems of personal revelation through choices in décor by psychotherapists, see Penelope Green, "What's in a Chair?," *New York Times* (March 6, 2008), http://www.nytimes.com/2008/03/06/garden/06shrink.html?ref=garden (last accessed July 31, 2008).

45. This brief account is based on Calvin Morrill, "Institutional Change Through Interstitial Emergence: The Growth of Alternative Dispute Resolution in American Law, 1965–1995," in *How Institutions Change*, ed. Walter W. Powell and Daniel L. Jones (Chicago: University of Chicago Press, forthcoming).

46. See, e.g., Judith Resnik, "Managerial Judges," *Harvard Law Review* 96, no. 2 (December 1982): 374–448.

47. For American Internet use statistics, see http://www.internetworldstats.com/stats14.htm (last accessed July 31, 2008). The figures cited are for the year 2007.

48. http://en.wikipedia.org/wiki/Web_portal (last accessed July 31, 2008).

49. http://www.CyberSettle.com/info/main.aspx (last accessed July 31, 2008). The Web site claims that CyberSettle "reduces the time from offer to settlement" and "significantly impacts at least 2 major claims activities: Negotiation/Settlement: allowing adjusters to allocate more time to complex claims[;] Litigation, Arbitration, and Mediation Management: reducing legal fees & other defense costs." We can see from this that CyberSettle is taking advantage of the efficiencies of location in cyberspace to offer services to lawyers for insureds and their insurers to negotiate general liability claims settlements. The site offers three rounds of bidding by algorithm; if this fails, the parties can be moved to interpersonal facilitation over the phone. It is important to keep in mind that CyberSettle handles only certain kinds of cases, not disputes in general.

50. Another site, SquareTrade, was founded in 1999 to provide both warranties for purchases (a kind of insurance) on the auction site eBay and dispute resolution regarding transactions on the site. As of July 2008, however, SquareTrade is devoted solely to selling warranties for products of all kinds.

51. The official site for MARS (mediation, arbitration, resolution, settlement) is www.resolve-mydispute.com (last accessed July 31, 2008) (note the music when you open the page).

52. A completely different way of using digital technology to handle disputes has been proposed by Sanjana Hattotuwa, a media researcher and specialist in using information technology for conflict resolution. Hattotuwa is interested in exploring how information and communication devices (many handheld) might be used to cool down the world's political hot spots, a peacemaking version of the networked battlefield we discussed earlier. For instance, people who are in scattered locations could broadcast messages to everyone else in their problem-solving network. All could have access to maps and other important local information. He envisions offline knowledge repositories of indexed information pertaining to "past and on-going ADR and ODR processes," which could illuminate the players in a conflict, provide details of the

history of the conflict, and so on. See http://ict4peace.wordpress.com/2007/11/08/online-dispute-resolution (last accessed July 31, 2008).

The model contains potential problems. For example, the kinds of cell phone and VoIP (Voice over Internet Protocols) communications that are made in the field might or might not be of the sort that should be recorded. Hattotuwa specifies neither how this will be decided nor how those communications will be protected from being intercepted. In addition, databases are only as good as their structure (logic and indexing) and their contents, their "expertise" conditioned by these choices and the capabilities of their searches. Information that is unvetted but recorded, like informal off-the-cuff assessments of other people, may wind up adversely affecting outcomes in unpredictable ways.

53. Joseph W. Goodman, "The Pros and Cons of Online Dispute Resolution," www.law.duke.edu/journals/dltr/articles/2003dltr0004.html (last accessed July 31, 2008).

54. Edward H. Freeman, "Cyber Courts and the Future of Justice," *Information Systems Security* 14, no. 1 (2005): 5–9.

55. Lucille M. Ponte, "The Michigan Cyber Court: A Bold Experiment in the Development of the First Public Virtual Courthouse," *North Carolina Journal of Law and Technology* 4, no. 1 (Fall 2002): 59–65.

56. Ibid., 60.

57. Estimating the size of the virtual world populations is a complex problem. In Second Life, where anyone can open an account and create a basic avatar without incurring cost, the number of active participants must be lower than the "over five million in 2007" estimated by Edward Castronova (*Exodus to the Virtual World* [New York: Palgrave Macmillan, 2007], 6). An in-world blog, using data regularly collected inside Second Life, estimated the population to be 600,000 users (James Wagner, "Half a Million Member Metaverse: Second Life Plateaus at 538K Active Users," *New World Notes*, December 18, 2007, http://nwn.blogs.com/nwn/2007/12/half-a-million.html (last accessed July 31, 2008)). Complicating this still further is that one paid user can create multiple avatars, so it is hard to know how many users are in-world at any one time. It is also important to note that the virtual world itself is spread across many servers, and the users see only the other players who are assigned to the same servers (in contrast, for instance, to Eve, which maintains all users in the same copy of the virtual world). World of Warcraft claims a "population" of 9.3 million players, but how many accounts this represents is up for grabs. For instance, William Sims Bainbridge, program director of the Human-Centered Computing Cluster of the National Science Foundation, has said that he plays fifteen characters in that game (lecture, Yale University Technology and Ethics Working Group, New Haven, CT, March 26, 2008).

58. Social shaming, for instance, is a major means by which groups on the Internet "police" behavior. For example, some young Marines were caught on tape throwing a puppy down a precipice. One blog entry threatened legal retribution once the perpetrator was identified (http://federalism.typepad.com/crime_federalism/2008/03/david-motari-ab.html [last accessed July 31, 2008]). This was followed by a more mainstream media treatment of the story (Audrey MacAvoy, "Marine Expelled, Another Punished Over Puppy Video," http://abcnews.go.com/US/wireStory?id=5051580 [last accessed July 31, 2008]). In a second episode, postings to MySpace led a vulnerable young teen to commit suicide. Bob Tedeschi, "After Suicide, Blog Insults Are Debated," http://www.nytimes.com/2008/03/03/ business/media/03blog.html (last accessed July 31, 2008).

59. Behavior in Second Life deliberately aimed at "disrupt[ing] the experience of others" is called "griefing." Tom Boellstorff, *Coming of Age in Second Life* (Princeton: Princeton University Press, 2008), 187.

60. In Second Life at least, behavior tends to be dominated by generosity and altruism, qualities desirable but often in short supply in actual life, although the presence of an economy

in Second Life can pull against them. The behavioral economist Dan Ariely has studied the interaction of two different systems of norms: social norms and market norms. While studying people's willingness to work for free or for a salary, he and his team discovered that "for market norms to emerge, it is sufficient to mention money even when no money changes hands" (Dan Ariely, *Predictably Irrational: The Hidden Forces That Shape Our Decisions* [New York: Harper Collins, 2008], 74). Further, Ariely found that when market behavior was evoked in his subjects, they were more self-reliant, selfish, and individualistic and less social. We can find in Second Life the same tensions between these different norms, with regard to the behavior of players among themselves and as game platform owners having to deal with the communities that they have founded (and on which their livelihoods depend).

61. Issues of politics and self-governance have created tensions in Second Life. For instance, the influx of corporate presence has given rise to a resistance movement, the Second Life Liberation Army (SLLA) (http://secondlla.googlepages.com/ [last accessed July 31, 2008]); the Web page features video coverage of the organization of the SLLA. For a discussion of free speech issues in Massive Multiple Online Role Playing Games (MMORPGs), see Peter S. Jenkins, "The Virtual World as a Company Town—Freedom of Speech in Massively Multiple On-Line Role Playing Games," *Journal of Internet Law* 8, no. 1 (July 2004): 1–18.

62. In 2008 the ABA offered a program with CLE credit in Second Life (Jim Milles, "ABA Forms Committee on Virtual Worlds," posted September 7, 2007, http://bwtr.wordpress.com/2007/09/07/aba-forms-committee-on-virtual-worlds/ [last accessed August 1, 2008]; see also Martha Neil, "Law Firm Plans Real Life Practice at Virtual 'Second Life' Office," November 6, 2007, http://www.abajournal. com/weekly/law_firm_plans_real_life_practice_at_virtual_second_life _office [last accessed August 1, 2008]).

63. http://video.google.com/videosearch?hl=en&q=ocampo%20in%20second%20 life&um=%201&ie=UTF-8&sa=N&tab=wv# (last accessed August 1, 2008). At the same URL there is also a video of an accompanying art exhibition that involves "real" Second Life avatars, "art," and a "light show." The levels of reality here are truly baroque.

64. Linden Labs collects and monitors such reports in an effort to maintain civility in the virtual world. On Linden Labs' abuse reporting (AR) mechanism, see http://wiki.secondlife.com/wiki/Help:When_and_how_to_file_an_Abuse_Report (last accessed July 31, 2008).

65. http://www.secondlifeinsider.com/2007/07/27/portuguese-ministry-of-justice-launches-mediation-and-arbitration/ (last accessed July 31, 2008).

66. http://www.ejusticecenter.mj.pt/ficheiros/Regulamento_Arbitragem_v3_26072007.pdf (last accessed August 1, 2008).

67. As a model, the E-Justice Center has a clear statement of principles and a mandate limited to dealing with contractual disputes. The Linden dollar is worth roughly one-third of an American dollar, so the financial issues at stake are too small to litigate in the real world.

68. In another case, *Eros LLC vs. John Doe a/k/a Volkov Catteneo*, a nineteen-year-old copied and distributed pixels for an animated sex toy in Second Life, and the toy's copyright owner sued for infringement. (Eros LLC is the real-life company that sold the original item; Volkov Catteneo is the name of the Second Life avatar of Robert Leatherwood.) The case eventually settled; http://virtuallyblind.com/2008/03/14/leatherwood-settlement/avatar (last accessed August 1, 2008). Case documents can be found at http://www.docstoc.com/docs/514835/Eros-LLC-v-Doe (last accessed August 1, 2008).

69. For more on the influences of jurors' (and judges') habits of watching and using media (television, movies, computer gaming) on their decision making, see chapters 2 (Justice Scalia's invocation of Hollywood film as a template for understanding the evidentiary videotape in *Scott*), 3 (e.g., the appeal of the defendant's multimedia slide show in *Bontatibus* to jurors' television and film viewing experience), 4 (the "*CSI* Effect" as a possible influence on jurors'

receptivity to brain scan pictures), and 5 (in *Cona and McDarby*, the plaintiff's framing of closing argument as a television program).

70. See generally Neal Feigenson, *Legal Blame: How Jurors Think and Talk About Accidents* (Washington, DC: American Psychological Association, 2000).

71. Attorney Thomas Ullmann was able to interview some jurors after the trial (Thomas Ullmann, interview by authors, December 5, 2007; notes on file with the authors).

72. For a slightly different discussion, including a black and white illustration of the DVD menu, see Richard K. Sherwin, "Visual Literacy in Action," in *Visual Literacy*, ed. James Elkins (London: Routledge, 2008), 190–91. A collection of links to news coverage of the story may be found at http://www.dailymail.co.uk/news/article-201479/Soham-nmurders-story.html (last accessed February 4, 2009).

73. Dan M. Kahan, David A. Hoffman, and Donald Braman, "Whose Eyes Are You Going to Believe? An Empirical (and Normative) Assessment of Scott v. Harris," *Harvard Law Review* 122, no. 3 (January 2009): 837–906.

74. http://www.knowledgenetworks.com/index5.html (last accessed August 1, 2008).

75. This "virtual jury pool," however, very likely did not resemble the one from which the Georgia jury that would have decided the case, had it gone to trial, would have been selected.

76. Percepticon owns and operates this site at http://www.i-courthouse.com/main.taf (last accessed July 31, 2008). Note that, unlike CyberSettle, which is a site for lawyers and claims professionals and features a relaxed lawyer, arms raised, hands clasped behind his head as its iconic figure, iCourthouse very abstractly echoes a Greek pillar with "balances" of information on each side on the home page.

77. http://www.i-courthouse.com/main.taf?areal_id=jurysmart (last accessed September 23, 2008).

78. Examples of other sites that provide focus groups for lawyers to test their case strategies include Virtual Jury (http://www.virtualjury.com/focusgrp.htm [last accessed September 17, 2008]), which provides an evidence window, a chat window in which the panel can interact, and a window for voting a yes or no "verdict." The site claims that this allows lawyers to forecast verdicts, uncover biases, test their evidence, and gauge the value of the case. On another site, eJury (http://www.ejury.com/attys_learn_about.html [last accessed September 17, 2008]), lawyers provide a list of questions to which online participants respond, and the case is closed after fifty "jurors" have responded. Unlike Virtual Jury, there is no chat or other common conversation between jurors, and jurors are drawn only from the single county in which the case will be tried, which presumably bestows greater predictive value on the results. So eJury appears to give lawyers less insight (in some ways) into how prospective jurors might think about the case but a larger and more targeted pool of respondents.

79. For a detailed discussion of the history and practices of online juries, see Nancy S. Marder, "Cyberjuries: A New Role as Online Mock Juries," *University of Toledo Law Review* 38, no. 1 (Fall 2006): 239–69.

80. On a related note, compare the recent scandal caused in the sciences when a conference attendee photographed and disseminated a presentation of data that the speakers intended to keep confined to the room. Geoff Brumfiel, "Physicists Aflutter About Data Photographed at Conference," *Nature* 455, no. 7209 (September 4, 2008): 7.

81. For a description of a "sealed" PDF file, see "HOWTO: Defeat Sealed PDFs, A DRM Nightmare," http://twinturbo.org/security/sealed-pdf/ (last accessed July 31, 2008).

82. This is already an issue regarding jurors in bricks-and-mortar courts; see Julie Bykowicz, "When Jurors Google," *Baltimore Sun*, July 27, 2008, http://www.baltimoresun.com/news/bal-id.jurors27jul27,0,4443725.story (last accessed August 1, 2008).

83. For instance, the security expert Bruce Schneier has reported that Sears.com "is distributing spyware that tracks all your Internet usage—including banking logins, e-mail, and all other forms

of Internet usage—all in the name of 'community participation.'" Bruce Schneier, "Is Sears Engaging in Criminal Hacking Behavior?," http://www.schneier.com/blog/archives/2008/01/is_sears_engagi.html (posted January 3, 2008) (last accessed July 31, 2008). As we write, Congress and the public are debating whether the government should have broad electronic surveillance powers over American citizens. Both private entities and government have joined in data mining programs. For a detailed discussion of surveillance, see Robert O'Harrow, Jr., *No Place to Hide* (New York: Free Press, 2005). The walls around this Internet courthouse, therefore, might be very thin indeed, even when encryption is used. See discussion of internet voting in text.

84. Since the taping of some Kansas juries as part of a research project in the early 1950s, taping of jury deliberations has generally been proscribed. See Valerie P. Hans and Neil Vidmar, *Judging the Jury* (New York: Plenum Press, 1986), 99; Saul M. Kassin and Lawrence S. Wrightsman, *The American Jury on Trial* (Bristol, PA: Taylor and Francis, 1988), 13–14. Exceptions include a PBS *Frontline* program featuring deliberations in a Wisconsin criminal case (Alan M. Levin and Stephen J. Herzberg, *Inside the Jury Room* [Washington, DC: PBS, April 8, 1986] [television broadcast]) and a CBS program that featured excerpts from several Arizona trials and jury deliberations (Linda Mason, *Enter the Jury Room* [New York: CBS, April 16, 1997] [television broadcast]). More recently, Shari Diamond, Neil Vidmar, and others have conducted extensive jury research based on videotapes of deliberations in fifty-five civil trials in Arizona; for a report, see Neil Vidmar and Valerie Hans, *American Juries: The Verdict* (Amherst, NY: Prometheus Books, 2007), 137–145.

85. Federal Rule of Evidence 606(b) (St. Paul, MN: West, 2008).

86. Anthony D'Amato, "Can/Should Computers Replace Judges?" *Georgia Law Review* 11, no. 5 (September 1977): 1277–1301.

87. Danielle Keats Citron, "Technological Due Process," *Washington University Law Review* 85, no. 6 (2008): 1249–1313.

88. Ibid.

89. A computer system will exhibit a life of its own in any event. One can't predict the emergent qualities of a system; the only way to know them is to run the software. This is a piece of craft wisdom known by those who design and write the code for software systems. In computing, system architecture ("the conceptual design that defines the structure and/or behavior of a system," http://en.wikipedia.org/wiki/System_architecture [last accessed September 22, 2008]) begins not just as a software engineering problem but as a computing response to the needs of a "client." Software emerges as a combination of culture, science, and techne, and however much one may know of the relevant factors from any one point of view, their combination makes for a complex system whose qualities are not fully apparent before the software is run. For an overview of the problem of emergence, see Jeffrey Goldstein, "Emergence as a Construct: History and Issues," *Emergence* 1, no. 1 (1999): 49–72.

90. A related phenomenon is the use of computers to engage in automatic stock trading or arbitrage, which has had a tremendous effect on the values of particular stocks. For a discussion, focused on the example of United Airlines stock, which dropped precipitously as a result of automated stock trading in the wake of the undated republication of an old article on bankruptcy threats, see Tim Arango, "I Got the News Instantaneously, Oh Boy," *New York Times*, September 14, 2008. Automated stock trading resembles automatic decision making in public administration in that in both cases, the software is empowered to make decisions and to act upon them. It resembles electronic voting (discussed next in the text) in that the software constitutes a very large system that can be subjected to perturbations or "weather" with cascading effects.

91. Pub. L. 107–252, codified at 42 U.S.C. §§ 15301 et seq. (2009).

92. On August 21, 2008, Yahoo News published an Associated Press report on voting machines with the following lead: "A major voting machine maker has cautioned its customers in

34 states to look out for a programming error that may cause votes to be dropped." Stephen Majors, "Company Acknowledges Voting Machine Error," http://news.yahoo.com/s/ap/20080821/ap_on_re_us/voting_machines_4 (last accessed September 18, 2008).

93. This is not to say that there is no expertise involved in designing the interface for users; that, too, is made up of semiotic tasks of great importance. See Clarisse Siekenius de Souza, *The Semiotic Engineering of Human-Computer Interaction* (Cambridge, MA: MIT Press, 2005) for an extended discussion of this problem.

94. This discussion is based on http://en.wikipedia.org/wiki/Expert_system (last accessed July 31, 2008).

95. Richard E. Susskind, *Expert Systems in Law: A Jurisprudential Inquiry* (Oxford: Oxford University Press, 1987), 41.

96. James Popple, *A Pragmatic Legal Expert System* (Aldershot, UK: Dartmouth, 1996).

97. Ibid.

98. Ibid., 63.

99. Ibid., 290.

100. As in any coding scheme, defining the attributes is one function where all kinds of conceptual bias can enter any expert system: What features are how important, and according to what criteria?

101. Ibid., 111.

102. See also Wendell Wallach and Colin Allen, *Moral Machines* (Oxford: Oxford University Press, 2009), 129–31.

103. James Grimmelmann, "Virtual Worlds as Comparative Law," *New York Law School Law Review* 49, no. 1 (2004–2005): 153–84.

104. Anton Tomažič, "E-Justice Based on e-Law," paper presented at the 2008 E-Justice and E-Law conference at Portoroz, Slovenia, June 1–3, 2008.

105. Another issue beyond the scope of the text but worth flagging is the problem of offloading responsibility—functional, legal, ethical—to the impersonal machine. In a recent dispute concerning Google's arguably unfair leverage over online advertising, the complainant is quoted as saying that "Google . . . told me that it never made judgments of what was 'good' and 'bad' because it was all in the hands of the algorithm." Joe Nocera, "Stuck in Google's Doghouse," *New York Times*, September 13, 2008, http://www.nytimes.com/2008/09/13/technology/13nocera.html?_r=1&scp=2&sq=google&st=cse&oref=slogin (last accessed September 17, 2008).

106. See *The New Hacker's Dictionary*, http://www.ccil.org/jargon/jargon_38.html#SEC45 (last accessed August 1, 2008).

107. As we write, a disgruntled techie either allegedly modified a new network system used by the city government of San Francisco so that only he has top-level privileges or set it up that way to protect it. See http://www.pcworld. com/businesscenter/article/148669/the_story_behind_san_franciscos_rogue_network_admin.html (last accessed August 1, 2008). The article cited contains summary information on many other related episodes.

108. Data held only in RAM (random access memory) disappear when overwritten or when the machine is turned off.

109. See, e.g., Reeves and Nass, *The Media Equation*.

110. One of the most helpful things that computers can do is to keep track of things for us. The computer's operating system does this, for instance, by assigning a location on the disk drive for the file. But even more efficient for many kinds of uses is a software application called a database management system. (*Applications* are programs that work with operating systems to enable specific functions, such as word processing or picture editing.) Any kind of data can be in a database. Rather than having to "thumb through" files one by one, to aid in rapid retrieval, the machine uses tags, or keys, so that a search can quickly select records of interest without the user's having to read every detail of a record in the whole file to look for the datum needed. A doctor,

for instance, might want to know about all the patients who need flu immunizations for this year. A Wal-Mart manager might want to know exactly what was purchased when so that replacement stock can be efficiently ordered. Google wants to know exactly what users searched for and how long it took them to find what they wanted to know. At every step of the way, someone or some "agent" (maybe a small software agent called a "bot") has defined the tags. They are judgments, not absolute truths. These tags or keys are ordered or selected by another powerful organizing tool used by computers: indexes. Indexes, too, can help speed up information searches, but they also are constructed according to one heuristic or another, so using them may simplify the task or make it more complicated at the same time. Think of the Yellow Pages. If you want to get your hair done, what is the appropriate search term? Beauty salon? Haircutter? Barber shop? With or without a manicure? Your Yellow Pages search is dependent upon someone else's idea about the right words to use for indexing. The same is true of computing.

111. Nancy Marder, "Introduction to Secrecy in Litigation," *Chicago-Kent Law Review* 81, no. 2 (2006): 328–29; see also Minna J. Kotkin, "Secrecy in Context: The Shadowy Life of Civil Rights Litigation," *Chicago-Kent Law Review* 81, no. 2 (2006): 587–88.

112. Daniel J. Solove, *The Digital Person: Technology and Privacy in the Information Age* (New York: New York University Press, 2004).

113. For discussion of the no-fly lists, begin with http://www.tsa.gov/approach/secure_flight. shtm; http://www.aclu.org/safefree/discrim/16969prs20031204.html (last accessed July 31, 2008).

114. To believe that they are more "rational," we have to subscribe to old notions of the binary opposition of reason and feeling. Many neurobiologists and cognitive scientists hold, to the contrary, that reason includes recognizing and using one's emotions; see, e.g., Antonio Damasio, *Descartes' Error* (New York: Grosset/Putnam, 1994).

115. We are grateful to David Dill, professor of computer science at Stanford University, for offering this example.

116. This is the classic problem of "the-man-in-the-middle," outlined by the security expert Bruce Schneier with reference to a hostage rescue operation in Colombia (http://www.wired. com/politics/security/commentary/securitymatters/2008/07/securitymatters_0710 [last accessed July 25, 2008]).

117. See generally David Harel, *Computers Ltd: What They Really Can't Do* (Oxford: Oxford University Press, 2000); Georges Ifrah, *The Universal History of Computing From the Abacus to the Quantum Computer* (New York: Wiley, 2001); Pamela McCorduck, *Machines Who Think: A Personal Inquiry Into the History and Prospects of Artificial Intelligence* (Natick, MA: A. K. Peters, 2004).

118. On information design, see de Souza, *The Semiotic Engineering of Human-Computer Interaction*; on courthouse design, see, e.g., David Tait, "Court Architecture and Judicial Rituals: Executive Tour of French Courts 2005" [CD-ROM] (Court of the Future Network, 2005).

119. "Bug": "An unwanted and unintended property of a program or piece of hardware, especially one that causes it to malfunction." See http://www.computer-dictionary-online.org/ index.asp?q=bug (last accessed August 1, 2008) for the quote in context and for an amusing account of the derivation of the term.

120. See Robert Pear, "In Digital Age, Federal Files Blip Into Oblivion," *New York Times*, September 13, 2008, http://www.nytimes.com/2008/09/13/us/13records. html?scp=1&sq=electronic%20records&st=cse (last accessed September 17, 2008).

CHAPTER 7

1. See, e.g., Dennis E. Curtis and Judith Resnik, "Images of Justice," *Yale Law Journal* 96, no. 8 (July 1987): 1727. The blindfold, like any other image, is ambiguous. Its primary meaning is that Justice is impartial. But it also suggests other, partly conflicting meanings: judgment in reliance on reason and freedom from the "corruption" of the senses; a Kantian morality of deciding in

accordance with general, abstract rules; perhaps a disinclination to watch the violence inflicted in Justice's name. Ibid. at 1754–64; see also Martin Jay, "Must Justice Be Blind?," in *Law and the Image*, ed. Costas Douzinas and Lynda Nead (Chicago: University of Chicago Press, 1999), 19–35; Judith Resnik and Dennis E. Curtis, "Representing Justice: From Renaissance Iconography to Twenty-First-Century Courthouses," *Proceedings of the American Philosophical Society* 151, no. 2 (June 2007): 139–83. Justice's sight, however, has not always been constrained. In classical Rome and medieval Europe, she was typically shown without a blindfold, and in one sixteenth-century print, she appears with two faces, one blindfolded and one not. See Jay, "Must Justice Be Blind?"

2. American Bar Association, *Model Rules of Professional Conduct* 3.3(a)(1), 3.4(b) (St. Paul, MN: West Group, 2008).

3. Only against some accepted standard of what counts as accurate judgment does it make sense to speak of judgmental error or bias. So, to evaluate a judgment influenced by visual rhetoric for factual accuracy, we need something like a consensus view of "the fact of the matter," the outcome that the rest of the (nonvisual) evidence in the case dictates. But such a criterion of factual accuracy simply doesn't exist in most cases, and, if it doesn't, it's hard to see how any given level of visual rhetoric could pose a systemic threat (or benefit, for that matter) to accurate decision making. Nevertheless, the discussion in the text proceeds on the assumption that it is possible to identify in some meaningful number of cases what counts as a "correct" decision.

4. See Brad E. Bell and Elizabeth Loftus, "Vivid Persuasion in the Courtroom," *Journal of Personality Assessment* 49, no. 6 (December 1985): 659–64.

5. Shelly Chaiken, "Heuristic Versus Systematic Information Processing and the Use of Source Versus Message Cues in Persuasion," *Journal of Personality and Social Psychology* 39, no. 5 (November 1980): 752–66; Shelly Chaiken, "The Heuristic Model of Persuasion," in *Social Influence: The Ontario Symposium*, ed. M. P. Zanna, J. M. Olson, and C. P. Herman (Hillsdale, NJ: Erlbaum), 5:3–39; Serena Chen and Shelly Chaiken, "The Heuristic-Systematic Model in Its Broader Context," in *Dual-Process Theories in Social Psychology*, ed. Shelly Chaiken and Yaacov Trope (New York: Guilford Press, 1999), 73–96; *see also* Fredric I. Lederer, "The Road to the Virtual Courtroom? A Consideration of Today's—and Tomorrow's—High-Technology Courtrooms," *South Carolina Law Review* 50, no. 3 (Spring 1999): 814–15 (describing views of judges presiding over high-tech courtrooms that electronic evidence technology not only speeds trials but also increases juror comprehension, leading to "better justice").

6. See Dan Grigorovici, "Persuasive Effects of Presence in Immersive Virtual Environments," in *Being There: Concepts, Effects and Measurement of User Presence in Synthetic Environments*, ed. G. Riva, F. Davide, and W.A. Ijsselsteijn (Amsterdam, The Netherlands: Ios Press, 2003), 191–207; Michael A. Shapiro and T. Makana Chock, "Psychological Processes in Perceiving Reality," paper presented at the convention of the Association for Education in Journalism and Mass Communication, Baltimore, MD, August 5–8, 1998; Michael A. Shapiro and Daniel G. McDonald, "I'm Not a Real Doctor, But I Play One in Virtual Reality: Implications of Virtual Reality for Judgments About Reality," *Journal of Communication* 42, no. 4 (Autumn 1992): 94–114. The basic model here is what social psychologists have called the *elaboration likelihood model* (ELM) of persuasion and attitude change (Richard E. Petty and John Cacioppo, "The Elaboration Likelihood Model of Persuasion," in *Advances in Experimental Social Psychology*, vol. 19, ed. Leonard Berkowitz [Orlando: Academic Press, 1986], 123–205; Richard E. Petty and Duane T. Wegener, "The Elaboration Likelihood Model: Current Status and Controversies," in Chaiken and Trope, *Dual-Process Theories in Social Psychology*, 41–72). According to ELM, people process messages through a central and/or peripheral route. When people are engaged in central-route message processing, they consciously attend to message content, elaborate ideas about that content, and integrate those ideas into a more or less coherent position about the object of the message. When processing information via the peripheral route, by contrast, people are consciously or unconsciously influenced by noncontent cues (such as the attractiveness of the source of the

message). Because (according to ELM) people in general prefer to hold correct beliefs and because beliefs based on central route or content-based processing are more likely to be correct and stable, people will prefer to attend to message content—unless they are unable or unwilling to do so, in which case they are less likely to process message content systematically and critically and are more likely to be persuaded by peripheral, noncontent-based cues.

7. For instance, Saul Kassin and Meghan Dunn found that mock jurors who saw an animation that was biased to support one party's version of events were inclined to decide in accordance with the animation instead of with the physical evidence, which supported the other party's version. Saul M. Kassin and Meghan A. Dunn, "Computer-Animated Displays and the Jury: Facilitative and Prejudicial Effects," *Law and Human Behavior* 21, no. 3 (June 1997): 269–81. For a summary of the advantages and disadvantages of digital media for legal judgment, see Damian Schofield and Lorna Goodwin, "Using Graphical Technology to Present Evidence," in *Electronic Evidence: Discovery, Disclosure and Admissibility*, ed. Stephen Mason (Edinburgh: Lexis Nexis Butterworths, 2007), 107–11.

8. See, e.g., Christy Visher, "Juror Decision Making: The Importance of Evidence," *Law and Human Behavior* 11, no. 1 (March 1987): 1–17; Theodore Eisenberg and others, "Judge-Jury Agreement in Criminal Cases: A Partial Replication of Kalven and Zeisel's *The American Jury*," *Journal of Empirical Legal Studies* 2, no. 1 (March 2005): 171–206.

9. E.g., Federal Rule of Civil Procedure 11; American Bar Association *Model Rules of Professional Conduct* 3.3. (Later in this chapter we expand upon this by proposing guidelines for good legal visual practices.)

10. In these crucial respects, digital visual and multimedia evidence does not raise evidentiary issues that differ very much from those posed by more traditional forms of evidence. For a thorough discussion of the admissibility rules pertaining to digital visual evidence, see Fred Galves, "Where the Not-So-Wild Things Are: Computers in the Courtroom, the Federal Rules of Evidence, and the Need for Institutional Reform and More Judicial Acceptance," *Harvard Journal of Law and Technology* 13, no. 2 (Winter 2000): 165, 198–260; see also Fredric I. Lederer, "Technology-Augmented Courtrooms: Progress Amid a Few Complications, or the Problematic Interrelationship Between Court and Counsel," *New York University Annual Survey of American Law* 60, no. 4 (2005): 675, 678; and see chapters 3 and 4.

11. So, for instance, a computer-animated reconstruction of a crime or accident ought to be adequately supported by eyewitness testimony and/or expert forensic evidence or it will be considered irrelevant (and/or unreliable) and thus inadmissible. In *Dunkle v. State of Oklahoma*, 139 P.3d 228 (Okla. Crim. App. 2006), a murder case, the prosecution offered a computer animation presenting four versions of the fatal shooting—three that the prosecution claimed were inconsistent with the evidence and a fourth, the "real" version, in which the defendant shot the victim. The trial court admitted the animation and the jury convicted the defendant, but the appellate court found that the physical and testimonial evidence was insufficient to support the animation's depictions of the victim's body and the distance between the victim and the gun. For this and other reasons, the appellate court found that the trial court committed reversible error in admitting the animation (139 P.3d at 246–51). The appellate opinion reflects the kind of vigilant application of the authentication requirements that should keep such arguably irrelevant and unreliable displays out of court. But the trial court's admission of the animation indicates that jurors may indeed be exposed to, and influenced by, prejudicial visuals.

12. Illustrative aids are admissible if they merely help the jury to understand the testimony. Although helpfulness is arguably a proxy for the relevance required by Rules 401–402, there need be no inquiry into reliability if (in the court's view) the picture is being depended upon not as substantive evidence of legally relevant reality but only as an "illustration" of testimony.

13. The reference to "all" relevant and reliable evidence must, of course, be qualified. Privileges, constitutional rights, and other extrinsic policies may properly keep otherwise relevant

and reliable information from the trier of fact. In order to keep proceedings within manageable limits, information that is merely cumulative (i.e., duplicates other good evidence) may also be excluded (as Rule 403 provides). And practical considerations at least partly beyond the reach of legal rules (e.g., unavoidable losses of evidence over time) may also prevent judges and jurors from having before them "all" of the relevant and probative evidence they might desire.

14. Mark D. Alicke, "Culpable Control and the Psychology of Blame, *Psychological Bulletin* 126, no. 4 (July 2000): 556–74; Joshua Greene and Jonathan Haidt, "How (and Where) Does Moral Judgment Work?," *Trends in Cognitive Sciences* 6, no. 12 (December 2002): 517–23; Jonathan Haidt and Fredrik Bjorklund, "Social Intuitionists Answer Six Questions About Moral Psychology," in *Moral Psychology*, ed. W. Sinnott-Armstrong (Cambridge, MA: MIT Press, 2008), 2: 181–217.

15. Consider, for instance, the phenomenon of "change blindness blindness," which refers to people's inability to recognize a particular limitation of their visual perception, the ability to detect significant but gradual changes in the visual field; see Brian J. Scholl, Daniel J. Simons, and Daniel T. Levin, "'Change Blindness' Blindness: An Implicit Measure of a Metacognitive Error," in *Thinking and Seeing: Visual Metacognition in Adults and Children*, ed. Daniel T. Levin (Cambridge, MA: MIT Press, 2004), 145–63. One might also consider the many cases in which confident eyewitnesses have incorrectly identified the perpetrator of a crime and have been believed by juries, where DNA evidence subsequently proved that the identification was mistaken; see Barry Scheck, Peter Neufeld, and Jim Dwyer, *Actual Innocence* (New York: Doubleday, 2000).

16. See Richard Sherwin, Neal Feigenson, and Christina Spiesel, "Law in the Digital Age," *Boston University Journal of Science and Technology Law* 12, no. 2 (Summer 2006): 243–44. This is not inconsistent with the claim that law on the screen induces passivity —"chewing gum for the eyes," as television has famously been described (the quotation is variously attributed to the architect Frank Lloyd Wright, the humorist Fred Allen, and others, but it apparently originated with the critic John Mason Brown in 1955; see Ralph Keyes, *The Quote Verifier: Who Said What, Where, and When* [New York: St. Martin's Griffin, 2006], 218)—and reduces critical scrutiny for that reason. The long-term effects of screens with which we interact may be a different matter, however, as we discussed in chapter 3.

17. See Matthew D. Lieberman and others, "Putting Feelings Into Words: Affect Labeling Disrupts Amygdala Activity in Response to Affective Stimuli," *Psychological Science* 18, no. 5 (May 2007): 421–28. Marketing experts have developed methods for verbally eliciting consumers' otherwise unconscious reactions to products and companies, which the experts believe more accurately reflect consumers' attitudes than do their conscious expressions (see, e.g., Gerald Zaltman, *How Customers Think* [Boston: Harvard Business School Press, 2003]). Deliberations in which jurors are encouraged to spend some time free-associating in response to the parties' visual displays and then to discuss those responses could produce constructive insights into the effects of those displays.

18. For instance, Hany Farid, a mathematician, has been developing specialized software for detecting more subtle picture alterations; Hany Farid, "Digital Doctoring: How to Tell the Real From the Fake," *Significance* 3, no. 4 (2006): 162–66. And Mike Rossner, Editor-in-Chief of the *Journal of Cell Biology*, has shown how to use Photoshop to detect some manipulations; Mike Rossner, "How to Guard Against Image Fraud," *The Scientist* 20, no. 3 (2006): 24–25; see also Nicholas Wade, "It May Look Authentic; Here's How to Tell It Isn't," *New York Times*, January 24, 2006 (discussing work of Rossner, Farid, and others), and see chapter 4.

19. Richard K. Sherwin, "A Matter of Voice—and Plot: Belief and Suspicion in Legal Storytelling," *Michigan Law Review* 87, no. 3 (December 1988): 543–612.

20. See discussion of the Elaboration Likelihood Model of persuasion in n. 6.

21. Michael Skakel's lawyers made this argument on appeal to the Connecticut Supreme Court. See *Connecticut v. Skakel*, No. SC 16844, Defendant's Brief at 79 (filed Nov. 24, 2003).

22. Brian Carney and Neal Feigenson, "Visual Persuasion in the Michael Skakel Trial," *Criminal Justice* 19, no. 1 (Spring 2004): 31.

23. See *Musladin v. Lamarque*, 427 F.3d 653, 657 (9th Cir. 2005), *vacated, Carey v. Musladin*, 549 U.S. 70 (2006) (wearing of buttons by homicide victim's family featuring victim's photograph violated defendant's due process right to receive a fair trial by an impartial jury free from outside influences; the buttons communicated an implicit message accusing the defendant of guilt, a message "all the more dangerous precisely because it was not a formal accusation [and] not susceptible to traditional methods of refutation") (quoting *Norris v. Risley*, 918 F.2d 828, 833 (9th Cir. 1990)). This is not to imply that "cross-examining" pictures is easy even when their effects can be recognized; pictures always come in a communicative or rhetorical context consisting of words (and sometimes other pictures), and effective cross-examination has to take all of that into account.

24. Rudolf Arnheim, *Visual Thinking* (Berkeley: University of California Press, 1971), 227.

25. For a discussion of subconscious associational logic in the context of pictures used in advertising, see Robin Andersen, *Consumer Culture & TV Programming* (Boulder, CO: Westview Press, 1995), 80–85.

26. For an excellent collection of essays on this issue, see Susan Bandes, ed., *The Passions of Law* (New York: New York University Press, 1999).

27. David A. Bright and Jane Goodman-Delahunty, "Gruesome Evidence and Emotion: Anger, Blame, and Jury Decision-Making," *Law and Human Behavior* 30, no. 2 (April 2006): 183–202.

28. See discussion of this point in chapter 1 and elsewhere.

29. See psychological research on the primacy effect (e.g., Murray Glanzer and Anita R. Cunitz, "Two Storage Mechanisms in Free Recall," *Journal of Verbal Learning and Verbal Behavior* 5, no. 4 [1966]: 531–60; Bennett B. Murdock, Jr., "The Serial Position Effect of Free Recall," *Journal of Experimental Psychology* 64, no. 5 [November 1962]: 482–88) and related phenomena, such as the halo effect (e.g., Daniel T. Gilbert, "Ordinary Personology," in *The Handbook of Social Psychology*, 4th ed., ed. Daniel T. Gilbert, Susan T. Fiske, and Gardner Lindzey [Boston: McGraw-Hill, 1998], 2: 89–150).

30. See, e.g., Janet H. Murray, *Hamlet on the Holodeck* (Cambridge, MA: MIT Press, 1997).

31. See Sherwin, *When Law Goes Pop*.

32. See, e.g., Samuel A. Guiberson, "The Challenge of Technology in the New Practice of Law," *Ohio Northern University Law Review* 25, no. 4 (1999): 567.

33. The most frequently invoked phrase of Rule 403, the reference to "unfair prejudice," is aimed at avoiding decisions made on an improper basis, which includes decisions "based on bad logic as well as base passions" (Charles Alan Wright and Kenneth W. Graham, Jr., *Federal Practice and Procedure*, vol. 22 [St. Paul, MN: West, 1978], 275). The next two phrases, "confusion of the issues" and "misleading the jury," further show that the rule is meant to address threats to good thinking in general.

34. Federal Rule of Evidence 403. In many states, the balance is struck less permissively, authorizing the judge to exclude the evidence if its judgmental risks "outweigh," rather than "substantially outweigh," its probative value.

35. As is the case regarding the admissibility of evidence generally, the dynamics are different in a bench trial, when the judge sits without a jury. Although the same rules of evidence apply, judges take a more relaxed attitude toward admissibility when there are no jurors to protect from irrelevant, confusing, or prejudicial information (e.g., Kenneth S. Broun and others, *McCormick on Evidence*, 6th ed. [St. Paul, MN: Thompson West, 2006], 113). And, of course, the judge cannot unsee a display once he or she has been exposed to it. (If the display is offered as substantive evidence [see discussion in chapter 3], the judge could look at it and then decline to consider it, although research indicates that judges, like jurors, are influenced

by exposure to evidence later determined to be inadmissible; see, e.g., Andrew J. Wistrich, Chris Guthrie, and Jeffrey J. Rachlinski, "Can Judges Ignore Inadmissible Information? The Difficulty of Deliberately Disregarding," *University of Pennsylvania Law Review* 153, no. 4 [March 2005]: 1251–1345.)

36. Of course there are exceptions to this generalization, but, since judges tend to be older than the average juror and to have reached their positions through immersion and success in a traditionally verbal (and even document-based) domain, they would seem less likely than jurors collectively to be conversant with digital visual culture.

37. Conversely, anecdotal evidence indicates that jurors are capable of recognizing at least relatively blatant attempts to use new media to bias their judgment; see Lederer, "The Road to the Virtual Courtroom?," 817–18 (reporting results of experiment involving use of vivid graphics during opening statement).

38. Cass R. Sunstein, *Infotopia: How Many Minds Produce Knowledge* (Oxford: Oxford University Press, 2006).

39. American Bar Association, *Principles for Juries & Jury Trials* (Chicago: Author, 2005), Principle 13.G, 93.

40. Just as the jury scholars Shari Seidman Diamond and Mary Rose have recommended that the best way to deal with the problem of "embedded experts" on the jury (nurses, engineers, and others who claim and disclose to their fellow jurors special knowledge relevant to a substantive aspect of the case) is not to try to prevent the hidden experts from sharing their expertise (which would be futile anyway, given the limitations on impeachment of jury verdicts) but instead to alert all jurors to the issue and to guide them in evaluating what their fellow jurors may say (e.g., that their views have not been subjected to cross-examination) (Shari Seidman Diamond and Mary Rose, "Embedded Experts on the Jury," presentation at First Annual Conference on Empirical Legal Studies, Austin, TX, October 28, 2006), so we believe that letting jurors see (most of) the pictures and encouraging them to scrutinize those pictures as carefully as possible is the best way to achieve the delicate balance between empowering the decision makers and guiding them so that they may decide as well as possible.

41. The first three of these sources of enhanced insight into visuals and multimedia would apply as well in bench trials, where the judge is the trier of fact.

42. Federal Judicial Center/National Institute for Trial Advocacy, *Effective Use of Courtroom Technology* (Washington, DC: Author, 2001), 186–209.

43. For instance, one of the authors (Spiesel) presented a workshop, "Law's Digital Way," at a plenary session of the Connecticut Judges Institute's annual meeting on June 27, 2007.

44. See *Dunkle v. State*, 139 P.3d 228, 251–52 (Okla. Crim. App. 2006); see also James E. Carbine and Lynn McLain, "Proposed Model Rules Governing the Admissibility of Computer-Generated Evidence," *Santa Clara Computer and High Technology Law Journal* 15, no. 1 (January 1999): 1–72. In *Commonwealth v. Serge*, 837 A.2d 1255, 1263–64 (Pa. App. 2003), the appellate court quoted the trial judge's instructions on computer animation:

> Members of the jury, parties in a case are permitted to use photographs, drawings and other exhibits to illustrate a point they are attempting to make in a case. This is what we refer to as demonstrative evidence. We refer to this type of evidence as demonstrative evidence, as opposed to substantive evidence, since it is offered merely to demonstrate or illustrate a point rather than as actual proof of that point.
>
> With the advent of the digital age, computers are now used to produce this type of demonstrative evidence. You heard testimony from Dr. Gary Ross and Trooper Brad Beach that the computer-generated animation, which will now be shown to you, is a fair and accurate illustration of the opinions that they

formed as to how this shooting allegedly occurred. You also heard this witness describe how he produced the three-dimensional drawings with computer software to depict those opinions, and thereafter transform them onto this DVD to produce moving images, which will be played for you. What you are about to be shown is commonly referred to as a computer-generated exhibit. There are two types of computer-generated exhibits, and you heard the witness refer to them. The first is what we call a simulation, and the second is what we refer to as an animation.

In a simulation, data is entered into a computer, which is preprogrammed to perform certain calculations by applying, for example, the laws of physics, mathematical formulas, and other scientific principles in order for the computer itself to draw conclusions and to attempt to recreate an incident. The end product of a simulation represents the computer program's conclusion of what happened. And the results of the computer simulation serve as the basis for the testifying expert's opinion of what happened.

In contrast, an animation is simply a graphic depiction, or illustration, of an opinion that an expert has already formed based upon his or her own independent investigation, computations, and analysis. With an animation, the computer does not perform any scientific calculations or develop any opinions, as is the case with the simulation. An animation consists of computer-generated drawings which are assembled frame by frame, and, when viewed sequentially, produce the image of motion. Thus, an animation is merely a graphic depiction or illustration of an opinion or recreation which an expert witness in the case has already devised through his or her own independent calculations and analysis.

Please understand that what you are about to view is an animation, not a simulation. This computer-generated animation is a demonstrative exhibit, not substantive evidence, and it is being offered solely as an illustration of the Commonwealth's version of events as recreated by Dr. Gary Ross and Trooper Brad Beach. You should not confuse art with reality and should not view the animation as a definitive recreation of the actual incident. The series of pictures which have been drawn by the computer and transferred on to the tape for your review are no different from a witness sketching a series of drawings on paper and then fanning those pages to portray moving images of his or her opinion.

Remember, the demonstrative animation is only as good as the underlying testimony, data, assumptions, and opinions that serve as the basis for its images, and the computer maxim, "garbage in, garbage out," applies equally to computer animations. Like all other evidence in the case, you may accept it or reject it, that is, the computer-generated animation, in whole or in part. I caution you again that the animation may only be considered for demonstrative purposes to illustrate the opinions of Dr. Gary Ross and Trooper Bradley Beach. Always bear in mind that the Commonwealth must still meet its burden of proving all of the elements of the offense charged beyond a reasonable doubt.

Both the appellate court and the state supreme court (586 Pa. 671, 696–98 (2006)) quoted these instructions approvingly. The supreme court did state, however, that, while such instructions "are a powerful tool in limiting prejudice, and . . . a trial court would be wise to issue them," the trial judge should not be required to do so (ibid. at 698 n. 12).

45. Greater specificity, such as alerting jurors to particular effects that particular visual elements might produce, seems neither justified (given the limited psychological research) nor feasible (given the nearly infinite variety of pictures and their possible effects). And it is not necessary to obtain the desired result: helping jurors to become conscious of at least some of the effects that visual displays may have on them, and thus enabling them to reflect critically on those displays.

46. On the limited efficacy of jury instructions, especially those that purport to restrict jurors from ignoring inadmissible evidence or using admissible evidence for one purpose but not another, see, e.g., Joel D. Lieberman and Jamie Arndt, "Understanding the Limits of Limiting Instructions," *Psychology, Public Policy, and Law* 6, no. 3 (September 2000): 677–711.

47. Shari Seidman Diamond and Jonathan Casper, "Blindfolding the Jury to Verdict Consequences: Damages, Experts, and the Civil Jury," *Law and Society Review* 26, no. 3 (1992): 513–63; Vicki Smith, "When Prior Knowledge and Law Collide: Helping Jurors Use the Law," *Law and Human Behavior* 17, no. 5 (October 1993): 507–35.

48. We would like to thank the sociologist David Tait, who has graciously shared with us instructions that he and his colleagues have drafted for use in an experimental study of the effects of interactive visual evidence on juries. These instructions include advising jurors that they should share their differing perspectives on visual (and other) evidence with their fellow jurors during deliberations.

49. Federal Judicial Center, *An Introduction to the Patent System* (2002), http://www.fjc.gov/library/fjc_catalog.nsf/ (last accessed July 31, 2008). Savvy lawyers may find that parts of the video have rhetorical value that helps one side or the other and thus may prefer that only certain parts be shown and/or may not consent to its use (attorney Robert Cote, interview by authors, September 25, 2006).

50. See, e.g., XVIVO Scientific Animation, http://www.xvivo.net (last accessed July 31, 2008).

51. See, e.g., the Center for Legal and Court Technology (formerly Courtroom 21) at the William and Mary Law School, www.courtroom21.net/ (last accessed July 31, 2008); Kenneth J. Hirsh and Wayne Miller, "Law School Education in the 21st Century: Adding Information Technology Instruction to the Curriculum," *William and Mary Bill of Rights Journal* 12, no. 2 (April 2004): 873–85.

52. The National Institute for Trial Advocacy, for instance, has offered trial practice instruction featuring new technologies, as has the Center for Legal and Court Technology; see Lederer, "Technology-Augmented Courtrooms," 684.

53. Whether such performances should be required for more complicated digital productions such as computer animations (as suggested by Elan E. Weinreb, "'Counselor, Proceed With Caution': The Use of Integrated Evidence Presentation Systems and Computer-Generated Evidence in the Courtroom," *Cardozo Law Review* 23, no. 1 [November 2001]: 423–40), may depend on whether improvements in software and hardware make such real-time demonstrations feasible, whether the courtroom is equipped to handle it, and the importance to the case of the visual display and the facts it is offered to explain or prove.

54. See Elizabeth Loftus, *Eyewitness Testimony* (Cambridge, MA: Harvard University Press, rev. ed. 1996).

55. For a detailed review of the law, see Courtroom 21 Project, "The Use of Technology in the Jury Room to Enhance Deliberations" (Williamsburg, VA: Author, n.d.), Appendix B (available at http://www.courtroom21.net/publications/articles/juryroomtechnologyreport.pdf [last accessed July 31, 2008]); see also Federal Judicial Center/National Institute for Trial Advocacy, *Effective Use of Courtroom Technology*, 120. The American Bar Association's *Principles*, 15.B, 113, affirm that (admitted) exhibits should ordinarily go to the jury room but are silent about demonstratives that are not admitted as full exhibits (see also Principle 13.B, 91 [recommended trial notebooks should contain "selected exhibits which have been ruled admissible"]). Indeed,

Federal Judicial Center/National Institute for Trial Advocacy, *Effective Use of Courtroom Technology*, 148, observes that "the practice of allowing evidentiary exhibits to go to the jury room but withholding illustrative aids is a mystery to most jurors," even as it proposes preliminary jury instructions maintaining and clarifying this distinction.

56. See, e.g., Gordon Bermant, "Courting the Virtual: Federal Courts in an Age of Complete Inter-Connectedness," *Ohio Northern University Law Review* 25, no. 4 (1999): 550.

57. Also, jurors ordinarily will have unlimited access to displays admitted as substantive evidence (i.e., as full evidentiary exhibits), despite a similar potential concern (that jurors will give evidence that happens to take tangible form too much weight relative to testimonial evidence).

58. See, e.g., Nancy S. Marder, "Juries and Technology: Equipping Jurors for the Twenty-First Century," *Brooklyn Law Review* 66, no. 4 (2001): 1276–77; American Bar Association, *Principles*, Principle 13.A, 91 ("Jurors should be allowed to take notes during the trial").

59. Whenever a judge, pursuant to the jury's request during its deliberations, reads back testimony to the jury, there are the risks that jurors may give too much emphasis to that testimony and/or may take the testimony out of context. The decision whether to comply with the jury's request is left to the discretion of the trial judge, who should consider both the reasonableness of the request and the difficulty of complying with it. See, e.g., *United States v. Padin*, 787 F.2d 1071, 1076–77 (6th Cir. 1986). We contend that the same principles ought to guide the judge's decision to read back testimony that the jury believes it needs to fully comprehend visual displays introduced during trial to illustrate expert testimony. (See also Marder, "Juries and Technology," 1274 [recommending use of videoconferencing to present remote expert testimony and pointing out that jury should be allowed to take the video into the jury room to "collectively review the expert's demeanor and credibility rather than rely on the recollections of individual jurors"]; *State of Hawai'i v. Robinson*, 903 P.2d 1289 (Haw. 1995) [jury given unsupervised, unlimited access during deliberations to defendant's audio- and videotaped confessions; court reasoned that tapes had "passed all tests of admissibility and . . . been duly received into evidence"]). Although these sources support allowing jury to have access to out-of-court statements admitted into evidence, the same reasoning should apply to demonstratives that have been found probative and clear enough to be shown in court and that the opponent has had the opportunity to question and criticize.

60. Indeed, one of us (Feigenson) raised these and other concerns in an earlier article (Carney and Feigenson, "Visual Persuasion").

61. E.g., Neil Vidmar and Valerie P. Hans, *American Juries: The Verdict* (Amherst, NY: Prometheus Books, 2007).

62. Federal District Court Judge Nancy Gertner, for instance, seems to support the use of new visual technologies but has expressed the following frustration: "I have the courtroom of the 21st century and the jury room of the 18th . . . so jurors lack the tools to do what they need to do with the [high-tech] material [shown during trial]" (remarks at conference, "The *CSI* Effect: Litigation Strategies and Courtroom Dynamics," Suffolk University Law School, May 10, 2007; notes on file with authors). Indeed, as recently as a few years ago, the most detailed study of the subject stated that "[d]eliberation room technology, including VCR's and the like, appears to be rare" (Courtroom 21 Project, "The Use of Technology in the Jury Room," 21). Given the rapidly increasing availability of visual and multimedia technologies, however, the situation could easily change if judicial branch administrators and judges were so inclined. See Fredric I. Lederer, "Courtroom Technology: A Status Report" (Williamsburg, VA: Courtroom 21 Project, 2005), http://www.courtroom21.net/publications/articles/status.pdf: 12–13 (last accessed July 31, 2008).

63. For a review of several possible methods of jury review of digital visuals and multimedia, see Federal Judicial Center/National Institute for Trial Advocacy, *Effective Use of Courtroom Technology*, 212–14. For more on the benefits and drawbacks of having jurors review visual displays in the courtroom instead of the jury room, or, if the review takes place in the jury room,

of having a court officer instead of jurors replay the visual display, see Lederer, "The Road to the Virtual Courtroom," 818–19; see also Carney and Feigenson, "Visual Persuasion," 29.

64. American Bar Association, *Principles*, Principle 13.G. Conflicts between this recommended practice of jury access to visuals and other rules (e.g., Federal Rule of Evidence 803(18), which allows learned treatises to be read to the jury but not taken to the jury room) would have to be reconciled (see Carbine and McLain, "Proposed Model Rules," 27–28).

65. 896 A.2d 1170, 1185 (Pa. 2006).

66. See, e.g., Meghan A. Dunn, Peter Salovey, and Neal Feigenson, "The Jury Persuaded (and Not): Computer Animation in the Courtroom," *Law & Policy* 28, no. 2 (April 2006): 228–48 (in one of two accident scenarios, animations most affected verdicts when plaintiff used an animation but defendant did not); Jaihyun Park and Neal Feigenson, "Effects of PowerPoint on Mock Juror Decision Making" (unpublished manuscript on file with authors) (in discrimination scenario, graphics reduced defendant's judged liability when defendant used them but plaintiffs did not).

67. Galves, "Where the Not-So-Wild Things Are," 290–95, agrees and makes the additional point that tolerating pervasive economic inequality in the American adversarial system (e.g., with regard to staffing of cases, hiring experts, and hiring jury consultants) but objecting to it only with regard to the use of computer generated evidence is an unfairly selective criticism. See also Federal Judicial Center/National Institute for Trial Advocacy, *Effective Use of Courtroom Technology*, 50–51. For other appraisals of the issues of cost and access, see Lederer, "The Road to the Virtual Courtroom?," 831–36; Anne Wallace, "Towards Virtual Civil Litigation?," paper presented at 30th International Congress on Law and Mental Health, Padua, Italy, June 26, 2007 (copy on file with authors).

68. See, e.g., *Serge*, 896 A.2d 1170, 1183 n. 10 (Pa. 2006) (reference to declining costs of digital technologies); Mina Kimes, "Courtroom Cartoons Help Win Legal Fights," http://money.cnn.com/2008/09/02/smallbusiness/courtroom_cartoons.fsb/ (last accessed September 18, 2008) (courtroom animations declining in cost and spreading in use; reporting an ABA study indicating that a quarter of law firms with fifty to ninety-nine lawyers used animations in 2007, up from 4 percent the previous year). For example, the animation in *Murtha* (chapter 5) cost about $12,000, according to attorney Hugh Keefe (Hugh Keefe, interview by authors, November 22, 2006); a day-in-the-life movie may cost in the $4,000–6,000 range (Bill Buckley, interview by authors, June 11, 2005); and PowerPoint slide shows entail little if any out-of-pocket cost.

69. Galves, "Where the Not-So-Wild Things Are," 293–94; Lederer, "Technology-Augmented Courtrooms," 676–77.

70. Elizabeth C. Wiggins, Meghan A. Dunn, and George Cort, "Federal Judicial Center Survey on Courtroom Technology" (December 2003), http://www.fjc.gov/public/pdf.nsf/lookup/CT-tech03.pdf/$file/CTtech03.pdf (on file with authors). On the complications presented by lawyers' use of court-supplied technology and the respective obligations of court and counsel when the technology malfunctions, see generally Lederer, "Technology-Augmented Courtrooms."

71. In Connecticut, for instance, once a public defender is appointed, the Division of Public Defender Services covers all costs of representation. Should any Division attorney believe that an animation or other visual evidence is necessary to properly and zealously defend her client, she would file a "Request for Authorization to Incur Expenses" with the Deputy Chief Public Defender, setting forth the approximate cost of the special service and why it is believed necessary. These requests are routinely granted. (We would like to thank Elizabeth Inkster, Senior Assistant Public Defender, State of Connecticut, for this information; private communication, November 27, 2007 [e-mail on file with authors].) Inkster adds, however, that "Connecticut is light years ahead of other states in its public defender funding."

72. Yet such a proposal might discourage lawyers from using digital visual displays in the first place if they know that they will have to pay for the opponent's as well. Galves, "Where the Not-So-Wild Things Are," 297.

73. See generally Federal Judicial Center/National Institute for Trial Advocacy, *Effective Use of Courtroom Technology*, 99–115.

74. Carney and Feigenson, "Visual Persuasion," 34–35.

75. See Carbine and McLain, "Proposed Model Rules," 33–41; see Galves, "Where the Not-So-Wild Things Are," 205–7 on the advantages and disadvantages of early disclosure; Galves concludes that the advantages outweigh the disadvantages.

76. *Serge*, 896 A.2d at 1188 (Pa. 2006) (Cappy, J., concurring).

77. Ibid. at 1174 n. 2.

78. Carney and Feigenson, "Visual Persuasion," 34–35.

79. See, e.g., Federal Rule of Civil Procedure 26(b)(3); *Hickman v. Taylor*, 329 U.S. 495 (1947); Carney and Feigenson, "Visual Persuasion," 35. Another way of managing the tension between the benefits of disclosure and those of protecting attorney work product when it arises in the cross-examination of expert witnesses is proposed by the Federal Judicial Center/National Institute for Trial Advocacy, *Effective Use of Courtroom Technology*, 178–79: "[O]ffer counsel (or . . . make) a choice of one of the following alternatives. First, if the illustrative aids are disclosed to opposing counsel prior to or at the outset of the cross-examination, then rebuttal examination will proceed as usual immediately upon the conclusion of cross-examination. Second, if illustrative aids are not disclosed and if surprise is reasonably claimed, then an appropriate recess will be granted at the end of cross-examination, so that counsel can prepare any necessary illustrative aids for rebuttal."

80. Federal Judicial Center/National Institute for Trial Advocacy, *Effective Use of Courtroom Technology*, 210–11. For the much broader suggestion that the use of visual aids in closing argument might be limited to those approved "well in advance" by the court, see *United States v. Crockett*, 49 F.3d 1357, 1361 (8th Cir. 1995).

81. Remote testimony also raises other procedural justice concerns, including whether permitting an adverse witness to testify by videoconference violates a criminal defendant's Sixth Amendment Confrontation Clause rights. See *Maryland v. Craig*, 497 U.S. 836 (1990) (Confrontation Clause may be compromised under limited circumstances where "considerations of public policy and necessities of the case" require; upholding state rule of criminal procedure allowing child abuse victims to testify from remote location via one-way closed circuit television); *United States v. Yates*, 438 F.3d 1307 (11th Cir. 2006) (permitting witnesses in mail fraud and conspiracy case to testify from Australia via two-way live videoconferencing violated defendants' Confrontation Clause rights where no case-specific factual showing was made that witnesses could not have given videotaped deposition under Federal Rule of Criminal Procedure 15). Three dissenting judges in *Yates* contended that testimony by two-way videoconferencing was not only constitutional but superior to testimony by videotaped deposition, because the witnesses, as they testified, could observe the lawyers, the defendant, and the jurors, and the judge and jurors could observe the witnesses (*Yates*, 438 F.3d at 1334–36) (Marcus, J., dissenting).

82. The court also needs to be sensitive to the need of the remote defendant for adequate legal representation during the proceedings; choices may have to be made between having counsel present with the client at the remote location or before the judge in the courtroom. See Patricia Raburn-Remfry, "Due Process Concerns in Video Production of Defendants," *Stetson Law Review* 23, no. 3 (Summer 1994): 805–41.

83. See Edward T. Hall, *The Hidden Dimension* (Garden City, NY: Doubleday, 1966).

84. For discussions of these and other effects of the videoconferencing medium on viewers' perceptions, see Aaron Haas, "Videoconferencing in Immigration Proceedings," *Pierce Law Review* 5, no. 3 (2006): 59–90; Anne Bowen Poulin, "Criminal Justice and Videoconferencing Technology: The Remote Defendant," *Tulane Law Review* 78, no. 4 (March 2004): 1089–1167.

85. For a thorough discussion of the responsibilities of court and counsel regarding courtroom technology generally, see Lederer, "Technology-Augmented Courtrooms." The Courtroom

21 Court Affiliates Protocols for Use by Lawyers of Courtroom Technology (which Professor Lederer collected and edited), ibid., 691–709, do not impose on the courts an obligation to supply counsel with any technology (§3-10.00) but do obligate courts to ensure that any technology they do supply is fully functional (§4-20.00).

86. Maryland Rule 2-504.3(f) (2006).

87. Carbine and McLain, "Proposed Model Rules," 32. Any such recording system will have to grapple with point of view, whether the camera is fixed or moving, and other videographical issues that can affect the meaning of the resulting picture.

88. See, e.g., Peter W. Martin, "Reconfiguring Law Reports and the Concept of Precedent for a Digital Age," *Villanova Law Review* 53, no. 1 (2008): 40–42 (briefly discussing gradual incorporation of nontextual material in electronic case reports). Here, too, many issues will have to be confronted, including the platforms for legal publishing, copyright implications regarding courtroom displays, and so on.

89. For a good discussion of other process issues relating to the use of new courtroom technologies, focusing on the allocation of responsibilities between the court and the trial lawyers, see Lederer, "Technology-Augmented Courtrooms."

90. For a thorough analysis and critique of expressivism as a jurisprudential theory, see Matthew D. Adler, "Expressive Theories of Law: A Skeptical Overview," *University of Pennsylvania Law Review* 148, no. 5 (May 2000): 1363–1501.

91. Law's public expression of any values depends, of course, on how what happens in the legal system is communicated to the public at large via news coverage, dramatic fictions, and otherwise, a topic that we have not addressed in this book. See, e.g., William Haltom, *Reporting on the Courts* (Chicago: Nelson Hall, 1998); William Haltom and Michael McCann, *Distorting the Law* (Chicago: University of Chicago Press, 2004).

92. Charles Nesson, "The Evidence or the Event? On Judicial Proof and the Acceptability of Verdicts," *Harvard Law Review* 98, no. 7 (May 1985): 1357–92.

93. For biological science, see, e.g., Rossner, "How to Guard Against Image Fraud" (describing policies of *Journal of Cell Biology*, of which he is editor-in-chief); *Nature*, http://www.nature.com/authors/editorial_policies/image.html (2006) (last accessed July 31, 2008) (detailed digital image guidelines for *Nature* family of journals). For forensic science, see Scientific Working Group on Imaging Technology (SWGIT), Section 1, "Overview of SWGIT and the Use of Imaging Technology in the Criminal Justice System," Version 3.0 2006.01.09 (2006); Section 11, "Best Practices for Documenting Image Enhancement," Version 1.2 2004.03.04 (2004). For photojournalism, see, e.g., David Schlesinger, "The Use of Photoshop," http://blogs.reuters.com/author/davidschlesinger/ (January 18, 2007) (last accessed July 26, 2008) (Reuters policy); Associated Press, "The Associated Press Statement of News Values and Principles," http://www.ap.org/news-values/index.html (last accessed July 31, 2008).

94. Cf. Max Holland and Joann Rush, "J.F.K.'s Death, Re-Framed," *New York Times*, November 22, 2007 (discussing how Abraham Zapruder's film of the Kennedy assassination has long been believed to be a complete visual record of the assassination, leading to misconceptions about a third shot, which other evidence indicates must have been fired while Zapruder's camera was turned off); Maryanne Garry, Deryn Strange, Daniel M. Bernstein, and Toni Kinzett, "Photographs Can Distort Memory for the News," *Applied Cognitive Psychology* 21, no. 8 (December 2007): 995–1004 (participants asked to edit a news story about a hurricane for typographical errors who saw a photo showing a village after the hurricane were three times more likely to claim afterwards that they had read about personal injuries or death [there was no such information in the article] than participants who saw a photo showing an undamaged village before the hurricane); Maryanne Garry and Matthew P. Gerrie, "When Photographs Create False Memories," *Current Directions in Psychological Science* 14, no. 6 (December 2005): 321–25 (both doctored and true photographs can create false memories for personal experiences).

95. ABA *Model Rules of Professional Conduct* 3.3(a)(1), 3.4(b).

96. See Federal Rules of Evidence 403, 901(a). For instance, the prosecution's proffer of the altered videotape in the *Dunlop* case (discussed in chapter 2) obviously violates this ethical norm, just as it violates already existing rules of professional conduct.

97. The Connecticut Supreme Court's decision in *Skakel* is a good example. The defendant's recorded words "I had a feeling of panic" could have meant any number of things: Was Michael Skakel panicked, as his lawyers claimed, by the thought that someone had observed him masturbating in a tree the night before? Was he panicked by answering the door hung over and finding Martha's mother there? Or was he panicked by memories of what he had done to his friend the night before? The prosecution argued for the last of these and, to make this point, showed the jury the defendant's words next to a picture of the victim's battered body under a tree. Just because the defense strongly disputed the prosecution's interpretation of the words does not mean that the prosecution's use of multimedia to explain its theory was misleading.

98. For instance, the kinds of photo manipulations reflected in the stock photos used in the Vioxx opening statements and closing arguments discussed in chapter 5—the cropped and tinted ATM machine, the orange-hued nose-diving plane—would not run afoul of our proposed norm proposed here because those altered photos did not purport to depict case-relevant reality. Instead, they were visual metaphors, illustrations of the lawyer's theory of the case, and as such did not mislead jurors or distort, much less falsify, reality.

99. Reuters' guidelines may be getting at something like this when they require that "photographers must remain contactable until their work is published" in order to answer questions if the photo caption does not fully explain the image (Schlesinger, "The Use of Photoshop").

100. For details regarding documentation of Photoshop alterations, see, e.g., Lisa Podolski and Neal Feigenson, "Digitally Processed Images in Connecticut Courts After *Swinton*," *Connecticut Trial Lawyers Association Forum* 25, no. 1 (Winter 2007): 37.

101. The proposed guideline is limited to pictures offered as depictions of reality, by which we mean unenhanced and enhanced photos, videos, X-rays, and the like. We might, however, extend the principle of transparency to diagrammatic pictures, including charts, graphs, models, and so on. The makers of these pictures might be required, for instance, to make available the sources for the information on which the pictures are based—not to include it as part of the display but to be ready to provide the source data if asked. (When, as is frequently the case, diagrammatic pictures are offered to illustrate expert testimony, the source data as well as the pictures themselves would presumably already be available through pretrial discovery, at least in civil cases; see Federal Rule of Civil Procedure 26(a)(2), (3).)

102. ABA *Model Rule of Professional Conduct* 1.1.

103. Nearly a decade ago, one trial lawyer wrote of courtroom technology: "This is not an option for lawyers, this is an imperative. Lawyers who choose not to engage themselves in this training, in this reformation of the concept of how to be advocates, will soon be like aging gorillas stumbling through the mists, hunting for clients under flat rocks in some remote Amazonian jungle. There will be no practice of law for those [who] do not employ these tools." Guiberson, "The Challenge of Technology," 567. To the same effect was the comment of another contributor to the same symposium: "An understanding of technological advocacy should be no less a part of an attorney's repertoire than is a keen ability to spot legal issues in a given fact situation." Paul L. Johns, "Technology-Augmented Advocacy: Raising the Trial Lawyer's Standard of Care; Changing Traditional Legal Education; and Creating New Judicial Responsibilities," *Ohio Northern University Law Review* 25, no. 4 (1999): 576. Johns also points out, though, that lawyers "wishing to utilize technology [also] have an ethical obligation not to overuse it" (p. 578)—that is, not to use it for its own sake, just to "bring pizzazz into the courtroom." (The notion that lawyers should not use new media or any pictures just to impress and possibly distract their audiences is captured by our first proposed guideline.) See also Lederer, "Technology-Augmented

Courtrooms," 685 (using courtroom technology should be considered an aspect of lawyers' general professional ethical duty of competence).

Still, the legal system and the academy have not yet generally heeded this warning. For instance, courts have not yet tended to recognize PowerPoint or TrialDirector as "reasonably necessary" presentation technologies for purposes of awards of costs under 28 U.S.C. § 1920—although that may change as the technologies become more common. As for legal education, the last comprehensive statement of the "fundamental lawyering skills and professional values" recommended for all new lawyers does not include visual communication skills among the requisite "effective methods of communication." American Bar Association, *Legal Education and Professional Development—An Educational Continuum; Report of the Task Force on Law Schools and the Profession: Narrowing the Gap* (the "MacCrate Report") (Chicago: Author, 1992), 139, 172–76. We, of course, strongly believe that the otherwise excellent recommendations of the MacCrate Report should be updated in this respect.

104. The Courtroom 21 (now Center for Legal and Court Technology) Court Affiliate Protocols for the Use by Lawyers of Courtroom Technology provide, among other things, that lawyers who use courtroom technology have an ethical obligation to do so competently (2-10.00). Lederer, "Technology-Augmented Courtrooms," 694–95.

105. Marc Galanter, *Lowering the Bar* (Madison: University of Wisconsin Press, 2006).

106. Consider, for instance, the many judges (such as the majority of the Supreme Court in *Scott*) who seem to think that all they have to do to ensure the proper use of a picture is to ascertain that it hasn't been materially altered, as if meanings will otherwise take care of themselves. For an excellent discussion of the naïve realist-iconoclast dichotomy in postmodernist and other academic thinking about pictures and an analysis of film makers whose work transcends it, see Ann Kibbey, *Theory of the Image* (Bloomington: Indiana University Press, 2005).

107. Yochai Benkler, *The Wealth of Networks: How Social Production Transforms Markets and Freedom* (New Haven: Yale University Press, 2006).

108. For a discussion of how the Web might encourage democracy, see Beth Simone Noveck, "Democracy, the Video Game, Virtual Worlds and the Future of Collective Action," in *The State of Play: Law, Games, and Virtual Worlds*, ed. Jack M. Balkin and Beth Simone Noveck (New York: New York University Press, 2006), 257–82. The Web has also produced an emergent new economy, with new markets and new kinds of property; adjusting to these changes, adapting the new to the older economy, is an ongoing challenge—witness the legal battles over music downloading being carried on by the Motion Picture Association of American and the Recording Industry Association of America, battles over issues of privacy and surveillance in the debates concerning the renewal of the Foreign Intelligence Surveillance Act (FISA) in 2008, and efforts by various interested parties to impose a top-down control on cyberspace by eliminating network neutrality (to name only a few of the areas of conflict in the news as we write). The Web is also making possible new understandings of market systems; see Benkler, *The Wealth of Networks*; Bernardo A. Huberman, *The Laws of the Web: Patterns in the Ecology of Information* (Cambridge, MA: MIT Press, 2001).

109. Readers may not know that hardware carries code—programming—that is fixed in the chips that reside on the hardware boards inside the computer. The programming of those chips can be subject to cultural bias or deliberate efforts to gain competitive advantage that have nothing to do with delivering a superior product. For a story that unfolded in the summer of 2008, see Ubuntu forums, http://ubuntu-virginia.ubuntuforums.org/showthread.php?t=869249 (last accessed July 30, 2008), featuring a debate over whether a supplier of boards, Foxconn, deliberately disabled use if customers chose to put a Linux operating system on their machines. See http://hehe2.net/thedarkside/microsoft/even-more-incriminating-evidence-in-the-foxconn-debacle/ (last accessed July 30, 2008). A year earlier, a technical blogger leveled a similar complaint about a board made by a company called Phoenix at http://blog.linuxoss.com/2007/04/

phoenix-bios-locks-out-all-oss-except-vista/ (last accessed July 30, 2008). Bruce Schneier, a se-curity expert, has written about efforts to insert remote government and corporate control over personal computers through hardware; see, e.g., Bruce Schneier, "I've Seen the Future and It has a Kill Switch," http://www.wired.com/politics/security/commentary/securitymatters/2008/06/securitymatters_0626 (last accessed July 30, 2008).

110. See, e.g., http://blog.secondlife.com/2006/08/10/forums-take-a-new-turn/ (last accessed July 26, 2008).

111. http://en.wikipedia.org/wiki/EVE_Online (last accessed July 26, 2008). One issue, of course, is that Eve exists on one set of servers, so it is possible for the whole community in that virtual world to gather. World of Warcraft and Second Life, by contrast, are made up of smaller collectives running on servers in many places. Coverage of the conflict in Eve is at http://www.nytimes.com/2007/06/07/arts/07eve.html?scp=1&sq=on-line%20gasming%20EVE&st=cse; the first meeting of Stellar Management is covered at http://www.nytimes.com/2008/06/28/arts/television/28eve.html?scp=3&sq=STELLAR%20MANAGEMENT&st=cse (last accessed July 30, 2008).

112. John Markoff and Scott Shane, "Documents Show Link Between AT&T and Agency in Eavesdropping Case," *New York Times*, April 13, 2006; Ryan Singel, "Spying in the Death Star: The AT&T Whistle-Blower Tells His Story," http://www.wired.com/politics/onlinerights/news/2007/05/kleininterview (last accessed July 31, 2008).

113. The shift to cloud computing, ongoing as we write, amplifies these issues of data owner-ship, privacy, and control. The Internet and the World Wide Web were initially thought of as com-munications devices that "published" or "broadcast" information. Now the Web has developed to the point that it is itself a platform; it enables us to do all kinds of things by accessing software that resides not on our personal computers but on Web sites. This is what is meant by "cloud comput-ing." Individuals will no longer have their own software on their personal computers; they will instead use Web-based applications to do their work and to store their documents. Whatever entity owns the servers that store the files will have access to all of the data, from whatever source. The im-plications for industrial spying, government surveillance, and related issues have barely been con-templated. See, e.g., Tim O'Reilly, "What Is Web 2.0, Design Patterns and Business Models for the Next Generation of Software," http://www.oreilly.com/pub/a/oreilly/tim/news/2005/09/30/what-is-web-20.html (last accessed July 31, 2008). It is possible to think of Google as a database bringing together businesses as if they were entries in a vast file system; among the companies reported in 2006 as having recently done deals with Google were eBay, YouTube, News Corp.'s Fox Interactive Media, Viacom's MTV Networks, NBC, Dell, Adobe Systems, AOL, and Skype. Eric Auchard (no title) (August 28, 2006), http://today.reuters.com/news/articleinvesting.aspx?view=CN&symbol=&storyID=2006-08-28T205744Z_01_N28210335_RTRIDST_0_TECH-INTERNET-PARTNER-SHIPS-FACTBOX.XML&pageNumber=0&WTModLoc=InvArt-C1-ArticlePage2&sz=13 (last accessed July 31, 2008).

114. Dan Ariely, *Predictably Irrational* (New York: HarperCollins, 2008).

115. See Martha Minow, *Partners, Not Rivals: Privatization and the Public Good* (Boston: Beacon Press, 2002).

116. Andrew Hawkins of Microsoft has presented a vision of the near future in which police, prosecutors, courts, prisons, and probation offices are all connected through a single informa-tion system that uses "partner justice applications," with citizens having an Internet interface. Microsoft has already been setting up database systems to manage information and cases for Slovenia, Iceland, Northern Ireland, Israel, and Brazil. With backdoor access to information from all the countries using its software, Microsoft could well be creating a system of international law outside formal treaties and agreements. Andrew Hawkins, "Innovation in Justice: E-Justice Collaboration and Information Sharing," PowerPoint presentation delivered at the E-Justice and E-Law Conference, Portorož, Slovenia, June 2, 2008, www.ejustice2008.si/presentations/

ejustice_trends_1/ejustice_a_showcase_of_european_and_global_innovation.ppt (last accessed July 31, 2008).

117. Recognizing that the ideal public system may not be achievable, service contracts need to include these sorts of provisions, and more that we have not yet envisioned, to maintain a balance of power between private entity as purveyor and/or provider of technology and services and client government agencies.

118. E.g., Lawrence Rosen, *Law as Culture* (Princeton: Princeton University Press, 2006).

119. Ming Hsu, Cédric Anen, and Steven R. Quartz, "The Right and the Good: Distributive Justice and Neural Encoding of Equity and Efficiency," *Sciencexpress*, www.sciencexpress.org (May 8, 2008).

120. The law professor Milner Ball maintains that the performance of justice is an essential part of redirecting aggression within a society and imaging a social order: "Those who would quit judicial theater either overtly because of its injustices or covertly because of its economic inefficiencies have not reckoned its puissance: to give place to an expression of humanity wherein even the least member of the community may find 'a local habitation and a name.' We will do well to ponder, before relinquishing it, whether this humanizing dimension of theater is not critical to the capacity of our courts for justice." Milner S. Ball, "The Play's the Thing: An Unscientific Reflection on Courts Under the Rubric of Theater," *Stanford Law Review* 28, no. 1 (November 1975): 81–115.

121. This might be equally possible in a virtual world like Second Life or in an immersive virtual reality environment.

122. The task, to borrow a few words from Jack Balkin, is to "find the meaning of the old in the new." Jack M. Balkin, "Digital Speech and Democratic Culture: A Theory of Freedom of Expression for the Information Society," *New York University Law Review* 79, no. 1 (April 2004): 53.

Index

AARP Bulletin, 223n6
Abelson, Reed, 275n70
Abelson, Robert, 248n83
Abu Ghraib photographs, 27, 78–79, 228–29n68, 233n48, 245n59
accounting, 63–67, 81
accuracy of decision making, 195, 196–97, 293n3
actor-observer effect, 97
adjudication, 180, 192, 196, 201; Anglo-American, 187; multimediated, 179; as public event, 219–20. *See also* judging machines
Adler, Matthew, 303n90
advertisements and advertising: confusion of fact and fiction, 15–16; as model for legal argument, 4, 200, 271n25; referring viewers to Web sites, 27; about Vioxx, used in *Cona and McDarby* closing argument, 155–56, 200; visual rhetorics of, 199
advocacy. *See* argument; closing arguments; digital technologies, rhetorical potential of; lawyers, adopting new digital technologies; pictures, rhetorical potential of; rhetoric; theory of the case. *See also specific cases*
algorithms, 185, 187, 189–90, 192, 219; bidding by, 286n49; and online advertising, Google's management of, 291n105; proprietary or protected as trade secrets, 191–93
Alicke, Mark, 295n14
Allen, Colin, 291n102
Allen, Fred, 295n16
Allen, James, 228n67
Allison, Wes, 235n62
Alpers, Svetlana, 231n19
alternative dispute resolution (ADR), 132–33, 172–73, 176, 286n52

alternative press online, 28
amateur filmmaking. *See* video and videotape, amateur
American Bar Association (ABA), 176, 202, 207, 213, 239n1, 269n11, 293n2, 294n9, 297n39, 299n55, 300n58, 301n64, 304nn95, 102, 305n103; offered program with CLE credit in Second Life, 288n62
American Board of Forensic Odontology, 262n88
American Idol, 27
America's Army, 19
analog media: compared to digital, 65–66, 76, 77–78, 84, 86, 109, 139–41, 242–43n40; VHS, 46, 52–53, 236n71, 244n55. *See also specific analog media*
Andersen, Robin, 226nn33, 35, 296n25
Anen, Cédric, 307n119
Angell, Marcia, 273n57, 274n59
Animation Technologies, Inc. (ATI), 72–74, 76
animations, 6, 27, 71, 90–98, 102, 197, 200, 211; and actor-observer effect, 252n123; in *Dunkle* case, 294n11; cost of, 301n68; contrasted to IVEs, 283n17; addressed in jury instructions, 203–4, 297–98n44 (*Commonwealth v. Serge*); in *Murtha* case, 92–99, 204; as function in PowerPoint, 84, 157; pretrial ruling recommended, 209; psychology of, 91–92; scientific, 204; contrasted to simulations for admissibility purposes, 298n44; use at trial recommended by ABA, 203
APPROVe (Vioxx clinical study), 275n70
arbitration and arbitrators, 132, 172–73, 176, 215
"Arbitration and Mediation Rules" (of E-Justice Center), 176
Archibald, Randall, 239n88

About the Authors

NEAL FEIGENSON is a professor at Quinnipiac University School of Law and author of *Legal Blame: How Jurors Think and Talk About Accidents*.

CHRISTINA SPIESEL is a senior research scholar at Yale Law School and an adjunct professor of law at Quinnipiac University School of Law and New York Law School.